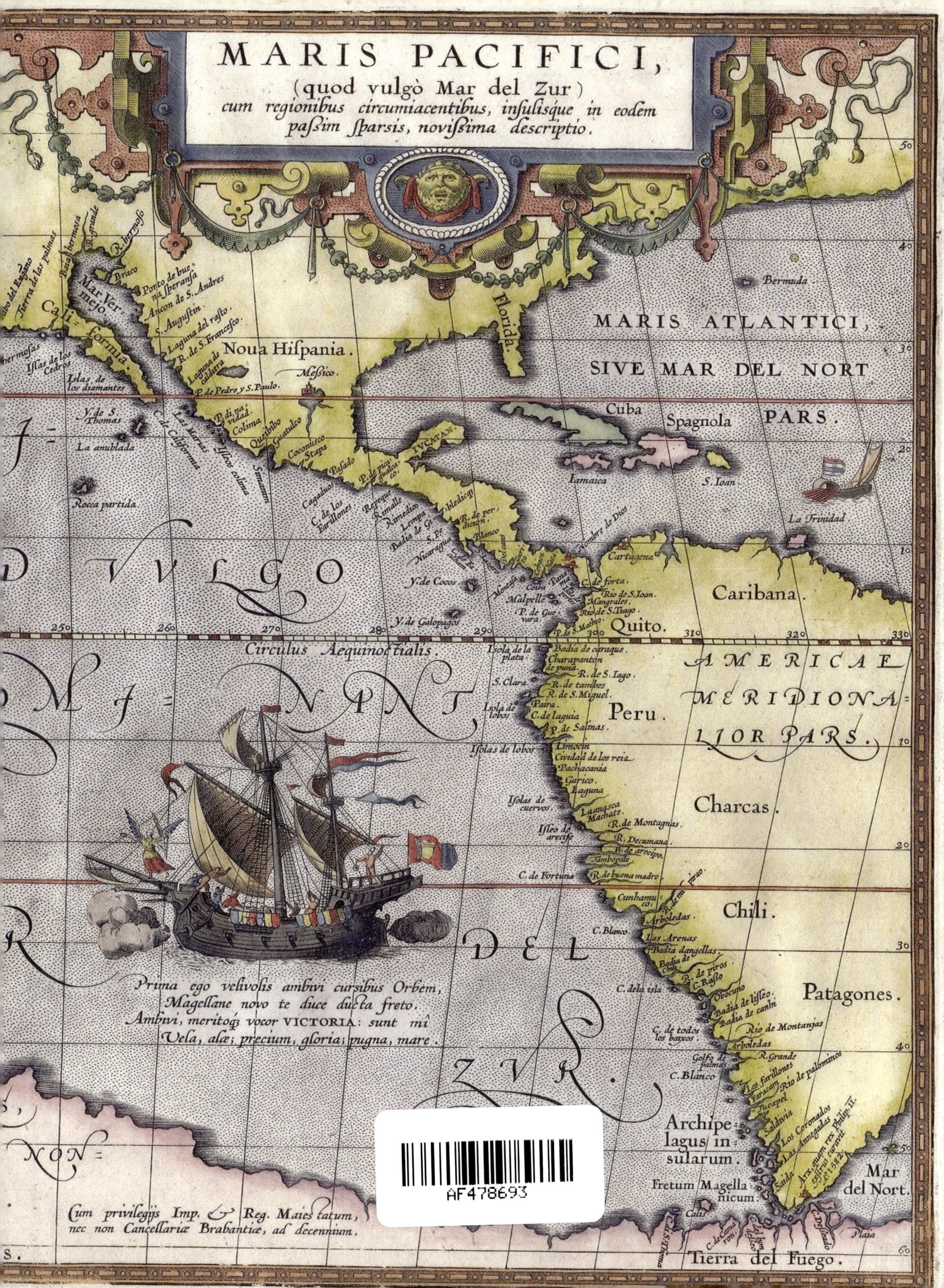

MARIS PACIFICI,
(quod vulgò Mar del Zur)
cum regionibus circumiacentibus, insulisque in eodem
passim sparsis, novissima descriptio.
MARIS ATLANTICI,
SIVE MAR DEL NORT PARS.
Noua Hispania.
Mar Vermejo.
Cali-forma.
Florida.
Bermuda
Mexico
Cuba
Spagnola
Iamaica
S. Ioan
La Trinidad
Caribana
Cartagena
Nombre de Dios
Quito.
AMERICAE
MERIDIONA-
LIOR PARS.
Circulus Aequinoctialis
Peru.
Charcas.
Chili.
Patagones.
VVLGO
MF = NANT,
DEL
ZVR.
NON=
Prima ego velivolis ambivi cursibus Orbèm,
Magellane novo te duce ducta freto.
Ambivi, meritoꝗ vocor VICTORIA: sunt mi
Vela, alæ; precium, gloria; pugna, mare.
C. de Fortuna
C. Blanco
C. dela isla
Golfo de S. palmas
C. Blanco
Archipe-
lagus in-
sularum
Fretum Magella-
nicum.
Mar
del Nort.
Tierra del Fuego.
Cum privilegijs Imp. & Reg. Maiestatum,
nec non Cancellariæ Brabantiæ, ad decennium.

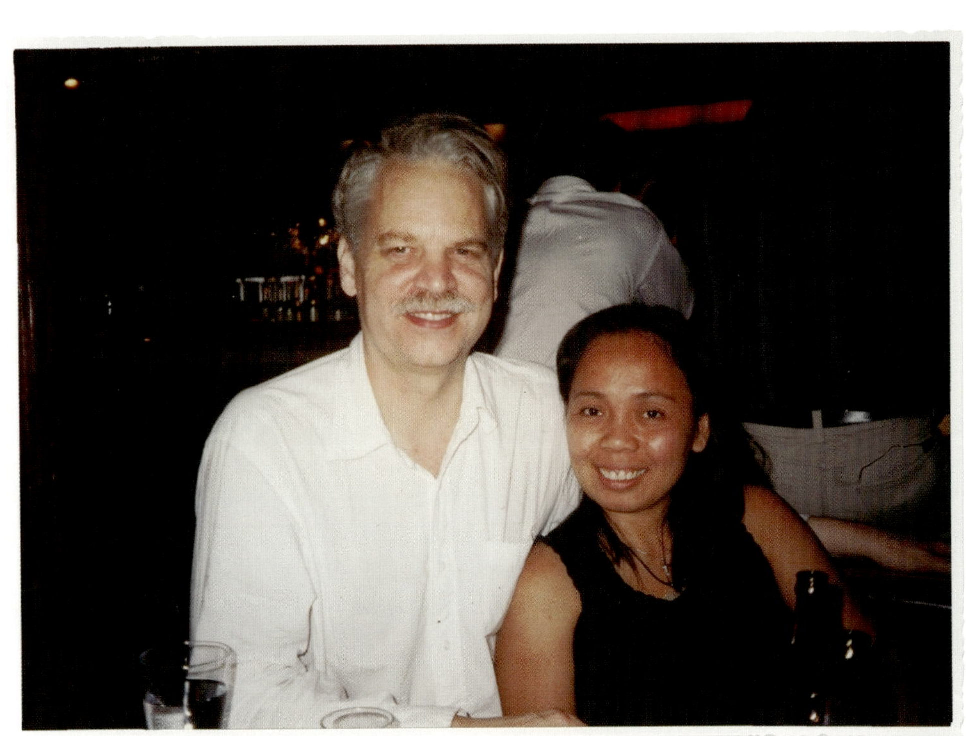

Our Family Album

John Libbey Publishing
United Kingdom

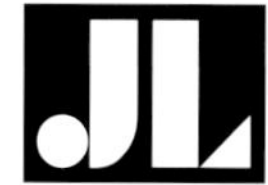

Cover image: *John Carlos Leon Thelonious Serana Musser with his sister-cousin Ziphora Serana Parks (age 3)*

Our Family Album
Essays-Script-Annotations-Images

Charles Musser
with Threese Serana

additional contributions by
Nick Deocampo, Thomas Allen Harris,
Lorna Johnson and Laura Wexler

British Library Cataloguing in Publication Data

Our Family Album: Essays-Script-Annotations-Images

A catalogue entry for this book is available from the British Library

ISBN: 9780 86196741 4 (Casebound)

Published by
John Libbey Publishing, 205 Crescent Road, East Barnet, Herts EN4 85B
United Kingdom
Email: john.libbey@orange.fr   www.johnlibbey.com

Distributed Worldwide by **Indiana University Press**
Hermanm B Wells Library – 350 1320 E. 10th St., Bloomington, IN 47405-3907
http://www.iupress.indiana.edu

Printed and bound in China by 1010 Printing.

For Peter Davis

In memory of

Gerry Williams

Other Works by Charles Musser

An American Potter: Gerry Williams (1976, film)
Before the Nickelodeon: The Early Cinema of Edwin S. Porter (1982, film)
Before Hollywood: Turn of the Century American Films –curated and edited
    with Jay Leyda (1987, exhibition catalog)
The Emergence of Cinema: The American Screen to 1907 (1990, book)
Resisting Images: Essays on Cinema and History –edited with Robert Sklar (1991, book)
High-Class Moving Pictures: Lyman H. Howe and the Forgotten Era of Traveling Exhibition
    –with Carol Nelson (1991, book)
Before the Nickelodeon: Edwin S. Porter and the Edison Manufacturing Company (1991, book)
Edison Motion Pictures, 1890-1900: An Annotated Filmography (1997, catalog raisonné)
Oscar Micheaux and His Circle: African American Filmmaking and Race Cinema of the Silent Era –curated and
    edited with Pearl Bowser and Jane Gaines (2001, exhibition catalog)
Edison: The Invention of the Movies, 1891-1918 –curated with Stephen Higgins (2005, DVD set)
Errol Morris: A Lightning Sketch (2014, film)
Pioneers of African American Filmmaking –curated with Jackie Stewart (2016, DVD set)
Politicking and Emergent Media: U.S. Presidential Elections of the 1890s (2016, book)

America is in the hearts of men that died for freedom; it is also in the eyes of men that are building a new world.

— Carlos Bulosan

Table of Contents

Acknowledgements

When two people from opposite ends of the world and quite different cultures meet and fall in love, how do they build a life together? How do they generate ties of ever greater intimacy and substance? Long before this book-film project began, in the very early stages of our relationship, Threese Serana and I read Carlos Bulosan's *America Is in the Heart* (1946). Neither one of us knew this book before we met: it was a shared discovery. It is an autobiographical account by a Filipino who came to the United States to work in its agricultural fields and canneries, eventually becoming a prominent contributor to the nation's Popular Front culture. He recounts his experiences as a working-class immigrant who encountered numerous instances of brutal racism yet somehow remained upbeat, hopeful and even celebratory. Thus, we chose a selection from that work as this volume's epigraph.

Our connection with Bulosan goes well beyond that book. His career took off with the essay "The Freedom from Want," published in the *Saturday Evening Post* on March 6, 1943. Not unlike Bulosan, Threese sometimes had to forage for food to feed herself and her younger siblings (when her father's paycheck failed to appear, wild spinach was sometimes quite literally a lifesaver). Today, getting food to the hungry of New Haven remains her ongoing concern. Moreover, as the discerning reader might suspect, our son John Carlos was named after Carlos Bulosan. We want him to know, in a profound sense, his Filipino roots as well as be reminded of his mother's experiences as an immigrant—some of which she discusses in her essay in this volume. Moreover, Bulosan's commentary on cultural production resonates with our own aspirations in making this film:

> Now culture being a social product, I firmly believe that any work of art should have a social function – to beautify, to glorify, to dignify man. This assertion has always been true, and it applies to all social systems…. Since any social system is forced to change to another by concrete economic forces, its art changes also to be recharged, reshaped, and revitalized by the new conditions. Thus, if the writer has any significance, [he] should write about the world in which he lives: interpret his time and envision the future through his knowledge of historical reality.[1]

Our Family Album is very much about the world in which we live even as it engages our historical reality and looks towards the future—most specifically the future of John Carlos and his generation. Certainly, it shares an autobiographical disposition with *America Is in the Heart.*

I can only hope that John Carlos will find a group of mentors and father figures like those I encountered in my late teens and early twenties. Three men changed my life, showing me how to understand and engage the world. The first was Gerry Williams (1926-2014), a studio potter who brought me on as a part-time apprentice. Some of what I learned from him can be found in the documentary we later made together: *An American Potter* (1976). In dedicating this book to his memory, I want to express my continuing appreciation and sense of debt for all that Gerry provided me. The second individual was my teacher and eventual collaborator, Jay Leyda (1910-1988). A cultural historian and filmmaker, he is never far from my thoughts. Not surprisingly, I have already dedicated a book to his memory.

The final member of that group, Peter Davis, is happily still with us; to him this book is dedicated as well. Peter hired me in October 1972, as an assistant editor, to work on a documentary project about the Vietnam War. Famously, he told me I was hired for two weeks, not two years. Yet somehow, I managed to stay on that film, the Oscar-winning *Hearts and Minds* (1974), until after its world premiere at the May 1974 Cannes Film Festival. Peter taught me how to write books as well as make films through that remarkable apprenticeship. He had mastered a rigorous process that precluded skipping steps while always moving forward with deliberate speed. My debt to Peter was and is multi-faceted and profound. Not least of all, he assembled a remarkable team of filmmakers to whom I am likewise indebted—most notably Richard Pierce, Lynzee Klingman, Tom Cohen, Brennon Jones and Susan Martin. I also benefited from his uncommon patience and generosity.

Peter viewed a fine cut of *An American Potter* and provided feedback that made that film significantly stronger. It was a moment when these two participated in a shared creative project.

I learned a lot about making documentaries from Gerry, Jay and Peter; but what I realize now, as I write this, is that all three of these individuals in some small way helped to prepare me for my encounter with Threese and Southeast Asia. *Hearts and Minds* was one long lesson on the United States' projection of military power into Southeast Asia, which really began with its re-colonization of the Philippines in 1899. Jay, who lived in China and wrote a book on Chinese cinema, was married to the modern dancer Si-lan Chen who, like Threese, was part Chinese. Gerry grew up in India where his father was a close associate of Mahatma Gandhi.

This book—like its film counterpart—was made possible by the contributions of others. Many of these individuals are acknowledged in the film's end credits at the end of this volume, so listing them again is not always necessary. Nevertheless, we were fortunate that all our family members were eager to share their images with us. My mother, Marilyn Keach (Musser) Bernart, was particularly generous in providing us with her photo collection and agreeing to talk about it on camera. My sisters, Jane and Nancy, also helped out. Threese's brother, David Buffet Gates Serana, likewise shared images at crucial moments. So did Guillerma Bejagan Enriquez, her mother Lola Bejagan and Shirley Dicdiquin. Victoriano Bejagan, Nemesio "Meling" Dicdiquin, Juan "Papa Jojo" Dicdiquin and Ferdinand Klebold all agreed to discuss family history on camera. This appreciation extends to our extended family in the barangay of Manlapay and the municipality of Dalaguete.

This book-film project is an exploration of the family album as a practice. My colleagues—filmmakers, many of whom are also scholars and archivists—contributed invaluably to this book-film project as they talked about their own family albums: Paolo Cherchi Usai, Lorna Johnson, Vanessa Toulmin, Ashish Chadha, Nick Deocampo and Thomas Elsaesser. We owe a special debt to Victor Gross, his wife Jade, his sons John and Edward Gross, his daughter Emy Gross and her husband Chad Borja. An especially heartfelt note of appreciation goes to their daughter Gabrielle Gross, who wrote and performed the closing song, "A Song Inspired by You." There is always an imbalance in a filmmaker's relationship to his subjects. We spent 24 hours with the Gross family, but I have encountered them again and again while editing this film. As I see them talk and perform over and over again, they seemingly become the most familiar of friends. And yet for the Gross family, they only remember us from our brief visit. In contrast, we see our documentary's most basic inspiration—our son, John Carlos Leon Thelonious Serana Musser—much more often than his representations in this film. How can we thank him? Perhaps by asking Carlito to forgive the film's shortcomings—and those of the book as well. That is true for our nephew, Binhi Chua Serana, as well.

My fellow documentary filmmakers and students of documentary here at Yale and in New Haven have actively participated in this film's making or otherwise nurtured its underlying aspirations. The film was begun in a Yale workshop taught by Thomas Allen Harris, but many other colleagues provided an intellectual framework of support including Laura Wexler, John MacKay, Zareena Grewal, Elihu Rubin, Sandra Luckow, Michael Roemer, Matt Jacobson, Raisa Sidenova, Tram Luong, Anna Marra, Josh Glick, Masha Shpolberg, Josh Sperling, jub Sankofa, Wills Glasspiegel, Gorman Bechard, Karyl Evans, Lindsay Thompson, John Lucas and the many students of Documentary Film Workshop. Inspiration, guidance and support came from many filmmaker friends and colleagues, including Alexis Krasilovsky, Charles Lyon, Iris Cahn, Laura Poitras, Chris Hegedus, D.A. Pennebaker, Lisa Molomot, Jacob Bricca, Gaspar Gonzalez, George Stoney, Alex Gibney, Su Friedrich, Robb Moss, Hanna Rose Shell and Errol Morris. A special shout-out goes to Michael Moore whose documentary *Where To Invade Next* turned John Carlos into a journalist whose class newspaper, *The Worthington Pride*, has fought for an eatable school lunch, more recess and less homework. He also wonders if his Danish heritage might enable him to move to Finland. As a scholar-practitioner I am much indebted to my colleagues in documentary studies, notably Jane Gaines, Brian Winston, Bill Nichols, Michael Renov, Jonathan Kahana, Josh Malitsky, Bao Feng and Ruby Rich.

To transform this documentary into a book is no small task. Most of that work took place in the offices of Yale's Film and Media Studies Program—the place where I spend more of my waking hours than anyplace else. Thanks to my colleagues Dudley Andrew, Brigitte Peucker, Aaron Gerow, Katerina Clark, Katie Trumpener, Millicent Marcus, J. D. Connor, Marc Lapadula, Camille Thomasson, Francesco Casetti, Anthony Sudol, Katherine Germano, and Edith Rotkopf. Many of these colleagues are involved in NHdocs: The New Haven Documentary Film Festival, where *Our Family Album* was first shown as a work in progress. This and the Film and Media Studies Program are largely based in the Whitney Humanities Center where its director Gary Tomlinson, Associate Director Mark Bauer, Laurene Asmus, and other staff members offer support and inspiration of all kinds.

Our Family Album owes a special debt to those who contributed essays, to the book's publisher John Libbey, to copyeditor Dana Benelli and to its designer John Lucas. It was published with the assistance of the Frederick W. Hilles Publication Fund of Yale University.

Charles Musser
New Haven, CT.
August 2019

[1] Carlos Bulosan, "The Writer as Worker," in *On Becoming Filipino: Selected Writings of Carlos Bulosan* edited with an introduction by E. San Juan, Jr. (Philadelphia: Temple University Press, 1995), 143.

Essays

Making Sense of the Family Album:
An Introduction

By Charles Musser

Making a documentary—or producing a book—that engages the family album has difficulty garnering critical attention in the world of serious cultural engagement (perhaps most of all in the world of academia). Family photo albums are considered to be "not art" or "non-art." They are not a form of mass culture. Nor are they recognized as an adequate form of autobiography. They are not proper cultural artifacts like books, feature fiction films, television shows or social-issue documentaries. They are not about encounters with famous people or earth-shattering events but are typically centered on the lives of young children and their families. Family albums are about the everyday, the quotidian. They might be considered a kind of folk art, in that they are of domestic origin. Yet because they are at once too singular and too personal, they cannot be easily transferred from hand to hand. Putting a quilt purchased at a flea market on one's bed is different from putting a similarly acquired family album on the coffee table.

Family albums are so common—very few of us escape them entirely, either growing up or as adults—that they are not considered worthy of individual assessment and critique. Yet, for this very reason, family albums can function outside dominant frameworks even when at first glance they seem to be typical. Family albums do more than represent a group of people at their Sunday best—a charade in which family secrets generally remain secret or are gussied up for semi-public consumption. They do more than testify to the tyranny of family patriarchy as a mode of social organization and control. They are statements—to be sure, often partial statements—about how people have chosen to live and represent their lives. In small but often discernible ways, they work against the grain and testify to what people hold most dear. Evoking Michel de Certeau, we might say that they are potentially subversive of systems and norms.[1] They can also be understood as an important form of domestic ethnography, albeit a self-reflexive one.

Taking Certeau's observations a step further, Malin Wahlberg has suggested, "Family pictures offer suggestive material to documentary filmmaking precisely because of what is not shown: tensions in family relationships, forced smiles, rivalries and secret passions. An autobiographic narrative may reinvent these invisible intrigues within recollection, contemplation, and imagination."[2] And so Threese Serana and I offer *Our Family Album*—a 97-minute audio-visual, digital media program that reconsiders what has not been revealed even as it inevitably conceals what can still not yet be said or shown. We have described this endeavor as "an essay film about love, war and the power of photography" and "a documentary about finding family at opposite ends of the world." Those opposite ends of the world are the Philippines, where Threese spent the first thirty-three years of her life, and the Northeastern United States, where I grew up and we now live. Screened in near finished form for our son John Carlos as a present on his eleventh birthday, this film essay is addressed to him in the proximate present—but also to his future self—whatever that may prove to be. At the same time this form of address is a literary conceit, for the documentary was also made to be seen (and now read) not just by Carlito, his family and friends but by a larger public.

Viewers have seemed inclined to look at *Our Family Album* as a personal account of our family's journey from our initial romantic encounter until John Carlos turns eleven. Certainly, this is one strand of our documentary and admittedly the first to be introduced; nevertheless, the epigraph for this essay film asks viewers to keep in mind other elements, for our documentary is also about other people's family albums: how friends, relatives and colleagues make use of family photographs. My mother's family album, a fairly conventional product of post-WWII white suburbia, serves as a useful foil for subsequent comparisons. My own discomfort with my parents' album is echoed by Paolo Cherchi-Usai, a senior curator at the world's oldest photography museum, who grew up hating his parents' endeavors at creating photographic memories. As a result, he keeps his own family images in his head. His stance is a modernist refusal: a radical affirmation of silence in conjunction with personal reflection that evokes a somewhat similar stance by Marcel Duchamp.[3] Admittedly, *Our*

Family Album breaks with that silence—a silence I shared for many years—to imagine a possible alternative.

I am fascinated by the comparison of our efforts at familial representations with those of Lorna Johnson and her husband Richard Frizell. Lorna left the mundane task of family documentation to her husband and focused her own efforts on more avant-garde film celebrations of familial love. Then there is Ferd Klebold, my uncle. A widower in his 90s who has no direct descendants, he anticipated his death by throwing away his treasure trove of family memories. Even so, there are a few images he could not bear to live without. Perhaps because my Uncle Ferd is actually a prominent local historian, I sometimes contrast his actions to those of Vanessa Toulmin, a scholar who grew up on the fairground and built a publicly-funded archive precisely to rescue documents that were likely to be junked—mostly family photographs of carnival, or "carney," culture. The resulting National Fairground Archive was made possible by the complex web of familial relationships in which Toulmin herself participates. Another friend, filmmaker Ashish Chadha, turns his family albums into artist's books. Film and media scholar Thomas Elsaesser used his family's archive to make *The Sun Island* (2017), an essay film about his grandfather, the architect Martin Elsaesser.[4] *Our Family Album* asks its viewers and readers to think about this diversity and how they deploy their family albums and what meaning such albums might convey.

Words are slippery units of meaning. They might appear to signify something quite specific and yet turn out to contain multiple and surprisingly open-ended denotations. Such is the case with the three words that make up the title *Our Family Album*. Viewers of the film seem predisposed to think that this documentary is about our *nuclear* family—the three of us living in a modest townhouse near downtown New Haven, Connecticut. Such an assumption proves far too narrow, and not merely because our nephew and John Carlos's brother (to follow Filipino kinship terminology) has become a fourth family member. The documentary also offers a sustained encounter with our *extended* family—both historically (genealogically) and in the present day. Moreover, the phrase "our family" is used in a still broader, more colloquial sense. Our

documentary was made with the full involvement of family friends. Tito Nick (Deocampo), Auntie Lorna (Johnson) and the rest count as family members as well. In making this documentary we also connected with Victor Gross and his family—our familial counterparts. Victor's father Edward Meyer Gross, a New York Jew, and his Filipina wife, Antonia Molina, made the first feature fiction films in the Philippines in 1912.[5] And here we are—a New Yorker and his Filipina wife—making a documentary about family photography and incorporating Gross family stories and photographs into our own family album.

One should understand this documentary as a *collective exploration* of the family photo album as a mode of expression. The forms that these albums can take—as well as their meanings and values for those involved—are surprisingly diverse. The individuals appearing in this film come from very different parts of the world, and—if the reader will indulge my own presumptuousness for a moment—this documentary endeavor points towards and evokes the larger notion of a "family of man." Of course, that was the title of a famous photo exhibition at the Museum of Modern Art (NYC), which was then put in book form, making it a kind of photo album. While the differences between that photo album and this one may be obvious, some underlying similarities might also be acknowledged. As Edward Steichen wrote about his exhibition in expansive terms: "We sought and selected photographs, made in all parts of the world, of the gamut of life from birth to death with emphasis on the daily relationships of man to himself, to his family, to the community and to the world we live in."[6] In fact, this idea of a "family of man" is very much the utopic ambition of our film's executive producer, Thomas Allen Harris, with his Digital Diaspora Family Reunion project. But then, as A. J. Jacobs argues, we *are* actually all related to each other.[7] It is just a question of tracing the connections. In this respect, you the reader might consider this book to be a photo album made by some of your more distant relatives.

We should also consider the term "album." The family album is a subset of the photo album, which Wikipedia describes as "a series of photographic prints collected by an individual person or family in the form of a book." The family album is a more private variant that is tied to personal life and typically has a single curator or author who selects and assembles the material. It is a creative act in which individuals assume the role of family chroniclers or historians. The compilers usually take many of the photographs, but rarely are all the photographs taken by the person assembling the work. Their provenance is diverse, often including images taken by friends and relatives—even strangers who are briefly handed a camera to take a group portrait. Although photographs are readily reproducible, and multiple copies of individual photos can be printed and shared with relatives and acquaintances (even more so in the era of digital photography!), the family album is generally a unique object. But not always. Sally Mann's photo album *Immediate Family,* published by Aperture in 1992, is a case in point. Langston Hughes and Roy DeCarava's *Sweet Fly Paper of Life*, published by Simon and Schuster in 1955, is a more unorthodox example. However, the family album can also appear in different media forms. Variants now live on the web, where people keep private albums that are shared (and built) with other family members. Likewise, Facebook provides a more informal, open-ended and public variant.

Although the family album has its motion picture counterpart in home movies and videos, there are documentaries that take on the subject. I am particularly intrigued by Alfred Guzzetti's *Family Portrait Sittings* (1975). Promotional literature notes that it "traces the history of the filmmaker's family from their origins in the Abruzzi region of Italy, through immigration to the United States early in the 20th century, their struggles to become established, understand the world, and raise children…. It is a film about how people struggle to make sense of their lives, how they shape it into stories, and how these stories convey what the family is." Guzzetti begins his film with the title "For my son Benjamin" very much as *Our Family Album* declares it is "For John Carlos." This is echoed by a shot later in the film, as a home movie of his three-year-old son ends with a fleeting freeze frame. Even so, both films clearly have a wider audience in mind. In contrast, Alain Berliner's *The Family Album* (1988) offers a far more distanced and impersonal approach as it reflects on the home movie. More recently, Nassim Amaouche, Mais Darwazah, Erige Sehiri and Sameh Zoabi have compiled four short films under the title *Family Album* (2012). Lorna Johnson's unfinished documentary *About Love*, excerpted in *Our Family Album*, is another compelling instance.

We have doubled down on the family album as an expressive form in that what follows is a book counterpart to our documentary film *Our Family Album*. Publishing film scripts, even of documentaries, is hardly new. Yet this is less a script than a photo album counterpart as imagined by and through *Our Family Album.* In the late nineteenth and early twentieth century, many creators of nonfiction screen programs—people such as John Stoddard, E. Burton Holmes and Dwight Elmendorf—published book versions of their illustrated lectures. Their printed variants balanced images with texts in ways that are somewhat analogous to our present endeavor. More recent instances of documentary-film-to-book translations are comparatively rare, but examples from the mid-twentieth century include Pare Lorentz's *The River* (1937/8), Joris Ivens's *The Song of the Rivers* (1954/7), nine of Chris Marker's documentaries from the 1950s and early 1960s, John Berger's *Ways of Seeing* (1972/3) and Claude Lanzmann's *Shoah* (1985).[8] The goal here is not only to reproduce text and selected images but also to provide annotations and commentary that will be helpful or of potential interest to the reader (and the viewer-turned-reader).

Most family albums suffer from a fundamental weakness: they are not really self-contained entities. They are composed primarily of images and generally have little—or even no—text. A succession of carefully chosen images, they are designed to be accompanied by extra-textual commentary. The authors/curators have these stories in their heads and will narrate them to almost anyone who is willing to listen. (Family albums are an early form of interactive documentary almost by design!) Near the beginning of my mother's family album, there is a photo accompanied by the caption "Four Generations!" This is, I think, an archetypical image that expresses family continuity across generations.[9] But who are these people? In particular, who is its oldest member? Fortunately, I was able to ask my 89-year-old mother, who was delighted to enlighten me. However, creators of family albums are inevitably separated from their creations by circumstance or death. Stories are lost—though not necessarily all at once since the people appearing in the albums are likely to know or recall some of the stories that were told. Nevertheless, there is an inevitable process of degradation. A recent conference on vernacular photography seemed to privilege those family albums that had been orphaned—bought on eBay or at flea markets—in which the connection between album and family had been completely severed.[10] Our documentary and this book, in contrast, exemplify efforts to slow, if not entirely halt that process by capturing some family stories and connecting them with the photo images as well as by providing cinematic and textual contexts. In this respect, *The Family of Man* with its commitment to universality comes at the expense of historical specificity. The anonymity of the images makes them emblematic of a certain vernacular modernism that our family album resists.

At its core, *Our Family Album* is a collaborative or co-creative undertaking in which Threese and I take turns voicing the narration. Our motivations for joining forces in this joint endeavor are similar if not always identical. Although we often lead quite independent lives, our happiest and most meaningful times as a couple have often involved working together on some project. While our joint endeavors may be as small and mundane as cooking a dinner, our biggest and most protracted adventure together is raising our son, John Carlos. Making this film has been a mid-sized undertaking, but it is hardly coincidence that these two projects overlap. In ways that are both obvious and far from evident, filmmaking and parenting have enhanced each other. The process of making a documentary in fact lends itself to a collaborative venture of "co-creation." In a world dominated by corporate hierarchies and claims to individualized self-expression, critics and scholars often overlook the value and frequency of partnerships. While fiction filmmaking generally involves a complex hierarchical chain of responsibility and authority, the mode of documentary offers numerous exceptions.[11]

We also share a mutual interest in photography. Although we have both used photography in conjunction with our work, our broader interests have been quite different. At the risk of indulging in cultural stereotyping, Threese possesses a longstanding and quite common Filipino passion for taking photographs that are largely focused on friends and family. (Take a look at her Facebook page!) My interests have had somewhat more academic origins. I taught a course on documentary film and photography for several years with my colleague Laura Wexler. This provided a starting point for much of my recent scholarship, which has investigated the work of American photographer-filmmakers such as Paul Strand and Weegee (Arthur Fellig).[12] So the opportunity to think creatively about the relationship of film to photography on one hand and the idea of bringing images—both stills and frame grabs—together in a photo album on the other hand has had particular appeal.

Documentary filmmaking provides a license to explore as well as to engage. As filmmakers we have been able to ask questions and go places that would have otherwise been difficult or impossible. In the process, we have learned more about our respective families. My mother offers a commentary on the family album that she assembled as her children were growing up—a conversation we had never had in my almost 50 years of adulthood. Threese's great uncle confirms that her mother's side of the family were Converso Jews from Spain and that within living memory her great-great-grandfather was still saying his Jewish prayers. By recording what they told us, their remarks became evidentiary fragments that we could juxtapose with others in ways that produce new understandings and insights—a new, revised and enriched family narrative. In asking family members how they make use of personal photographs, we have had to reflect on the way photographs and the new forms of technology that deploy them (i.e., social media) have impacted all our lives.

We have just begun to screen *Our Family Album* to audiences. The film can be read in any number of ways, depending on the context. In some respects, it can be seen as a twenty-first century version of Steichen's *The Family of Man*—a more intimate and integrated version that reflects a world made smaller by the Internet, a global economy and immigration. For many in the United States, it also speaks to an increasingly diverse America. In the Philippines, it has been received quite differently—as advocating for the value of a Cebuano cultural heritage and by extension other local cultures that are being pushed aside by national and global economies. Bringing John Carlos all the way from the United States to the mountains of Cebu, where he attends school in the local language, stands in counterpoint to the attitudes of many middle-class professionals living in Cebu City whose children are brought up only speaking English.

This endeavor is imagined as the start of an on-going book-film project, eventually to include a second volume tentatively entitled *Reflections: On Documentary, Photography and "Our Family Album."* Moving far beyond what can be done through annotation, this forthcoming volume will use the film as a starting point to engage a wide range of topics—the task of the scholar-practitioner, the film's own genealogy, the circulation of photographs and their functions within families, a reassessment of documentary reenactments and the nature of filmmaker-subject dynamics. Thomas Allen Harris has posed a number of important questions about this undertaking, which need to be addressed: as he has pointed out, *Our Family Album* treads lightly on what J. P. Sniadecki calls "the cruelty of the social."[13] Perhaps it is a characteristic of family albums that they omit many moments of pain, conflict and discomfort. They are not so much sites of overt resistance but quiet refusals. Showing the family at its Sunday best, as Thomas Elsaesser has characterized most family albums, is an effort to construct a parallel world—a counter narrative—in which cruelty is kept outside the gates. Family albums are about love much more than war, about friendship more than squabbles. Albums such as ours, which are immersed in a multi-cultural milieu, often exclude casual humiliations, microaggressions and the specific types of anxieties we have for our children's future. They are not what we want to memorialize. They are daily burdens that are evident only around the edges, almost as subtext—a structuring absence. Volume two will bring them back into the conversation.

The essays in this volume are written by people who are more than friends and colleagues—they are extended family. Threese Serana, my collaborator and spouse, discusses what she hopes our son John Carlos might learn or remember from *Our Family Album.* Filmmaker and co-director Lorna Johnson reflects on her own complicated, changing relationship to family photography and documentary. Co-producer Nick Deocampo considers the ways images–particularly those of photography and film—bear historical witness to the troubled relationships between two peoples and how individual bonds of love and affection have reshaped aspects of that history over time. Thomas Allen Harris, who works extensively with family images and whose workshop provided the nurturing environment from which *Our Family Album* began, assesses our overlapping set of concerns. Laura Wexler, a prominent scholar of photography, has walked beside this project throughout its creation. She offers a perspective on how *Our Family Album* might be appreciated and understood.

Endnotes

1 Michel de Certeau, *The Practice of Everyday Life* trans. Steven Rendall (Berkeley, CA: University of California Press, 1984).

2 Malin Wahlberg, *Documentary Time: Film and Phenomenology* (Minneapolis: University of Minnesota Press, 2008), 110.

3 Francis M. Naumann, *Marcel Duchamp: The Art of Making Art in the Age of Mechanical Reproduction* (New York: Harry Abrams, 1999). If this comparison of Paolo Cherchi-Usai to Duchamp seems farfetched, the reader should investigate Cherchi Usai's work as a filmmaker.

4 Thomas Elsaesser, "The Home Movie as Essay Film: On Making Memory Posthumously," in Julia Vassilieva and Deane Williams (eds.), *Beyond the Essay Film: Subjectivity, Textuality and Technology* (Amsterdam: Amsterdam University Press, forthcoming).

5 Edward Meyer Gross made *The Life and Death of Dr. Jose Rizal* in 1912 with Antonia Molina (star of the Zarzuela Theater in Manila).

6 Museum of Modern Art, New York, *The Family of Man: The greatest photographic exhibition of all time—503 pictures from 68 countries—created by Edward Steichen for the Museum of Modern Art*, prologue by Carl Sandburg (New York: Maco Magazine Corporation, 1955), 7.

7 A. J. Jacobs, *It's All Relative: Adventures Up and Down the World's Family Tree* (New York: Simon & Schuster, 2017).

8 Pare Lorentz, *The River* (New York: Stackpole Sons, 1938); Joris Ivens and Vladimir Pozner, *Lied der Ströme* (Berlin: Tribune, 1957); Chris Marker, *Commentaires* (Paris: Éditions du Seuil, 1961) later reissued as *Commentaires 1* in 1967 along with *Commentaires 2* (Paris: Éditions du Seuil, 1967); John Berger, *Ways of Seeing* (London: British Broadcasting Corporation and Penguin Books, 1973); Claude Lanzmann, *Shoah: An Oral History of the Holocaust* (New York: Pantheon, 1985).

9 There is another photo of four generations in our family album, showing Grace Greene Musser, Robert John Musser, me and Hannah Grace Zeavin Musser (as a baby). They are assertions of generational continuity—the very old and the very new.

10 Imagining Everyday Life: Engagements with Vernacular Photography (Columbia University), 19-20 October 2018.

11 Like many others, we have recognised the benefits of collaborative filmmaking. After the pioneering *cinema verité* filmmakers at Drew Associates moved on, there were the Maysles Brothers while Robert Drew worked with Anne Gilbert—soon Anne Drew. D.A. Pennebaker worked with a succession of collaborators including Ricky Leacock, but his company and filmmaking fortunes stabilized when he teamed up with Chris Hegedus. Joe Berlinger and Bruce Sinofsky, Chris Choy and Renee Tajima, Spike Lee and Sam Pollard, Steven Ascher and Jeanne Jordan, Steven Bognar and Julia Reichert— the list goes on and on. Katerina Cizek and William Uricchio, *Collective Wisdom: Co-Creating media within communities, across disciplines and with algorithms* (1st ed.). Retrieved from wip.pubpub.org/ collectivewisdom.

12 Charles Musser, "Charles Sheeler and Paul Strand: Friends, Collaborators, Rivals," in Kirsten M. Jensen, ed., *Charles Sheeler: Fashion, Photography and Sculptural Form* (Doylestown, PA: James Michener Art Museum, 2017) 155-177; Charles Musser, "Cameras at Coney, 1940-1953," in Robin Jaffee Frank, ed., *Coney Island: Visions of an American Dreamland* (New Haven, CT: Yale University Press, 2015), 228-247.

13 John Paul Sniadecki, "Digital Jianghu: Independent Documentary in a Beijing Art Village" (Ph.D. dissertation, Harvard University, 2013), iv.

How I Want John Carlos to See Himself Through *Our Family Album*

By Maria-Threese Serana

When you try to stand up and look the world in the face as if you had a right to be here, you have attacked the entire power structure of the western world. —James Baldwin

Whatever we do or think speaks for the identity that we claim and how we, knowingly or unknowingly, want that identity represented in public. I would like to think that my involvement in the making of *Our Family Album* revolves around this premise. We want our audience to recognize the many layers of circumstance and particularity portrayed in this documentary even though it offers only a very thin slice of the life that Charlie and I share as spouses and parents to our son, John Carlos Leon Thelonious Serana Musser; as guardians to Binhi Chua Serana (our nephew); and as individuals navigating the two very different worlds we have decided to somehow merge. The complexity of this project inevitably reflects the many intertwined layers present in multi-ethnic families and communities from which many of us come.

Obviously, there's only so much a feature-length documentary can show, and there are many things that I would have wanted included or certain scenes removed. However, I believe that the film succeeds in reminding John Carlos that he is more than just the color of his white skin, blonde hair, and hazel eyes that he inherited from his father's European-American DNA. The project documents an important stage in his childhood in which he gets to live and play with his dark-haired, darker-skinned friends and relatives in the Philippines, particularly in the mountains of Manlapay where John Carlos depends on their generosity as he struggles to learn the local Cebuano language. Their supportive kindness is something he has reciprocated in a wide range of situations: with new classmates in his school in the U.S., who are not yet fluent in English; with homeless people on the street; and so forth.

John Carlos and I are frequent travelers. We often take the train to New York to see friends and relatives, to participate in marches and rallies, or to go to museums and other cultural events. He has witnessed several instances where I was treated badly, or differently from the way he is treated for the obvious reason that I am not white and could easily pass as his nanny. He has also been exposed to instances of white Americans being hostile to, or acting atrociously toward, non-white people—especially Blacks, Hispanics, and Muslims. This has resulted in moments when he loathes the associations of privilege and arrogance that come with his white skin. In one heartbreaking moment, John Carlos told me, "Mom, I may be white but I will never hurt you or treat you with disrespect because you are brown. I wish I'm not white." Yet John Carlos embraces different aspects of his heritage—whether the Chinese-Sephardic Jewish-Filipino ancestors on my side or the Swiss and Scandinavian progenitors on his father's side. For the moment, Charlie's Danish ancestry has allowed him to occasionally embrace a "tough" Viking imaginary.

One of the interesting aspects we have explored in *Our Family Album* is my mother's story of our Jewish ancestors. To be honest, I have often felt uncomfortable including this strand of our documentary because it remains controversial in my family (I have a brother who is a priest) and we have no detailed evidence to support this claim. This Jewish heritage excited John Carlos because it brings him closer to his sister, Hannah Grace, who—like her mother—identifies as Jewish. John Carlos's desire to be more than just a half-brother to Hannah touched me deeply. I do feel this claim to be true in my heart; this history makes me cry each time I think of it, for reasons I cannot explain. Perhaps, it pains me to imagine my ancestors forced to flee Europe for survival in the strange New World simply for being Jews. It was always a mystery to me, each time I came to visit in the summer growing up, why my grandparents and their parents decided to settle in these remote mountain villages, so far away from "civilization" and where life is very hard. There was lots of walking on dirt roads with sharp rocks and no electricity. It was only in the late 2000s, as our documentary captures, that the roads were beginning to be widened and paved with concrete. I am inclined to believe that it's the Jewish part of me that makes me identify with peoples who are persecuted and oppressed and which makes me want to courageously fight for justice or help bring light to darkness.

Arguably, life's journey is about finding out who we are, shaping ourselves into the person we aspire to be, and not allowing others to define us. As Toni Morrison said in *Beloved*, "definitions are for the definers, not the defined." This philosophy can never be overemphasized when you're an immigrant in a country that wants to relegate you to the corners or demands that you shed your "inferiority" by embracing the mainstream definition of standard, if not superior, citizenship. Filipinos sometimes call themselves "little brown Americans." It is a playful if somewhat ironic comment on our post-colonial status. When I moved to the U.S. in 2005, married Charlie, and lived in New Haven, I was living in a bubble for some time. This bubble gave me the impression that the color of my skin, my Third World origin, and my accent did not matter. I felt that I was treated as an equal. The bubble burst soon after John Carlos was born. People on the train would question how my "employer could allow my charge to travel" with me on public transportation; or they would ask me "how much do you get paid for that?" meaning for breastfeeding my baby (as a wet nurse); or if I adopted my baby; or say, "Wow, he calls you Mommy?" There are many other instances that I, in hindsight, realize were instrumental in helping me to dispel the stupid notion I was beginning to entertain that I could pass as white. As one well-intentioned acquaintance remarked when she expressed horror at how people could think I am too dark to be the mother of my fair-skinned son: "You could pass for an Italian-American." (This was at Charlie's high school reunion at St. Paul's School, in New Hampshire.) I couldn't help but wonder if my ability to pass for white was contingent on my being married to an alumnus of a prestigious prep school, someone who graduated from Yale where he is now a professor. Nevertheless, at a Yale party, a faculty member assumed that I must be part of the help and complained that I was not doing my job—cleaning the dirty wine glasses. One can also look at this from another point of view: for elderly Chinese couples pushing their grandchild's stroller around Yale, I must be Chinese and so they do not hesitate to speak to me in Chinese. Or a Lyft driver will start a conversation in Spanish assuming I'm Hispanic. I share these stories with John Carlos, telling him that it's my ancestors' way of reminding me who I am and, therefore, reminding him that "they" are in him, too.

Our Family Album bears witness to the fact that our friends and neighbors in the United States come from many different ethnic, racial and religious backgrounds and possess a wide range of social/gender orientations. In New Haven, Connecticut, John Carlos's "first friend," Ahad, and second mom (Mommy Subiya) are Muslim South Asians. Later he divided his week between two pre-schools—one filled with the children of Yale faculty and staff while the other was populated by African American kids drawn from a housing facility in our local neighborhood. Not all of this found its way into *Our Family Album,* but the documentary reminds us of the ways that John Carlos has been making connections between different worlds from a very early age. Our hope is that from these experiences, John Carlos will more fully recognize that we, humans, are all the same regardless of our skin color, where we live, and our economic background: We have a universal need to love and be loved, to learn, to play, to belong.

I want John Carlos to realize that his experience is not typical either of America or of the world. It is one he is able to enjoy because his father is a Yale professor and we live in downtown New Haven. He attends the Worthington Hooker School where the general student population comes from all over the world—thanks largely to Yale University. His annual class photos look like they were taken at a little United Nations event. This is balanced by his experience living in the remote village of Manlapay without hot running water, without Internet access and without access to regular public transportation. Schools are without libraries, and there is just one copy of a tattered dictionary for the entire high school. Children as young as preschoolers walk some kilometers to and from school, rain or shine. All this provides the necessary contrast and, hopefully, moral grounding for him. Our hope is for John Carlos to recognize the privileges he was born into and to use those privileges to help correct the injustices he is already beginning to identify on his own.

Just as the experience of racialized microaggressions have metaphorically put me back in my place, we hope this documentary will remind John Carlos that he carries within himself a rich global culture of humanity, of real people who are different yet also his relatives and friends. I want this film to remind him that he is more than just the color of his skin and hair, and that he needs to keep exploring the world, which is even richer (and more fraught) than what he has encountered so far. Indeed, we all need to remind ourselves of this reality as well.

What Photography Has Meant for Our Family

by Lorna Johnson-Frizell

Participating in the making of *Our Family Album* has made me reflect more seriously on the role that photography has played and continues to play in my life—and the life of my son Noah. For instance, I have never seen images of my parents as children. Born in the 1930's on the West Indies island of Jamaica, my parents were poor but ambitious. As they were born poor, photography was a luxury their parents could not afford. The earliest photographs of my parents that I have found are from their twenties—black and white images in which they were well dressed or in professional attire.

Born to agricultural workers, my parents' dream was to migrate into the professional classes. In my mother's case, she first left for Scotland, at age nineteen, to attend nursing school. She next went to England to work as a nurse midwife, then back to Jamaica and finally to the United States to continue working as a nurse. This was a common migration pattern for Caribbean folks. Though my parents left Jamaica they still identified as nationals. My mother, in particular, has chosen to build a home in Jamaica rather than purchase a home in the place in which she resides, the United States.

By the 1960's, my father had become the family photographer, capturing images of me and my siblings when we were infants and my parents were in their thirties. In contrast to the formal photographs of him and my mother, taken when they were young, our family photographs were less formal and captured social interactions. There is the photograph of one-year-old me seated on a blue rocking horse at the park. There is the photograph of my older sister Elaine, then two, looking at me—an infant with a perplexed expression. There is the photograph of my sister seated on a park bench next to my mother. These photographs documented the personal rather than professional. Somehow the color of the blue rocking horse remains fixed in my memory some fifty years later.

My husband, Richard, comes from a large Irish American family in New Jersey. As a baby-boomer, much of his childhood was chronicled with both still photographs and Super-8 film. There is a treasure trove of visual artifacts of his childhood which reveal just as much about his family as it does about mid-twentieth century America. Their value for me is in the memories that are not inherently mine, yet they evoke as much a reaction from me as if I had experienced the events myself. For me, they are what remains from a period of my husband's life that pre-dated me. Looking at the images I can deduce much about his nuclear family as well as societal norms and gender paradigms. The images serve both a cultural and personal role.

Unlike my parents whose formative years were in Jamaica, my siblings and I were not rooted in any given country. We were nomads. I immigrated to the United States when I was eleven years old. What I knew of America was what I had learned from the movies. Each Sunday there was a four p.m. movie on our one Jamaican channel. It projected the joys of whiteness, the privilege that was deeply embedded in those images. I just wanted "it." I wanted to be that happy, that rich, that pretty, that loved, that unbothered.

I became a filmmaker because, like my parents, I was "in search" of something. My young films searched for my own identity even as they questioned it. I was a puppy, lost in a vast world of images that told me I did not exist. It had never occurred to me as a child to question the veracity of those images. I was raised to drink the Kool Aid of America. My short films *Strands* (1996) and *My Wolverine* (1997) interrogated those images and probed my Jamaican American identity. They deal with what is left out of both those TV images and my father's family photos. In those films, I centralized my own story while questioning the role that race and gender play in determining what stories are traditionally told. *Strands* created a cinematic space where I could chronicle my own African diasporic experience—my life in England, Jamaica and America. I was thus able to project my own filmic image back onto myself. *My Wolverine* questions patriarchy, examining the insidious role micro-aggressions play in daily life. These early films were my search for and assertion of identity and self.

In 2001, I accepted a tenure-track position teaching film production. "How could students understand my work?" I asked. My subsequent films no longer interrogated identity in the same way. I used images for "work": work was teaching at a state college. I lost faith in my own filmmaking aesthetic and began work on "serious," social issue documentaries in an attempt to conform to the expectations of the position. *Freedom Road* (2004), distributed by Women Make Movies, was one result. Though I made films, I no longer travelled with a Super-8 camera as I had in my earlier years: I had somehow lost the desire to document, capture, record, see and share the personal and private with the world. As with those first photographs taken of my parents, I had separated image making from the personal space. *About Love*, several scenes of which appear in *Our Family Album*, was the major exception—perhaps one reason why it was never quite finished.

When my husband Richard and I met, neither of us owned a still camera. That changed when I became pregnant with Noah; Richard bought a camera and made it his mission to document everything. He became the new "family photographer," stepping into the role that his father and my father played in an earlier generation. Richard did not have the challenge of proving that this work "mattered" so he could effortlessly capture our lives without thought of how it would be "used." Here are some of the images Richard captured that I treasure so dearly:

- A series of photographs which reveal our three-year-old son's face gradually lighting up as he discovers his Christmas day present made by his dad—a train table.
- Noah's first day of school, looking excited and then dejected upon finding out we were leaving him there.
- An image of me sitting by the fireplace in a robe on Christmas day with Noah on my lap.
- Ten red cardinals perched on a white snow-covered tree next to our bird feeder in the middle of winter.

I am still flabbergasted by Richard's love of photography. In his photographs, he shared his appreciation of what was before him—the wonder of the world and the people in it. I had lost that carefree nature. Images have had to "mean" something and I had to prove their worth beyond personal pleasure.

One memorable example of Richard's audacity was when he photographed me giving birth to our son Noah. Though he had a desire to document this spiritually beautiful but physically gruesome moment I have yet to encounter one person who has any desire to see those photographs when invited. I stand by my belief that not everything needs to be captured and shared.

Richard was diagnosed with cancer in 2015. During his treatments, he asked me to document his radiation and chemotherapy. I found it hard to comply with this request but I did as he asked. I had no desire to capture him in a radiation mask or seated with a chemotherapy IV drip. I was traumatized by it all, but Richard, on the other hand, still had the desire to speak about and share his experience. I now understand the role the images played in demystifying the experience and humanizing our plight. I found it hard but Richard was so open with the world. It was as if his arms were extended and he was inviting the world into our lives.

This desire to document our lives did not lessen as his illness worsened. Midway through his treatment Rich could not breathe and we found ourselves in the emergency room yet again. He had to have a tracheostomy—a collar with a tube protruding from his neck. Later that year he had a radical neck dissection. He often asked me to photograph his neck so he could determine the speed with which his neck was healing. In these photographs, we looked for signs of hope. Just as my parents had used their images to project who they wanted to be, so we used these images to project what we wanted to be—better. It is very difficult for me to look at certain of these photographs. Despite this, Richard's work made me feel deeply—whether sadness or joy or love. I am immersed in the beauty of ten cardinals on a winter day or the sadness of an open neck wound.

Had Richard not insisted on taking photographs of our family or chronicling and sharing some of his journey, our story—our history—would probably die when we die. In combining his images with images of our family taken by others, I have a story to tell of our time here: the euphoria of our marriage and pregnancy, the quotidian details of our daily life together, the slow realization that cancer would ravage Rich's body, and the eventual acceptance of his death. It is our moments together that matter most, and Rich was cognizant enough to know that. He was cognizant enough to understand why he had to capture those images. Now Noah will have a story of his family spanning four countries. Like his friend, John Carlos, he will understand that his American story is a blend of continents, classes, skin tones, sheer joy and utter disappointment. Will these images matter to him in the decades to come? Will he feel as deeply about the images of his father as I do?

Rich died in 2017 when Noah was nine. He tells me he does not remember his father before he was riddled with cancer. The photographs of our family baking pies, at the beach and playing games together provide evidence of a time he cannot remember. They provide evidence that his father was once healthy and active. They suggest one form of memory—photographs—can triumph over another. They will also allow him to eventually pass these memories that are frozen in time on to another generation.

Rich gave us physical memories of our time as a family together. Rich packaged it and presented it to us as a gift that lives on beyond him and beyond us. Now that he is no longer here, I find myself taking up the camera and continuing his efforts along these lines. Noah will have memories of the two of us climbing glaciers in Iceland together, memories of celebrating Christmas by visiting family in Florida, and memories of traveling to the home of my birth in London. I have finally embraced what I spent most of a lifetime avoiding. I see now what it means to others. These images provide evidence of our family, our pain, our joy—our small moment in time. We were here…once, together.

Family Albums and Intersecting Diasporas

By Thomas Allen Harris

I first met Charlie Musser on December 6, 2006—one week before the birth of his son John Carlos, to whom the documentary *Our Family Album* is ostensibly addressed. I was visiting Yale University to screen my most recent film, *Twelve Disciples of Nelson Mandela: A Son's Tribute to Unsung Heroes* (2005). I had been traveling with the film nationally and internationally for nearly a year when Elizabeth Alexander, then a Yale Professor of English and African American Studies, invited me to the campus. I had known Elizabeth for a number of years and gladly accepted. (If had I visited Yale a week later or John Carlos had shown up a week earlier, much of the following story would have been different.)

At that time, I had been making deeply personal films for over fifteen years. Part documentary and part narrative, *Twelve Disciples of Nelson Mandela* is a film about my late South African stepfather, Pule Leinaeng (Lee), and the 11 comrades who left South Africa together to fight apartheid in 1960 and, unbeknownst to them, begin 30+ years of exile. Rather than make a straightforward historical documentary, I chose to engage a community of young South African actors with their forgotten history through Lee's photo album, which I had brought with me to South Africa after his death. Lee had joined our family when I was nine-years old and had raised me as his son although cultural differences—a traditional African father and an American son—often strained the relationship and the family.

I don't actually recall the screening or Q&A but I will never forget the dinner that followed. It was an intimate gathering of seven or eight people during which we continued to discuss issues raised by the film. The conversation quickly turned to the personal. Elizabeth Alexander's husband and father of her two sons, Ficre Ghebreyesus (1962-2012), left his native Eritrea as a political refugee like Lee. Charlie had been joined by his wife Maria Threese Serana, who had left behind her close-knit family and political activism in the Philippines.

So much of the conversation was about the nuances of navigating intercultural family dynamics with the reality of exile and its impacts on individuals and families. Reunions also became a topic, particularly when we were joined by one of Elizabeth's students, a senior named Mena Cammett. As a child, Mena had been in my first documentary feature, *VINTAGE–Families of Value* (1995)—a film that looked at African American families through the eyes of three groups of queer siblings (including Mena's mom and two aunts along with my brother and myself.) One underlying motive I had for making that film: to disrupt the misconception that if individuals embraced their queer selves, they would be forced to exile themselves from their families and church communities.

It was during that dinner that Elizabeth Alexander first told us to look out for a close friend of hers from her time in Chicago, who was launching a bid for President. He was a young Black senator named Baraka Obama, who also came from a multicultural background and spent formative years of childhood growing up outside of America—something both John Carlos and I share with him. It was at this dinner that the idea of the first Black American President became a possibility within my imaginary, though at the time I had no idea that two years later I'd be watching Alexander recite her poem "Praise Song for the Day" at the historic 2008 presidential inauguration of Barack Obama.

When viewed from today's vantage point, the context for this first meeting with Charlie takes on somewhat mythic proportion. In my mind's eye, I see that moment, that evening, as a kind of metaphysical crossroads—intersecting the present, past, and future and bringing narratives of diaspora (African, Asian, European) into dialogue with one another. For me it remains to this day a harbinger for both communication and change. It was at that dinner that Charlie and I began a conversation about film and teaching. By the end of the evening, he would ask me if I'd consider coming to Yale to teach. That special evening set the stage for the work and collaboration in which Charlie and I would subsequently engage—though it took nearly a decade to become a reality.

At the time I was moving into production on a new film, *Through A Lens Darkly: Black Photographers and the Emergence of a People*. Inspired by

Dr. Deborah Willis's groundbreaking publication, *Reflections in Black: Black Photographers from 1840-Present*, *Through A Lens Darkly* explores the role of photography in shaping the identity, aspirations and social emergence of African Americans from slavery to the present. The film brings into view previously hidden and largely unknown images by professional and vernacular African American photographers which add to our understanding of history by providing a window into lives, experiences and perspectives of Black families that is absent from the traditional historical canon.

For this film, I drew inspiration from the work of Marlon Riggs, particularly his pioneering *Tongues Untied*, in its assembly of a diverse yet focused community of storytellers to follow and transform a singular journey into both a communal journey of discovery and a call to action. *Through A Lens Darkly* highlights photographers, artists, and scholars who are rethinking the archive and its relevance to issues of identity and representation. The film addresses visual literacy in understanding the construction of race and representation—and the use of art and photography, in particular, as forms of activism challenging accepted stereotypes. The goal of this film, ultimately, was to encourage a re-valuation of the family photo archive as historical records which illuminate, inform and expand our understanding and shared values as members of a common culture.

While working on this project, I kept thinking about how my previous films repeatedly elicited audiences to ask me to build a platform that would allow them to creatively engage with their own family photographic archives. This desire to create a structure that would allow people to pursue their own historical investigations through their family archives lead to the formation of the transmedia project Digital Diaspora Family Reunion.

Initially conceived as primarily an Internet website, Digital Diaspora Family Reunion (DDFR) quickly morphed into a live performance event in 2009 and has since toured to over 50 cities/areas, generating an archive of 50,000 images and 3,000 interviews with ordinary people speaking about their family photographic archives. DDFR is a multimedia, socially engaged art project that has become a virtual space to activate the many stories and photographic images that had been slowly gathering dust in some overlooked corner of an attic or been buried in some half-forgotten folder on a hard drive.

Like other crowd-sourced story platforms such as Antiques Roadshow or StoryCorp, DDFR Roadshow gathers together the neglected shards of our past residing in our archives and repurposes them for a new generation seeking some connection between themselves and the world as they know it. DDFR's mission quickly evolved to focus on bringing together individual, family and community narratives within a context that helps to expose the commonalities of our shared experiences. Although it began as an engagement tool for my films, DDFR actually shifted the narrative of its companion documentary, *Through A Lens Darkly*. In this expanded form, it situated an analysis of the Black image within the mythic American family photo album.

It was *Through A Lens Darkly* and Digital Diaspora Family Reunion that brought Charlie and I together again in the Fall 2015, when Yale Art History Professor Kobena Mercer invited me to screen the film at Yale. At our second dinner together we were joined by a number of Yale students and faculty. Once again Charlie brought up the subject of my teaching at Yale. Unbeknownst to either of us, this second visit to Yale triggered a number of events that led to my teaching a non-credit workshop around Digital Diaspora Family Reunion in the School of Art in the Spring semester of 2016. While I was setting up the room for the class, Charlie walked in. Although he had signed up for the course, he wanted to make sure it would be okay for him to intrude on an opportunity designed largely for undergraduates. Charlie explained that he and Threese had been working on a film entitled *Visa Wives*, about Filipina family members who had come to the U.S. on fiancée visas. That project had become "stuck," and he wanted to use the class to think about other possibilities.

During this class, my friendship and working relationship with Charlie took root and grew. I encouraged participants in the workshop to bring in family photographs and use them to construct a range of creative work. Charlie was soon developing some of the scenes that would be crucial to *Our Family Album*—then entitled *For John Carlos: (Y)our Family Album*. We discussed a variety of family images, including many taken by Threese; coherent scenes and a variety of theoretic concerns emerged in the process. These included scenes of Charlie's first visit to the Philippines, where his colleague, the Filipino queer filmmaker Nick Deocampo, had him lecture on the first on-screen kiss, creating an occasion for Threese and Charlie to meet face to face. Charlie's emerging film already hinted at the ways their romance and relationship developed over time and space while each of them reflected on the meaning of the new family they were creating. At the end of the semester, all the class participants—several undergrads, two graduate students and Charlie—organized a set of successful public presentations of their work. One of the most exciting aspects of those segments of *For John Carlos* that were screened that night was the way Charlie was interweaving his life and work as a film scholar with new and inherited family narratives. The event was hosted by then Associate Dean for the Arts at Yale College, Susan Cahan, who had made the course possible. At the end of the evening Susan shared with me that not only did she find Charlie's short 10-minute film the most developed of the work screened but she was also unexpectedly surprised that Charlie's film had allowed her to see another dimension of a colleague she thought she knew.

Although the workshop had ended, Charlie and I were eager to continue to develop our shared intellectual engagement around film, family, diaspora and politics. It was at this point that he asked me if I would be willing to serve as Executive Producer for the feature-length version of *For John Carlos*, and I enthusiastically agreed to do so. For me, this project embodies the mission of Digital Diaspora Family Reunion: to help people creatively engage with their family photographic archives and in so doing make new work, whether films, art projects or books; to expand and enlarge our definitions and functions of the family photo album; and to investigate the complexity around our identities, subjectivities and origins while in the process enlarging the meaning of family beyond the narrow constraints of the nuclear model so prevalent in American mainstream culture and entertainment.

After the workshop, *For John Carlos* became Charlie and Threese's mutual endeavor. They cannibalized material they had shot for *Visa Wives*—scenes of family taken in the Philippines in 2013—and returned there again in 2017 to film additional material specifically for the new project. Given its ultimate length and complexity, the documentary that was eventually renamed *Our Family Album* developed quite quickly. I occasionally watched cuts of the film as it developed and provided feedback. [Editor's note: Thomas's feedback was consistently productive and in so many ways crucial.] The resulting essay film interweaves intersecting family narratives, Filipino cinema history, meditations about the family photo album, and interviews with a community of filmmakers, archivists and scholars who do double duty as extended family members.

Over the last four years of our working together, I have had the good fortune to develop a friendship with Charlie, his wife and son. Through Charlie's good services, I was invited to join the Yale faculty, appointed in both African American Studies and Film & Media Studies. Just as I supported his investigation into his family's photo archives, he has served as a mentor around teaching at Yale. These two strands have occasionally come together, for instance, when I screened *Our Family Album* for my course Family Narratives/Cultural Shifts. When I look through *Our Family Album*, I cannot help but see the life of a friend and colleague as he passes his song, his story, which is also a collective story, to the next generation. Likewise, I see the perseverance of Threese as she finds her way in an unfamiliar country while retaining ties to her native Philippines. And, finally, I follow John Carlos as he grows from a newborn to an eleven-year-old who is nearing puberty. I see a blended family that spans ethnicities, religions, geographies; I see a family that reflects the diversity and complexity of who we are.

Documents and Memories

By Nick Deocampo

Depending on where one locates oneself in the march of civilization, documents are there to mark time. Cavemen painted on walls; Egyptians wrote on papyrus; monks inscribed sacred texts on paper; Gutenberg mass produced books through the printing press; Beethoven put down his notations on score sheets; and when technology advanced, Niepce preserved images in photographs; Muybridge, Edison and Dickson, and later the Lumière brothers, made those still photographs move; computers globalized the circulation of images; and cell phones allowed us to make selfies. These landmarks in the history of mankind have generated documents that survive to tell the tale of its progress. Documents are what survive us. They constitute our memory as human civilization.

In our age, especially with the coming of the twenty-first century, the media available for us to record our memories as humans have exponentially exploded. From the humble paper of ancient history, we have technologized communication and memory. Many recording machines have made possible the encoding of our fleeting time on earth in forms which, if they survive, provide a continuum into the distant future. What remains will be what is kept, and what is kept depends on who remembers, what needs to be remembered, and where kept memories will be stored. In our age, documents in virtual form pose the challenge of keeping our memories alive and bringing the story of our age to its future.

Motion pictures offer new and myriad possibilities for keeping the memories of a generation mad with images. From the image of workers leaving a factory, cinema has become a recorder of life as it has been, of wars, microbes and galaxies, yellow brick roads and avatars, gangsters and ETs—all the narratives that crowd our reality and imagination. All this progress in motion pictures accelerated with the advent of digital technology, bringing the act of image production into the virtual world.

As we drown in a vast ocean of images, how do we discern the single drop of the individual image that makes us appreciate the nature of a moving picture or a photograph? After all, it is still the singular image, not the entire ocean, that captures our attention and affection. Whether still or moving, it is the singular experience of the *image* that provokes our senses and our imagination to hold on to that image as part of our memory. It is the image of a train arriving at a station, a Maharaja's cortege, an Eskimo hunting seals, cowboys chasing injuns, the dropping of a bomb, a colonizing invasion, landing on the moon, a president getting shot in a speeding car, and Forrest Gump giving us the wisdom of a generation. "Life is like a box of chocolates," pictures both cherished and reviled. Whichever memory we want to keep, the motion picture enables us to remember our time spent in this world and with one another.

It is in this flow of memories and machines that a film like Charlie Musser and Threese Serana's *Our Family Album* makes us appreciate the role that motion pictures play in giving testimony to life and to the role that the image plays in it. The documentary collects memories that are stories whose proximity to the filmmakers make them remote to us as viewers. Yet, no matter the disconnect, there is a compelling force that attracts us to the film because we, too, have fallen in love, created a family, interacted with one another across racially charged lines, talked to friends, and made records of our lives so people know that we have been here. That we lived. That we loved. That we left a legacy. And there—in that album, in that video, is kept *that* memory. A memory that is as universal as it is partisan, as collective as it is singular, as personal as it is political.

Our Family Album is one such memory. In its elastic capture of time, painful memories are told of how two races—American and Filipino—were once caught in a bitter war that led, a century later, into a sweet memory of two people falling for each other and defying that history of animosity to declare love and bond into a family. What better story is there to tell? However, there is also the story of a cinema that has borne witness to a narrative of the colonial relations between cultures but is now released from that role to become a medium that informs how those cultures can look respectfully at each other. What more enlightening narrative is there to show? Then there is the story of the *image* itself—resilient in its mandate to store not just a picture of the past but also the fondness, the nostalgia, the surprise, and all the remembered thoughts and emotions which an image conjures. Nothing could be more compelling.

While early film documents made about the Philippines were either actualities taken with a one-sided point-of-view (that of American camera-men capturing native images to be brought back and shown in America as a way to affirm America's colonial status) or re-constitutions of reality (cinematic caricatures of sanitized, romanticized imperialism), what we see in *Our Family Album* is a shared story by an American and Filipina honoring their union through a filmed story. History has come far for this plot to find expression on the screen. It breaks the legacy running through films such as Edison's 1899 "re-enactments" of the Philippine-American War, Dean C. Worcester's *Native Life in the Philippines* (1913) or (from a quite different perspective) Marlon Fuentes's *Bontoc Eulogy* (1995). Charlie and Threese create a radically different, more personal account of the coming together of races through the union of individual lives and families, with film to cement the relations.

In the film, the story of Charles and Threese is one to which we can all relate. Within the classic narrative of two people finding each other, we discover many other things: awareness of individual lives, the value of family, consciousness of races, attachment to documents…and through all these, enduring memory. It is memory that ties the documentary's disparate elements into a unified coherence for what would otherwise be an incoherent shuffle of peoples and places, time and events, objects and emotions. In one photograph John Carlos is born, in another he is grown. One moment the Serana-Mussers are in Cebu, the next time we see them are in New Haven. Some memories are preserved in photographs, others are digitally captured. Both Charles and Threese's film constitutes the narrative of their memory as individuals, as family, as humans. It gives testament to life. Not just their life, but also the life of documents.

Running as a sub-story to the main narrative is the story of photographs and motion pictures. They tell their own story as recorders. Their technological invention made it possible for contemporary people to mark their own moments in contemporary time. But just as people die, so do those machines. They are invented and they become obsolete. They have their own life span as people have. And so we have lost the cinématographe, nitrate film, open-reel tape recorders, Kodak instamatic cameras, Super-8 mm cameras, Steenbeck editing machines, Betamax tape, Umatic half-inch video, and many other machines that are first orphaned, then left for dead. But with their disuse, will the images they captured also fall into forgetfulness?

This is one reason why we admire documents. They are resilient for having survived centuries like the tablets containing the ancient hieroglyphs of Egypt or the pre-historic syllabary etched in the barks of trees found among the Palawan tribes in the Philippines. But although many documents have survived, they remain fragile as they can be destroyed by natural causes, disasters, wars, technological obsolescence, lack of archival facilities, human neglect, and capitalist greed among many other reasons. This is why documents need our utmost care: if they slip into the void, nothing remains as evidence of our past. Without a material basis, everything becomes imagined thought.

If we face the frightening prospect that the loss of documents will lead to a loss of memory, we can derive some comfort from *Our Family Album* as it redeems us from the growing amnesia that accompanies successive generations. The film does this by embracing the humble family album as a quaint personal practice of keeping family memories and personal recollections. While ably accomplishing this, the documentary moves even a step further by expanding its task to include the storing of racial memories, social history, technological progress, documentary awareness, and global consciousness. The family album which the documentary sets out to present, once unpacked, contains more than mere personal family anecdotes. Through the specificity of the races and the individuated stories it contains, it addresses in larger symbolic ways a history of humankind.

This is where a document like Charles and Threese's film derives its power to dialogue with the audience beyond the personal and the parochial, to embrace our larger humanity. Throughout the film there is a conscious iteration of what recorded documents can do to bring back memories and with them our endangered histories, arrested in time from slipping into oblivion. The film, as document, serves as a mirror by which we can gaze at our image and reflect on the person that we think we are. Or not. But unlike the mirror, the documentary holds the image of the past, preserves it, and makes it appear to us again, defying age and eschewing the bounds of temporal forgetfulness. Documents are ruthless witnesses to our past. It is not documents that fail to recall what has gone by. As we look at documents, we realize that it is we who have changed; they, those documents, remain faithful to our past.

Your Family Album: A Diasporic Story

By Laura Wexler

Deprived of a principle of marking, photographs are signs which don't take, which turn, as milk does. —Roland Barthes

Family photographs can be made to reveal secrets that they have long concealed. South African writer Terry Kurgan has parsed a set of discoveries she made while investigating a clutch of family snapshots left by her Polish Jewish grandfather, dating from just before the outbreak of World War II.[1] Her grandfather's detailed journals from the war years until the late 1950s, when he ceased to keep them, accompanied the photographs. Reading these diaries alongside and against this set of photographs she is able to clarify many of the scenes in the photographs, but this intense inspection also raises more questions. Learning about the family's successful escape from their home in Bielsko, Poland, just hours ahead of the invading Nazi soldiers—and their subsequent migrations to Bucharest, Istanbul, Ankara, Aleppo, Baghdad, Basra, Muscat, Karachi, Bombay, Mombasa and Cape Town—sharpens the stories she is able to pry from the images. Conversely, the silent pictures upend her earlier understandings not only of the war, but also of the record her grandfather kept of what had been going on in her own family, before the Nazis came.

Blowing up small portions of the photographs and focusing in illuminates the images, sometimes in stunning ways. For example, a much-loved photograph of Kurgan's mother, as a small child, sitting between her own mother (Kurgan's grandmother) and a handsome man on a set of lawn chairs at the Jasny Palac Hotel in the mountain resort town of Zacopane, in the Tatra Mountains, eventually resolves into the *mise-en-scene* of that grandmother's long affair with the handsome man. It is a family secret of the most mundane, yet shattering, kind. Kurgan writes, "This photograph in my family's album records a day in the summer of July or August, 1939. And, at the very outset of what was to become one of the greatest atrocities of the twentieth century, my grandmother was fucking Doctor Lax…. This photograph masks a secret. A secret that is too big for this page."[2]

More secrets are exposed. A diary entry records her grandfather's discovery of a propaganda pamphlet among the scattered effects that Terry's governess, Truda, had left behind when the women and children of the household fled the German invasion of Poland. Pausing briefly, before leaving forever, her grandfather notes in his diary that he picked up the pamphlet and read the *Ten Commandments of a Polish Nationalist*. Point 4 read: "Remember that the Jewish issue has to be solved drastically and our towns have to be made utterly Polish, so that food and work in Poland are guaranteed first of all to our countrymen, and not to foreign parasitic Jews." Yet the family photographs studied earlier show Truda seemingly well ensconced in her job, and looking kindly towards the little girl. Were these earlier photographs also a mask? Had there been nothing but dissimulation?

Kurgan has read another story about Bielsko in the memoir of holocaust survivor Gerda Weissman Klein.[3] Nazi soldiers entered Bielsko just after her grandfather fled, and an SS officer marching down a main thoroughfare lined with cheering townspeople carried a gift bouquet of fresh-picked roses in his hand. Klein writes of her shock that people her family had long considered friends flew the Nazi flag and adopted the Nazi salute. "She remembers," writes Kurgan, "how it angered her to notice that a neighbor had picked her mother's beautiful white roses and given them to a German officer, only to see the man drop them to the ground a moment later when he was handed a glass of schnapps."[4] Uncannily, these same roses —and the officer—appear in a YouTube video of old film footage that Kurgan comes across while doing her research. What are the chances of this coincidence? Come to think of it, what are the chances that any of it would have happened? And yet the photographs line up with the reality that history has exposed. Or, had it always been visible, only gone unseen in her Jewish family? As Roland Barthes puts it, photographs "*turn, as milk does.*"[5]

Terry Kurgan is but one of many writers who discover in photography a mode of inquiry that can reveal something quite distinct about family and history from that for which they had originally gone looking. Following the trail of the photographs backwards in time, from South Africa to Europe, and from her own to her grandfather's writing, challenges Kurgan's understanding of the lived reality of the war itself. The intimacy of Jewish life narrows the war while at the same time it unfolds portions of history. As she traces their flight, she loses her previous certainty about her characters. This loss of certitude is the secret that is too big for the page.

In a sense, Charlie Musser and Threese Serana are two more seekers in this vein. For them, photographic inquiry into family history also begins with the inheritance of images and stories. This leads to a journey of recovery, not only back to the Philippines, where they originally met, but eventually to Europe and Threese's Jewish heritage. Charlie and Threese's search proves consequential. The memory that they recover is sparked by an apparently anti-Semitic utterance that Threese's mother addressed to their son (her grandson), John Carlos—that "the Jews killed Jesus." This provocation ricocheted through the family, quickly reaching John Carlos's [half] sister, who is Jewish through matrilineal descent. The resulting turmoil proved crucial for unearthing the fact that Threese's mother's family were Converso Jews: Jews who fled the Spanish Inquisition (one quite possibly on Magellan's ships) and took refuge in the Philippines, eventually settling in a remote mountainous area of Cebu (the first island to be colonized by the Spanish). Some of her ancestors were apparently caught practicing their Jewish faith, taken to Mexico and executed. On learning this history, we are told, Threese "wept for a long time."

It is as if there had been no place for this Jewish history before because the inquisition and anti-Semitism had rendered it fugitive and dangerous even though they had not erased it. Through their drive for relation, between themselves and with others, Musser and Serana are able to enter this diasporic story into the family album, repairing a part of the past. Threese tells us that her mother had been told as a child that "you are not supposed to tell that we are Jewish because Christ was killed by the Jews." Later in the film, her mother's brother asserts they had been told as children that they must not try to read the strange Bible written in unintelligible script because it "would drive us crazy." For John Carlos this secret became a revelation that created an important bond that he could share with his sister. The film ends in a postscript with John Carlos reading the four questions aloud at his sister's Seder, as the youngest Jewish child. This is a story of survival that leaps from the frame.

While initially surprised to discover this lost history, Charlie Musser sees parallels with his ancestors who fled to North America because they were being persecuted as Anabaptists, later called Mennonites. As relatives disclose their family's hybrid racial, religious and cultural past, Charlie and Threese gain a firmer sense of historical possibilities. Unexpectedly, family lore acknowledges the kind of transcultural love that they themselves pursue, and buttresses the surmounting of stereotypes as represented by their son John Carlos, for whom this family album is being created.

Whereas Kurgan, like most writers about family photographs, narrows in, Charlie and Threese's world grows contrapuntally wider and more external the more they look for photographs and stories about the specific families they have joined. They are constantly finding new places to look for pictures, and new people to ask about what they find. They also take new pictures, memorializing their friendships and the new acquaintances they make. This important distinction demands further attention. Kurgan, as a writer, is most often working alone. The sparks of her intellect glance off of striking encounters with others but function largely in an interior space. One gets the sense—in fact she even says—that she would climb into the photographs if she could. "I long to be able to sit inside this photograph."[6] Musser and Serana, on the other hand, are filmmakers, occupying a collaborative social field. To me, this is the most distinctive charm of the film. The title of the film, *Our Family Album*, only seems to present a possessive *"our."* Actually, what happens is that through their joint endeavors—filmmaking, storytelling, parenting, befriending—Musser and Serana include more and more people in their own circle of interpretation. These other people have family pictures too, and stories, which soon become part of *"ours"* as well. In the film, social groupings—schools, conferences, fairgrounds—are repeatedly and explicitly said to be indistinguishable from family forms of kinship. This point is first delivered by the word "likewise" in the film, uttered by Musser as he shifts his attention from his own family photographs to those contained in the British National Fairground Archive, which preserves 150 years of historical documents of a group of people who, according to its founder Vanessa Toulmin, are related "by kinship, family, business, shared lifestyles." The point is further emphasized by the film's repeated shifts from private life to large communal gatherings. Because we share these kinds of social groupings, we also have a stake in *Our Family Album.*

Our Family Album brings to mind certain other films that ponder the family's photographic record: Rea Tajiri's brilliant re-construction, in *History and Memory: For Akiko and Takashige*, of the significance of a photograph she happens to come across in the National Archives of her grandmother making a little wooden carving of a bird while interned with other Japanese during World War II, the gateway to a personal memory of the family history she had not herself experienced; Thomas Allen Harris's trenchant suture of the paternal and maternal, the African and the American, the masculine and the feminine strands of contemporary Black families, his own family included, in *VINTAGE – Families of Value*; Socheata Poeuv's astonished discovery, driving *New Year Baby*, that her family photographs document a loving family that was literally constructed through surviving the Khmer Rouge; Arthur Dong's honorific exegesis of his family photograph as a form of collage, since his immigrant Chinese family was not actually, at the time it was taken, legally able to be physically all together and present with one another, in *Sewing Woman*; Cecilia Aldarondo's loving resurrection, in *Memories of a Penitent Heart*, of the memory of her uncle's lover, ghosted by the family because of the homosexuality they refuse to acknowledge even while her uncle dies of AIDS; and Alan Berliner's powerful "para-cinematic" confrontations with the men in his family and the idea of the American family itself, using multiple modes such as photographs, scrolls and collages in addition to his many documentary films.

Most scholarship on the meaning of family photographs is textual. Yet the printed text can only describe. In contrast to text, these films *animate* moments of discovery. They literally show the process of illumination at work. Writers such as Martha Langford and Tina Campt emphasize the oral and the haptic components of learning from family photographs. In her exploration of memory and the photo album, Langford parses the many ways in which the conversations that take place in the event of looking at family photographs are fundamental to making meaning. She writes: "Any photograph can be at cause, for any photograph is a potential kernel story, a discrete, catalytic reference to a longer story that is teased out and expanded in conversation."[7] As Campt goes on to observe, what is crucial to the listening practice developed here is a conception of photographs as deeply affective objects that implicate and leave impressions upon us through multiple forms of contact: visual contact (seeing), physical contact (touching), psychic contact (feeling), and most counterintuitively of all, the sonic contact (frequency) that requires us to listen to as well as view images.[8] How the "longer story" gets "teased out and expanded in conversation" is the story arc of all of the above films. How the search for photographs sounds and feels is a particular focus of *Our Family Album*, as boxes are discovered, photographs are unwrapped, and especially as the camera lingers on Serana's thumb as it moves back and forth across a stain on a newly shared photograph of her grandmother, digging in to the surface of the image in an attempt to scrape it off.

What Musser and Serana have uniquely, further done in *Our Family Album* is to make this process of oral and haptic illumination sharable beyond the family circle, to represent the "kernel" of reconstruction in real time, so to speak, so that widening circles of audience participate in making "them" into "us" without collapsing distance. That this is their real-life ambition as well should be acknowledged. More than the buried stories of the Jewish diaspora, the biggest "photographic turn" Charlie and Threese accomplish is to demonstrate just how powerfully two individuals, closely tracking their own distinctive family histories, can activate the filmed photograph's remarkable capacity to affiliate.

Endnotes

1 Terry Kurgan, *Everyone is Present: Essays on Photography, Memory, and Family* (Johannesburg, South Africa: Fourthwall Books, 2018).
2 Kurgan, *Everyone is Present,* 20.
3 Gerda Weissman Klein, *All But My Life* (New York: Hill and Wang, 1957).
4 Kurgan, *Everyone is Present,* 117.
5 Roland Barthes, *Camera Lucida: Reflections on Photography* translated by Richard Howard (New York: Hill and Wang, 1981), 6.
6 Kurgan, *Everyone is Present,* 15.

7 Martha Langford, *Suspended Conversations: The Afterlife of Memory in Photographic Albums* (Montreal: McGill-Queen's University Press, 2001), 150.

8 Tina Campt, *Image Matters: Archive, Photography and the African Diaspora in Europe* (Durham: Duke University Press, 2012).

Script

An Explanatory Key

What follows is the annotated script for the documentary *Our Family Album*. The transcribed script is in regular typeface. The annotations are *in italics*. Annotations provide contextualizing information for various scenes, identify people in the photographs, add comments and asides. Introductory annotations are generally ***in bold italics***. The film itself integrates interviews and cinema-verité-style scenes with voiceover commentary. When people appear in the diegetic world of the documentary, they are first identified by their full names, afterwards only by their first names. In this context, the filmmakers are identified as **Threese** and **Charlie**. Several interviews were conducted in Cebuano and appear with English subtitles. This book only provides the translation. The voiceover is delivered exclusively by Threese Serana and Charles Musser—indicated as **TS** and **CM** in what follows. While the film itself is a collaborative effort, Charlie Musser is responsible for the annotations and the selection of images accompanying the script.

Our epigraph is freely drawn from a popular quote (in the tradition of Werner Herzog) in Umberto Eco's "The Theory of Signs and the Role of the Reader," The Bulletin of the Midwest Modern Language Association, 14:1 (Spring, 1981), 36. Other epigraphs were considered. We particularly liked one that the United Nations published in the year of my birth, 1951: "As there is no reliable evidence that disadvantageous effects are produced thereby, no biological justification exists for prohibiting inter-marriage between races." (UNESCO, "Four Statements on the Race Question," [1969], 42) However, it felt a little too on point.

Thomas Allen Harris is the President & Chief Creative Officer of Digital Diaspora Family Reunion, LLC. He is this documentary's executive producer. Our Family Album was begun in a workshop that he conducted at Yale University and he has continued to provide invaluable support.

Photo Day at Worthington Hooker School, New Haven, Connecticut, for Patrick Hermann's Fourth Grade Class. We consider ourselves fortunate that our son John Carlos is a student at this school with its dedicated teachers and students who come—or whose parents come—from all parts of the world.

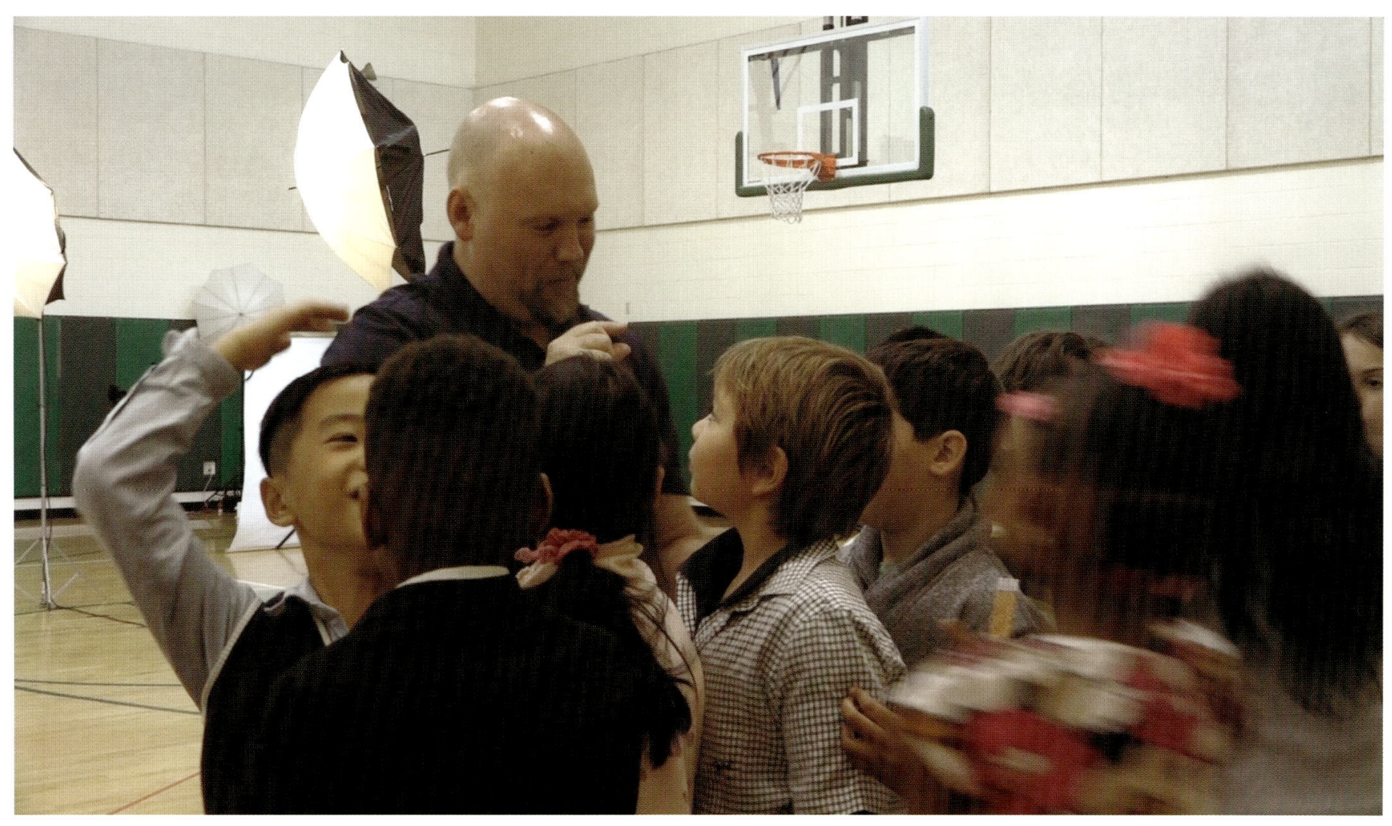

Patrick Hermann: Perfect. Perfect. Perfect. Just a little bit [shorter].

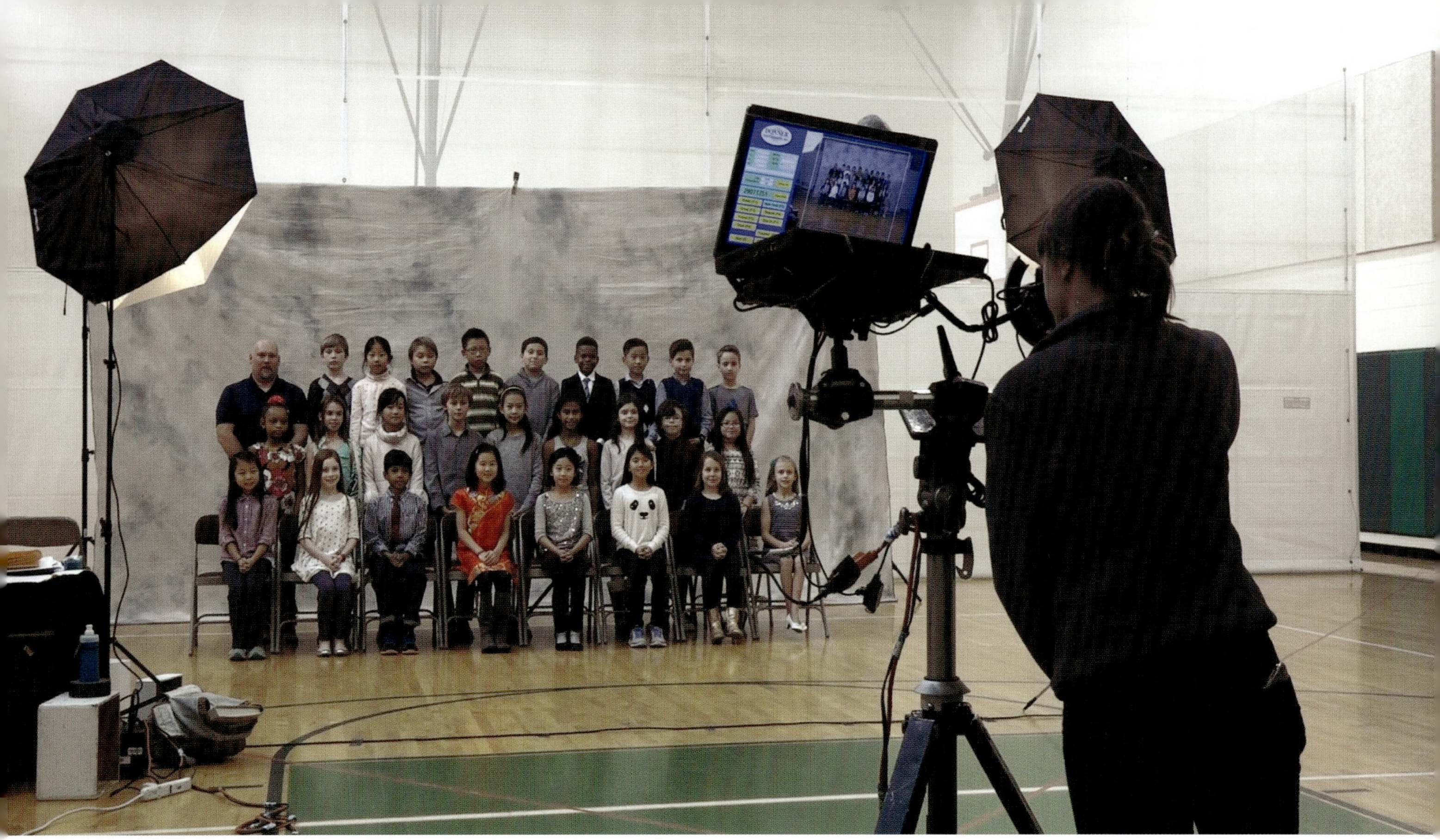

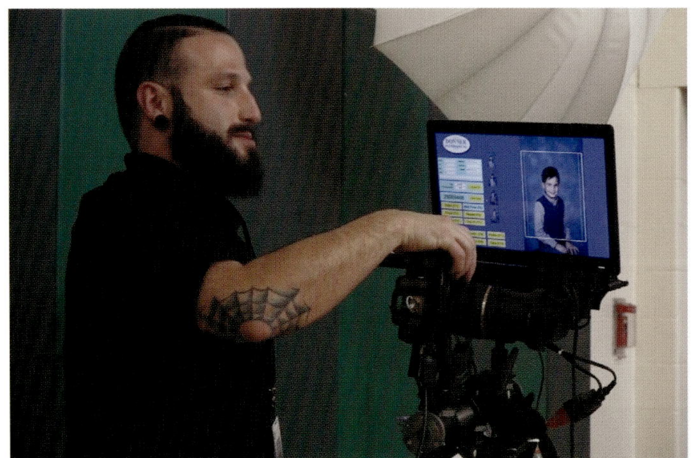

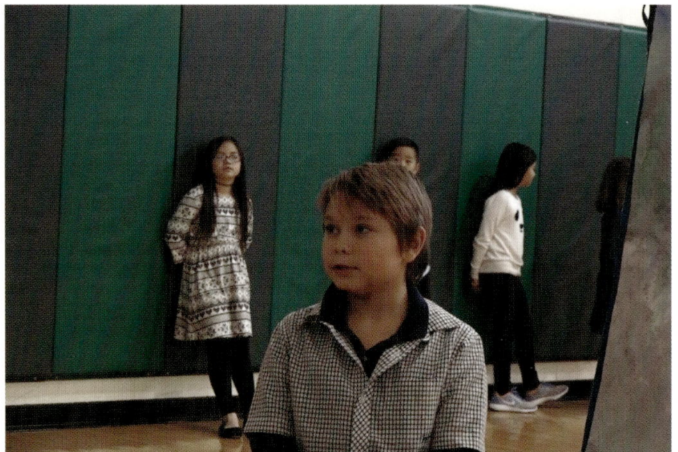

Photographer: Say "Chicken!"

For John Carlos...

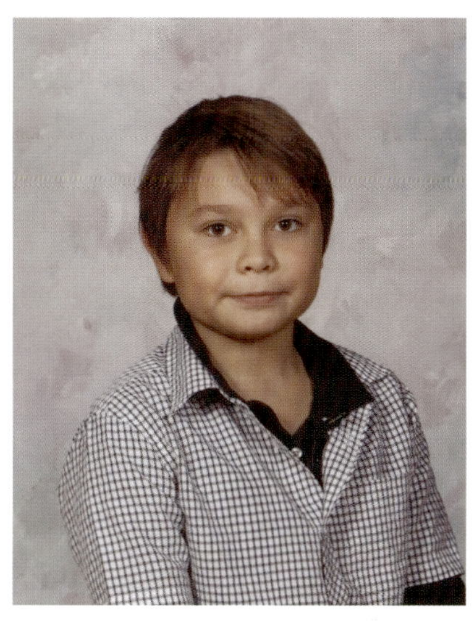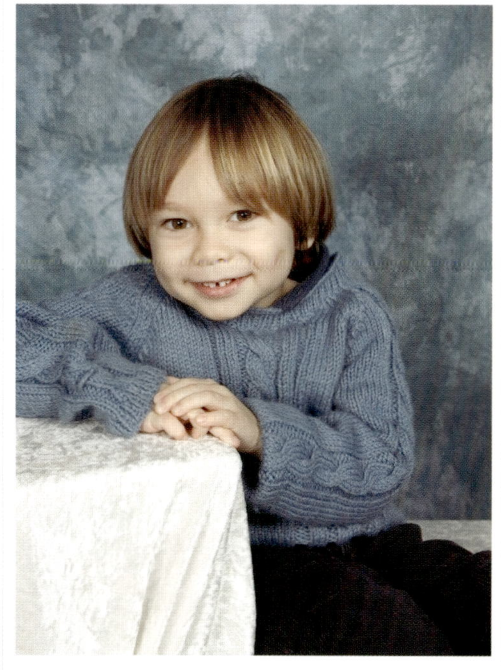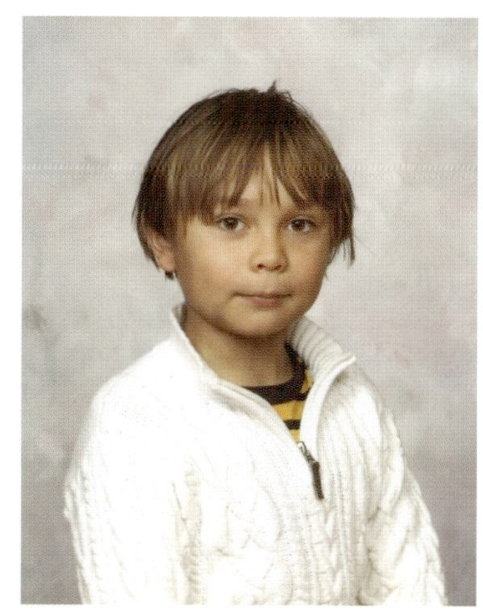

Threese Serana (TS): Carlito, we want to make you a family album.

Charles Musser (CM): And tell you something about the photographs.

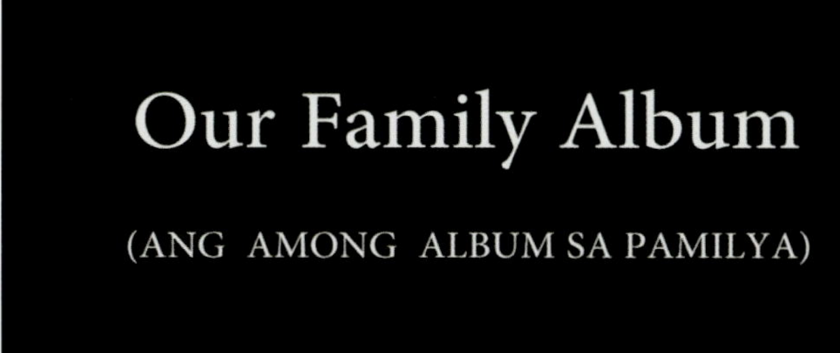

Our Family Album

(ANG AMONG ALBUM SA PAMILYA)

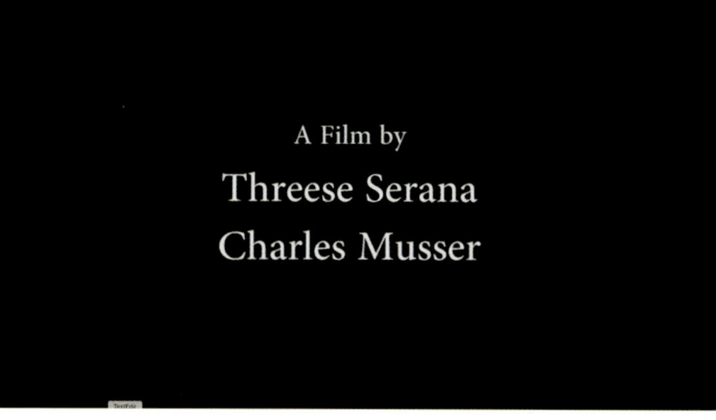

A Film by

Threese Serana
Charles Musser

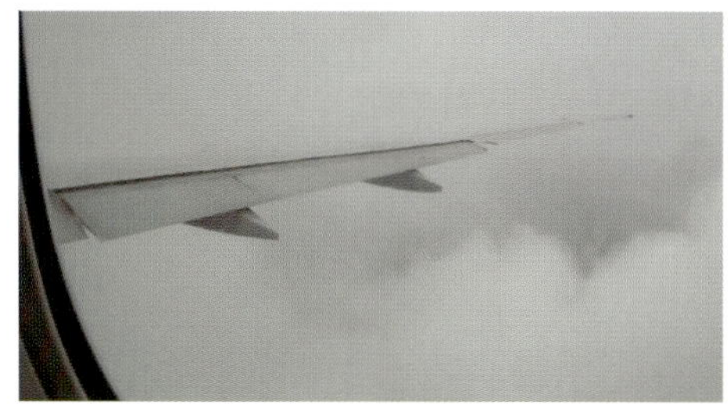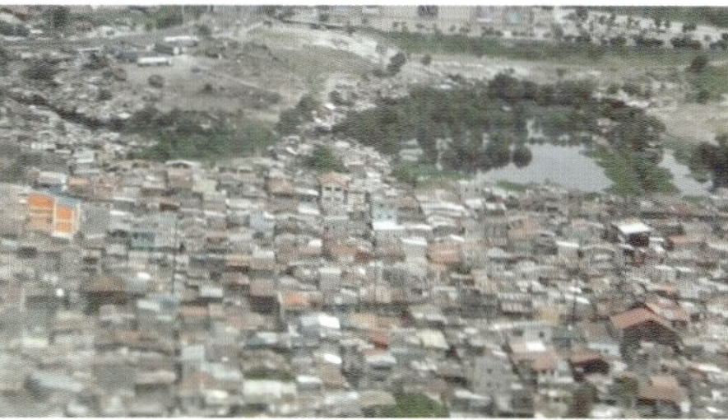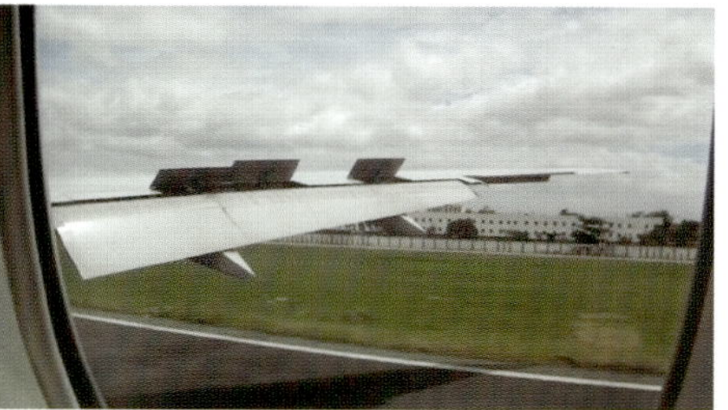

CM*:* Twelve years ago I was on a plane to Manila--on my way to meet a woman teaching Political Science at University of the Philippines-Cebu. We had connected on the Internet barely six weeks earlier. We shared many interests, even though as a political activist she had been far more courageous than I had even dreamt of being myself. Was this just another stupid idea or would there be chemistry?

Note*: "Twelve years ago" from when we started to make this film, fourteen years from when it was"finished," and perhaps fifteen years from when this book is published. In terms of the film's timeline, our narration has stayed as first written.*

In the era of pre-digital photography, few people could claim extensive photographic documentation of their first evening together, or of the many other formative moments in their relationship. We do because Nick Deocampo knew that these images could become valuable evidence down the road—if Threese was applying for permanent residence in the United States. As Laura Wexler has suggested in an academic article on "The State of the Album," the photo album is heavily shaped by the laws and needs of government. Without Uncle Sam's requirements, many of these pages would be blank.

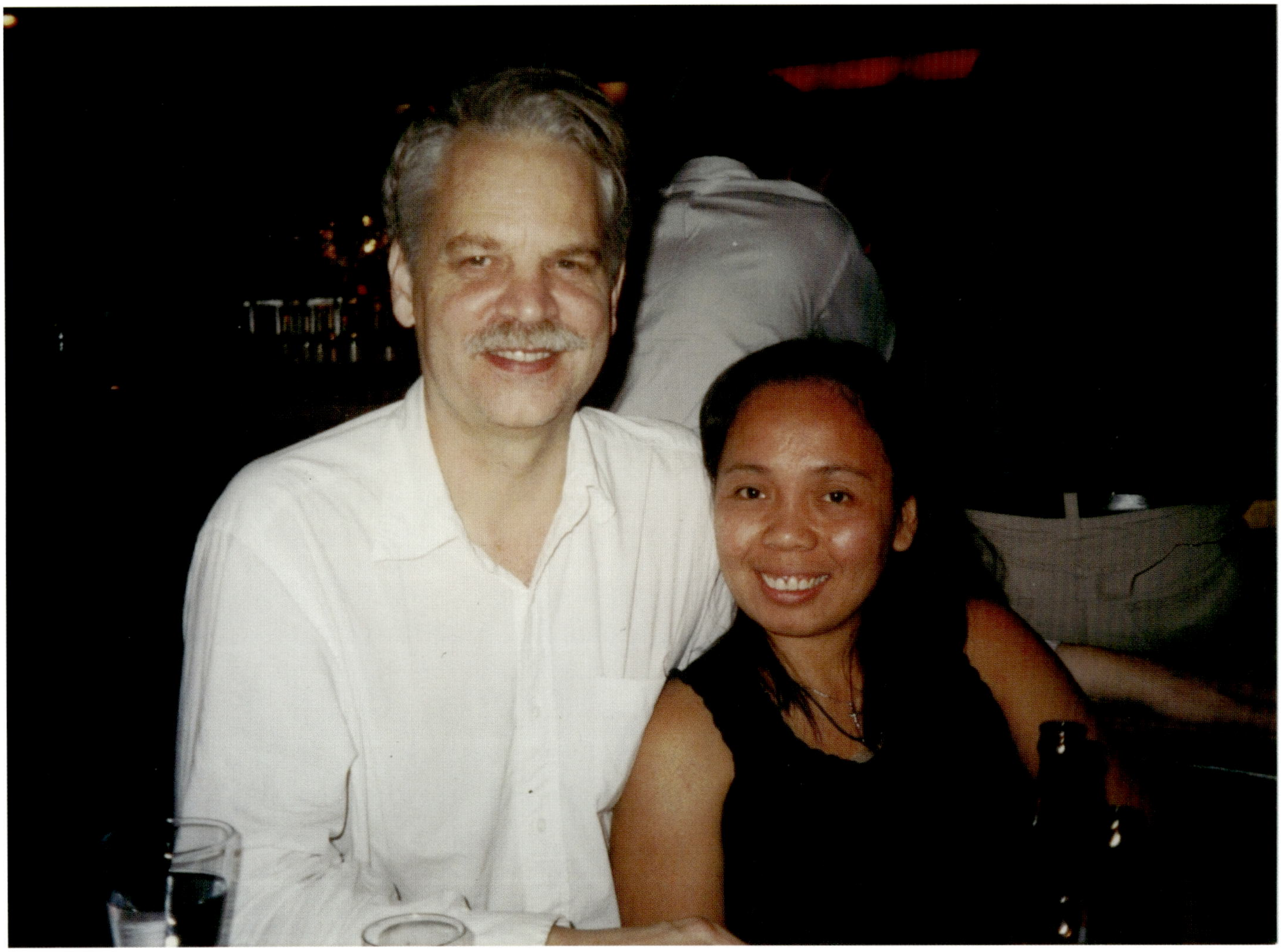

TS: This should be the first photo in your family album. It was taken the night your dad and I actually met.

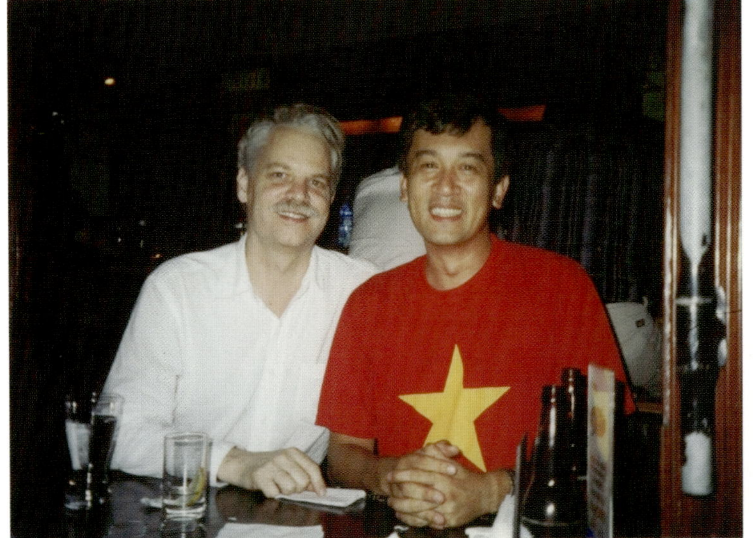

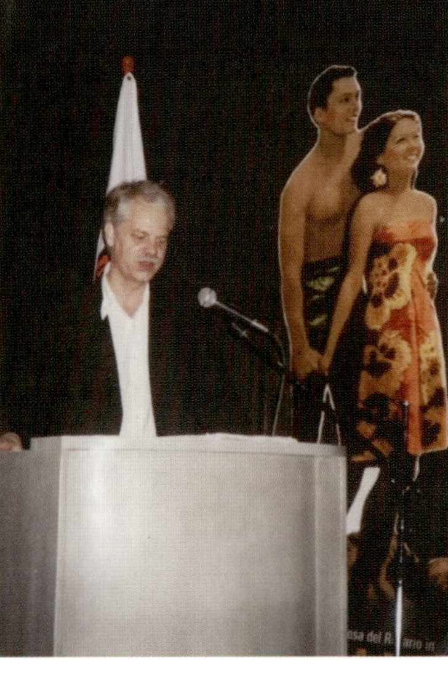

CM: Nick Deocampo played cupid. Your Tito Nick was planning a conference on early cinema in South East Asia at his film school in Quezon City. I came as a consultant and also gave a presentation.

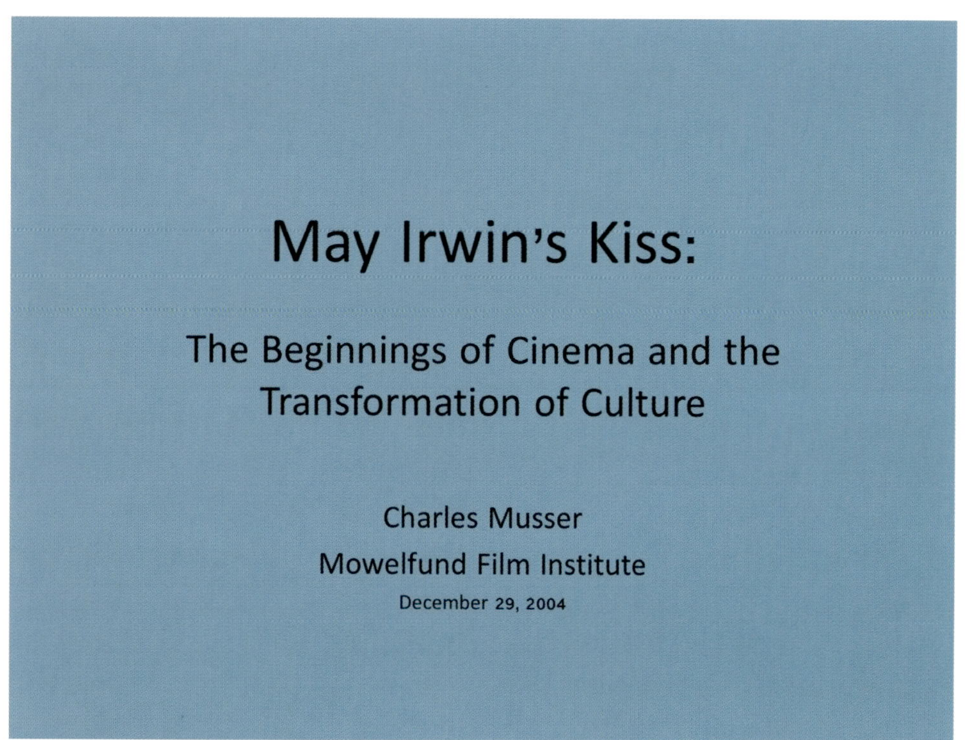

Nick Deocampo is not only an internationally renowned filmmaker and film scholar; he is the godfather of independent filmmaking in the Philippines. For many years Nick headed the Mowelfund Film Institute, which offered courses in filmmaking. The Mowelfund, or the Movie Workers Welfare Foundation, is an organization in the Philippines that provides for the welfare of workers in the film industry. It was established in 1974 by the film actor Joseph Estrada, who went on to become president of the Philippines.

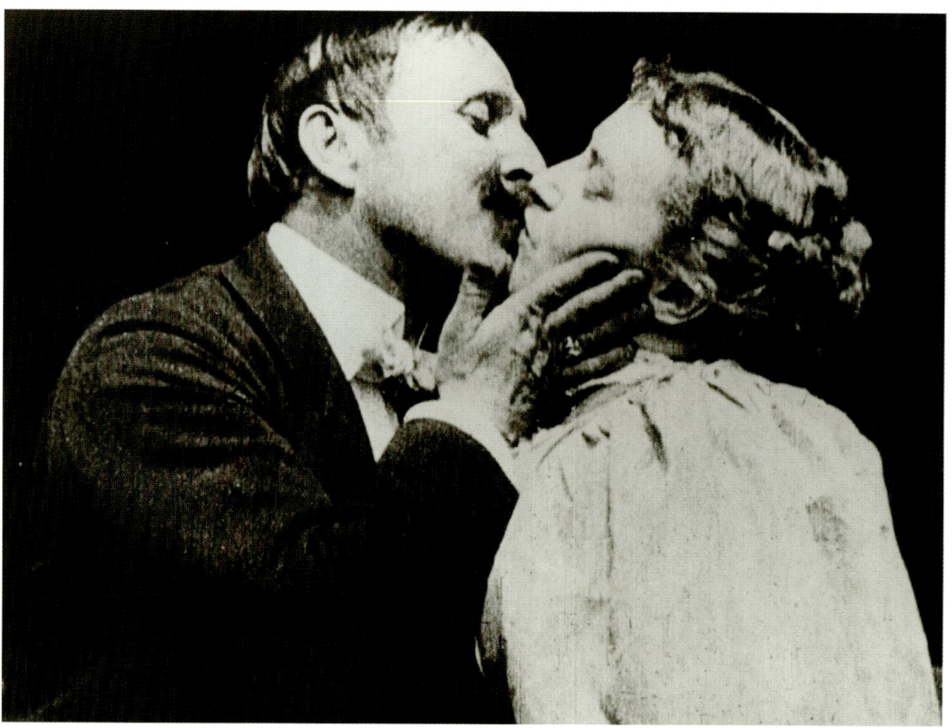

CM: It was about the first movie kiss.

The John C. Rice-May Irwin Kiss (1896) *was an immensely popular Edison film during the first year of projected motion pictures in the United States. The twenty-second film was generally shown as a loop, which meant the couple seemed to be kissing continuously. Kissing is a recurrent motif in our documentary—and this album.*

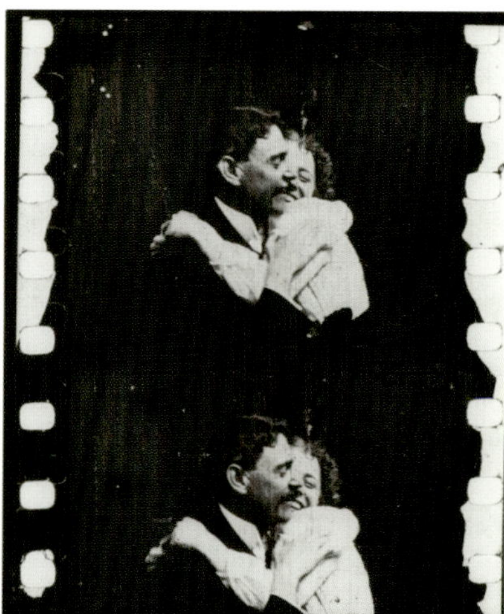

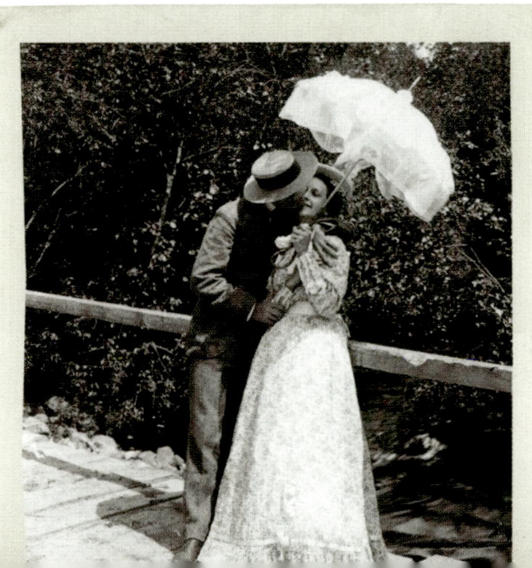

CM: John Rice became a kissing star. Afterwards there were lots of kiss films. Soon kissing in public became widely accepted.

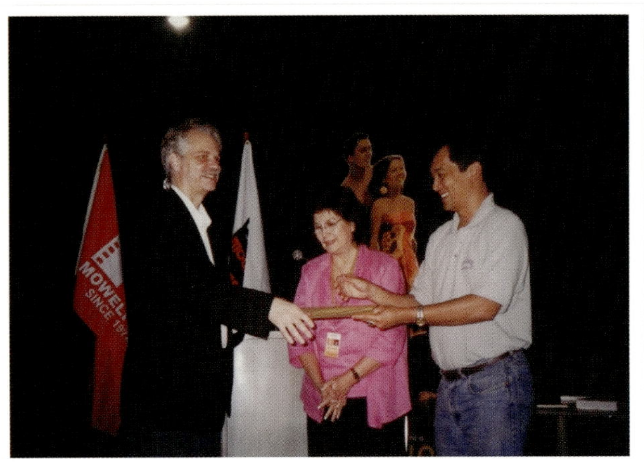

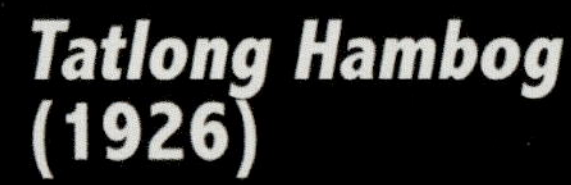
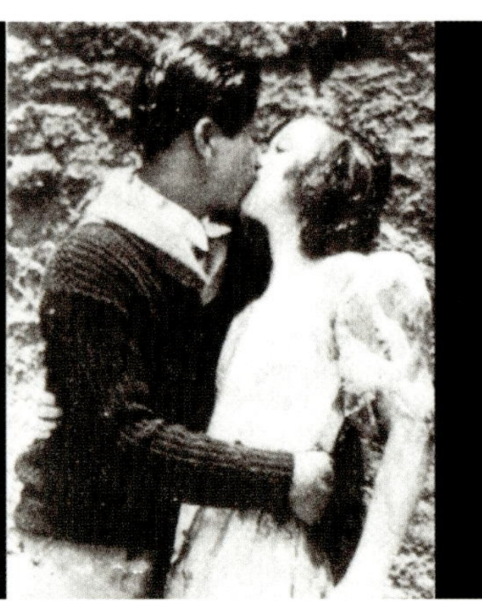

CM: My new colleagues told me about the first movie kiss in Filipino Cinema. The actress, Dimples Cooper, later became General Douglas McArthur's lover.

CM: I like to joke that I re-enacted that kiss with your mom during the Q & A session.

TS: But that's not quite true.

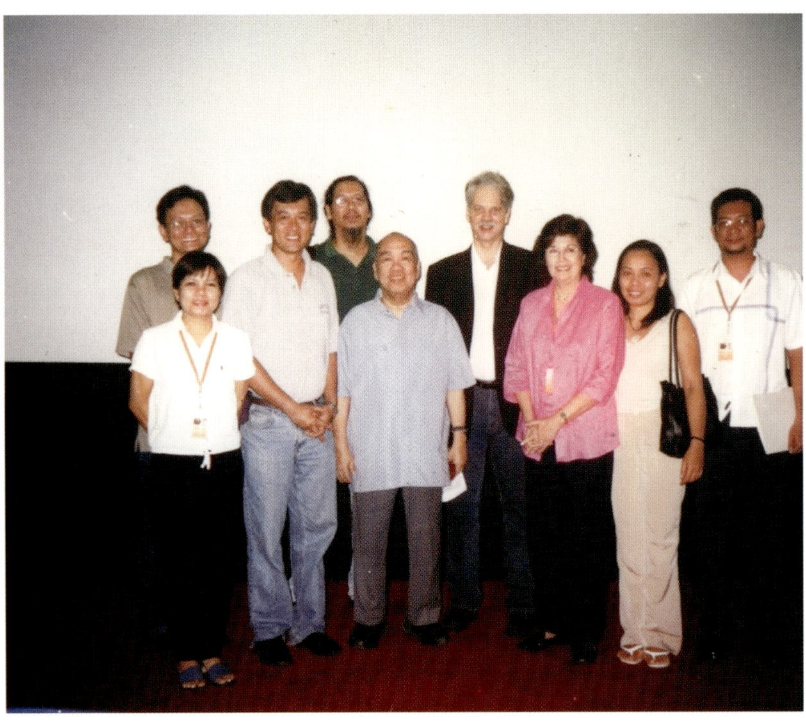

From left to right: Oscar Atadero (staff, Mowelfund), Sonia Cenidoza, Nick Deocampo, Teddy Co (currently Commissioner, National Commission for Culture and the Arts), Ernesto de Petro (film historian), Charlie, Boots Anson-Roa (President of Mowelfund), Threese, Ricky Orellana (staff, Mowelfund).

TS: Afterwards we secretly took an overnight from Manila to Cebu.

CM: There are no photographs that document those 24 hours. Photos would have been inadequate markers in any case. But whenever we go back to the Philippines, your mom and I take the Manila-Cebu Ferry as a way to recall our experience together.

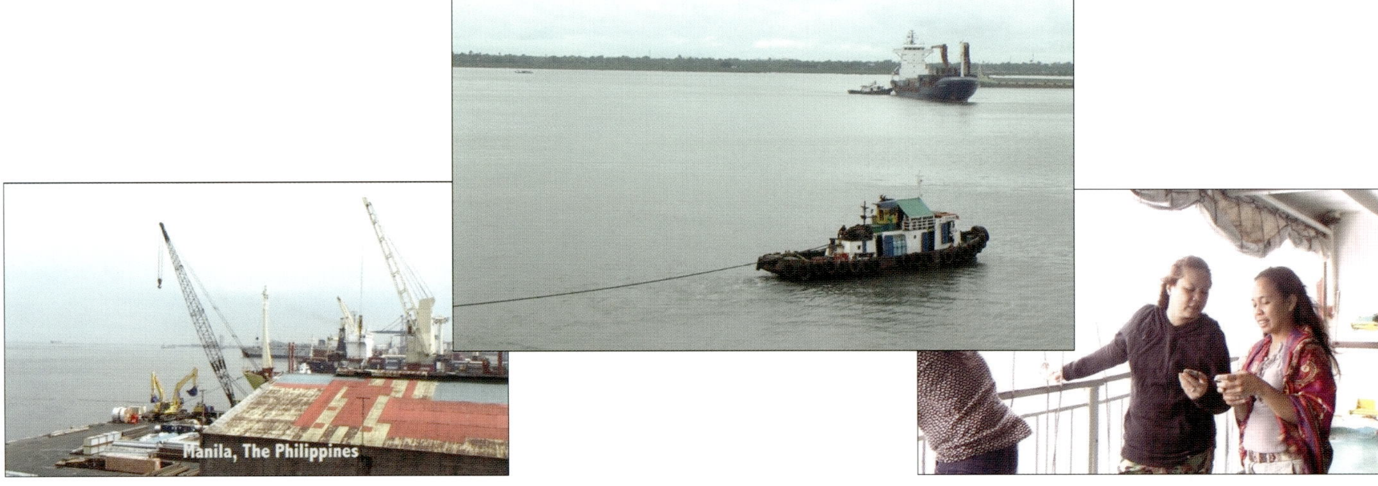

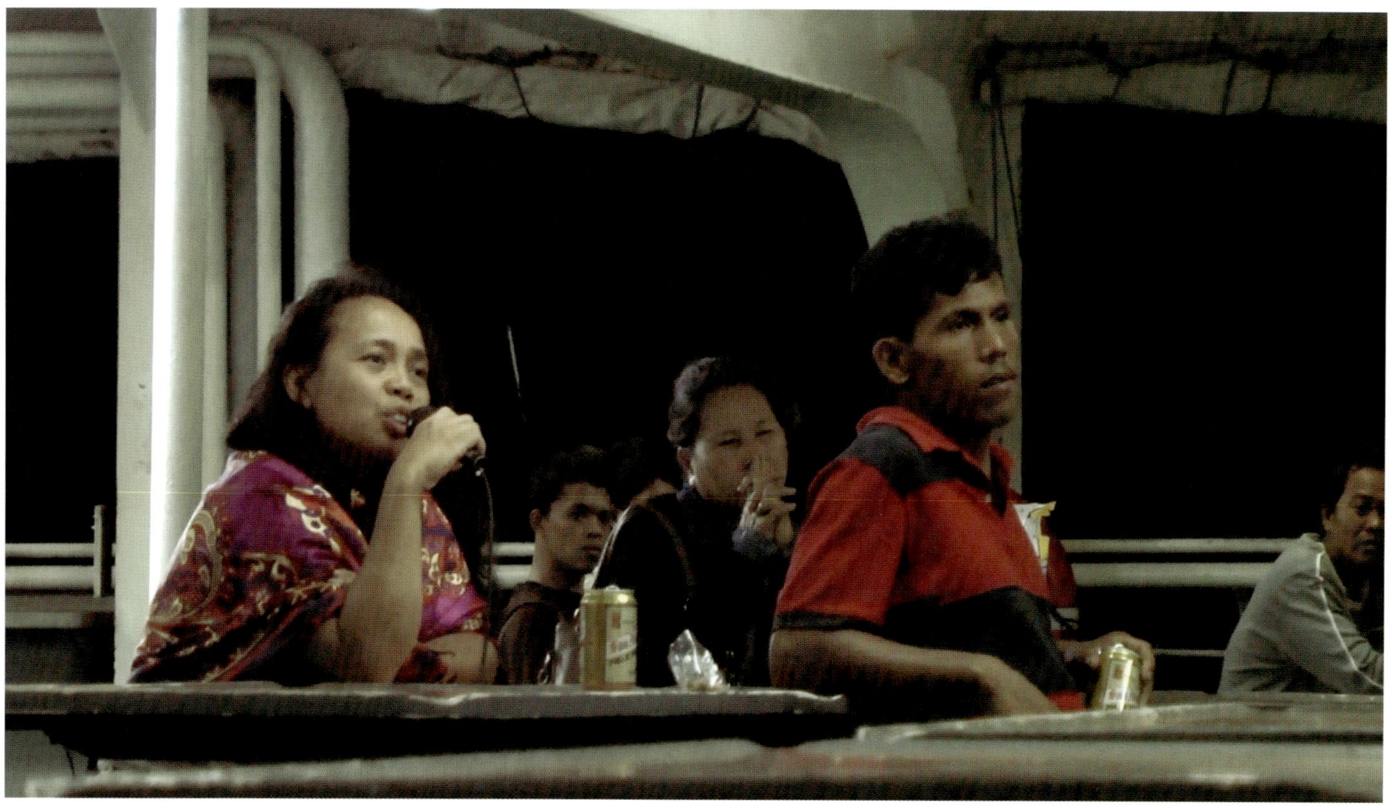

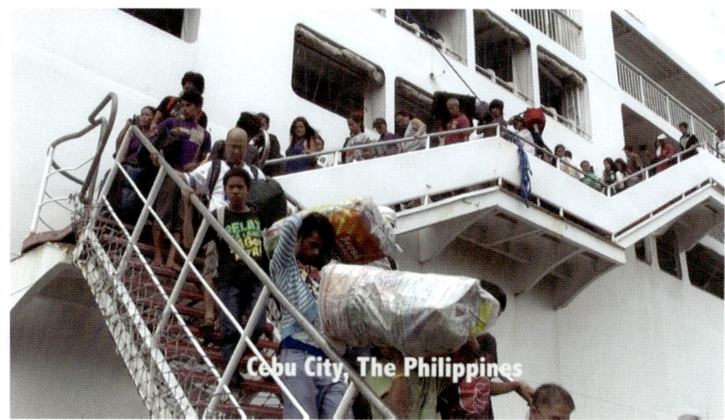

CM: I think I fell in love with your mom on that ferry ride.

TS: I thought we might go to the beach for a few days and if everything went well your dad might meet your grandmother, Mamay.

CM: Instead the whole family met us at the dock. The first question that Mamay asked me was: Did I intend to get married in the church? It was a slightly awkward exchange.

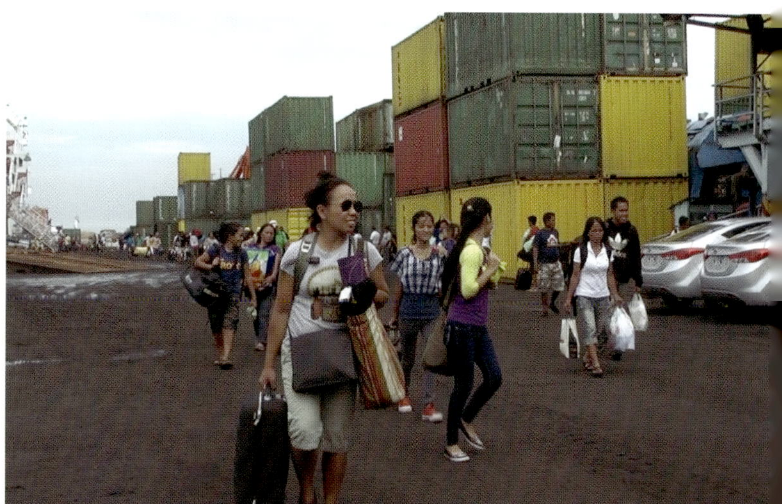

In a friendly interview, Threese and I discuss some of the photographs that were important in the early stages of our relationship. Why these, and what emotional meaning did they carry for us?

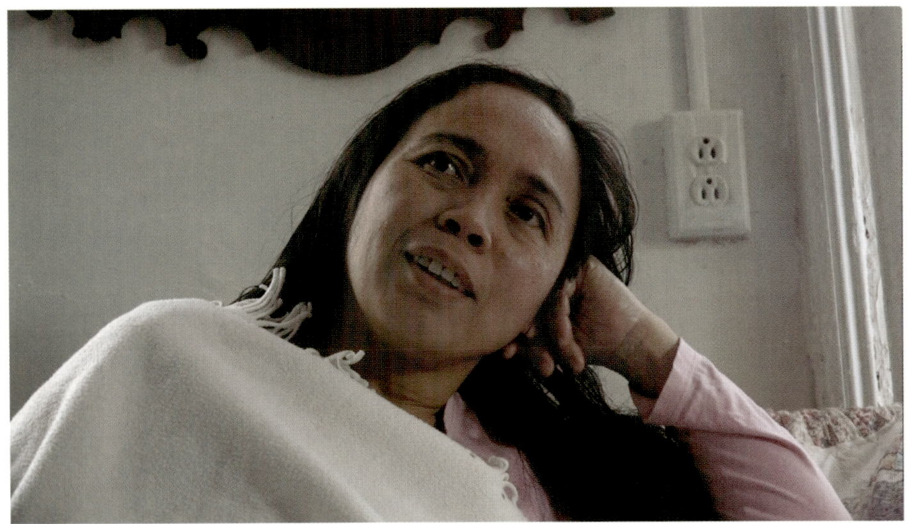

Charlie Musser (off camera): Did you think about taking a camera when you came to meet me?

Threese Serana (on camera): I thought I did. I thought I did have a camera. I don't remember.

Charlie: Do you remember any photographs being taken on that occasion?

Threese: (Laughs) Unfortunately no, though.

Charlie: What's interesting is that the two photos you have from that period are of Binhi.

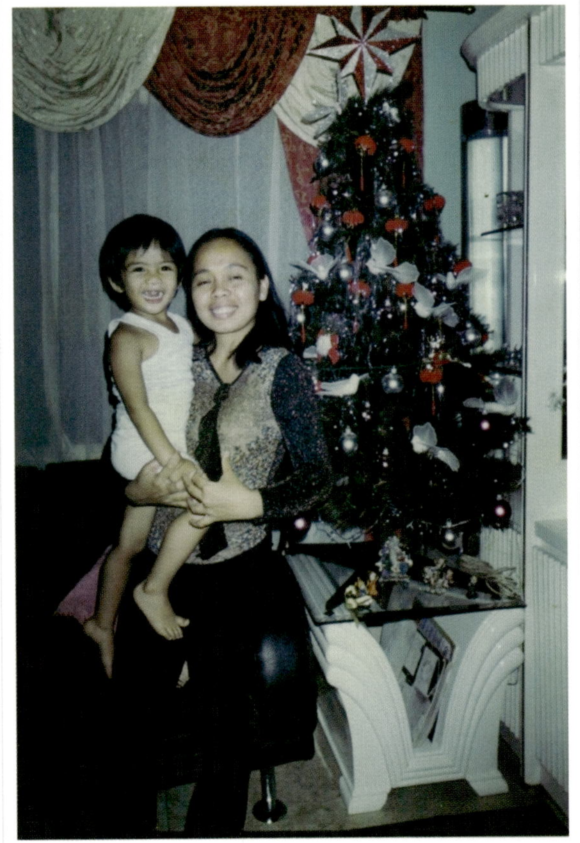

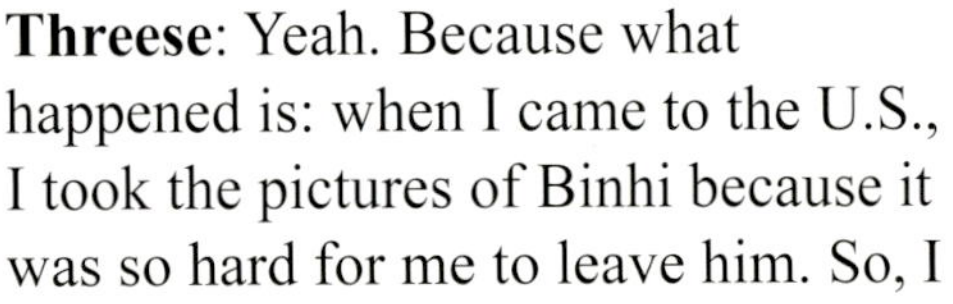

Threese: Yeah. Because what happened is: when I came to the U.S., I took the pictures of Binhi because it was so hard for me to leave him. So, I took pictures of him with me. The one in the frame and the one in my wallet.

CM: As the oldest child your mother was considered the third parent. Binhi called her Mommy Moon and they were so close that there were moments when I wondered if maybe she wasn't the first parent.

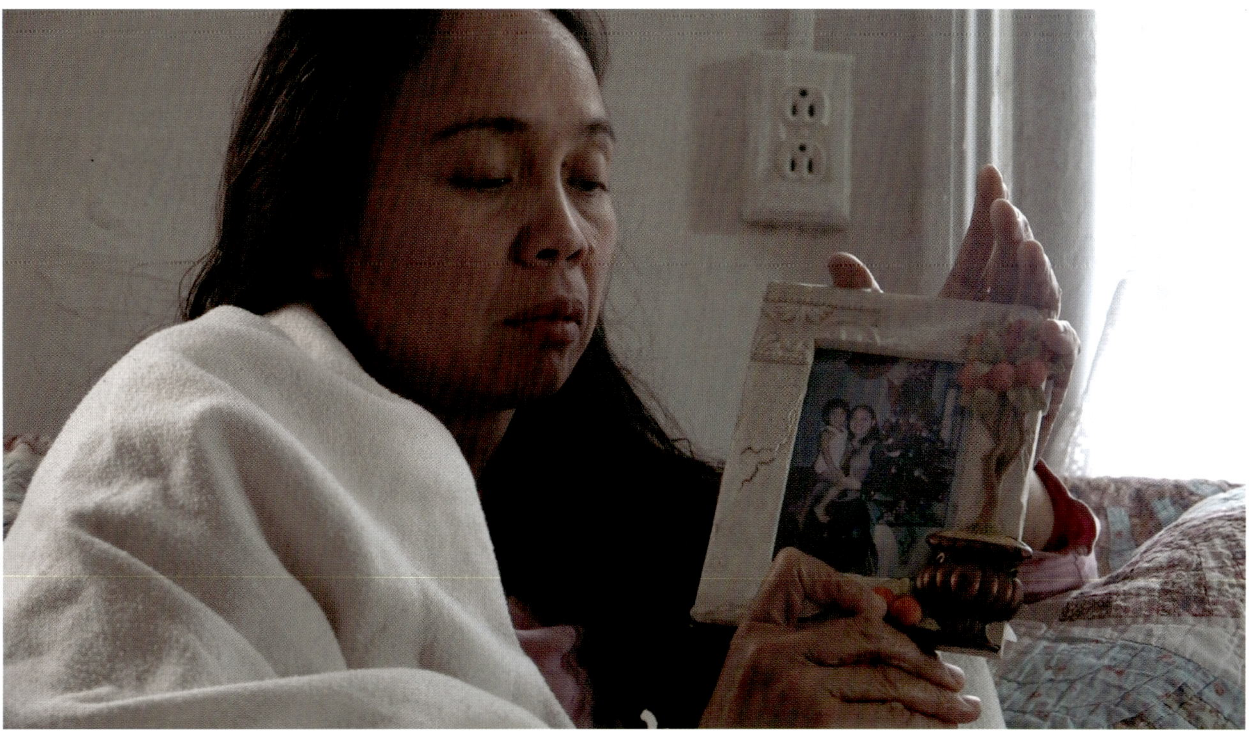

Threese: So, this picture was taken in December 2004. Yeah. So, I think this was after my father died. We said "Let's not be sad all the time," and we set up the Christmas tree. And I think this was when we took this picture. Binhi.

When he came to our family…the idea that a mother would just instantly, right after birth, abandon her baby was to me unthinkable, so he became the family baby and I took it on me to just be the mommy. Being the eldest in the family anyway, being the third parent. And then of course, when he became close to me, and he would call me "Mommy," and actually hug me and sleep with me. And then "Oh, it's such a beautiful thing."

A lot of this came from having him in my life…in the family's life. But particularly in my case, because I wasn't so keen about being married or having children of my own. It was just too much being the eldest of nine children. I'm done taking care of children. I'm not taking care of babies. I'm just not going to have them.

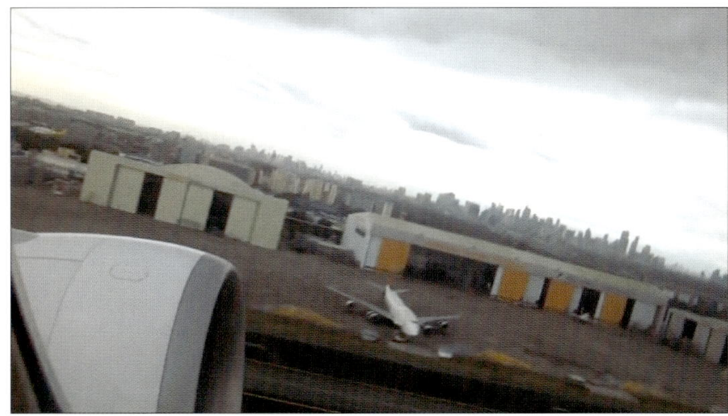

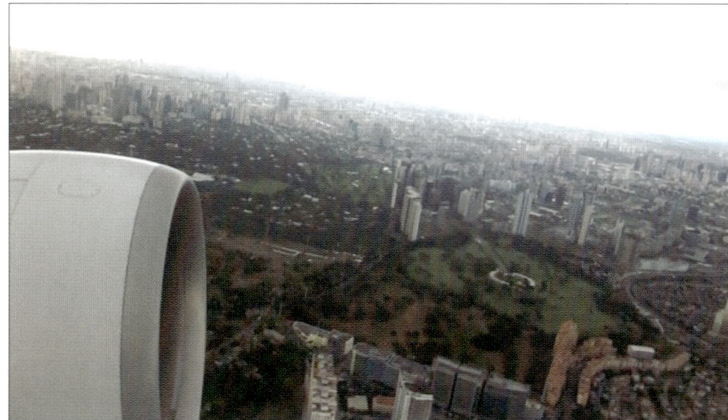

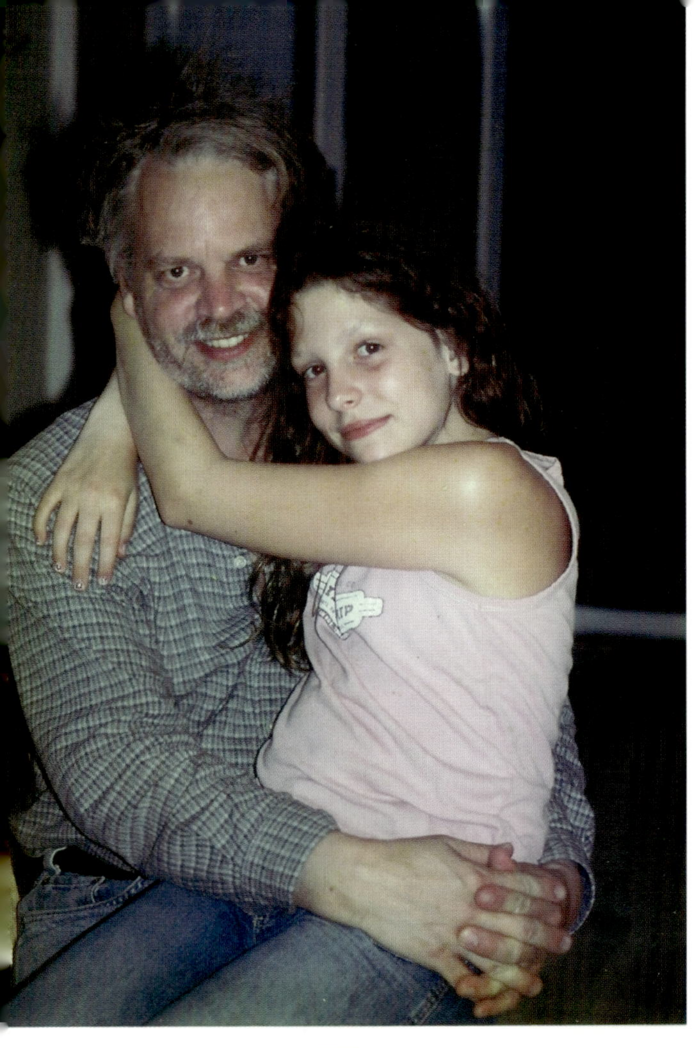

CM: I was only in the Philippines for eight days because I had to go to the Academy of Motion Picture Arts and Sciences to accept an award to write a book entitled *Film Truth, Documentary Practice.* Right now, I wonder how much truth—how many silences and how much dissembling—will be in this documentary.

But back then I wondered how I might get your mom to take me seriously. Giving a talk on the first movie kiss was clever, but it was a photo that actually did the trick.

Threese: This is the first picture you showed me and I'm like, "Oh, my goodness! This guy is really husband material. This is father material. I'm going to get married to this guy because look at this: There is so much love that he has for this child." So, I really thought that this was a decisive photo in my life.

The pictures of Threese and Binhi rhyme with the photo of me and my daughter Hannah. Inverted reflections of each other, their similarities seem more than just coincidence.

We imagined ourselves to be two academics who were conducting an international romance in the era of globalization. In terms of communication, the Internet had made all parts of the world equally accessible. Travel takes time and money but was manageable. It was borders, visas and governmental regulations that finally put an end to our illusions. We were too preoccupied with the task at hand to document our day devoted to getting Threese's visa.

So once again we re-visited those memorable places some eight years later—and did a little reenactment for the camera. The same coffee shop where I paced nervously, perhaps even the same uncomfortable chair where I sat, unable to concentrate on the book in front of me.

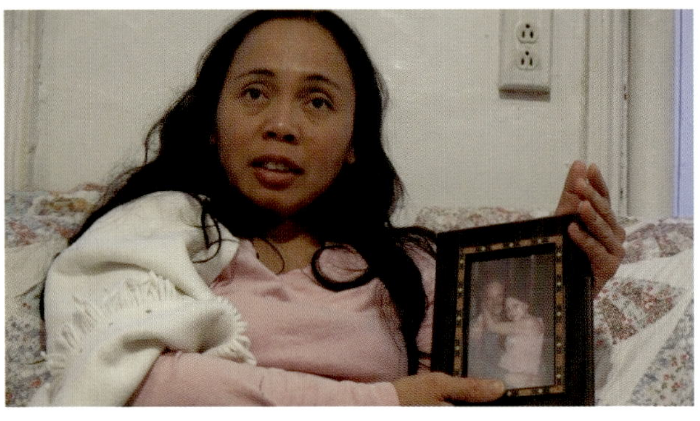

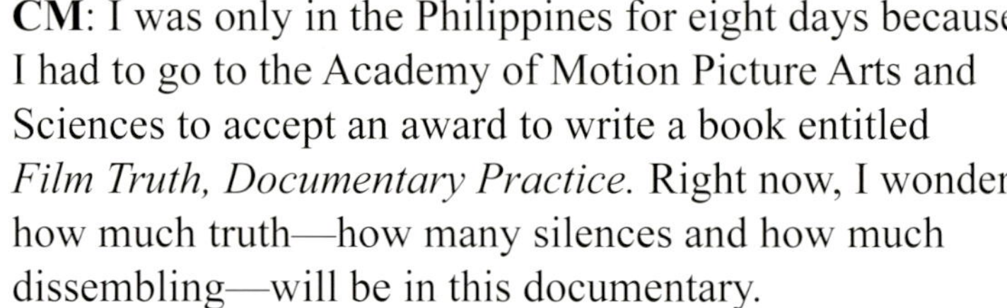

CM: Meanwhile, your mom had been accepted to give a talk at a Yale conference on Tropical Forests and Sustainability. I went back to Manila during Spring break and spent a day sitting in a coffee shop across from the American Embassy while your mom tried to get a visa.

TS: Very few Filipinos were getting visas. The Bush administration was busy punishing the Philippines because it had withdrawn from the Coalition of the Willing in Iraq.

CM: Your mom had assembled a huge dossier in support of her project.

TS: And I hoped to get a multiple entry visa so we could travel back and forth between our two countries.

CM: Finally, she returned. She had a visa—but it was only for a single entry

Threese: It was really a huge accomplishment to get a U.S. visa. It's like winning the lottery in the Philippines.

CM: We celebrated by going to a local photo shop and having our picture taken.

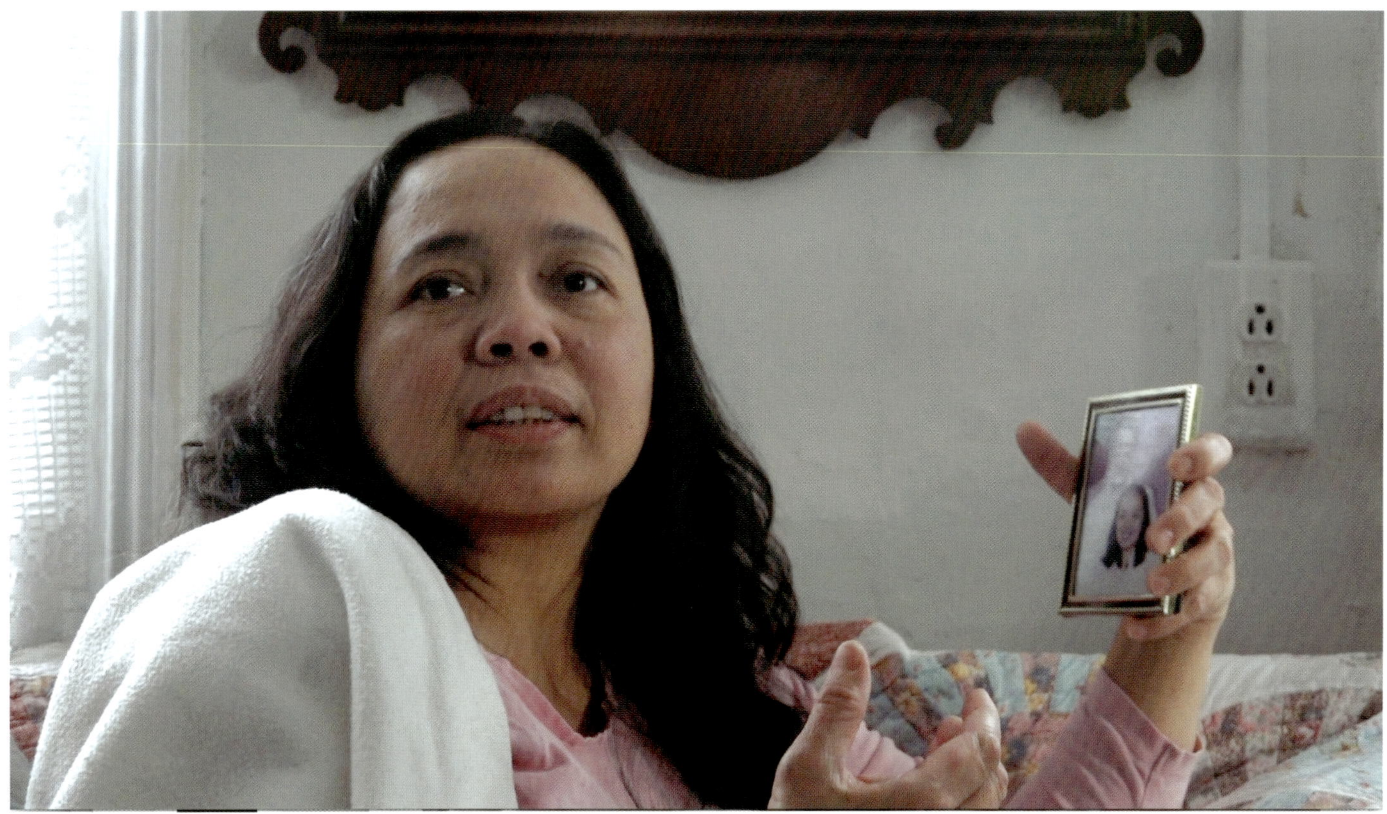

Threese: They had a lot of themes. There was a tropical theme. And mountains…nature. But we chose this.

CM: We purposefully selected their sappiest background.

Threese: At that time, it was kind of the logical thing to do. But then if you come to think about it, it has more meaning if you look at the photographs and you try actually to understand the whole process of which the photograph is only a part.

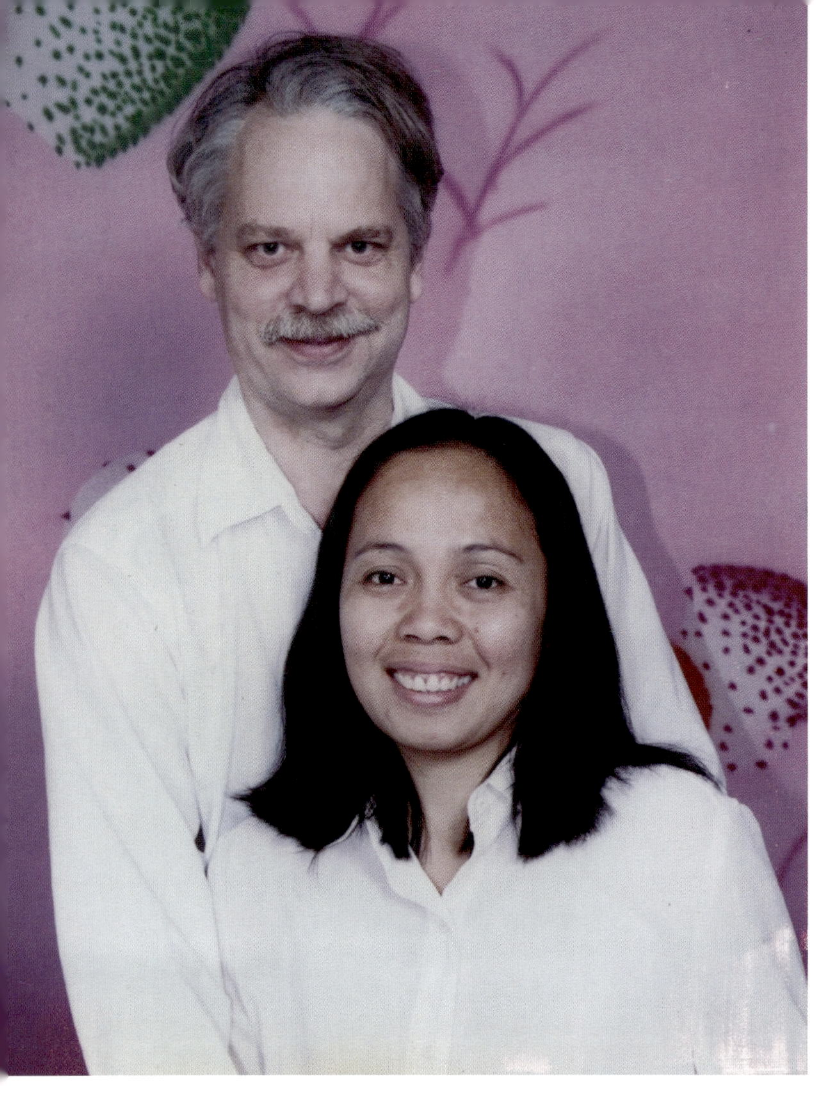

Charlie (off camera): So, what did you think of the photo while it was being taken.

Threese: I was very elated. I was like so happy. I felt giddy. And then of course taking the picture it was symbolic of the visa, the possibility of me coming to the US and the possibility of me being married to you.

CM: Happy. Yes. But I also knew we were destined to fit many people's stereotypes. I would be the older perhaps slightly lecherous and desperate white American. She was the younger Filipina ready to take a chance on love. What people see has changed over time, but how they see us has generally remained remarkably stable. And yet every couple conforms to some kind of type. So, what becomes important is not what people see—or think they see. In our case, we are at our best and happiest together when we share projects—like getting your Mom's visa, or having you, or making this film.

We returned to downtown Manila and searched for the storefront studio where our first photograph together was taken. It and its cohorts were all gone. Only a couple of convenience stores that made passport photographs remained. Although we filmed our search, we somehow misplaced the SD-card on which that scene was record. Perhaps we will find it one day or perhaps we might again reenact that search for the camera, but for the moment our efforts are illustrated by a squatters' area we filmed the next day. Threese hates using these images as stand-ins, but it is the best we have for the moment.

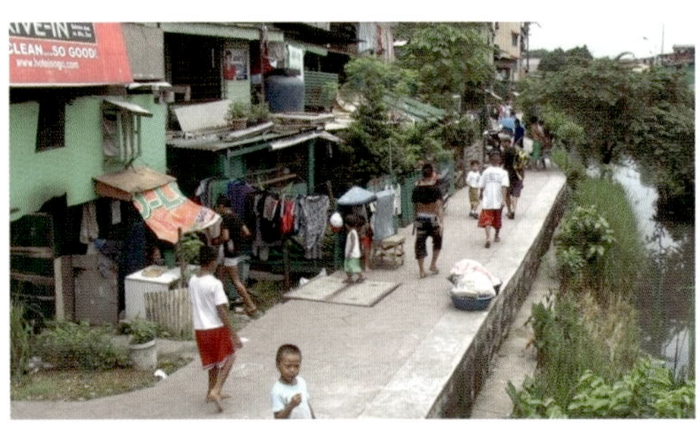
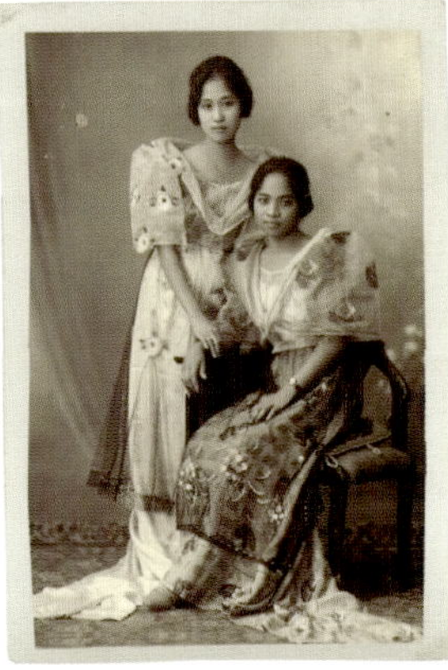
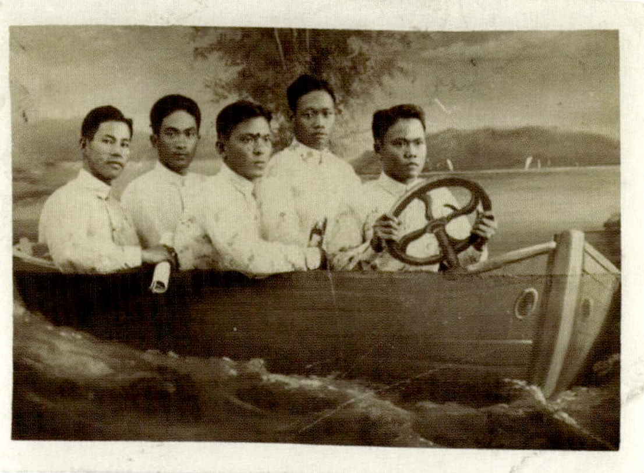

TS: Years later we went back to look for that photographic studio but all of them had closed. Digital photography had shut them down. The traditional photographer, who had existed for over 160 years and was deeply imbedded in Filipino culture, had essentially come to an end.

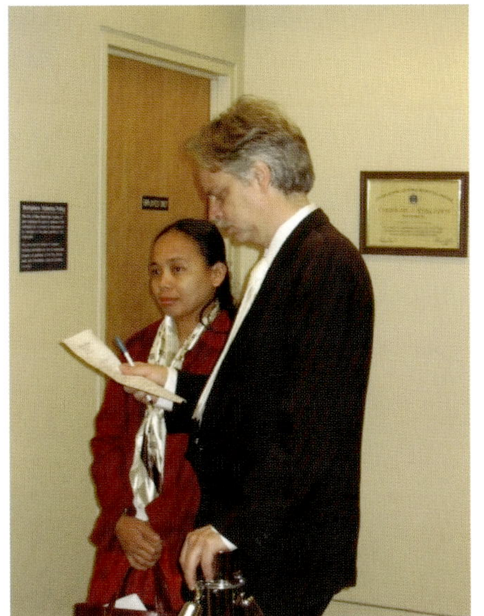 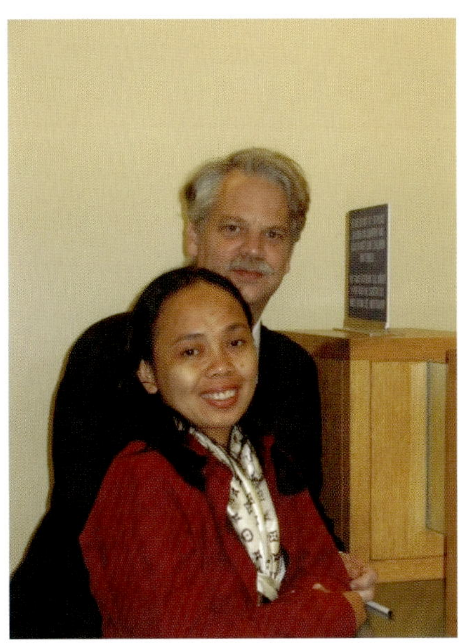 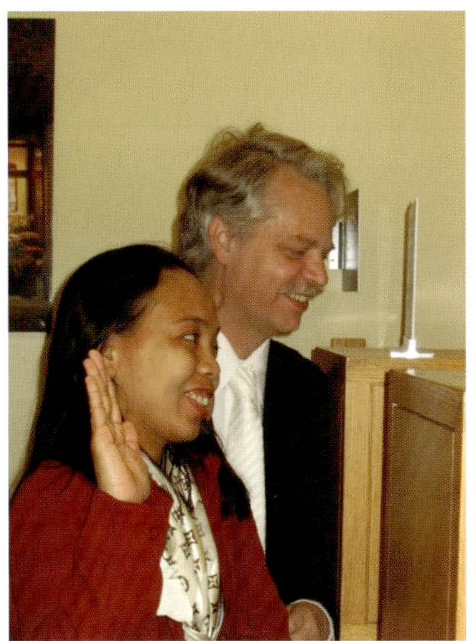

CM: It had been so difficult to get your mom into the U.S., that the prospect of going through the process again seemed overwhelming. But if she was to stay we had to get married quickly. Much too quickly so far as my family was concerned. My normally supportive aunt was sure that she was only interested in my money. Even though I only had debts. My mother thought she just wanted a green card. Her family was convinced we would not get married at all.

Threese: My mom was texting me, calling me every day. The pope just died. Why are you hanging out with this guy? Staying with him! You're not married yet. You're going to be causing my soul to burn in hell, or something to that effect. But yeah. That really was very stressful.

CM: Your Tito Dada even threatened to kill me.

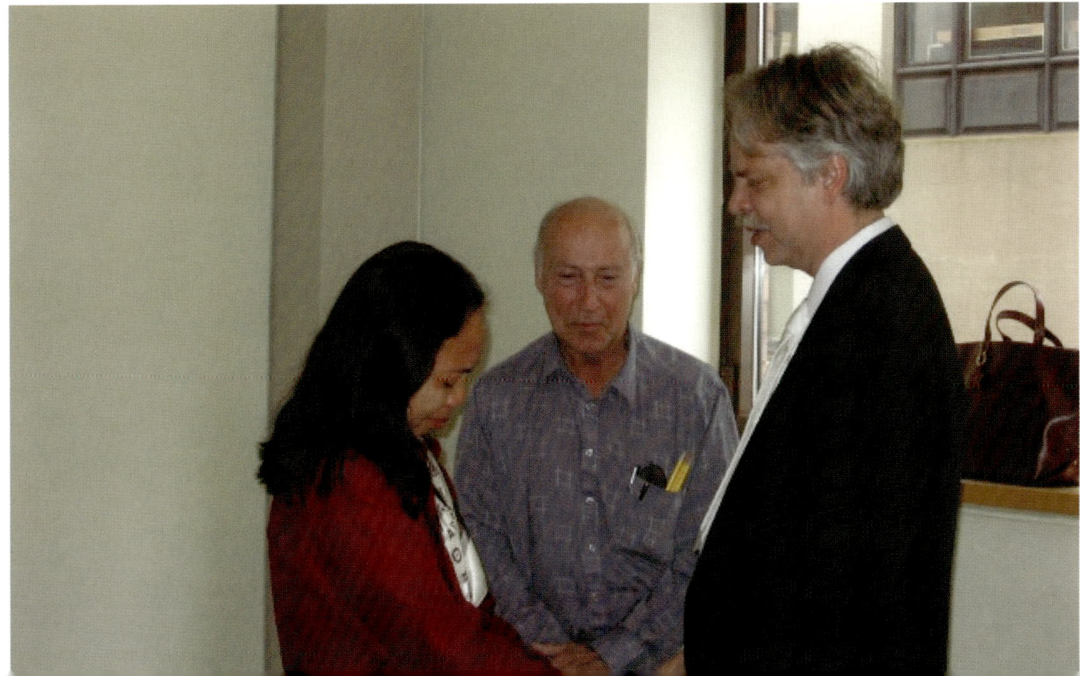

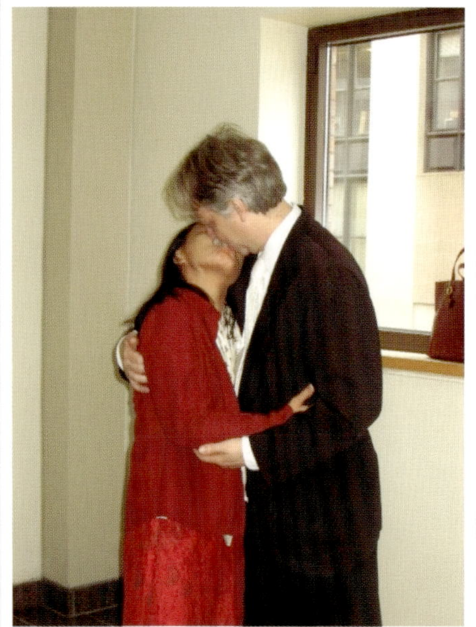
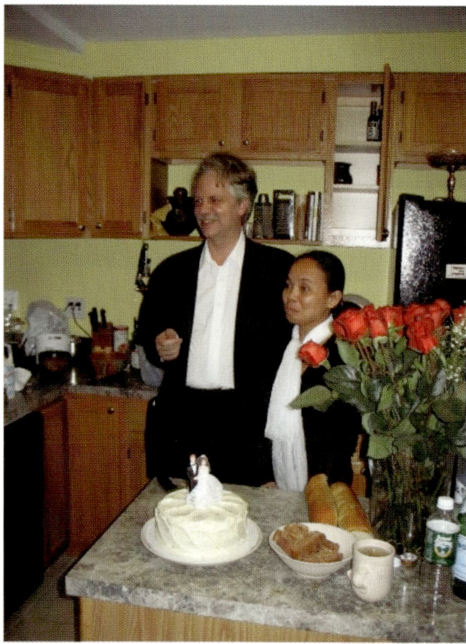
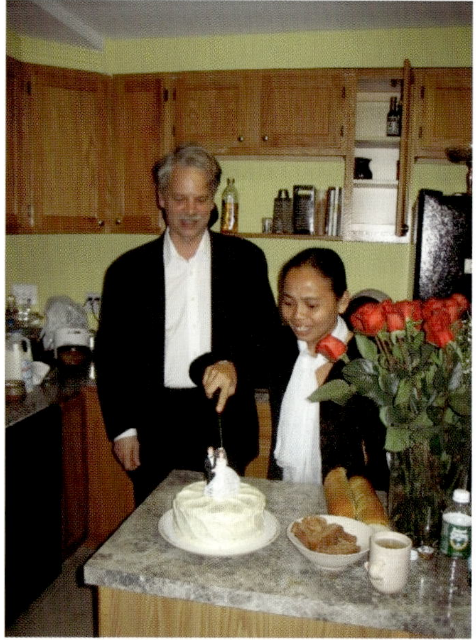

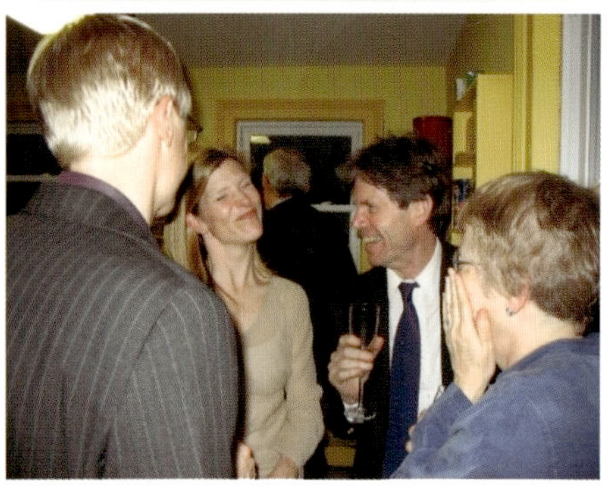
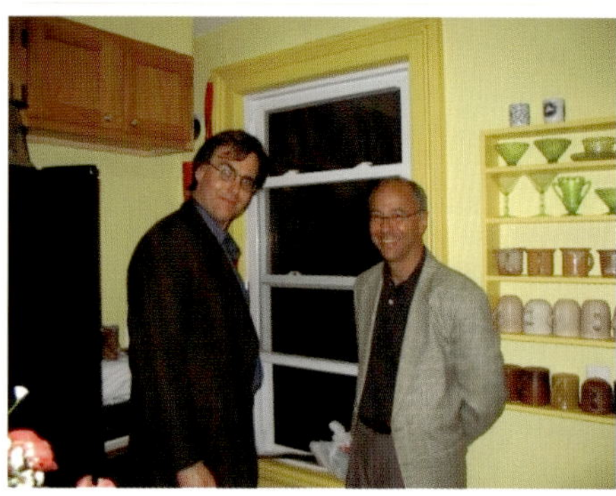
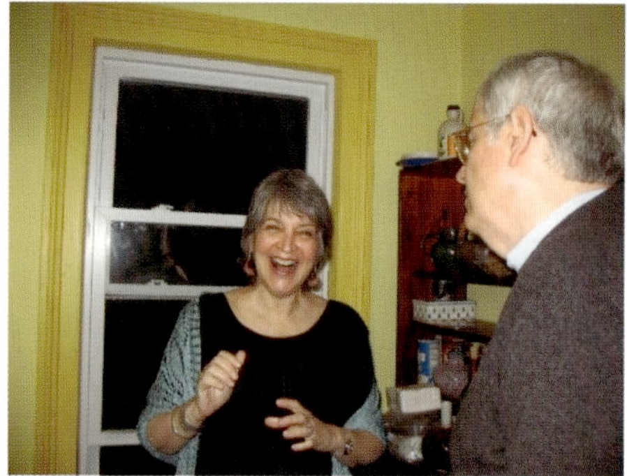

Guests included Tim and Anne Kern, Dudley and Stevie Andrew, John MacKay, Bruce and Laura Wexler and Joe Roach.

CM: The thing about getting married to a foreigner, particularly a woman from the Third World, is that one needs lots of photographs. We needed to prove to Immigration Services that this was a bona fide marriage. And if it wasn't for Uncle Sam, we probably would not have a single image from that day. One reason I like these photographs is that they were taken for such a practical purpose.

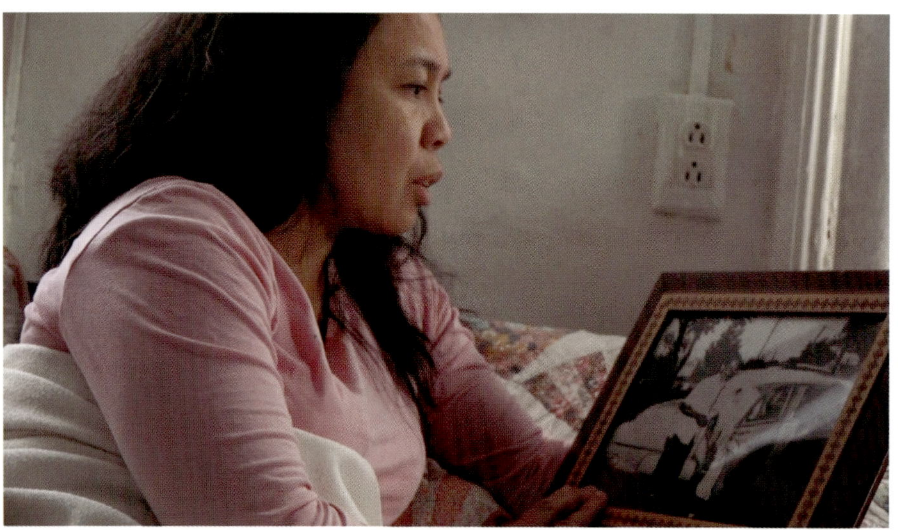

CM: What about photographs of our parents' weddings?

Threese: This is a picture of my grandfather taking my mom out of the car. And if I remember it correctly, this car is owned by my dad's commanding officer. My mom was one of those women who has ideas of how their wedding was going to be. So, she told my dad that he had to spend all his savings for the wedding. And I remember my dad actually…

Threese: The whole time during the marriage, my mother would give him a hard time because he wasn't earning enough. Of course, there were nine of us to begin with. Dad would say, "Your mom wanted a grand wedding. She made me spend our savings that we were going to use for a house and everything." There are other photos I couldn't find. Maybe we could find some of them when we go back to the Philippines.

CM: Indeed, we did go back. And we did find some small photographic proofs tucked away in a tiny album.

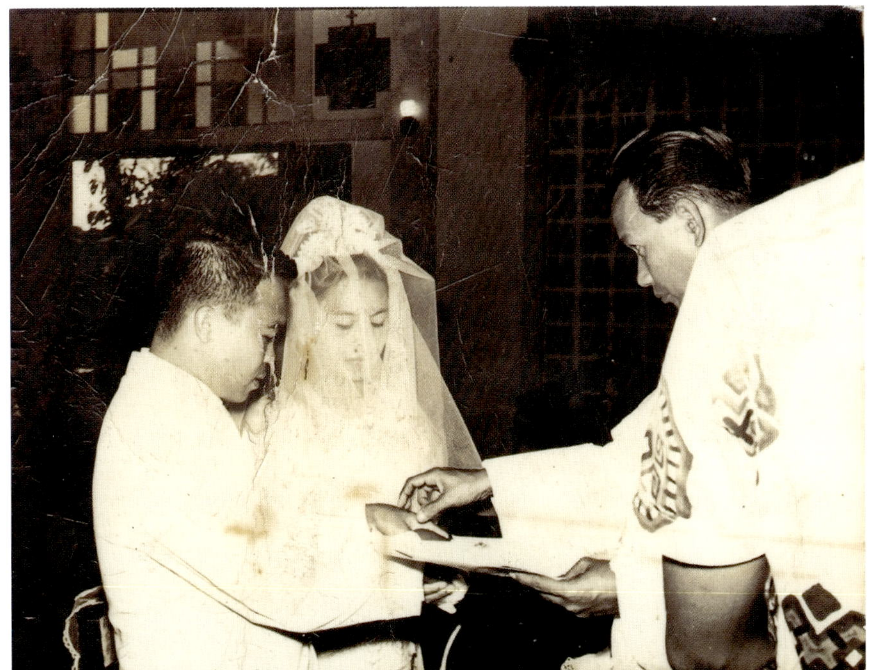

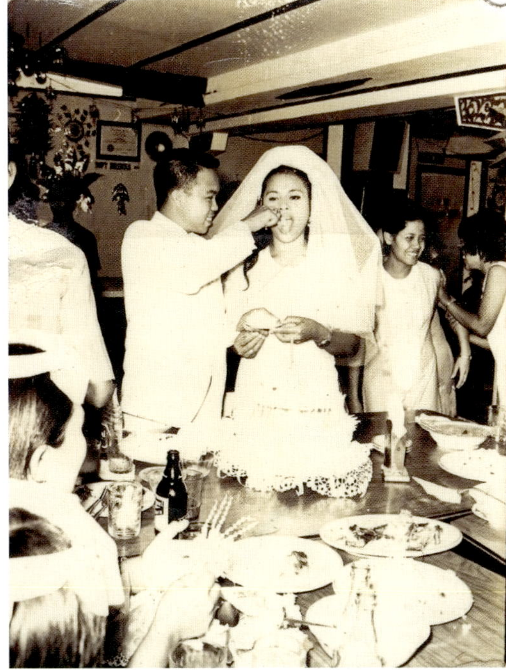

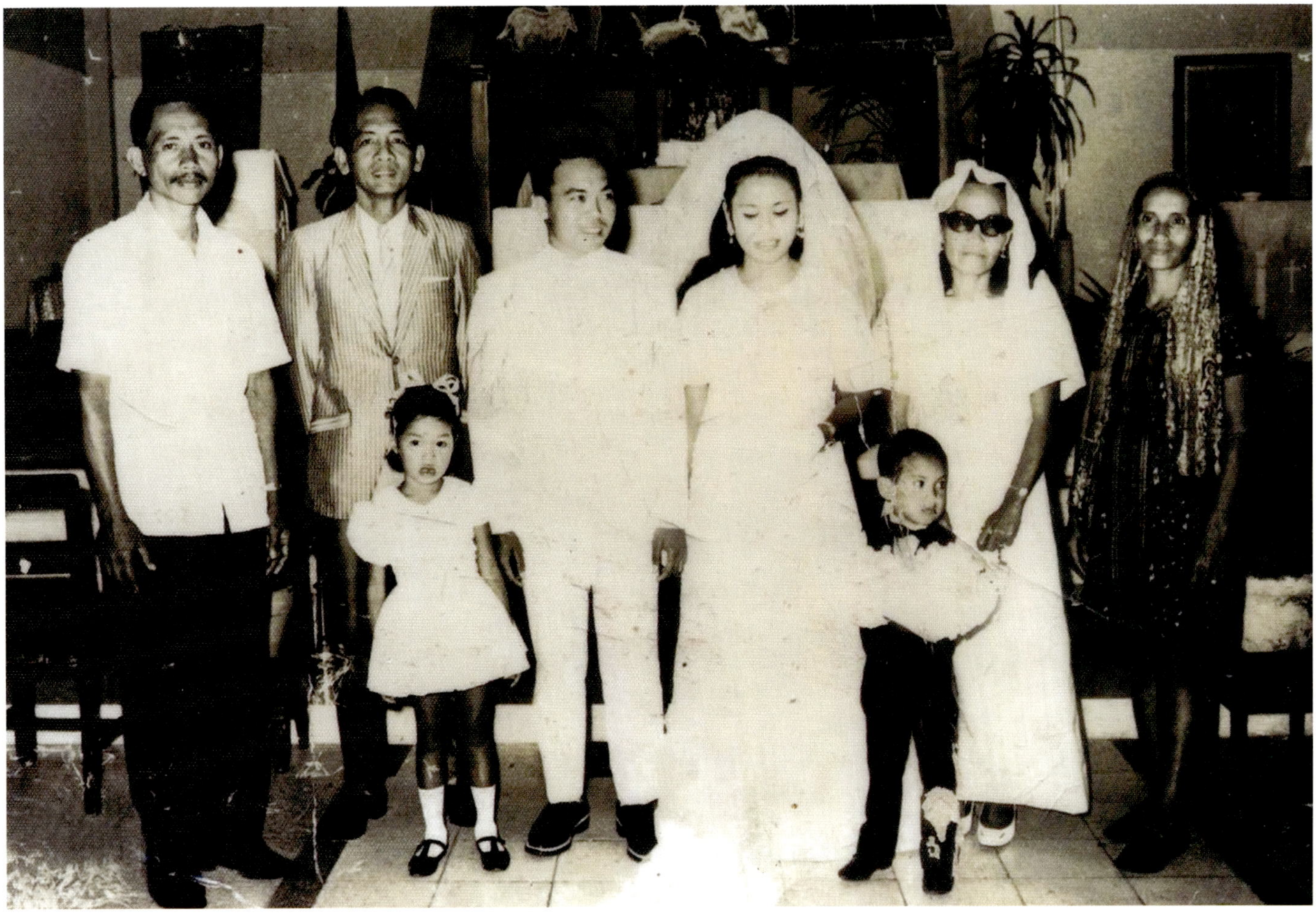

My sister Jane Musser Nelson lives in Concord, Massachusetts, where the American revolution effectively began. The oldest part of her house dates from 1740. Its attic is an ideal place to store family heirlooms.

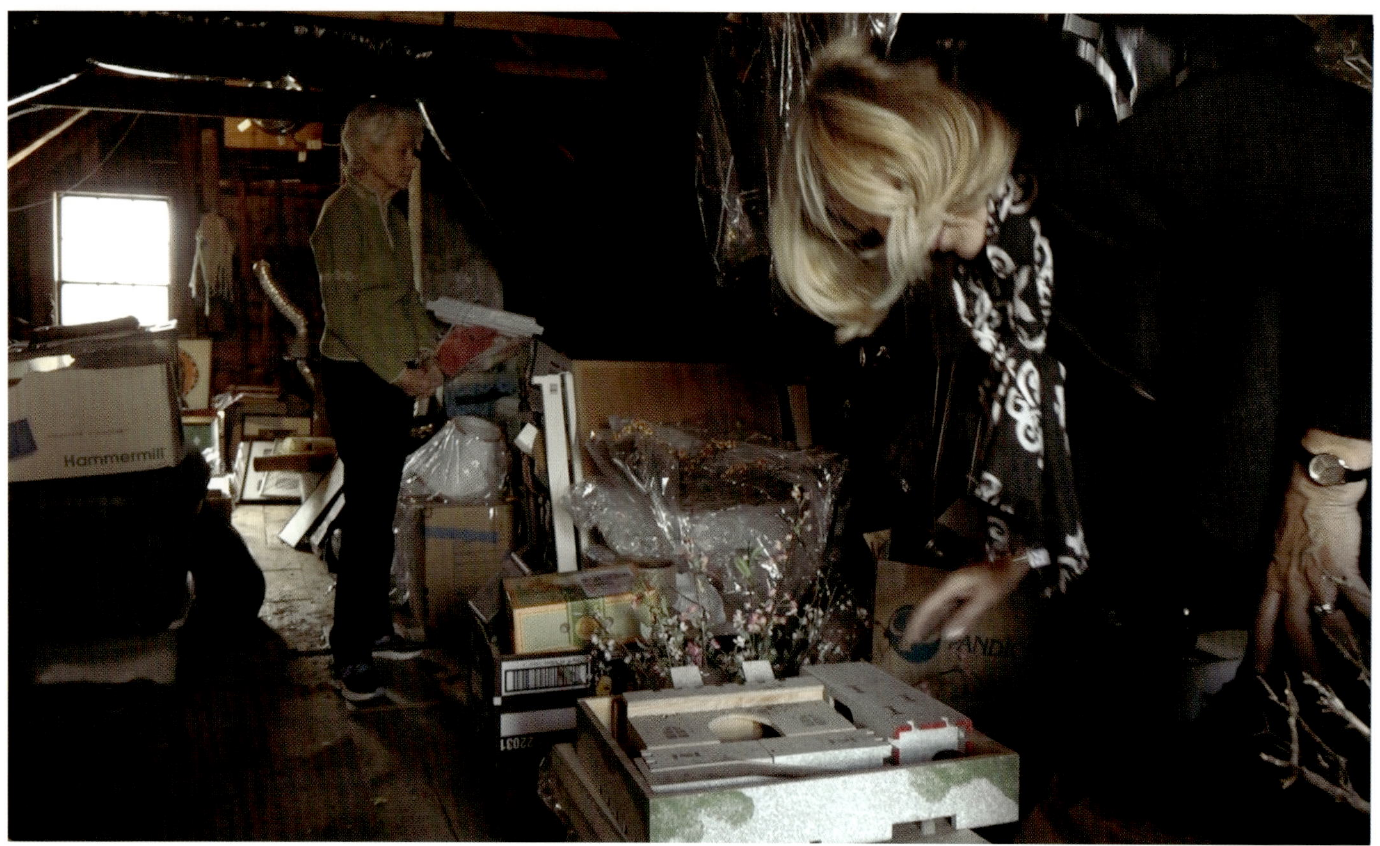

CM: I had vague memories of having seen my parents' wedding photos long ago. Eventually I learned that my sisters were each given wedding albums by my mother, but where were they?

Jane Musser Nelson: Hold on, Charlie. Wait a second.

Marilyn Keach [Musser]: Found a goodie?

Jane: We might have found something. Let's see what this is. This says," Mom's scrapbook: Kindergarten through Wheaton [College]." Not a photo album. We'll bring this down?

Charlie: Sure.

CM: We searched in your Aunt Jane's attic but came up empty handed.

Charlie: I have to say that I'm not convinced it's not here.

CM: My other sister [Nancy] had at least one and it was eventually shipped to my office.

That same weekend I interviewed my mother in our New Haven kitchen, where quite a few scenes for **Our Family Album** *were filmed and photographed. We discussed family photographs and the family album that my mother had assembled. Although we had not yet located her wedding pictures, and she had not seen them for more than a decade, her memory of the images and the stories that went with them proved to be razor sharp. My father's father, John Musser (1888-March 22, 1949) died less than two weeks before their marriage on April 2nd. Needless to say, we find the similarities and differences between these three sets of wedding pictures, taken over a period of more than 55 years and at opposite ends of the globe, to be quite intriguing.*

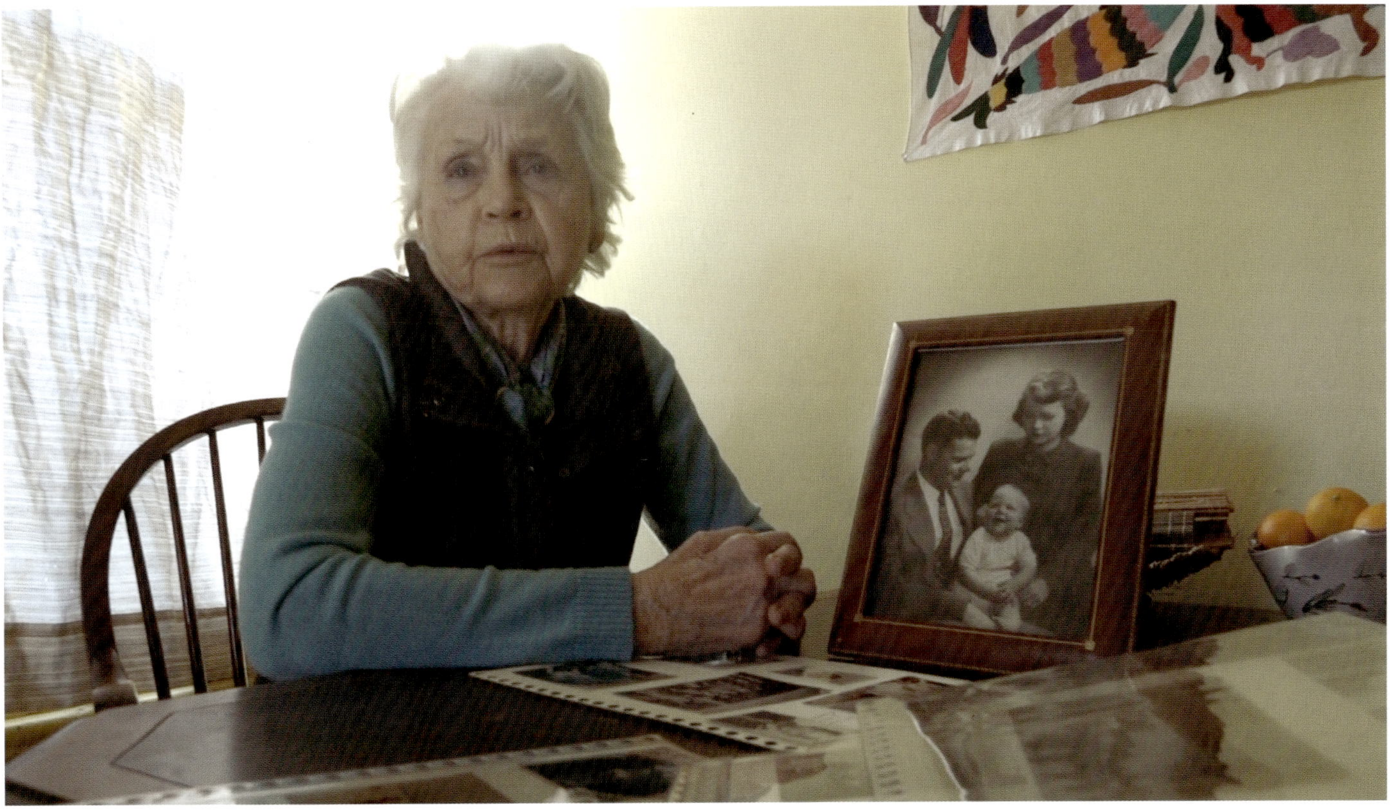

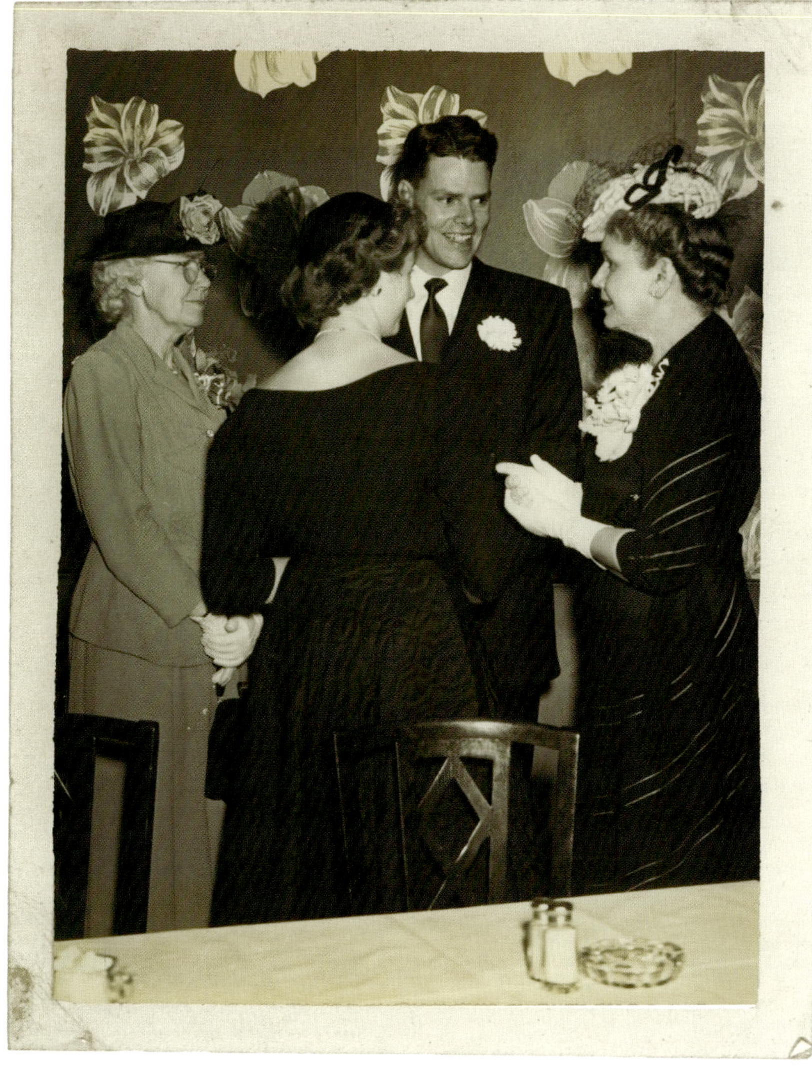

Charlie (off camera): Tell me a little bit about the wedding album. Dad's dad had just died. And so…

Marilyn: So, as a result our whole wedding was in Navy Blue. Muddy [Grace Winter Greene Musser] didn't want to put it off. She was insistent about us continuing to get married. So, it made it a little quieter affair than it might have been otherwise, but it was a happy affair. Everyone had a good time. My grandmother was there. And of course, Muddy was there. It's all big photographs. And it was everything from when we were fixing our hair at the last minute and then at the wedding. At that point, it was formal photography. We received a lot of proofs, and then picked out the photographs that we liked, and then they were put in an album, which was just the way it was done all the time.

My two grandmothers. Grace Winter Greene Musser (on the left) wore spring colors to emphasize her insistence that the wedding go ahead. Yarda Jergens Keach (on the right) doubtlessly devised the royal blue color scheme.

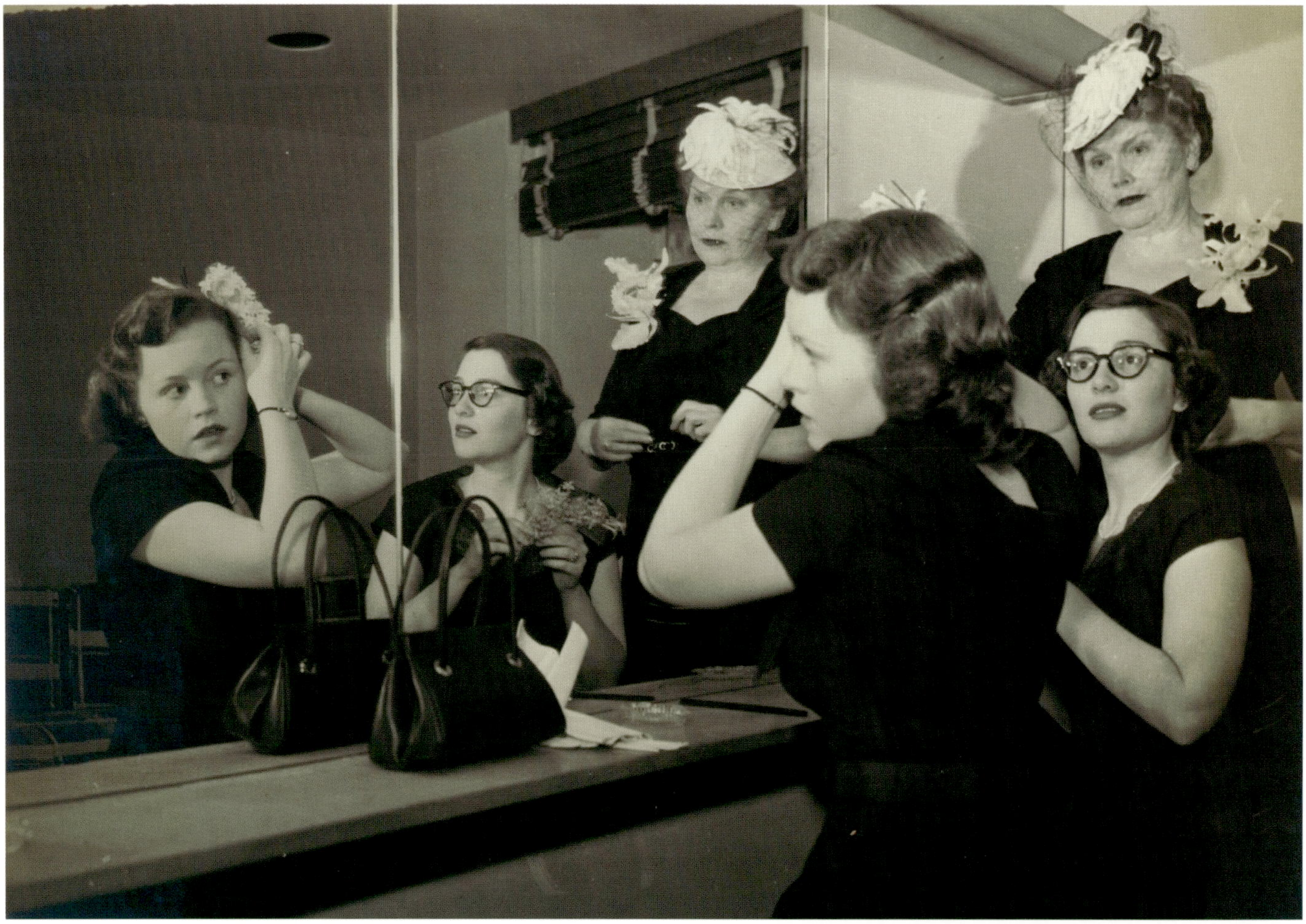

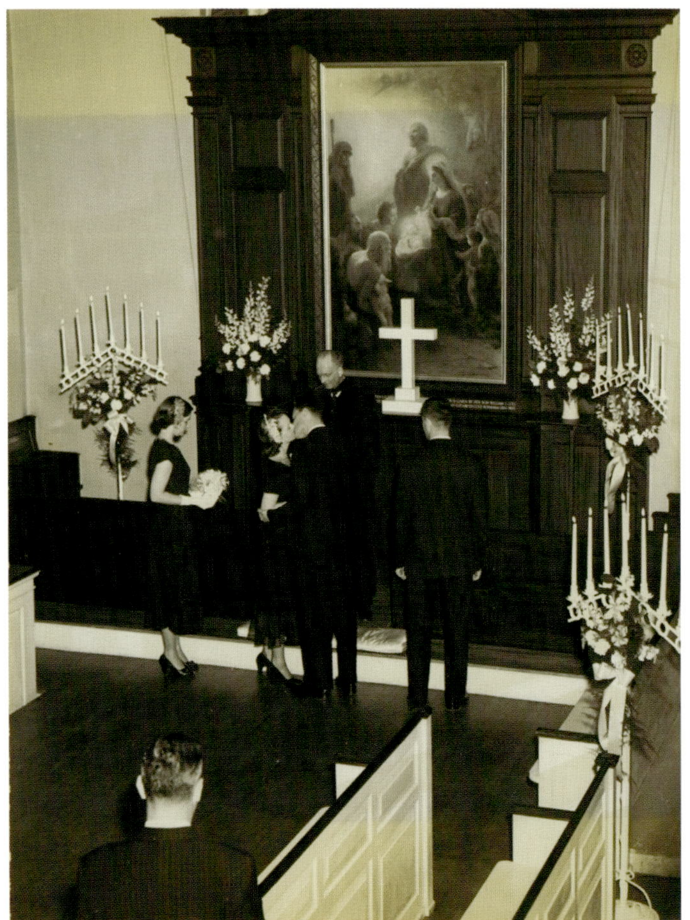

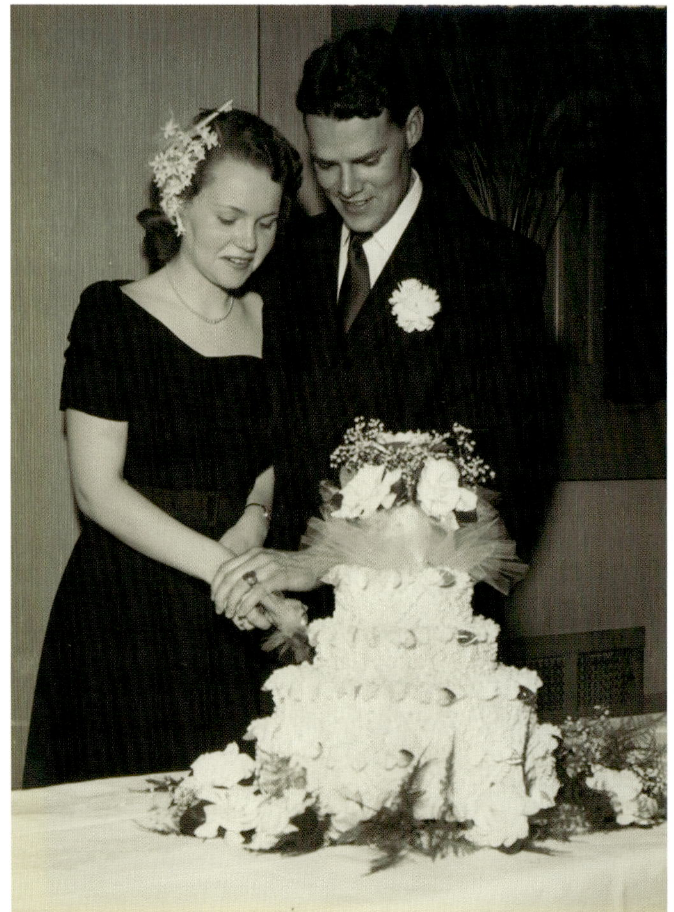

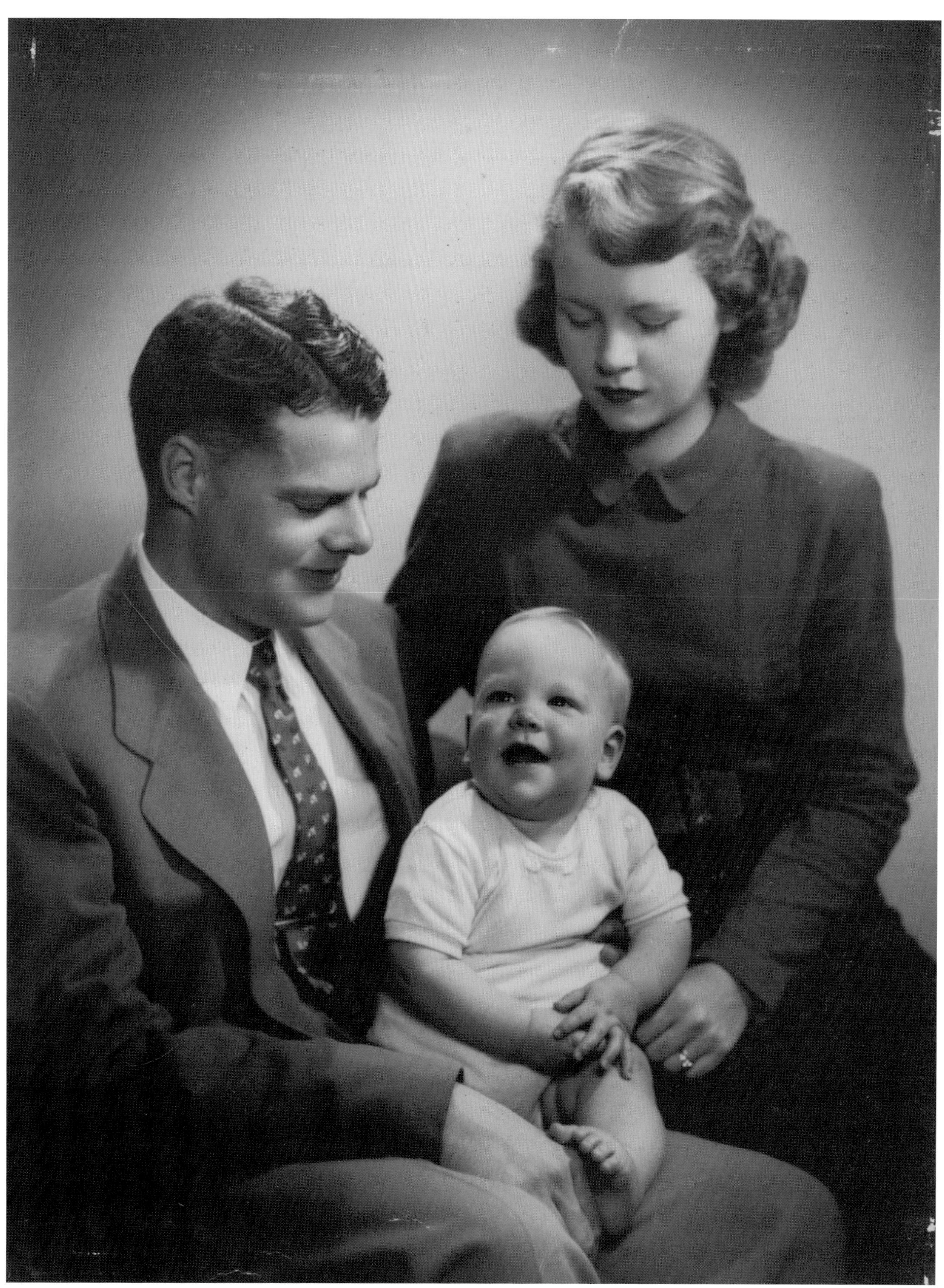

CM: I showed up less than two years later.

The family album that my mother made is a rich object of study. In this section of the documentary, I interrogate the gap between the images and my own experience. However, it also documents an all-white suburban world of what is now commonly referred to as "white privilege." I did have an African American piano teacher when I was in my early teens, and an African American woman came to clean the house once a week. Not surprisingly, they do not appear in my mother's album. The absence of racial markings is made to seem perfectly normal. In this respect, it quite accurately reflects the world I grew up in. However, it also reflects the world I was trying to escape—in which case, this film suggests the distance I travelled.

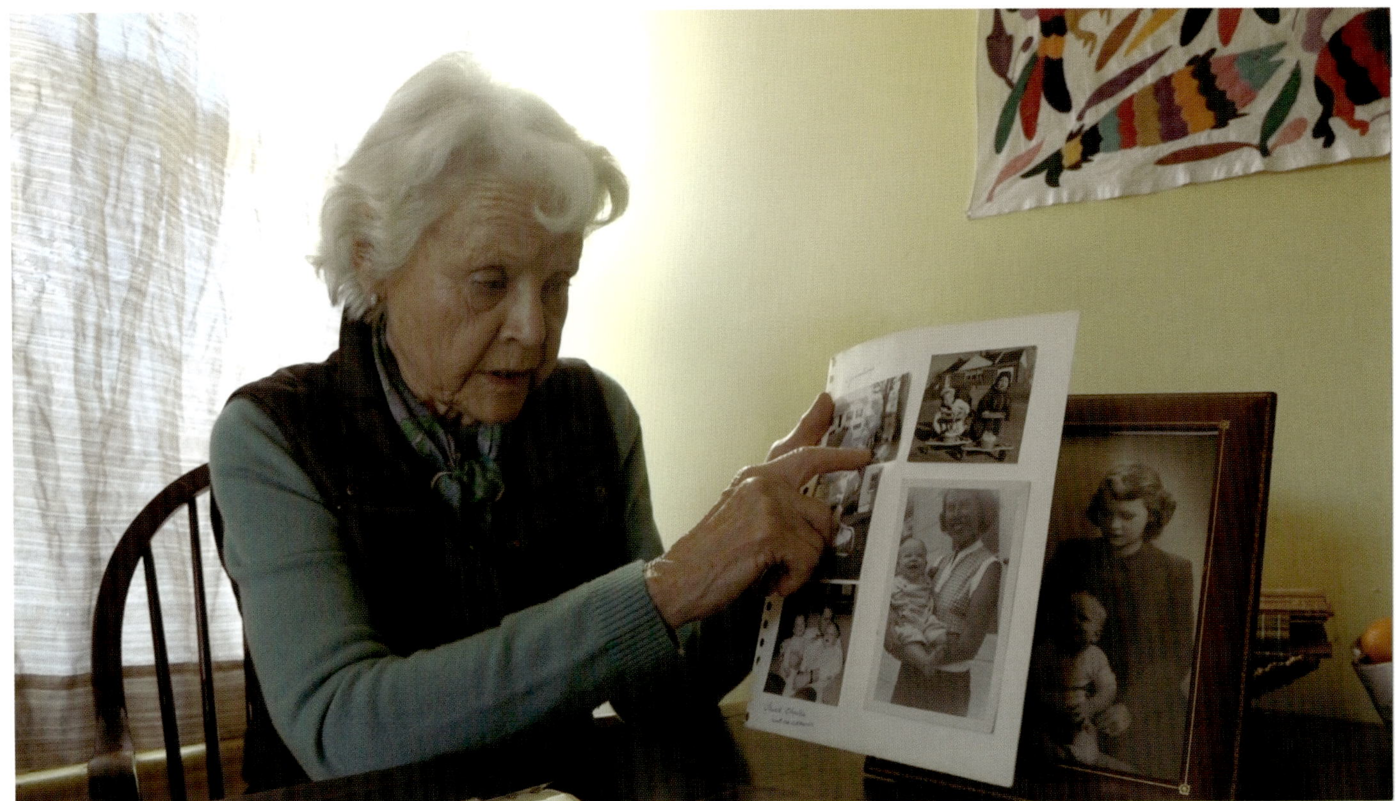

Marilyn: That's four generations.

Charlie: Four generations. Who…?

Marilyn: That's you, Charles. That's me, that's your granddad and your great grandmother. My father's mother.

Charlie: Right. And her name was?

Marilyn: Her name is Daisy Bird. Daisy Bird Keach. There you are with your Aunt Nancy, who thought you were mighty special. Let's see what is on this side.

CM: They are almost entirely of us children celebrating various holidays. We had what they had not had. Unlike my mother who was an only child, I had siblings. In many ways, it was a very white, ostensibly privileged upper-middle class existence. But not everything was perfect.

Charlie: It seemed like there was a gap between five… and then I think Dad got sick.

Marilyn: He got sick when you were seven…

Charlie: And the photo album sort of stops for a while and then resumes. Is that accurate?

Marilyn: That's pretty much it. Yeah. Yeah. Because you were seven, Nancy was five, and Jane was not yet born but born in March.

4 generations!

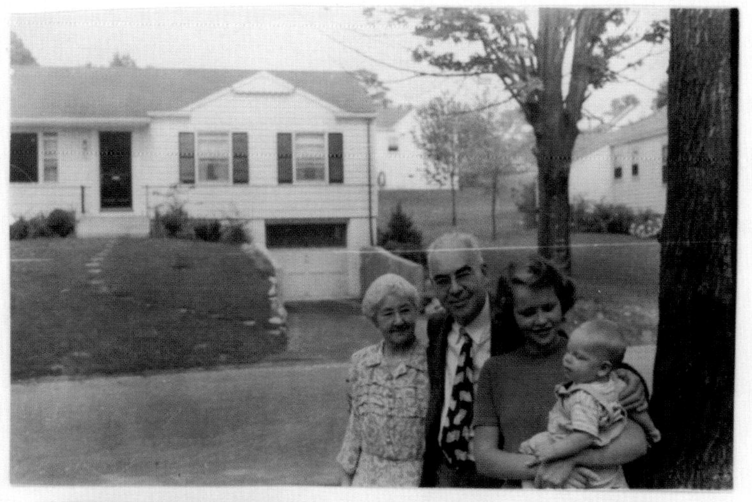

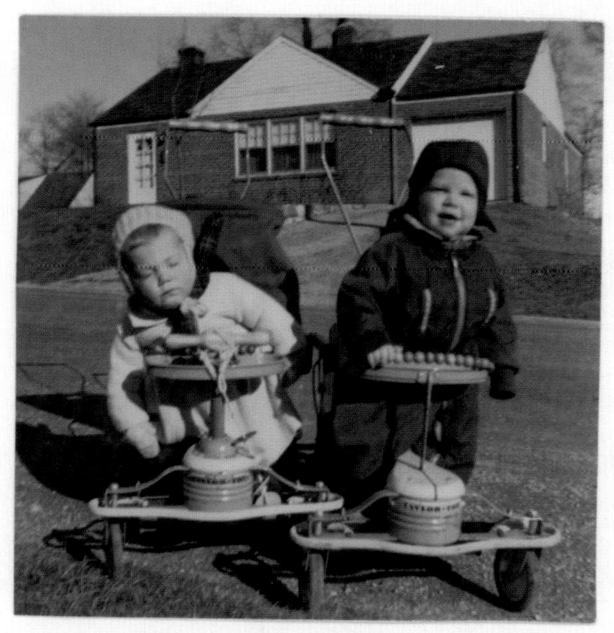

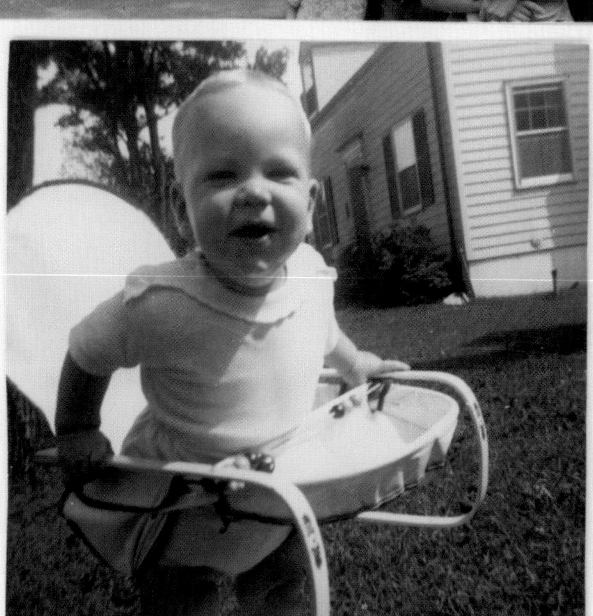

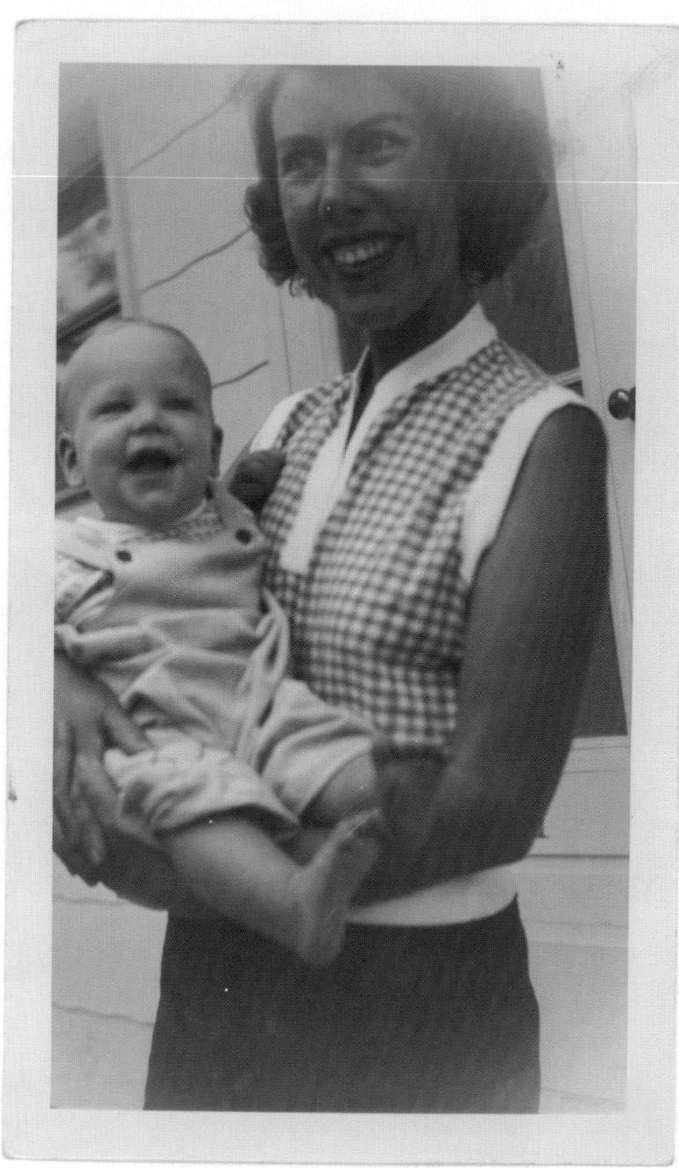

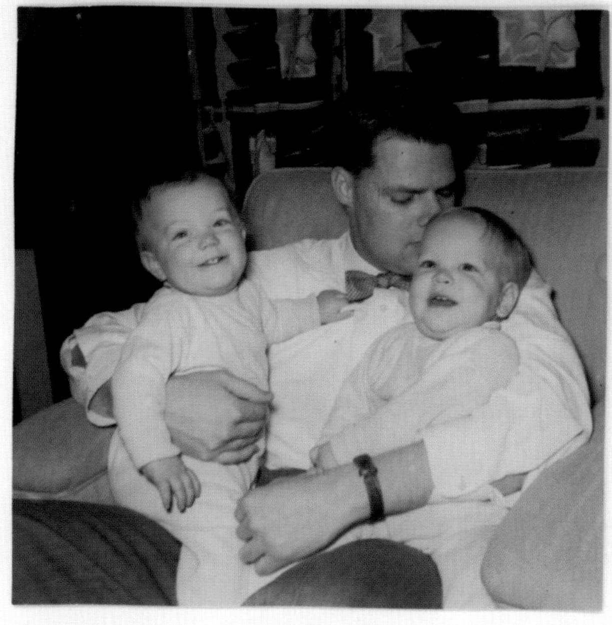

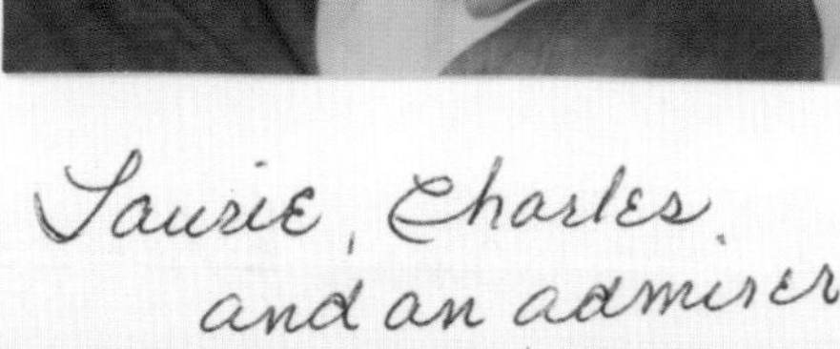

Laurie, Charles.
and an admirer

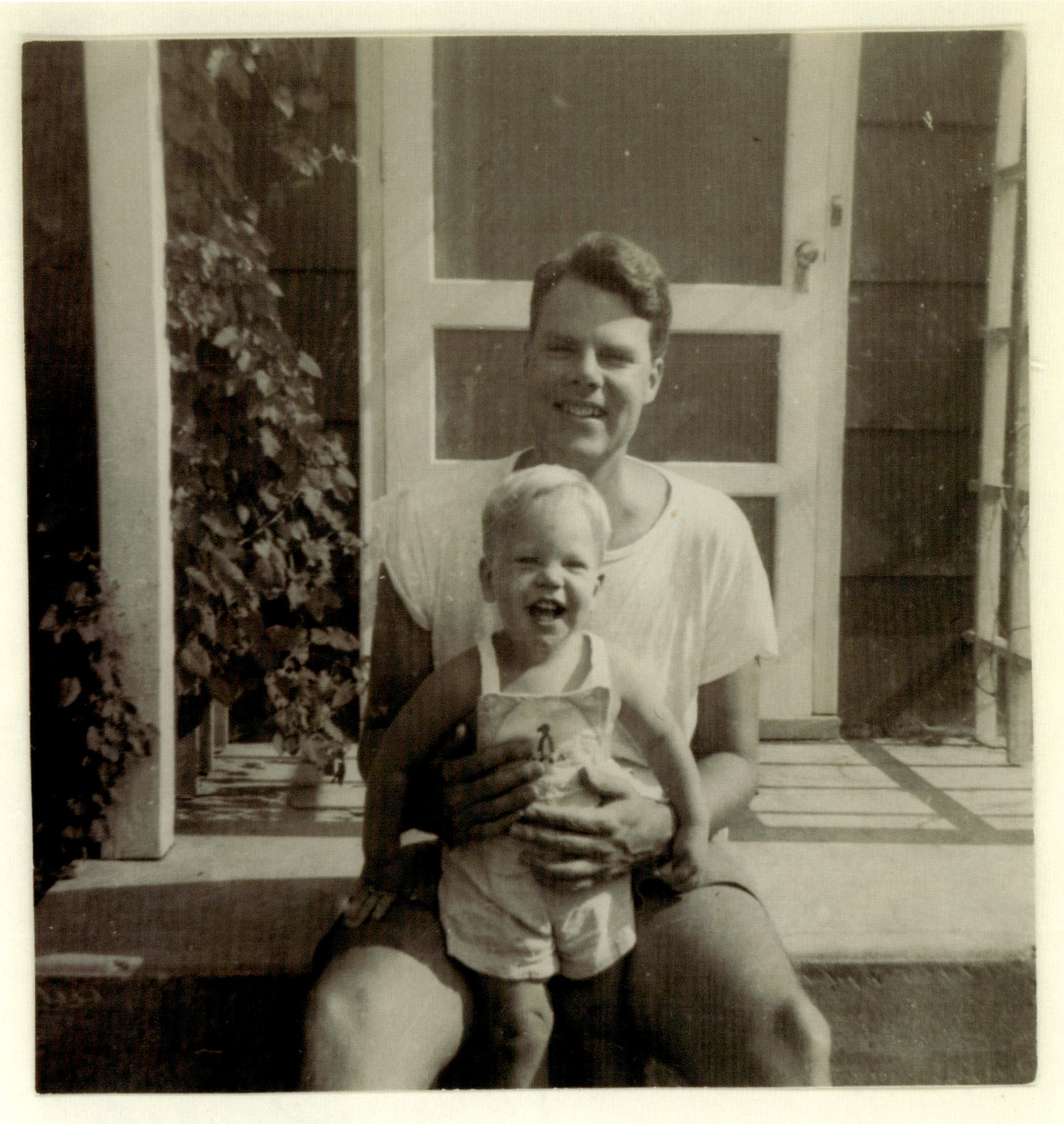

CM: My father was in an institution receiving electric shock therapy for manic depression and post-traumatic stress disorder that almost certainly came from his wartime experience.

Marilyn: But then we resumed and we had some wonderful times, of course.

CM: So why couldn't I remember them? Our family album always made me uncomfortable. Why was that? I thought it might be helpful to consult with my friend Paolo Cherchi Usai, who is a senior curator at the world's oldest photography museum. He's also a founder of the Silent Film Festival in Pordenone Italy.

I interviewed Paolo Cherchi Usai at the Giornate del Cinema Muto, an eight-day festival of silent films in Pordenone, Italy. Although we have known each other for more than thirty years, I had no idea as to his views on family photography. I only knew he would offer provocative insights, forcefully expressed. Not entirely surprisingly we share similar childhood experiences. Nonetheless, while highly critical of family photography, Paolo still keeps his own carefully curated private photo album in his head.

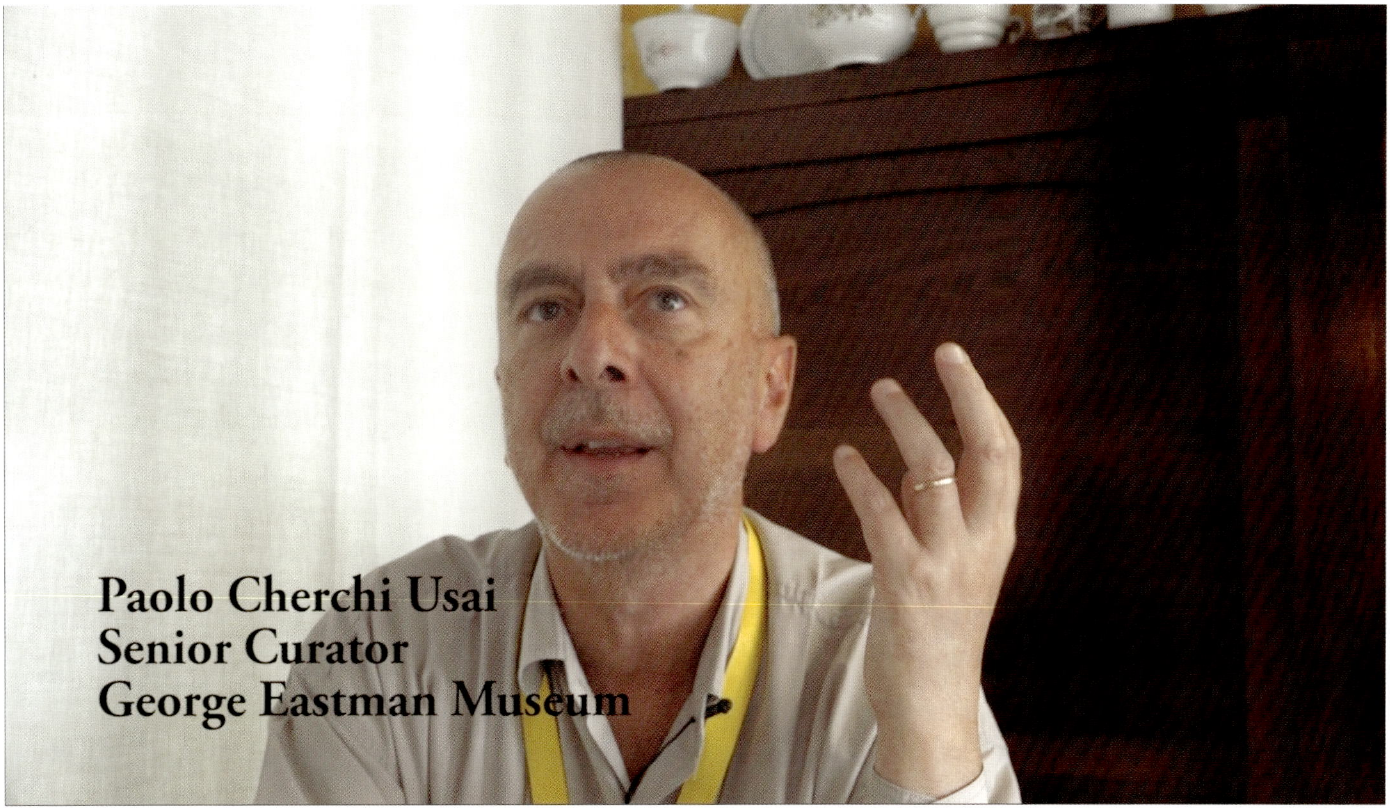

**Paolo Cherchi Usai
Senior Curator
George Eastman Museum**

Paolo Cherchi Usai: I don't like photographs in general, but particularly those that represent something in my life. And I've avoided doing photographs of my dear ones fundamentally for one reason. It's because the best pictures I have of my dear ones are here [in my head]. I take my pictures. There are those moment that I want to keep. I have made those images, I have framed them…I can recall them anytime I want and they're mine.

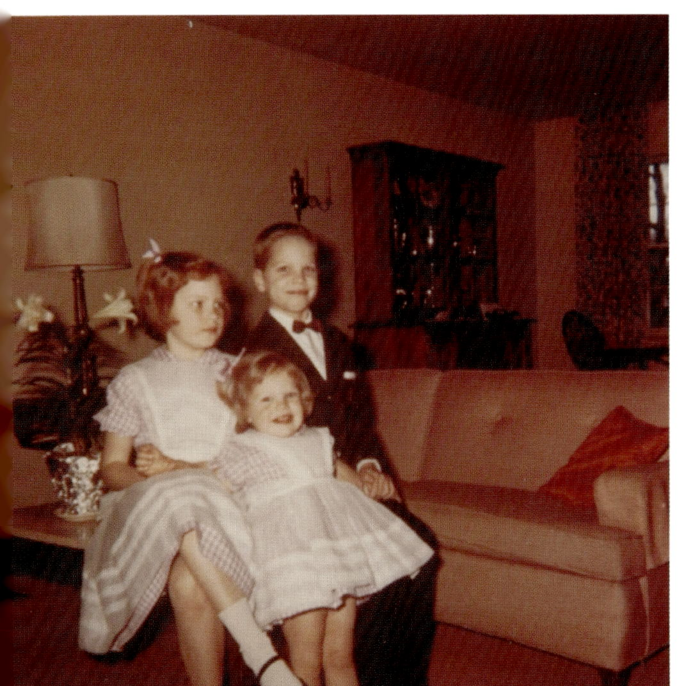

CM: Unfortunately, I lack a photographic memory, and these photographs now provide many of the crucial memories of my childhood. Indeed, they remind me again and again that the photograph itself often took priority over the event. We were dressed and expected to perform for the photograph, making it almost impossible to live in and simply enjoy the moment. The photograph as it might be experienced some day seemed more important than experiencing the present. I often felt like a performing seal. Was it worth it?

Paolo: I realize how much I dislike family albums. I despise them. I never wanted to be part of a family album. Whenever I knew I was going to be depicted in a photograph, I was trying to make sure that the photograph would be as unappealing as possible.

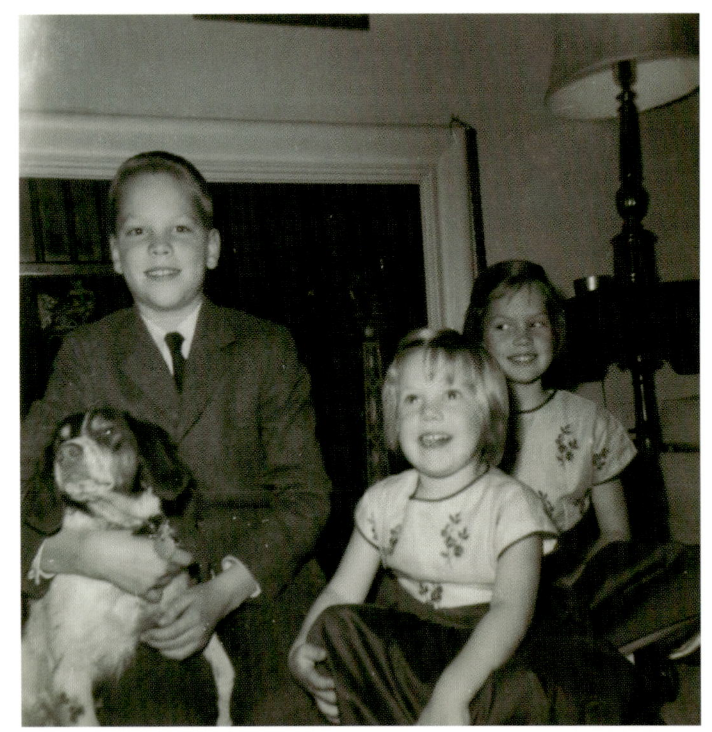

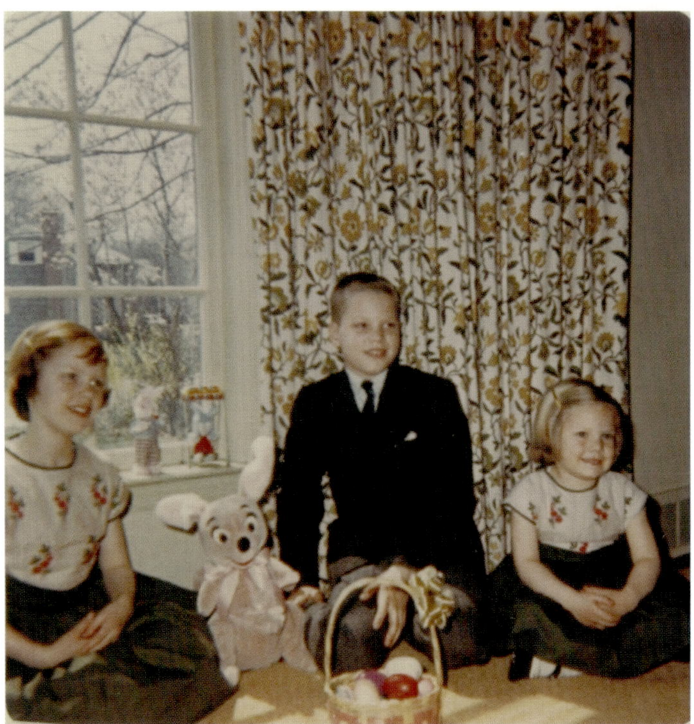

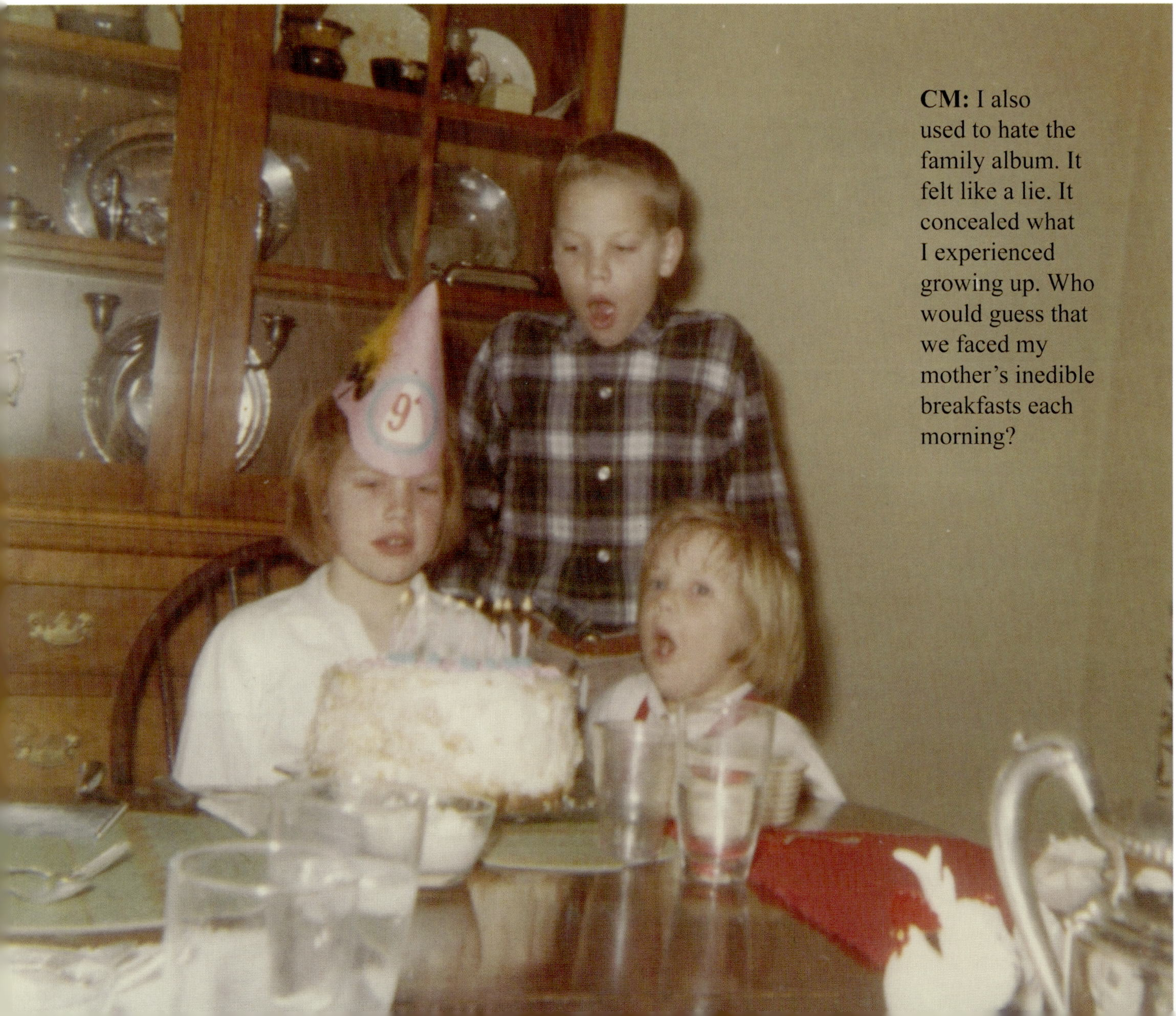

CM: I also used to hate the family album. It felt like a lie. It concealed what I experienced growing up. Who would guess that we faced my mother's inedible breakfasts each morning?

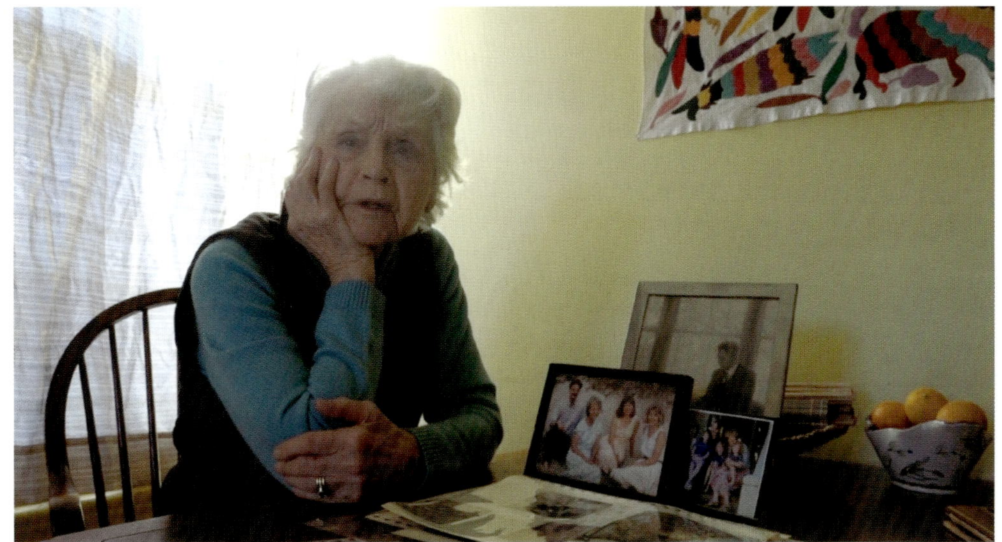

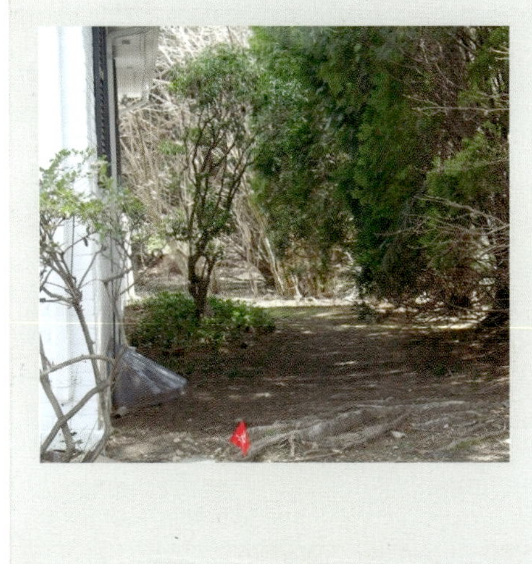

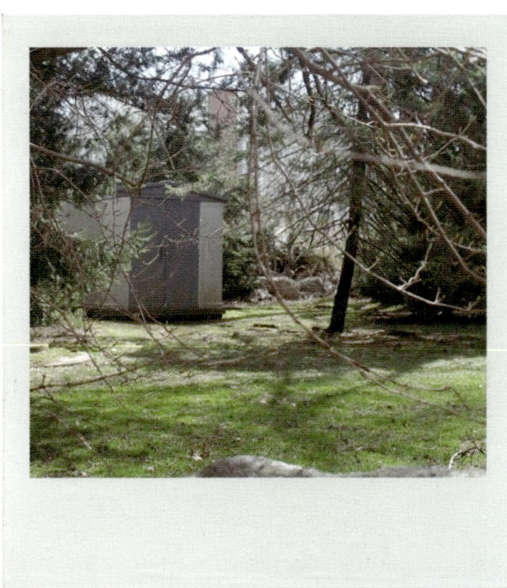

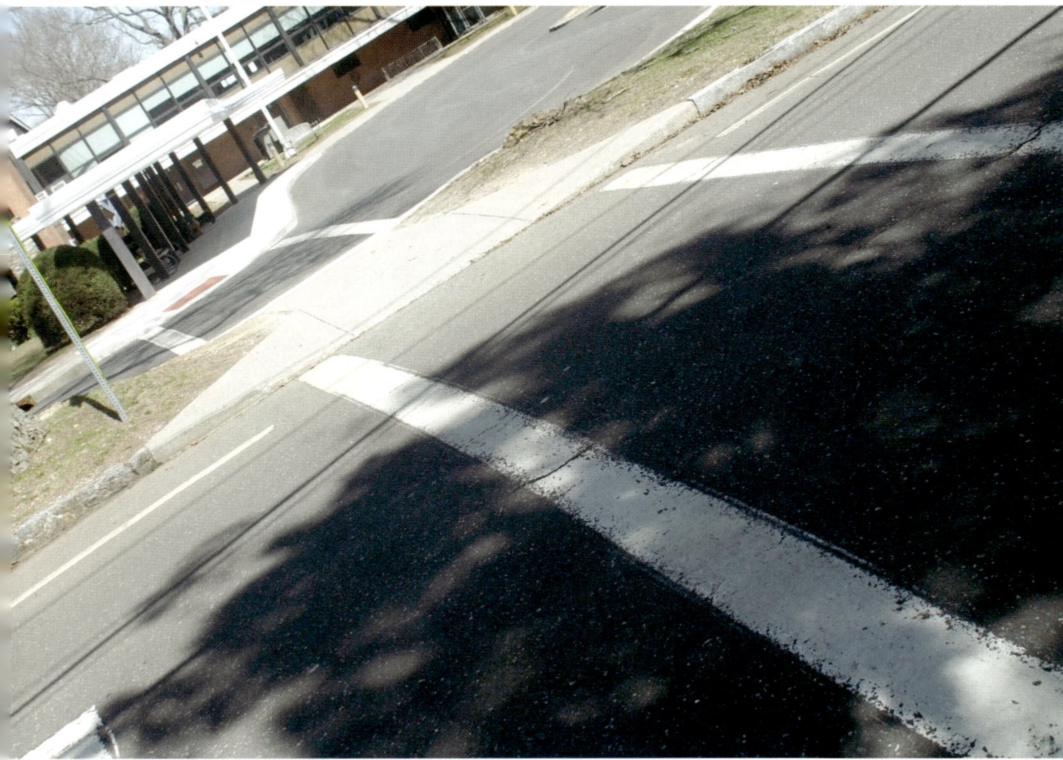

CM: Yes. I too, learned to hate the family album.

Marilyn: Tiger's Milk and all that stuff, you mean?

Charlie: Do you remember the exact combination?

Marilyn: No. It was black-strapped molasses for one thing. And it was soy milk. And it was some other stuff that was a health-food additive sort of thing that was very popular at the time, but I can't remember. But you didn't like it much.

Charlie: Wheat germ and Brewer's Yeast.

Mom: Wheat germ was part of it. I hope you still eat wheat germ.

CM: We performed happiness while my walks home from school were filled with terror, as I was stalked by and often battled boys two years older than me—the ones who had stayed back. I want the family album to mark those places. … HERE. And HERE.

CM: The last one took place HERE, in eighth grade, against the Murphy twins. It was a draw. One brother kicked me as hard as he could while I had his twin pinned to the ground, banging his head on the pavement, knowing it would be all over if I let him up.

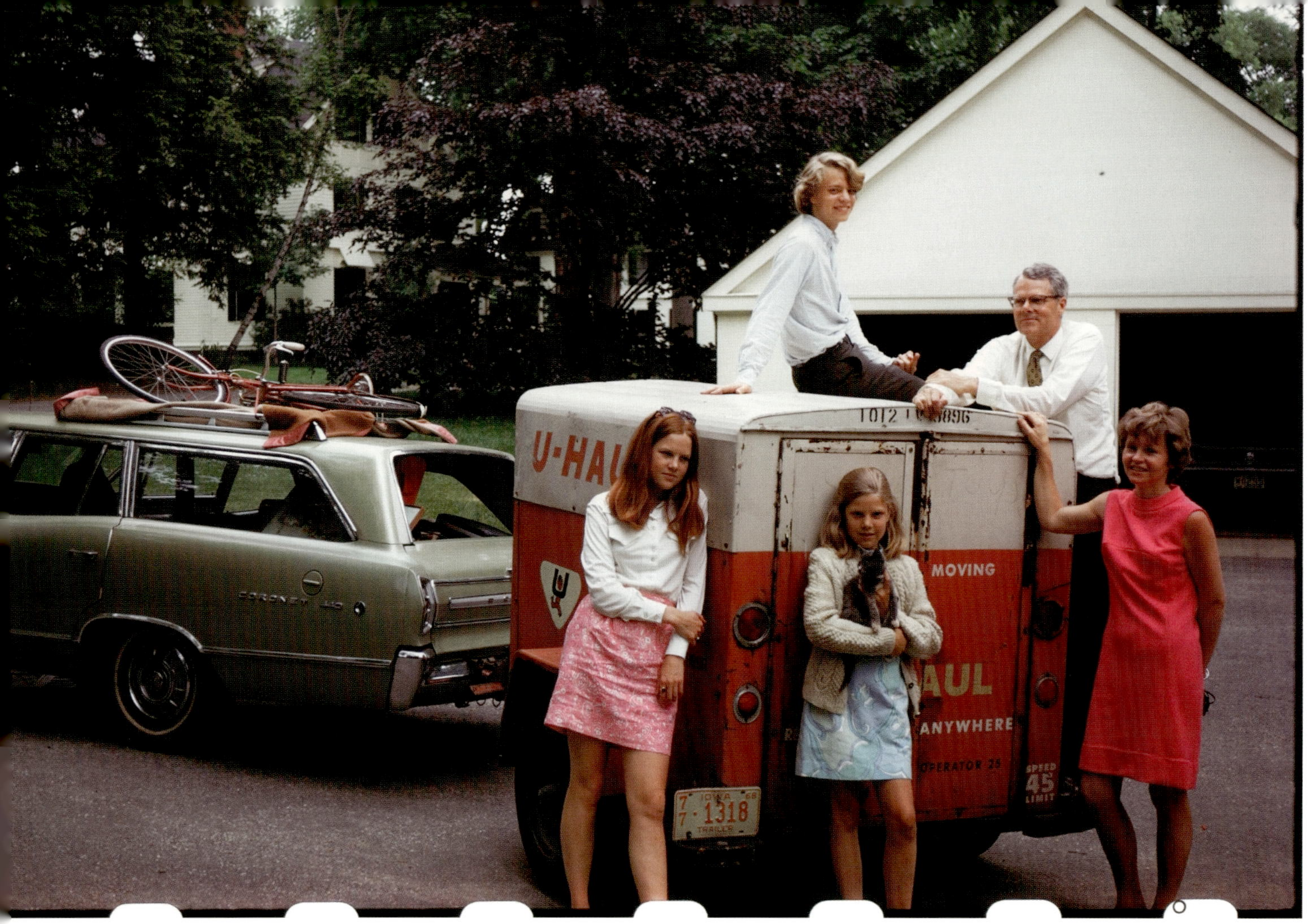

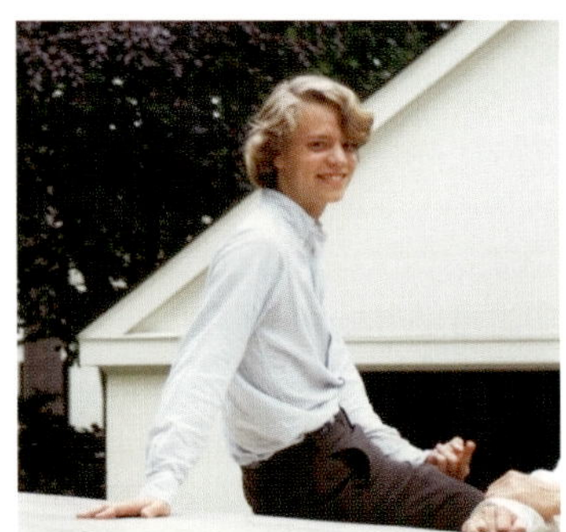

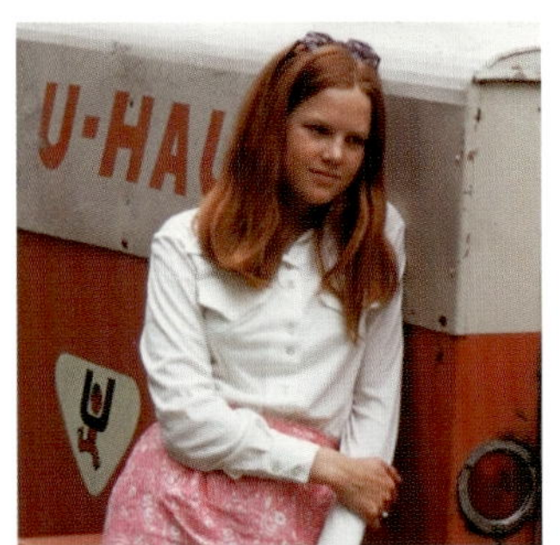

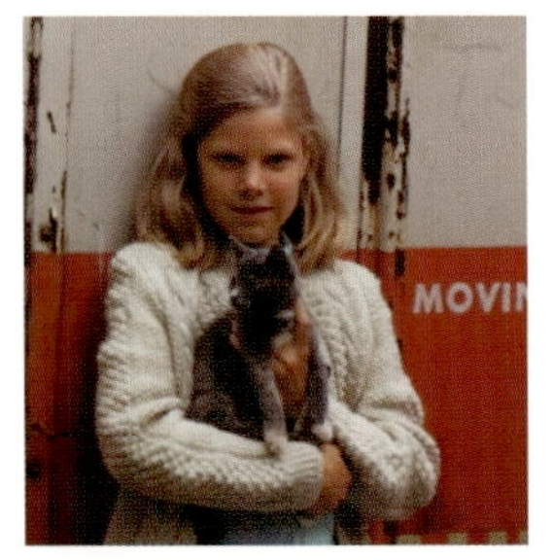

This photograph, taken as I was leaving St. Paul's School at the end of my senior year, calls out for an interpretive reading, beginning with my gleeful ruining of a family photo. I had been in full-out rebellion for several years. Rebellion became more focused as I began to apprentice with studio potter Gerry Williams, who grew up in India and whose father was a friend of Mahatma Gandhi. Gerry returned to the U.S. at the beginning of World War II, just in time to spend those years in CO camps. He became my first surrogate father, perhaps my first really positive role model—though I would be blessed to have others. With the Vietnam War in full swing, I too registered with the draft board as a conscientious objector—though I never had to face the real consequences due to the "Vietnamization" of the war.

My sister Nancy's posture and her sideways glance—her refusal to meet the camera's eye—speaks clearly, at least to me. Though not happy to be posing, she avoided outward mutiny. Having witnessed the consequences of my rebellion, she learned the art of staying under the radar and quietly going her own way. For a time that would be filled with hallucinogens. Eventually she became a therapist and drug counselor.

My youngest sister Jane would prove to be my parents' greatest success, reproducing if not improving on their lives and choices. She worked in finance, married a Harvard man and raised her family in the suburbs.

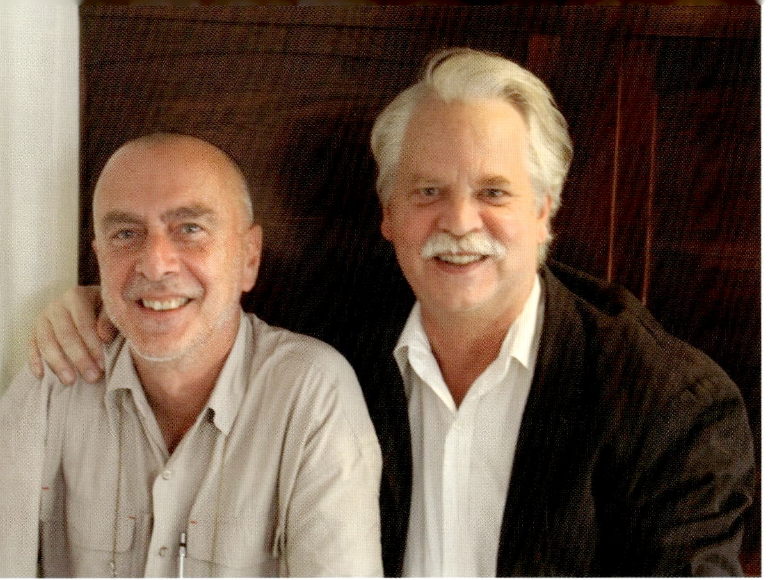

Paolo: A family album is fundamentally a form of emotional ideology. How we would like ourselves to be perceived by others.

My first Giornate was in 1985, and I have been a regular ever since. Although a professional convening of archivists and film scholars, long-time Giornate president David Robinson always launched the year's festivities by welcoming us home. We are, indeed, a kind of family (a family of rather off-beat obsessives), and this is our annual family reunion.

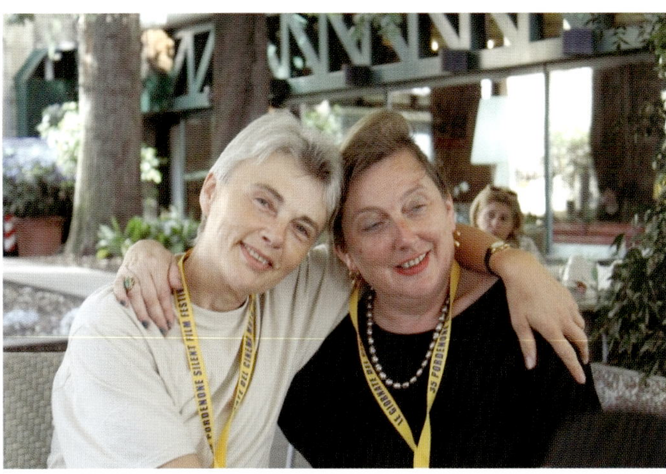

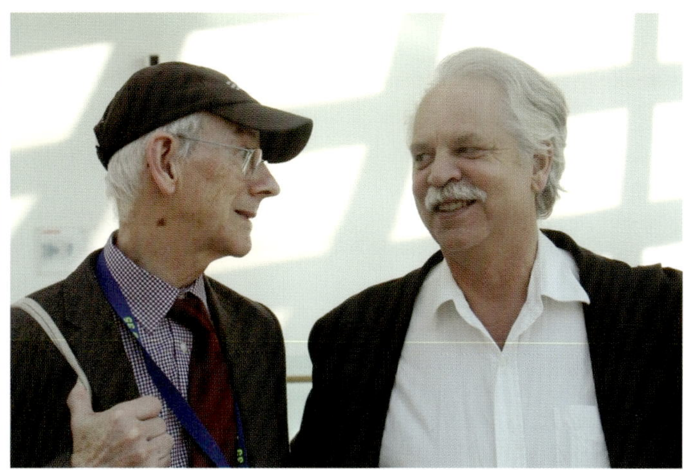

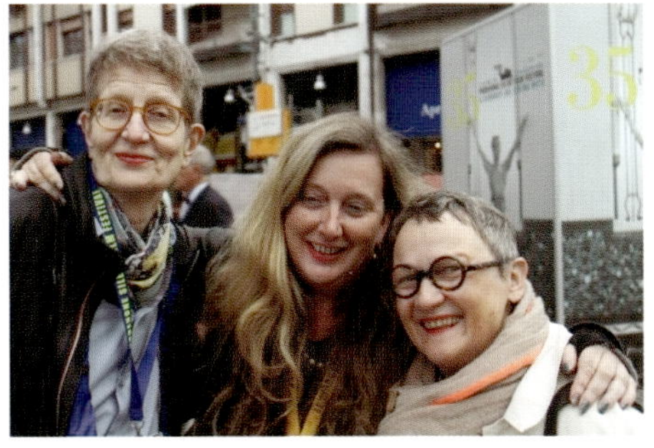

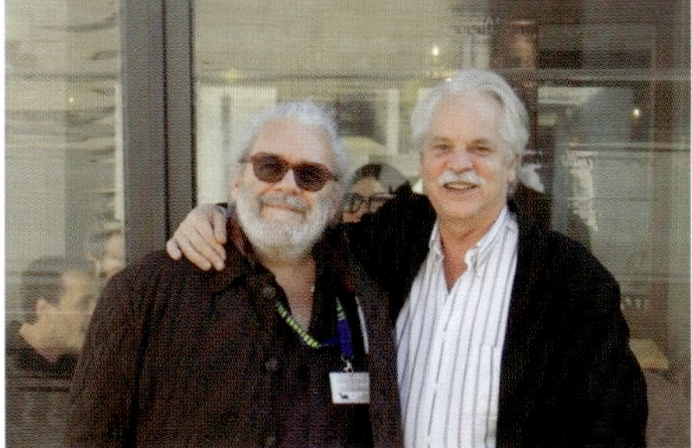

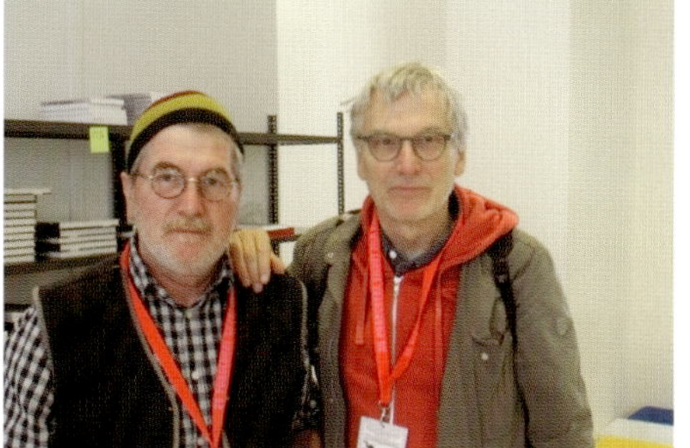

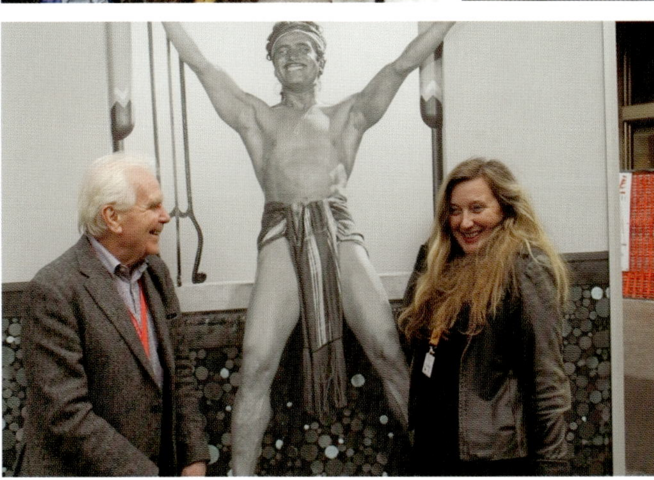

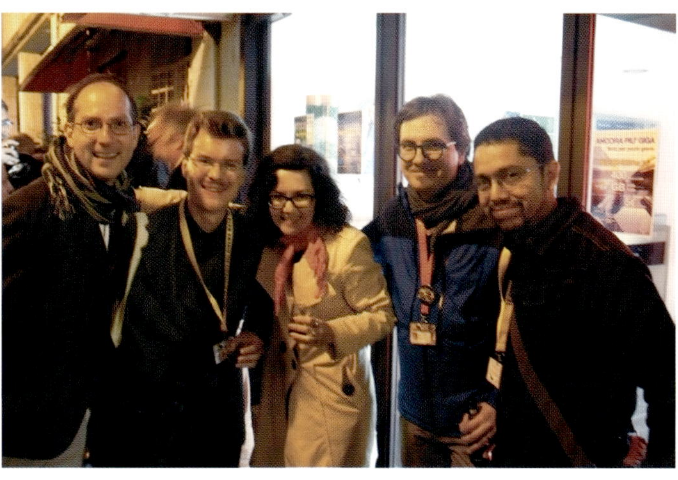

Top: Sabine Lenk and Vanessa Toulmin; Kevin Brownlow & CM. Middle: Heide Schlüpmann, VT & Karola Gramann; CM & André Gaudreault; Paolo Jacob & Livio Jacob (Giornate director). Bottom: David Robinson (Giornate past president) & VT; Jay Weissberg (Giornate president) & Co. October 2016.

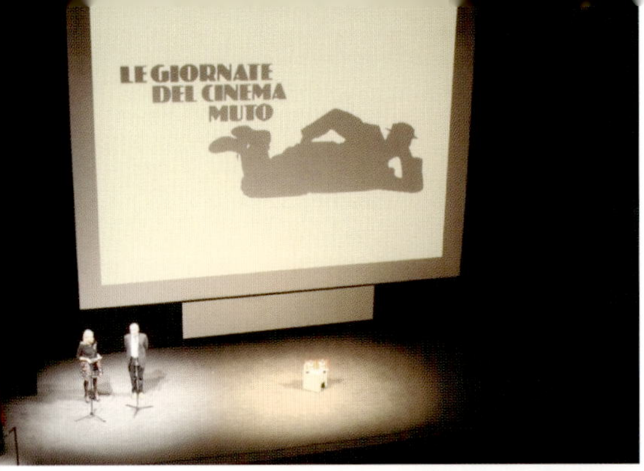

CM: Each year the Pordenone silent film festival provides a second home for many of us. It also boasts its own family album—images of when we were all much younger. Paolo looks so gorgeous.

Black and white photos by Paolo Jacob. His Giornate family album was on display at the festival book stall (below left). Paolo with Marguerite Engberg (below right).

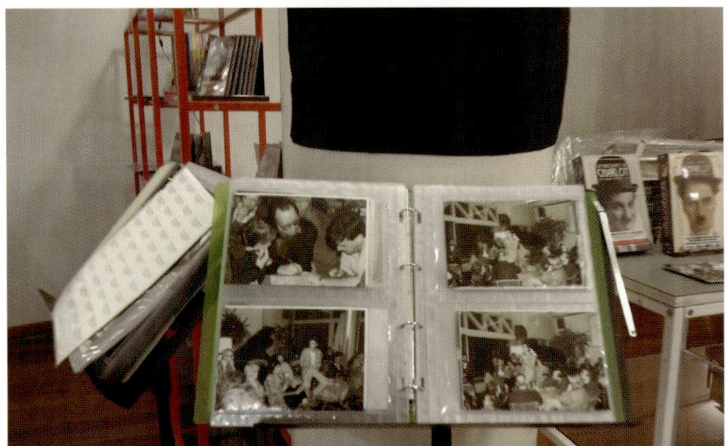

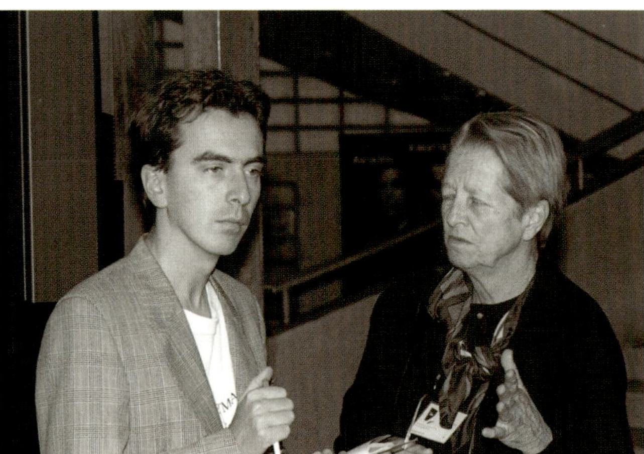

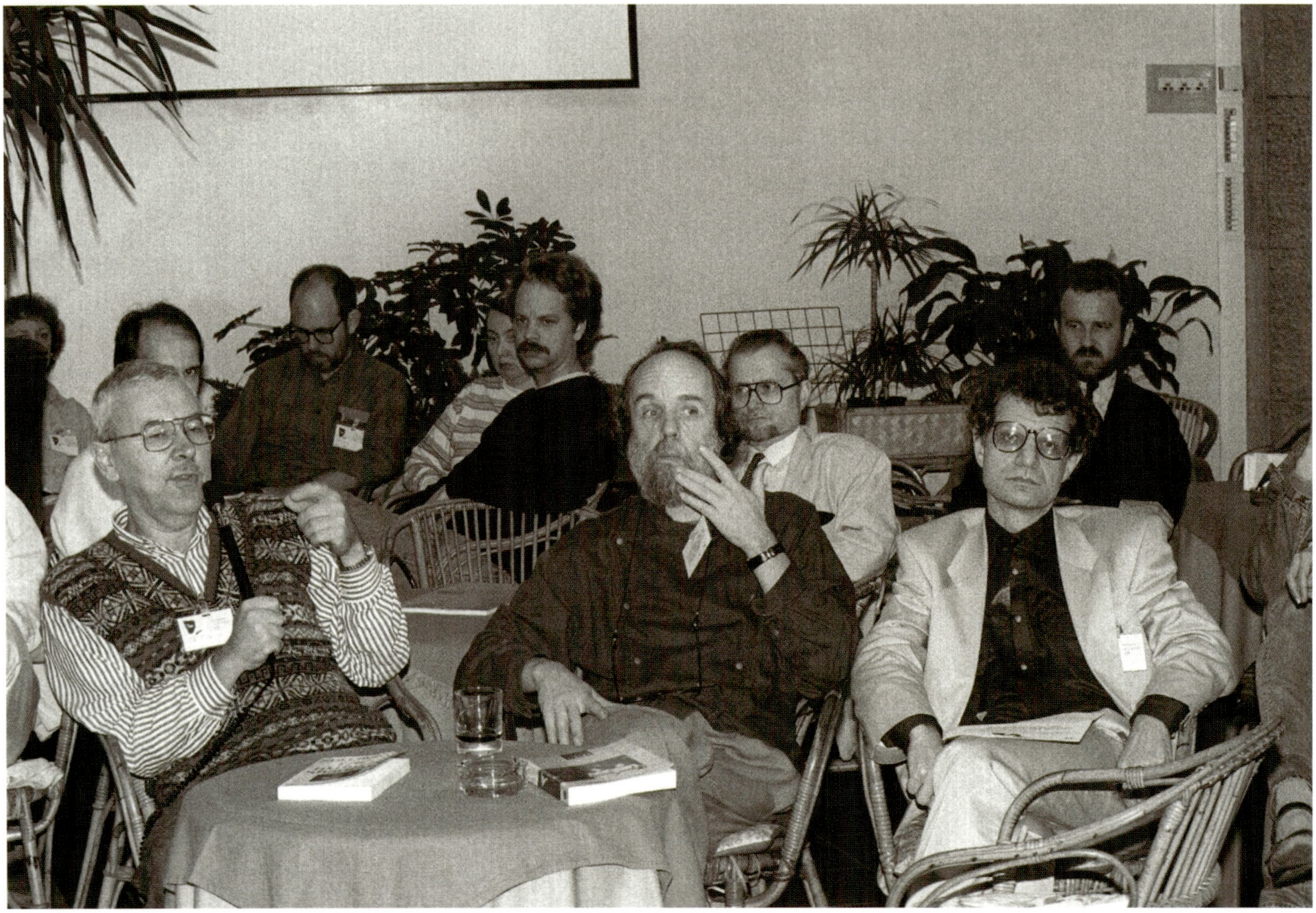

Front row, left to right: Geoffrey Nowell-Smith, Noël Burch and Thomas Elsaesser.

CM: And I had forgotten that I had spent time there with some of my heroes, like Noël Burch and Thomas Elsaesser.

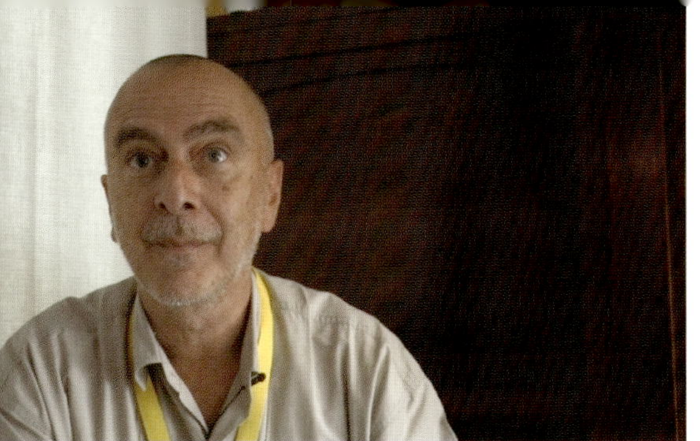

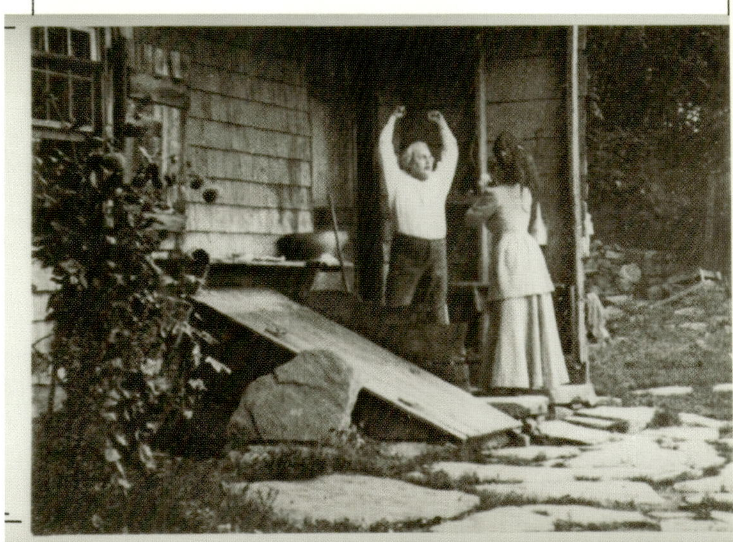

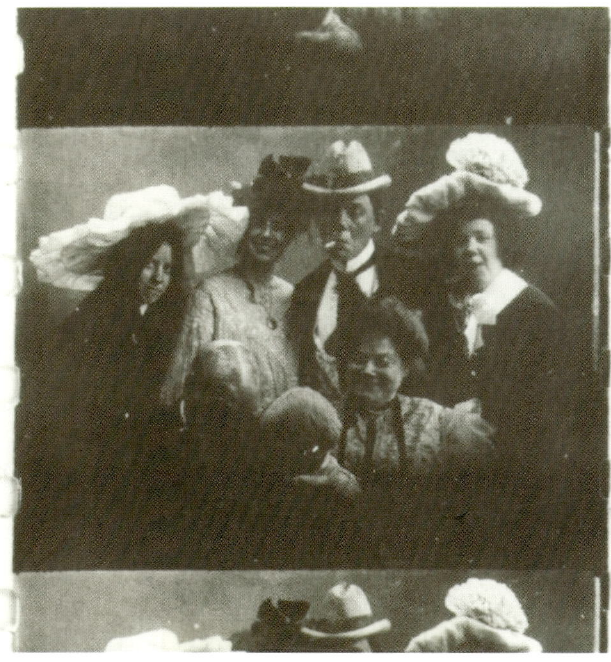

Paolo: There is something sacred about the image itself that I think should not be wasted in something as mundane and banal—for me, at least—as a family album.

My dissertation was on Edwin S. Porter, for whom family was a recurrent motif. Above: The Miller's Daughter *(Porter, 1905);* The Whole Dam Family and the Dam Dog *(Porter, 1905). Below:* Stolen by Gypsies *(Porter, 1905).*

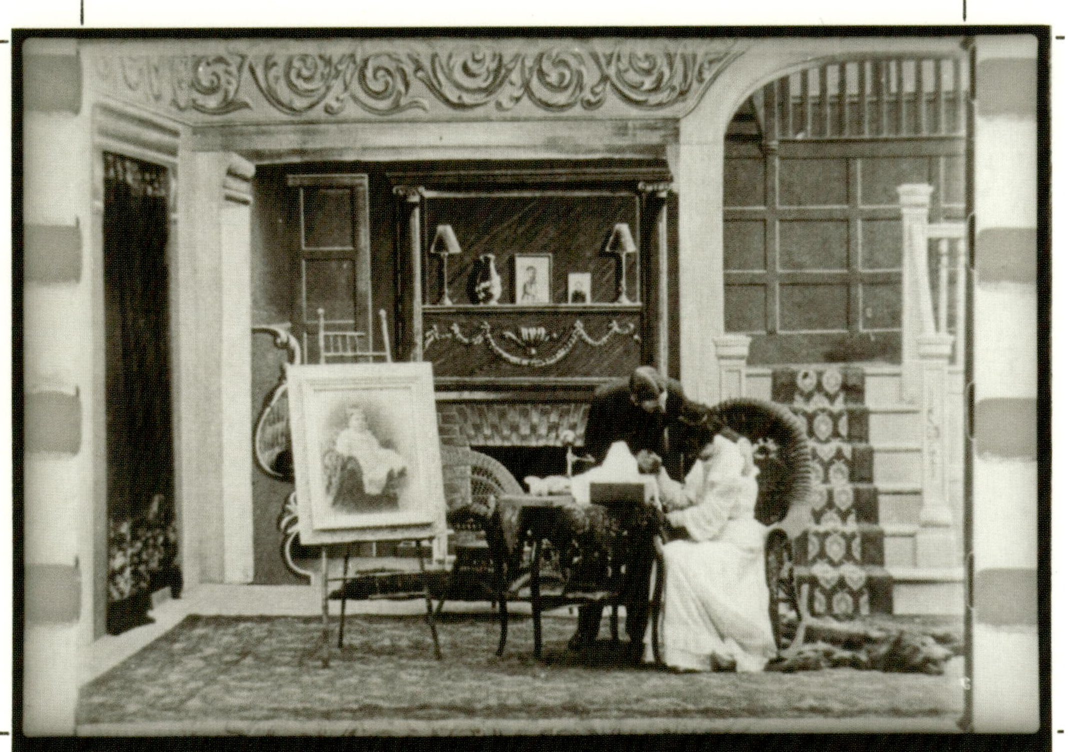

CM. For a long time I thought about the image very much like Paolo. I had a camera because I was taking photographs for my work. Without perhaps quite realizing it, these frame enlargements and other images were my alternative to the family album—the unfamily album of my 20s and 30s—as I sought to document everything that was shot for Thomas Edison by his employees. These were illustrations for articles, books and a documentary.

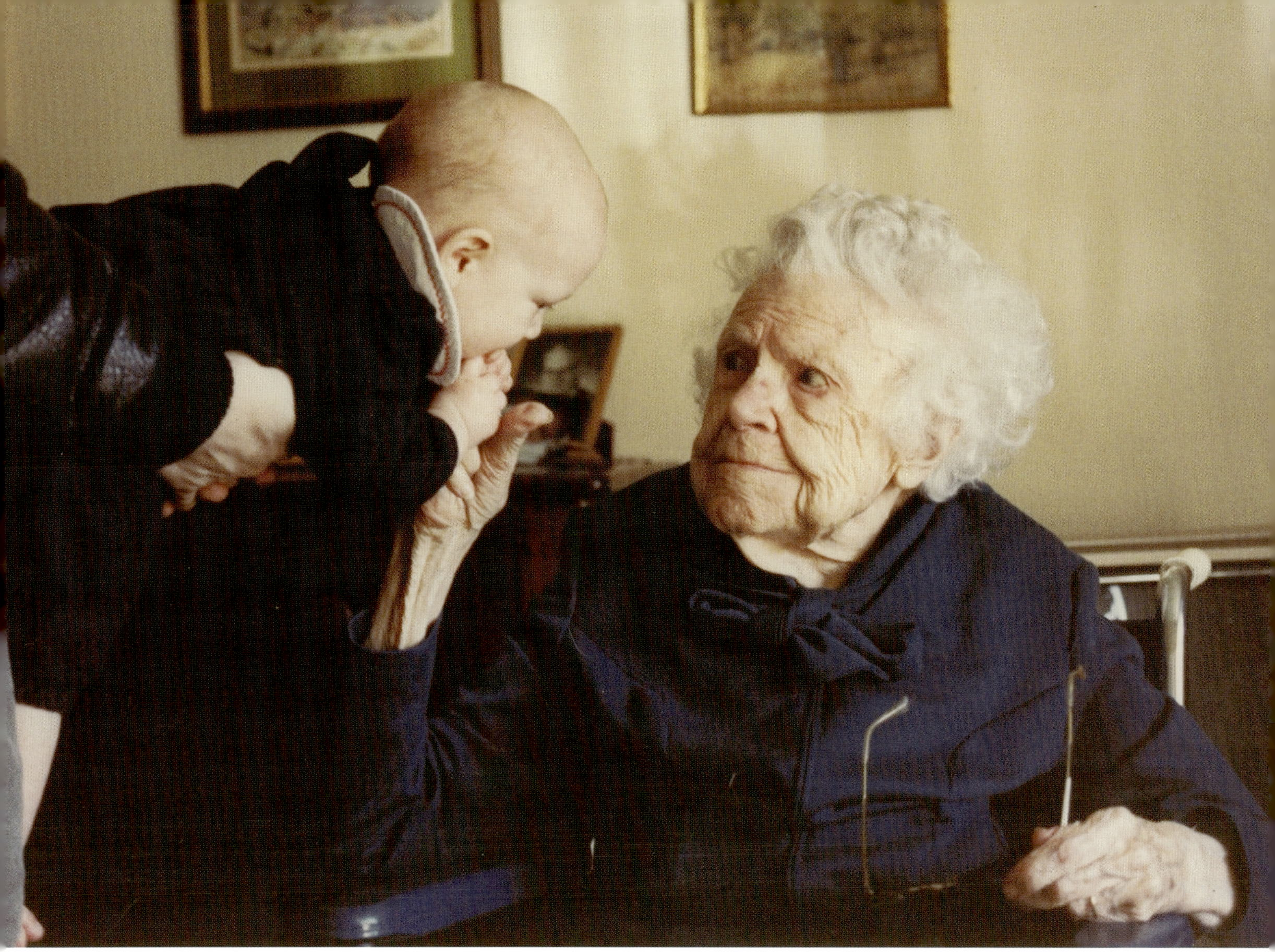

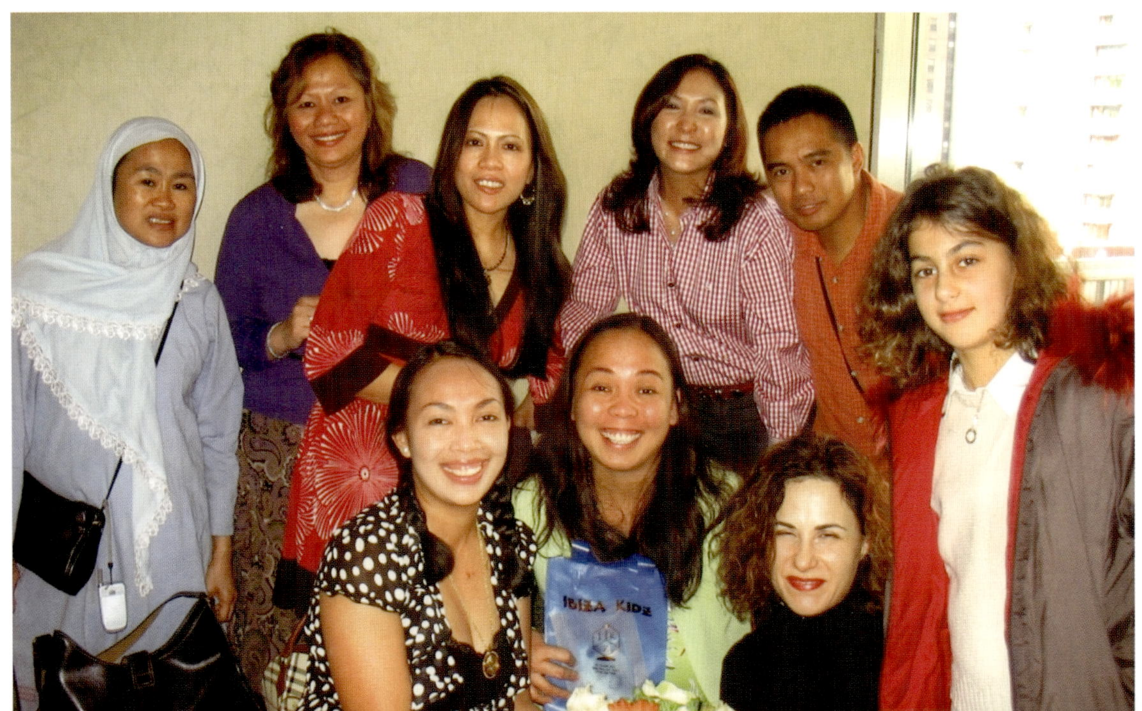

CM: And then, when your sister Hannah Grace was born, I wanted a photo of her and my 100-year-old grandmother, Grace Greene Musser, after whom she was named. But these two enterprises—the unfamily album and the family album—were worlds apart. And they stayed that way. It was generally Hannah's mom who took pictures for your sister's family album.

We celebrated Threese's baby shower in the hospital.

TS: Then at my baby shower someone gave us a small digital camera—our first.

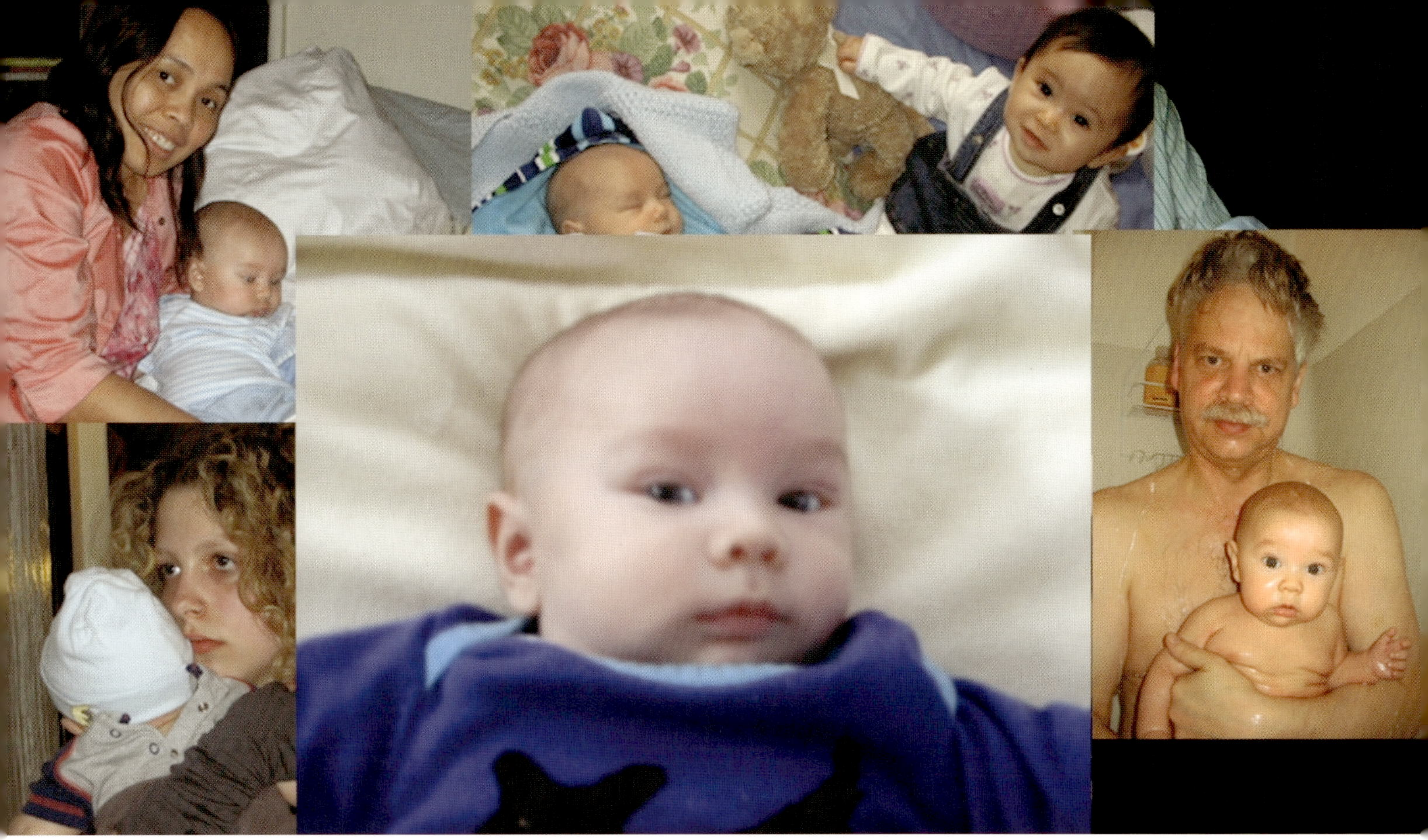

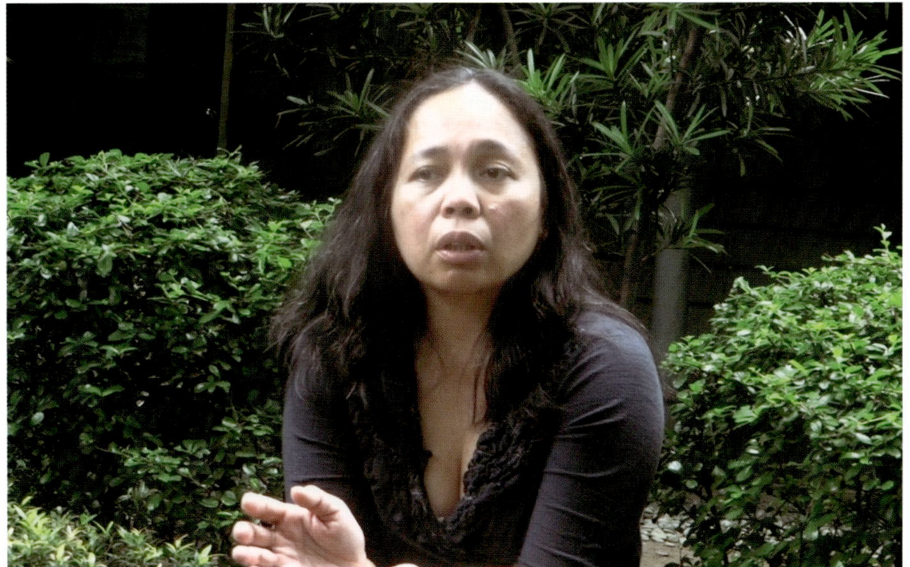

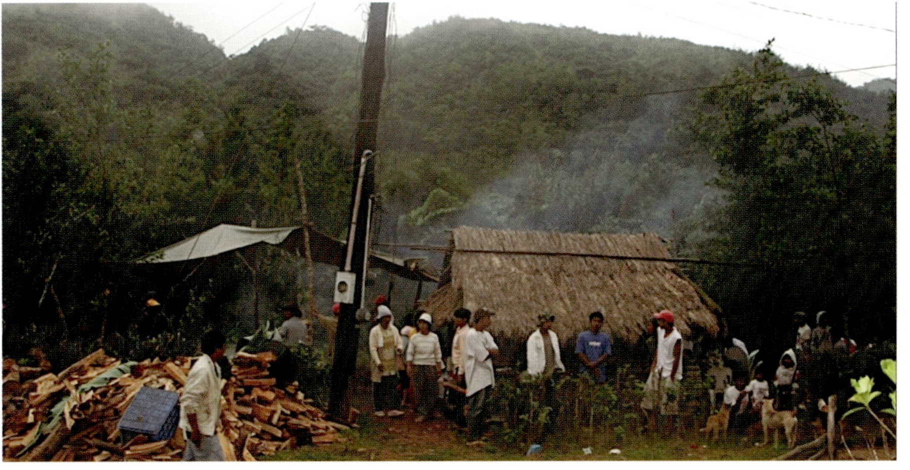

CM: When you were one and a half, your mom was heading back to the Philippines and you were going with her. She needed a more professional camera to document her master's thesis.

Threese: And so, my thesis work was on the Indigenous land use of the Kalahan Tribe. Here's a case of the tribal people, the Ikalahan in Nueva Vizcaya, who in 1972 actually formulated their own land use plan. And using that land use plan, they were able to secure rights and privileges to protect their own domain, which was not a lot, but it was good enough for the community and because of that they were able to preserve their forests.

CM: You quickly felt right at home.

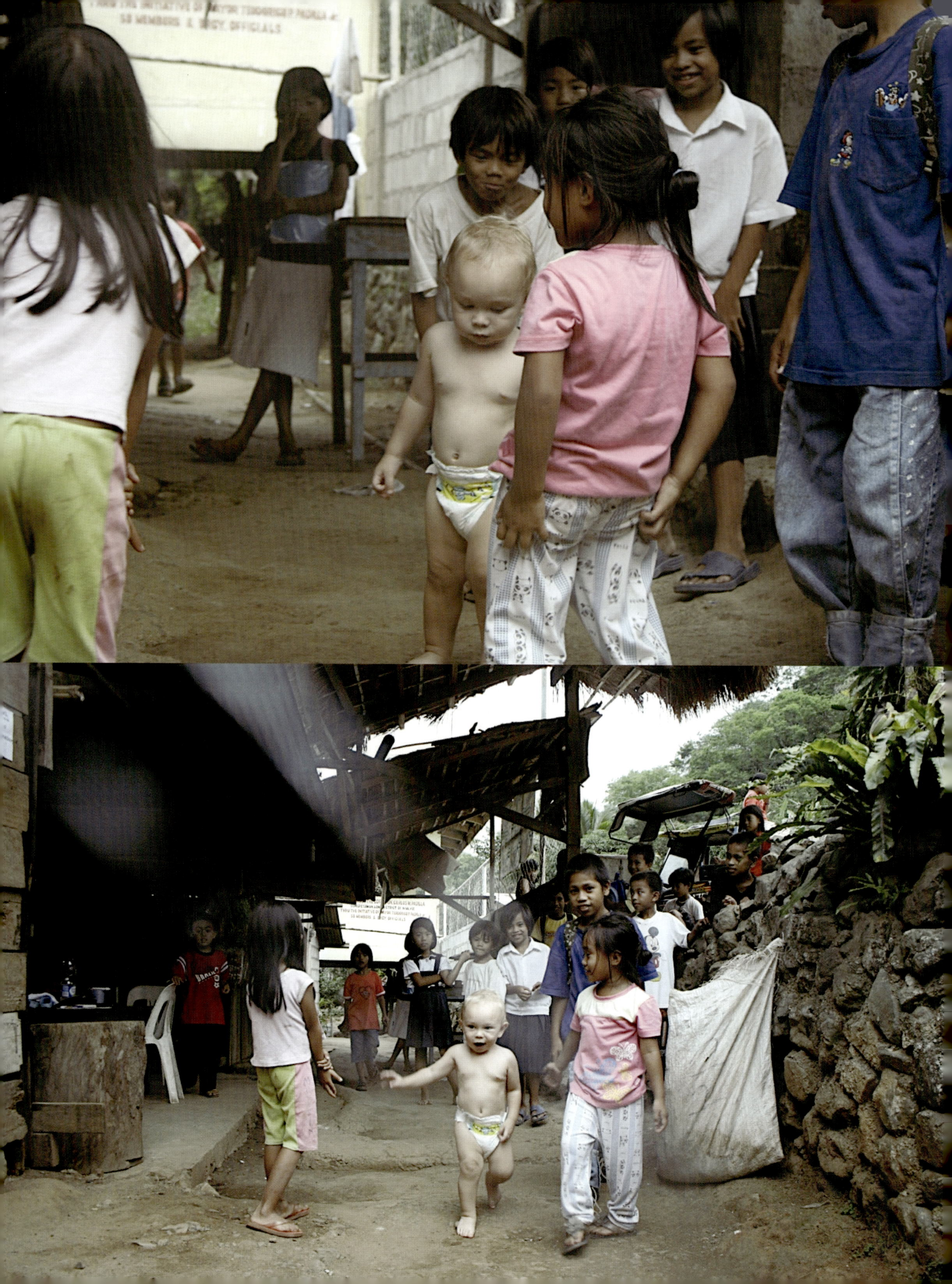

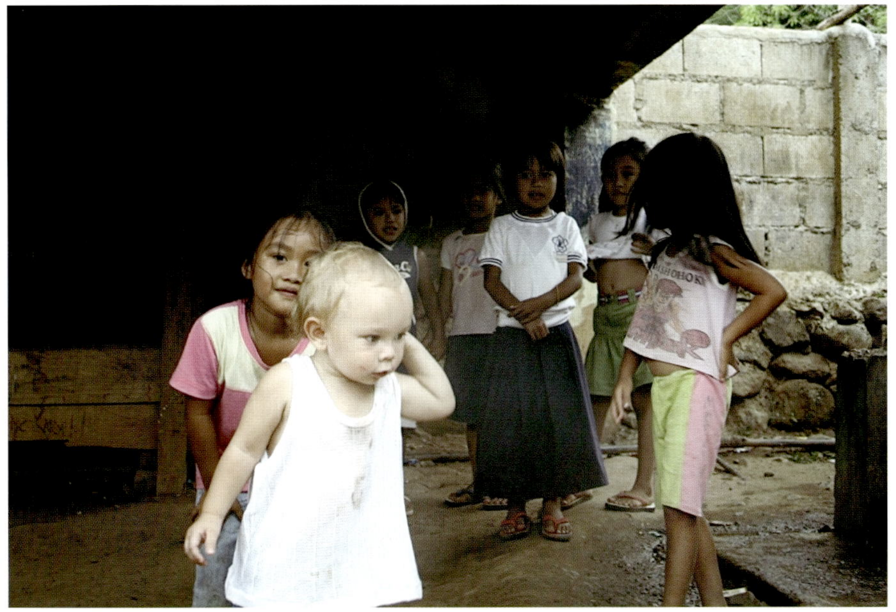

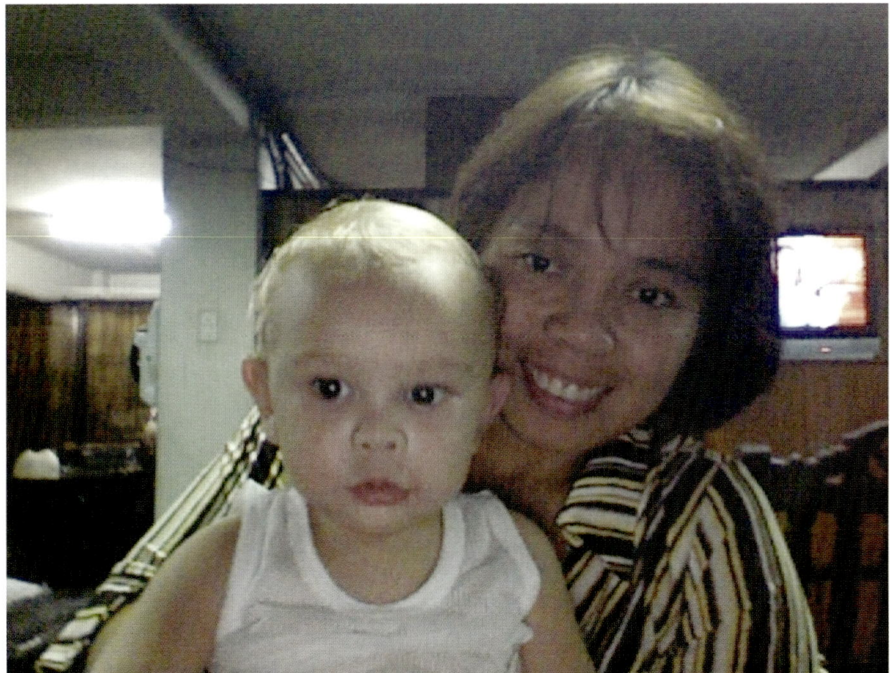

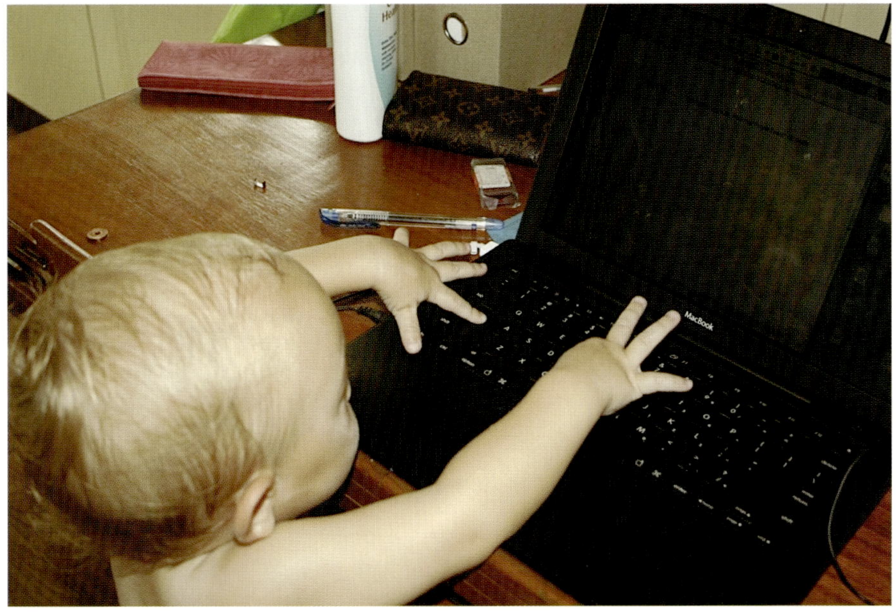

The Ikalahan live in the mountains of Northern Luzon, where Threese worked closely with Rev. Delbert Rice (January 24, 1928-May 8, 2014), whose many books include Ecology: Ti Urnos Ti Lubong *(1998) and* Life in the Forest: Ikalahan Folk Stories *(2011), which detail the traditional knowledge of the Ikalahan on ecology.*

CM: Later, when we skyped on our third wedding anniversary, your mom had some bad news. University of the Philippines told her that she had taken too much time to finish her thesis, and so would not receive her Master's Degree.

Threese: While trying to get my Master's Degree, I was faced with the responsibility of being the third parent. I was funding my own education so I had to work. My brother ran for Congress and I had to help him, and then, finally, my father got sick and I had to take care of him. He was dying of cancer. And of course, I went to the U.S., got married and had you, John Carlos. But of course, I'm not regretting anything.

CM: But it did seem that her professors were annoyed that she had gone off with an American and so had manipulated the clock, costing her a crucial academic credential. After teaching some of the best college students in the Philippines, your mom was about to become a pre-school teacher in New Haven, Connecticut. Hers became a classic immigrant story.

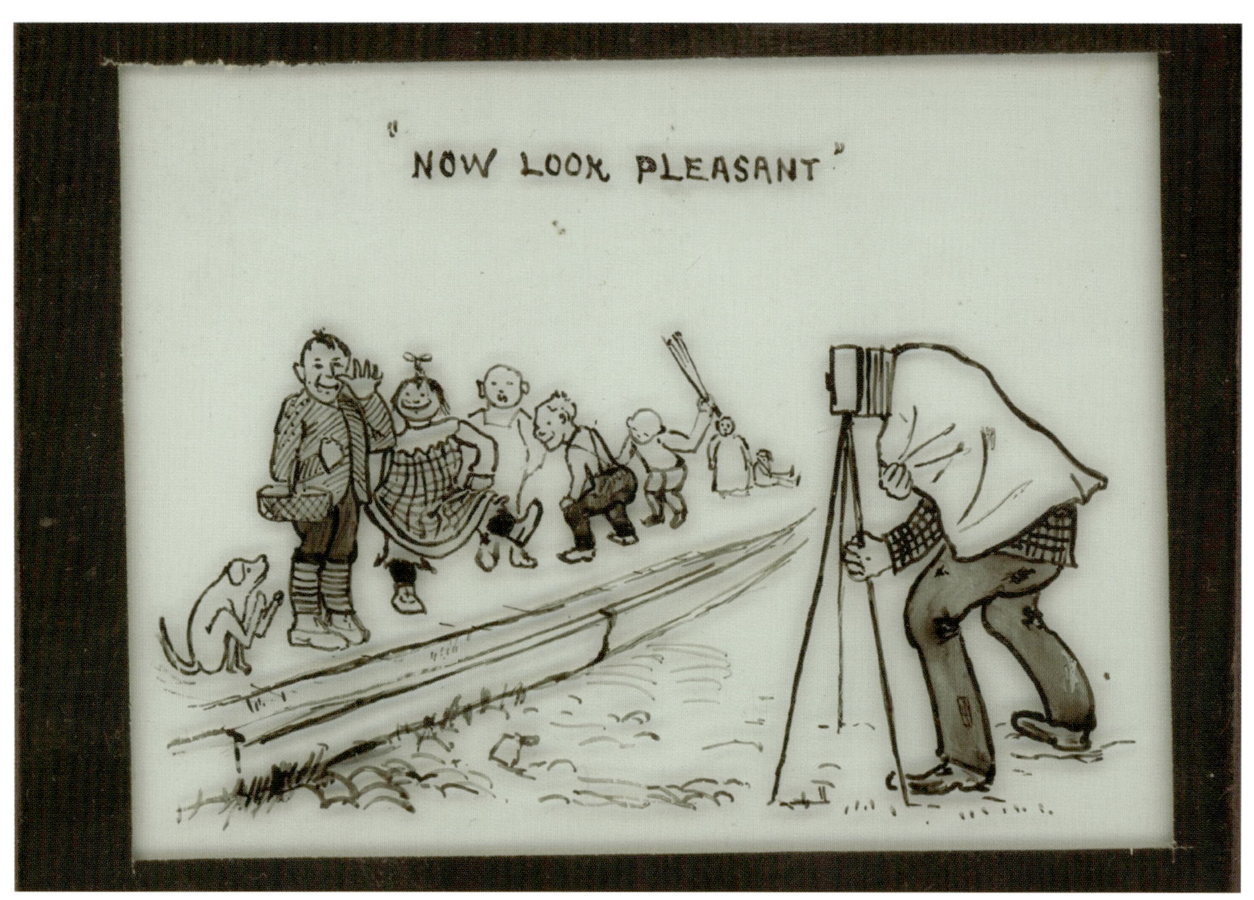

CM: The camera soon took on a new role. Filipinos love the camera and I loved your mom. Not wanting to be a stick in the mud, I changed.

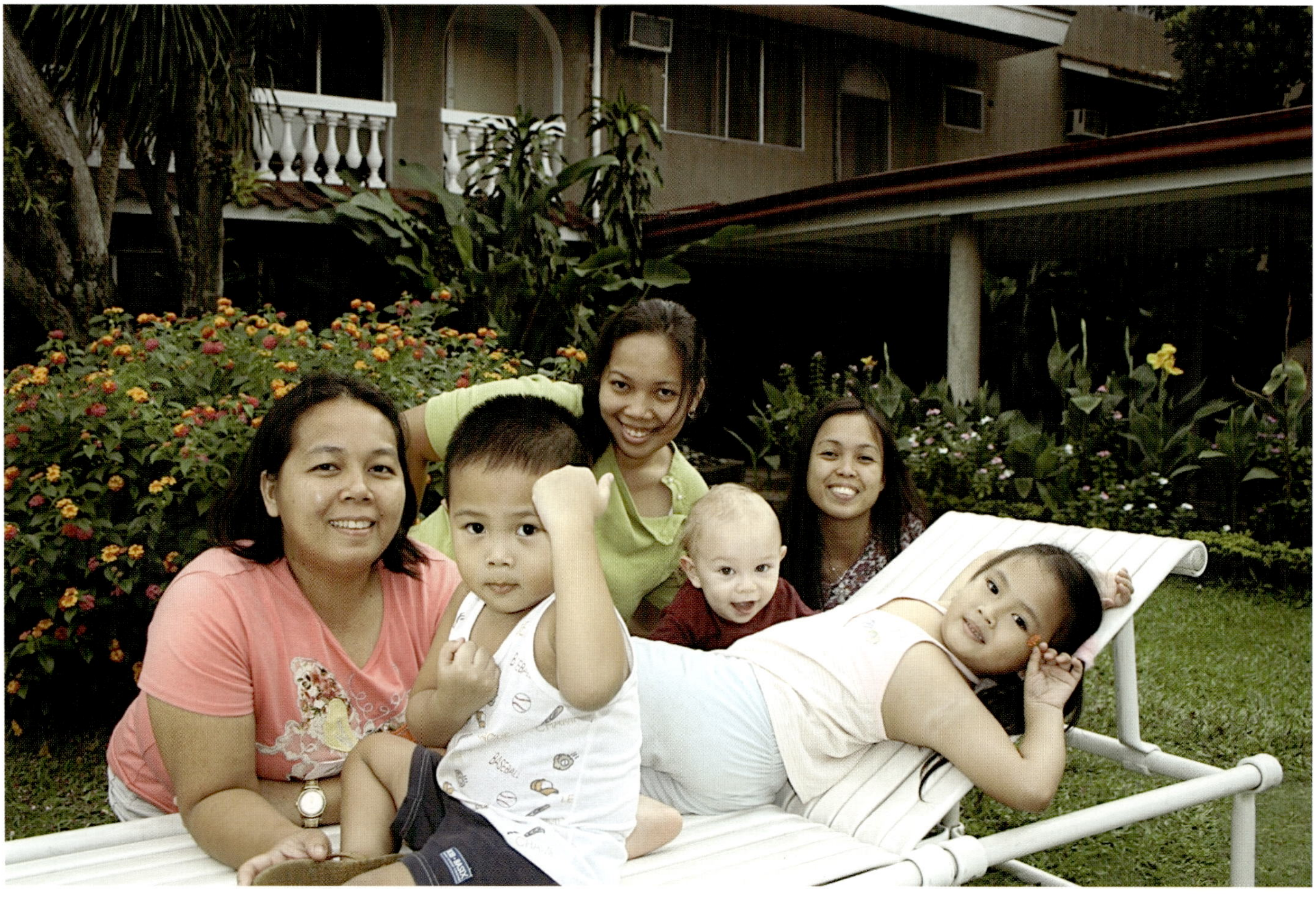

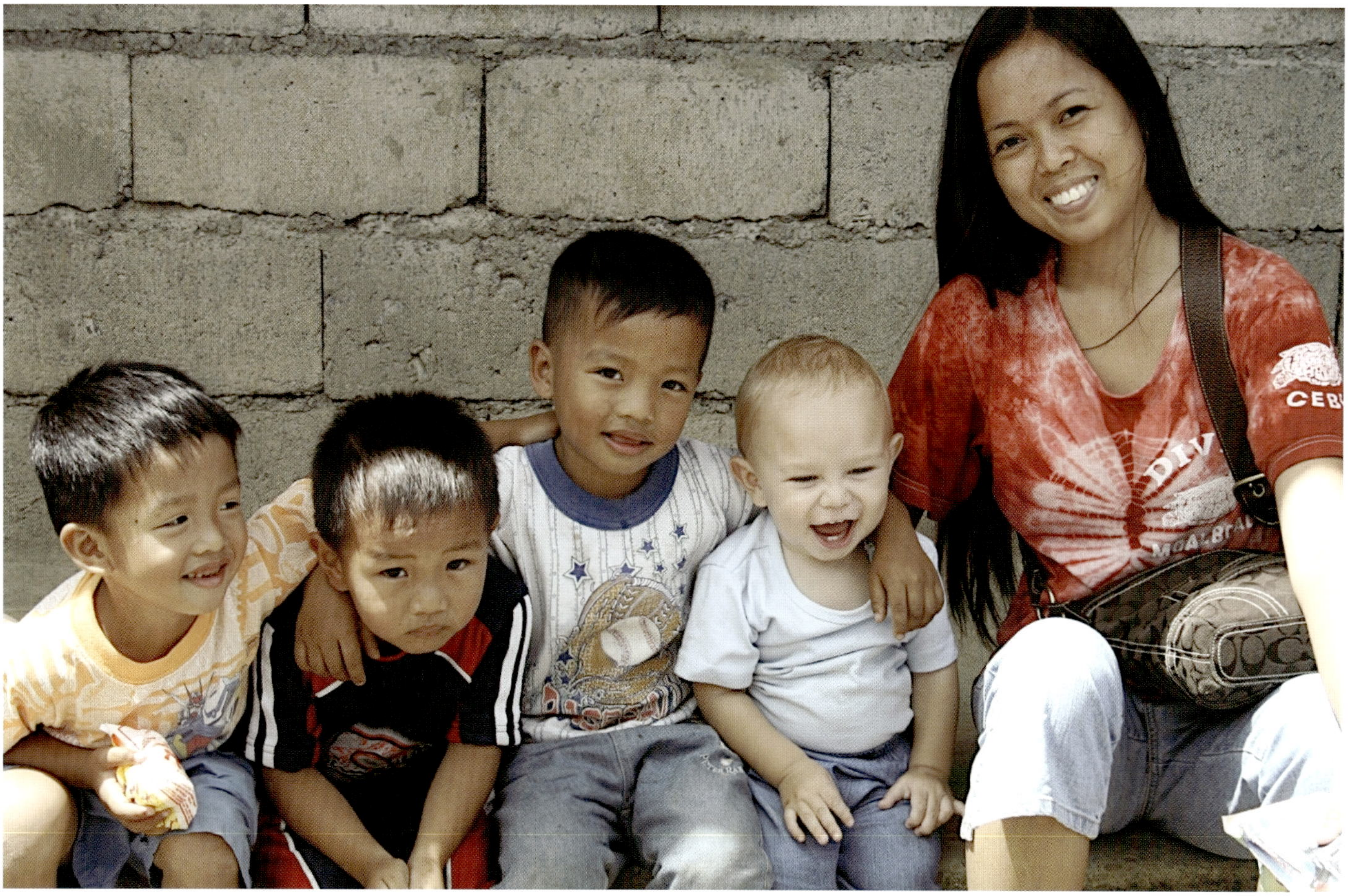

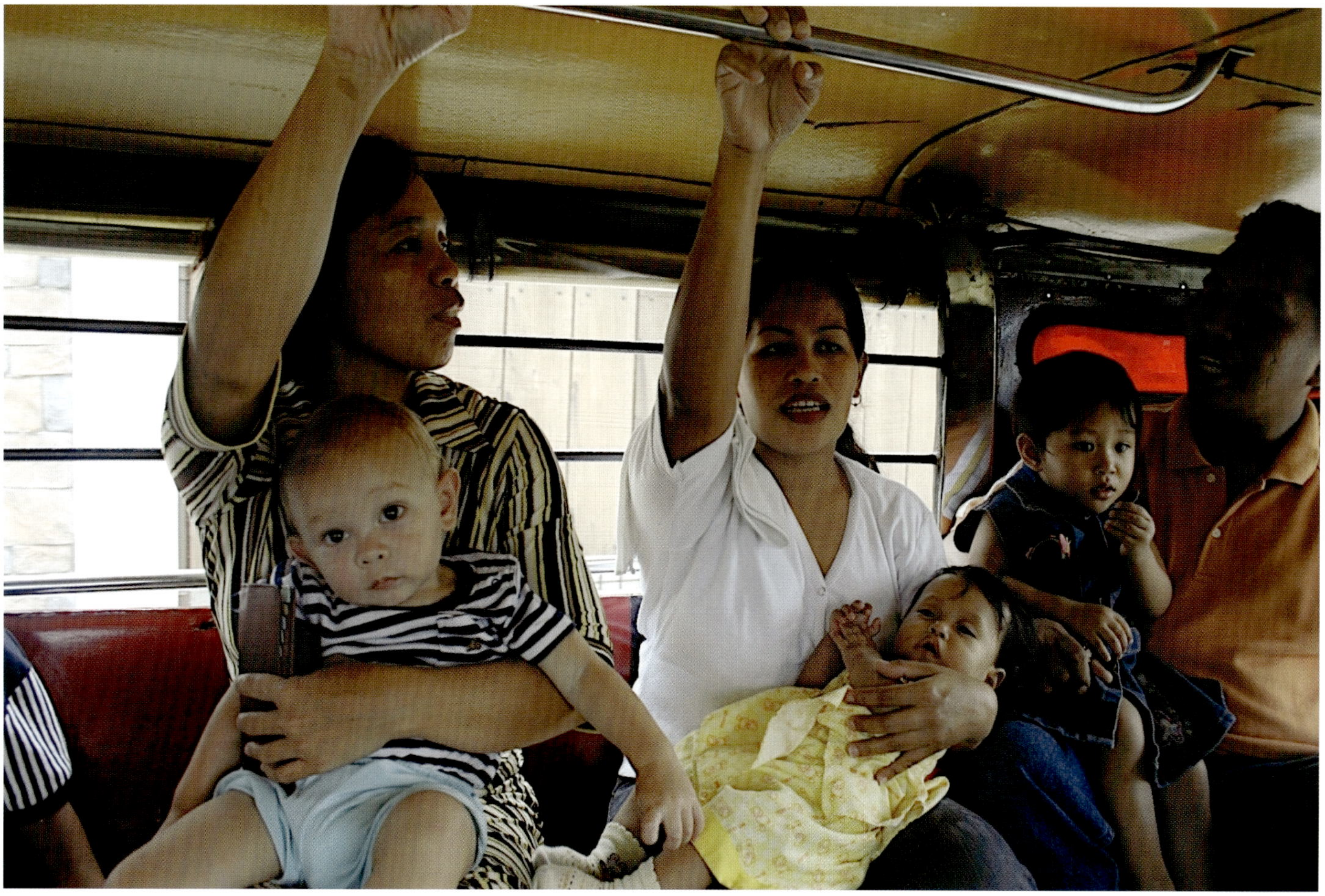

Top: John Carlos and friends with Cheerful Catherine ("Tita Kat") Serana.

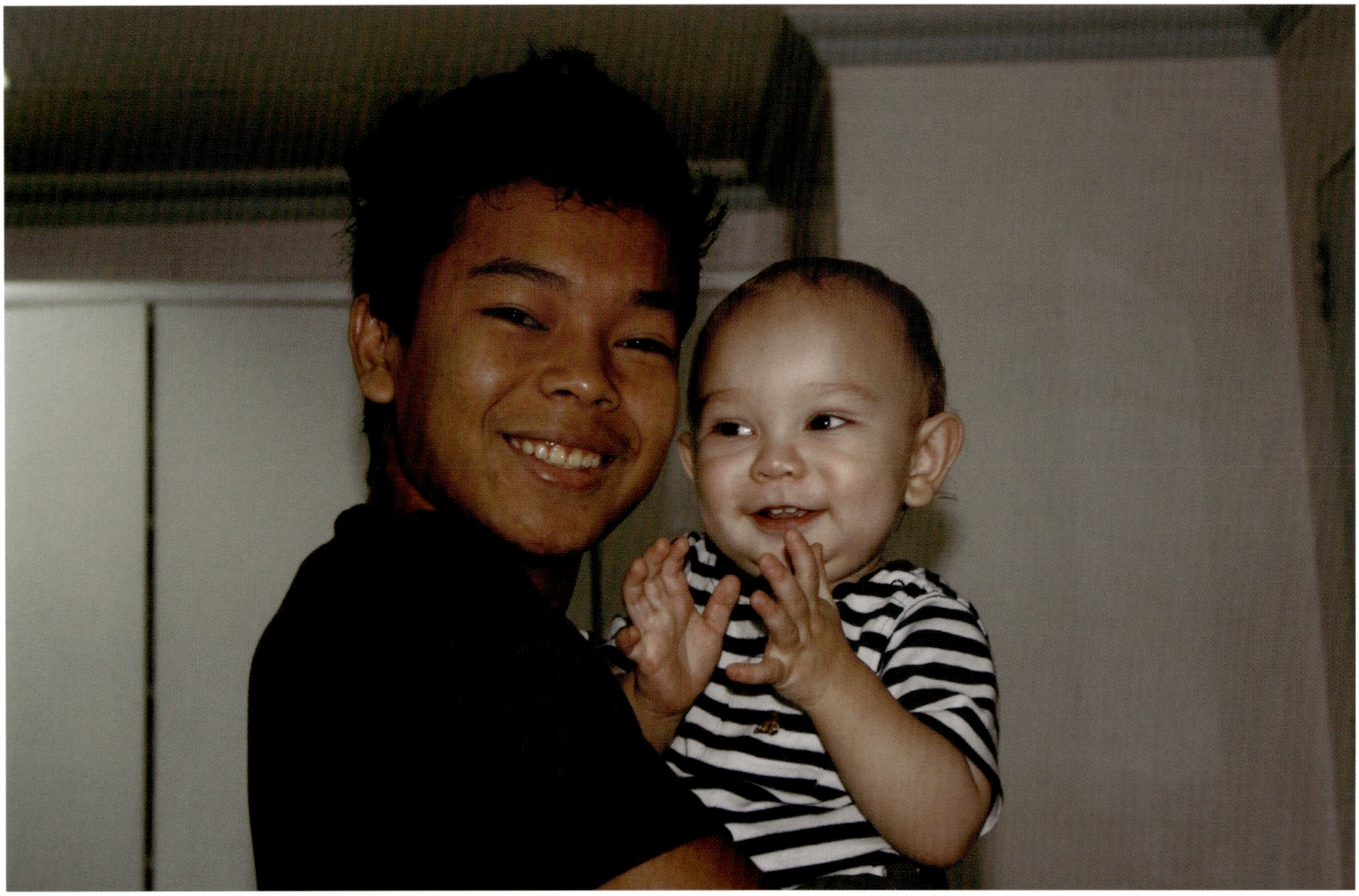

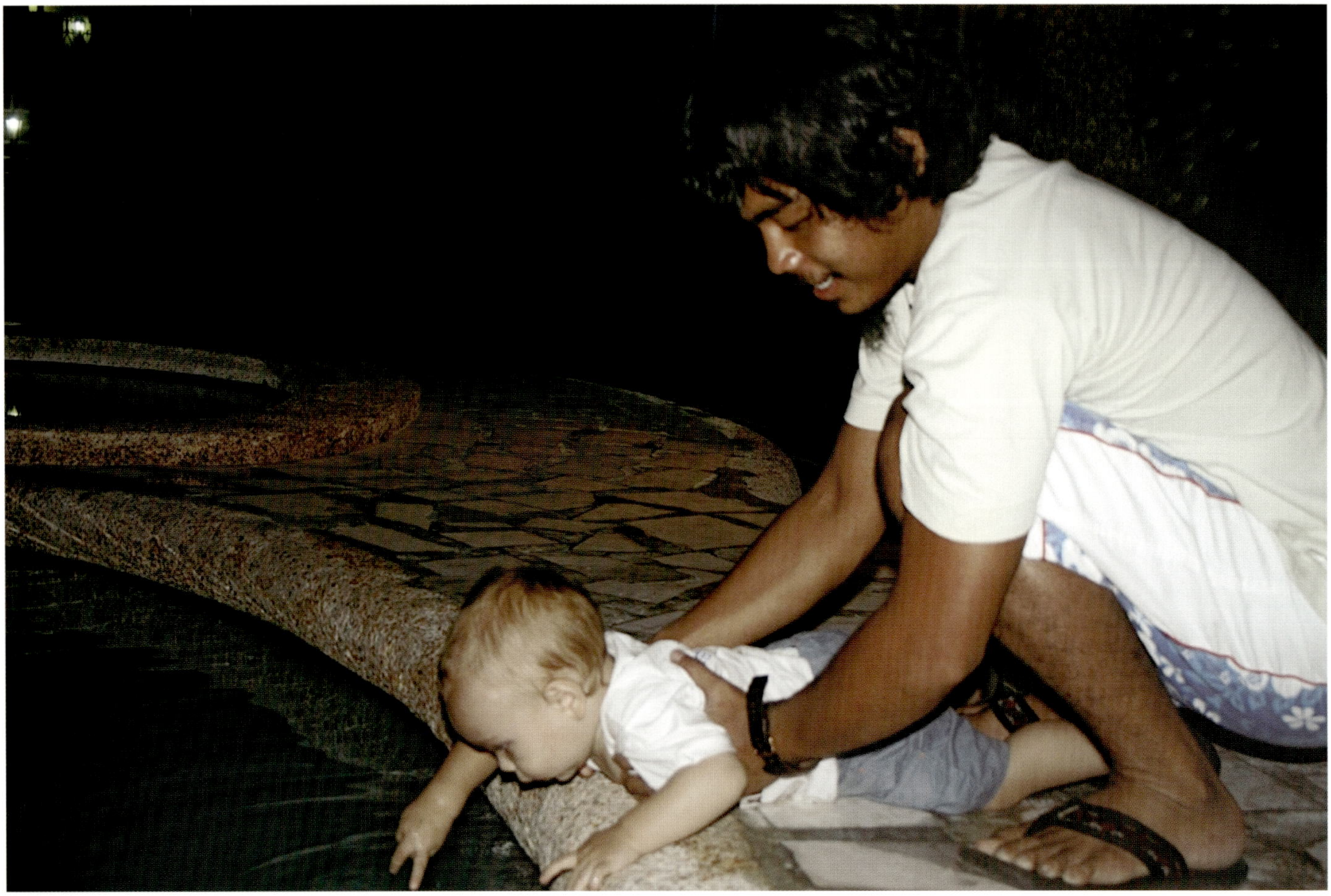

Top: John Carlos with Uncle Matthan. Bottom: With Uncle Bunbun (Chaumet Jethruvine Serana). Right: Hannah.

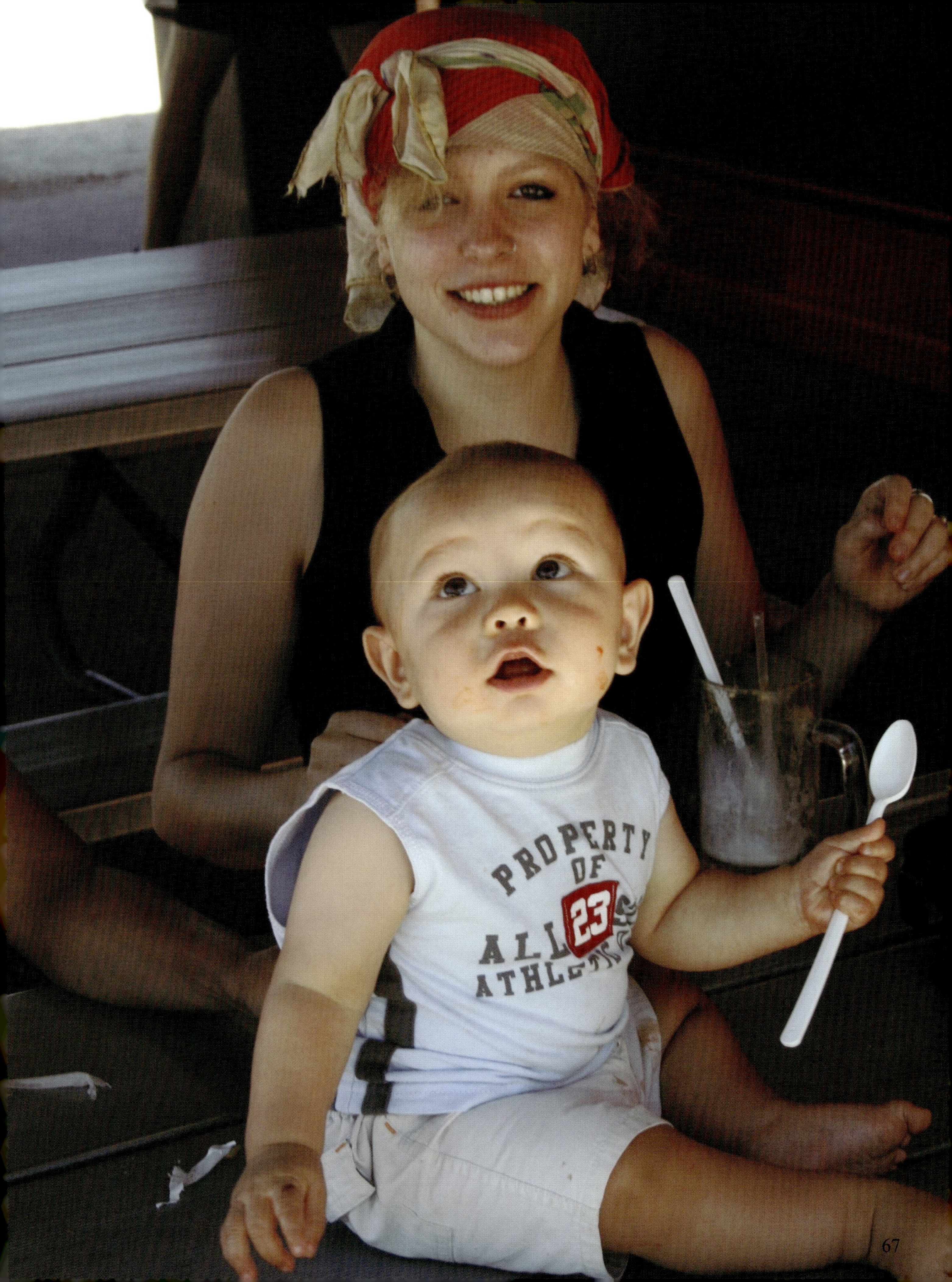
PROPERTY
OF
23
ALL
ATHLET

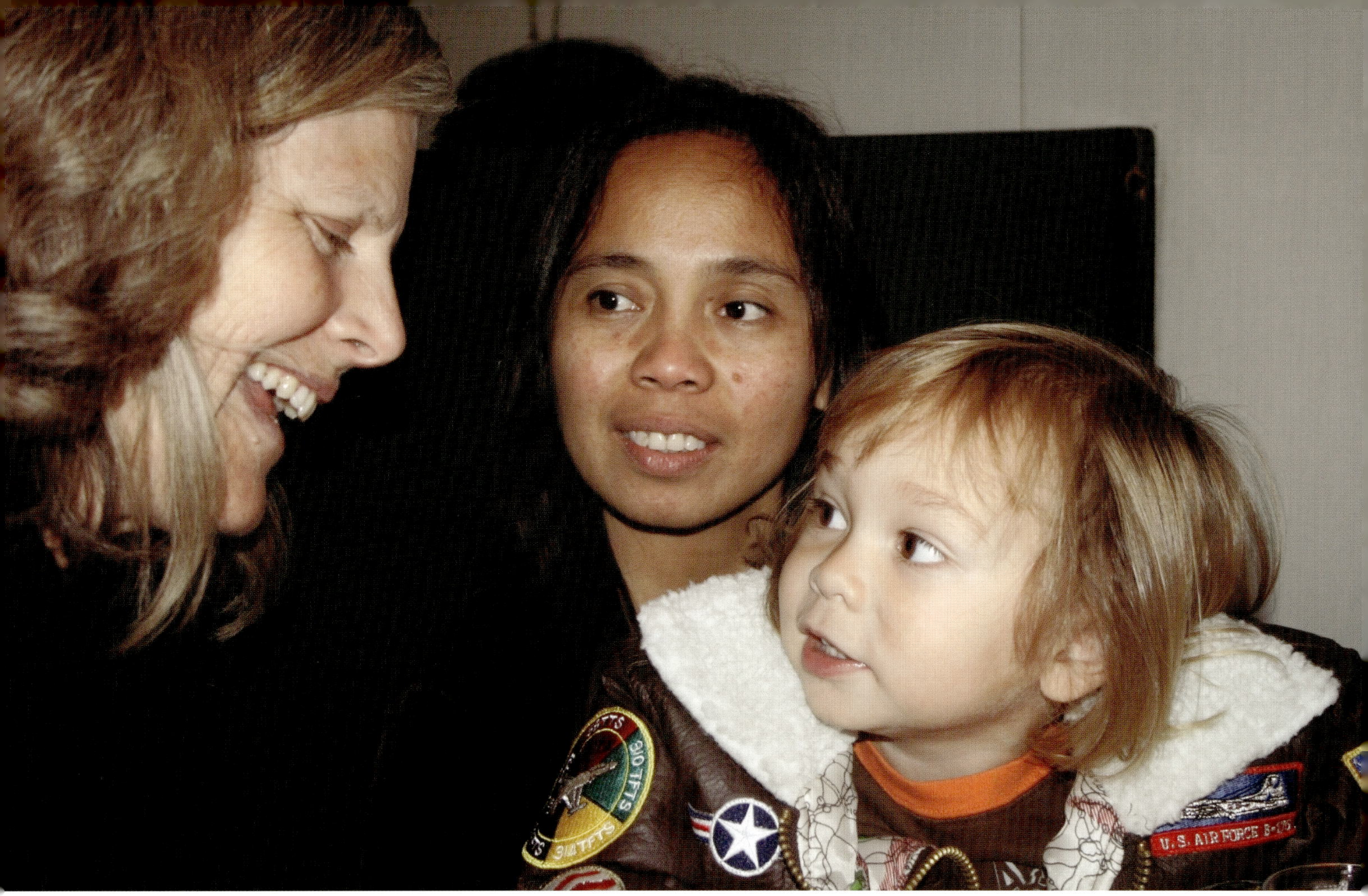

As I edited this sequence of images of John Carlos at roughly one-and-a-half-years old, family resemblance emerged as a unifying theme. He so often looks like a blond version of his mother, but then he also looks like his uncle Matthan, his sister Hannah and his Aunt Jane.

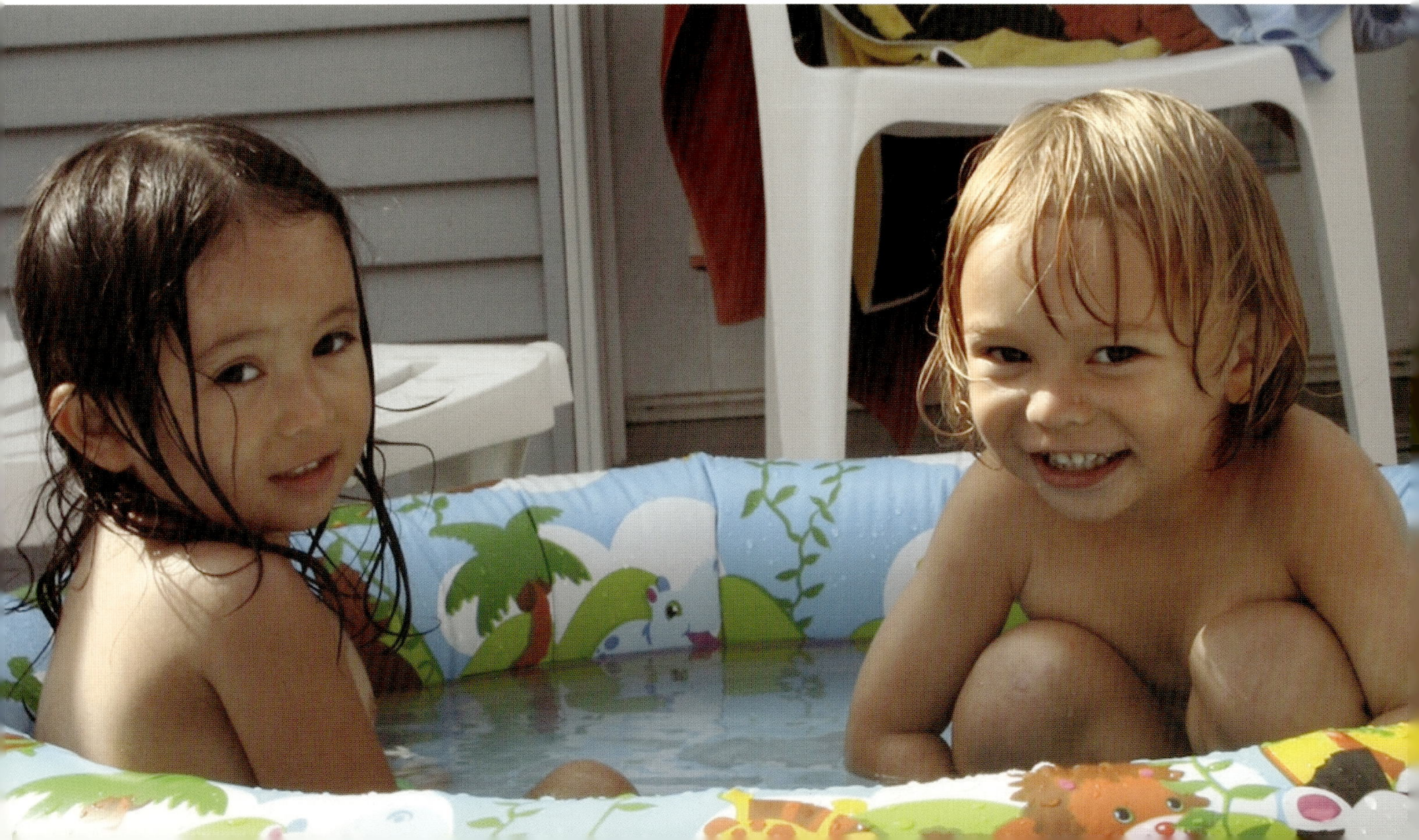

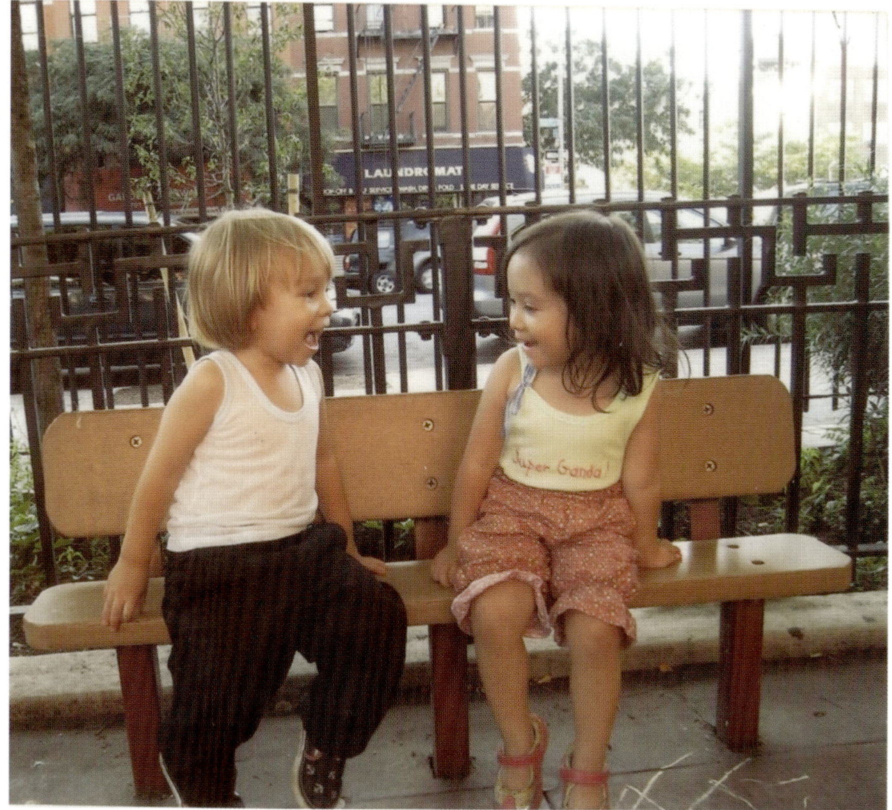

TS: For a long time your sister-cousin Ziphora and you were exactly the same height. At a party several years ago, someone asked if you were twins.

CM: "No," you both replied. Curious, the man wanted more information. Ziphora explained that you were only her brother. You said she was only your sister. Asked how old you were, you each said three—and ran off, leaving the poor man suitably confused.

TS: Clearly, he wasn't Filipino.

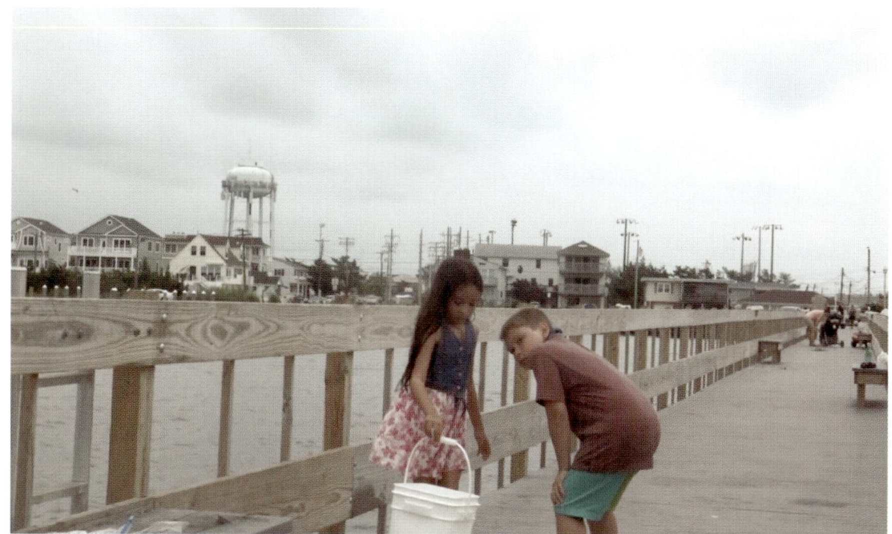

The Mussers have been going to Seaside Park, New Jersey, for roughly a century—ever since my father was four years old. My grandfather, John Musser, a university professor, spent his summers there sailing in Barnegat Bay. They owned an inexpensive summer house (their one piece of real estate). Although it was not winterized, my grandfather had to live there after he got sick and stopped working. After he died, my grandmother and Aunt Nancy moved across the bay to Toms River. Summers at Seaside Park and the neighboring Seaside Heights have many attractions: family, the amusement park, body surfing, and the local bakery with its donuts. The bayside has a children's beach and a pier that John Carlos and Ziphora use for crabbing.

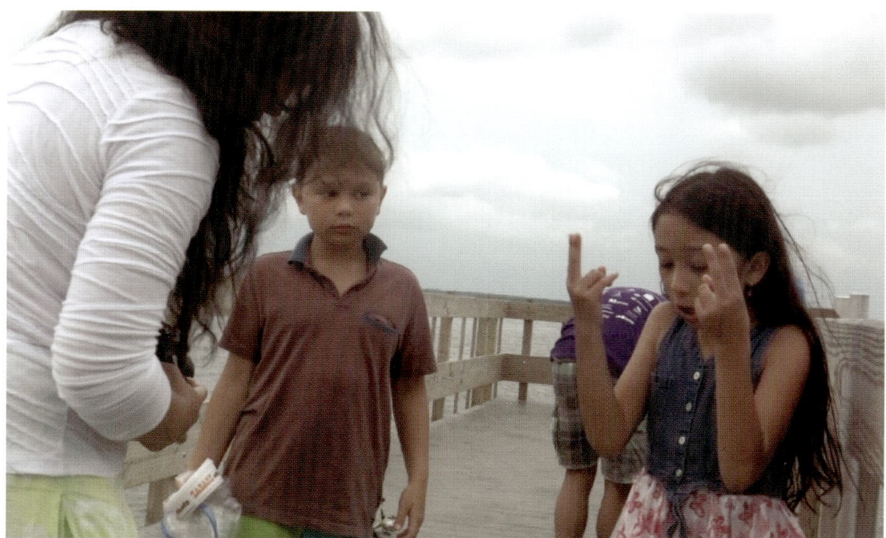

John Carlos Musser: Ziphora, where's the cage.

Ziphora Parks. In the water.

John Carlos: Oh, there.

Ziphora: Don't. Don't let it [the crab] go.

Threese: I won't let it go.

Ziphora: It has its claws out. He's going to bite you.

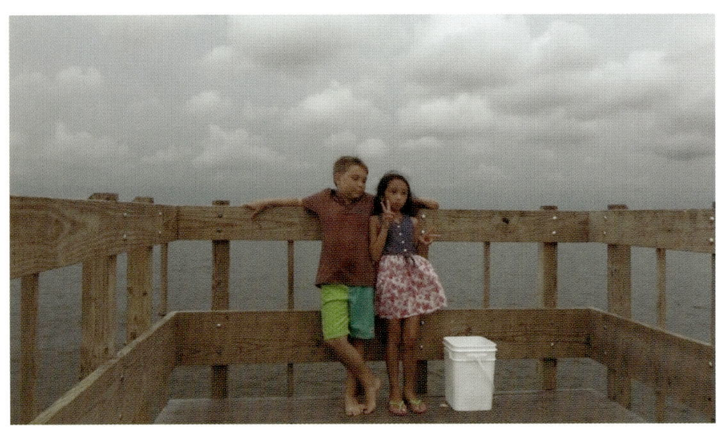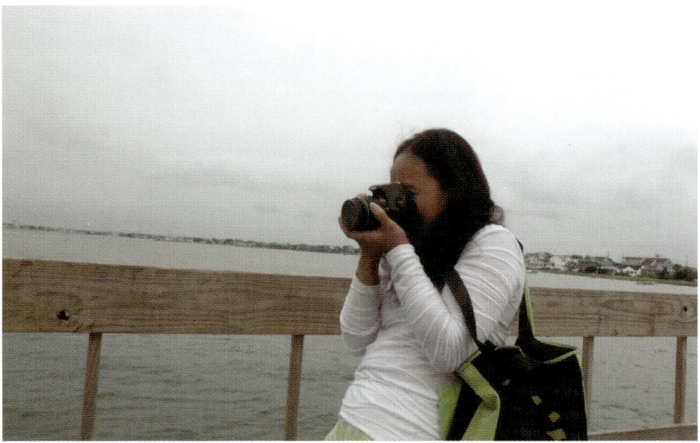

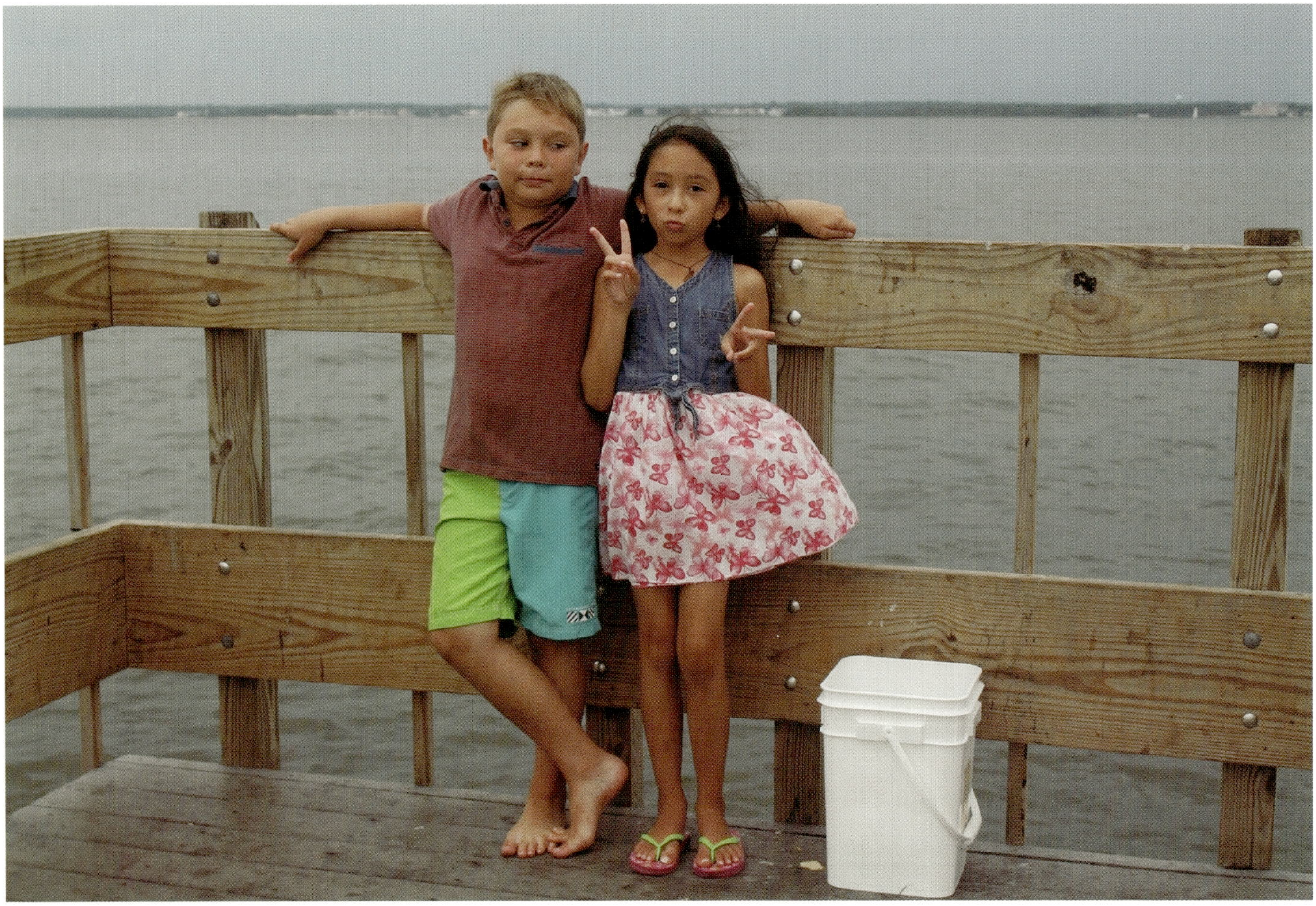

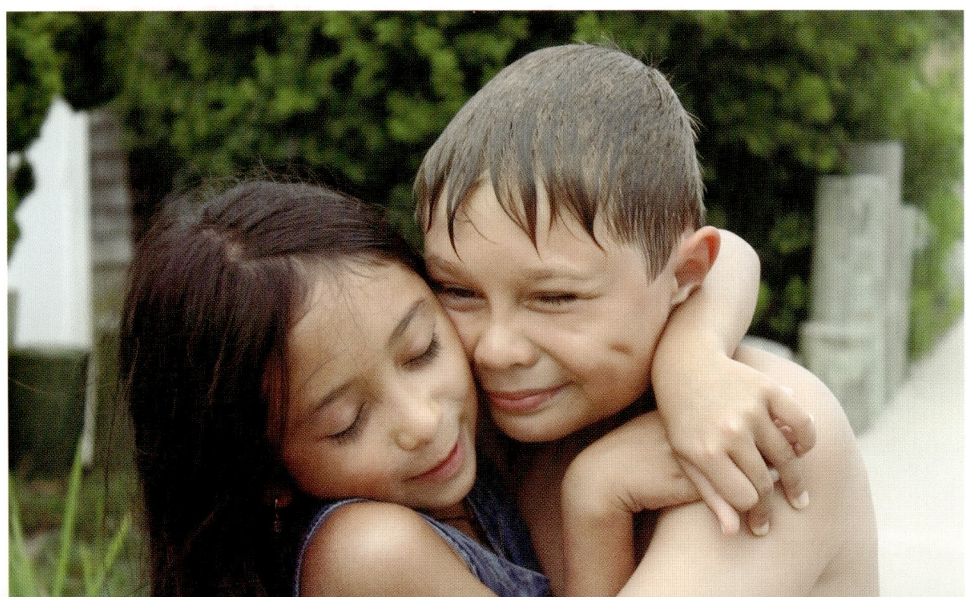

Only much later, as I looked over the video of John Carlos and his sister-cousin crabbing, did I realised that Ziphora's "peace sign" was something else: a hand gesture evoking the crab claws.

When they are posing for Threese, the photographer, are they also posing for me, the filmmaker?

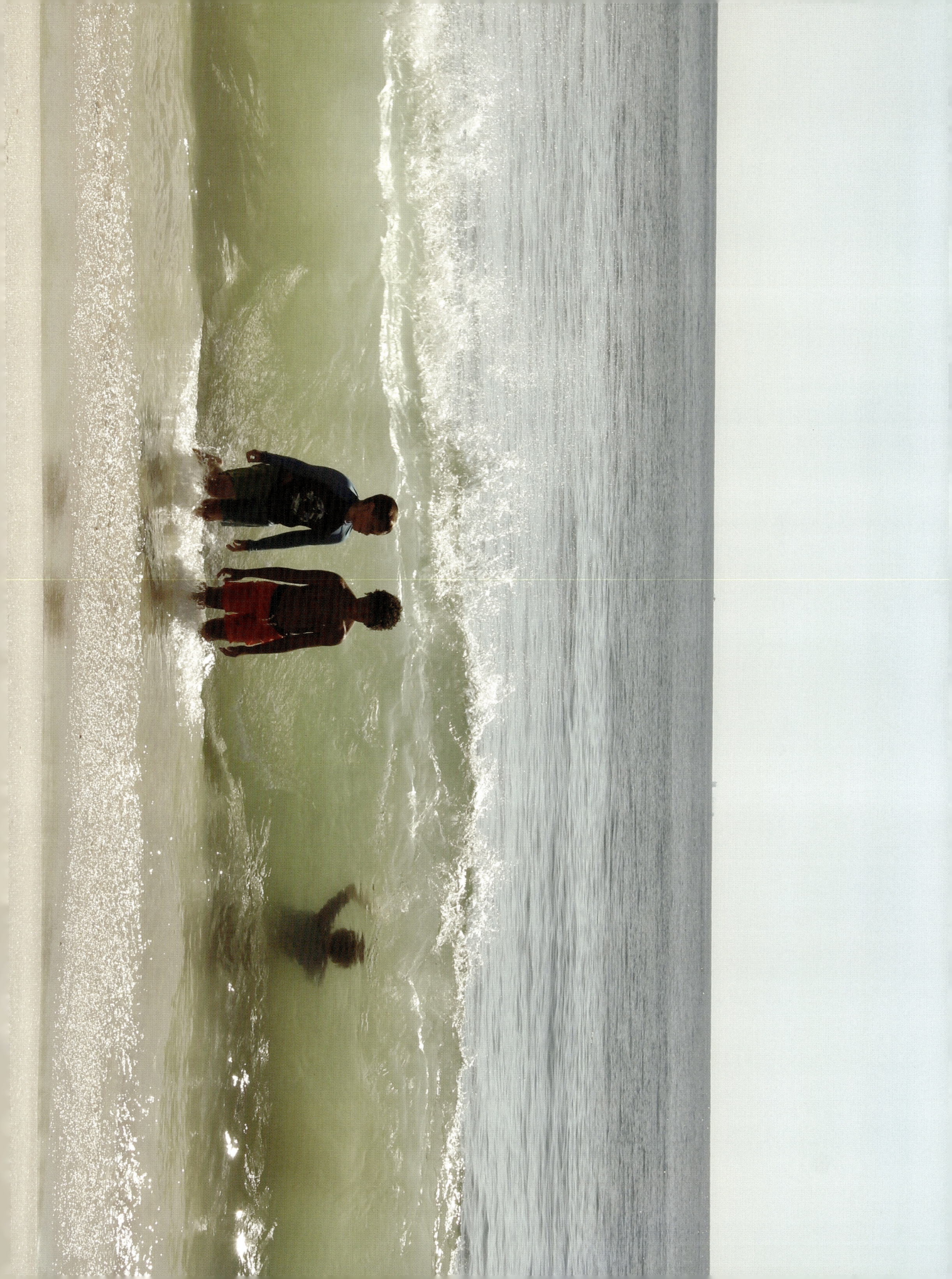

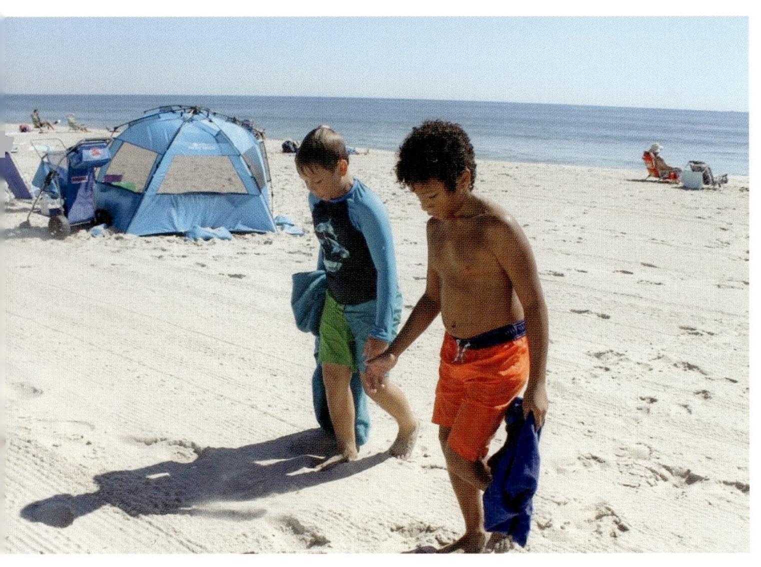 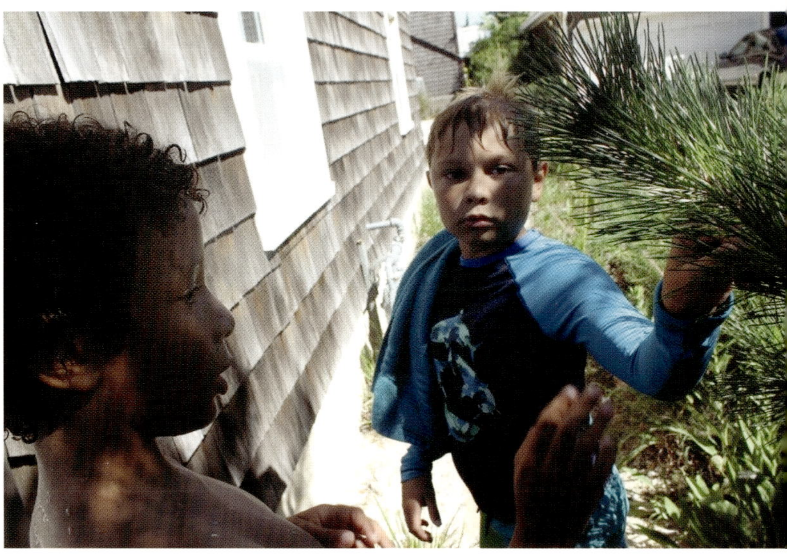

TS: Your steady friend at the Jersey shore has been Noah. His family has joined us there ever since you were born.

*My friendship with Noah's mom, Lorna Ann Johnson-Frizell, evolved slowly. Her two short experimental documentaries, **Strands** (1996) and **My Wolverine** (1997), are brilliant, personal works, which I showed in my courses. Eventually Lorna came to one of my classes as a visiting filmmaker. Coincidence—or was it fate—brought us much closer together. Marriage and children made us close friends as our families formed a tight-knit circle. The first person to whom I showed the following film sequence was not Lorna but her husband Richard Frizell. It made him cry.*

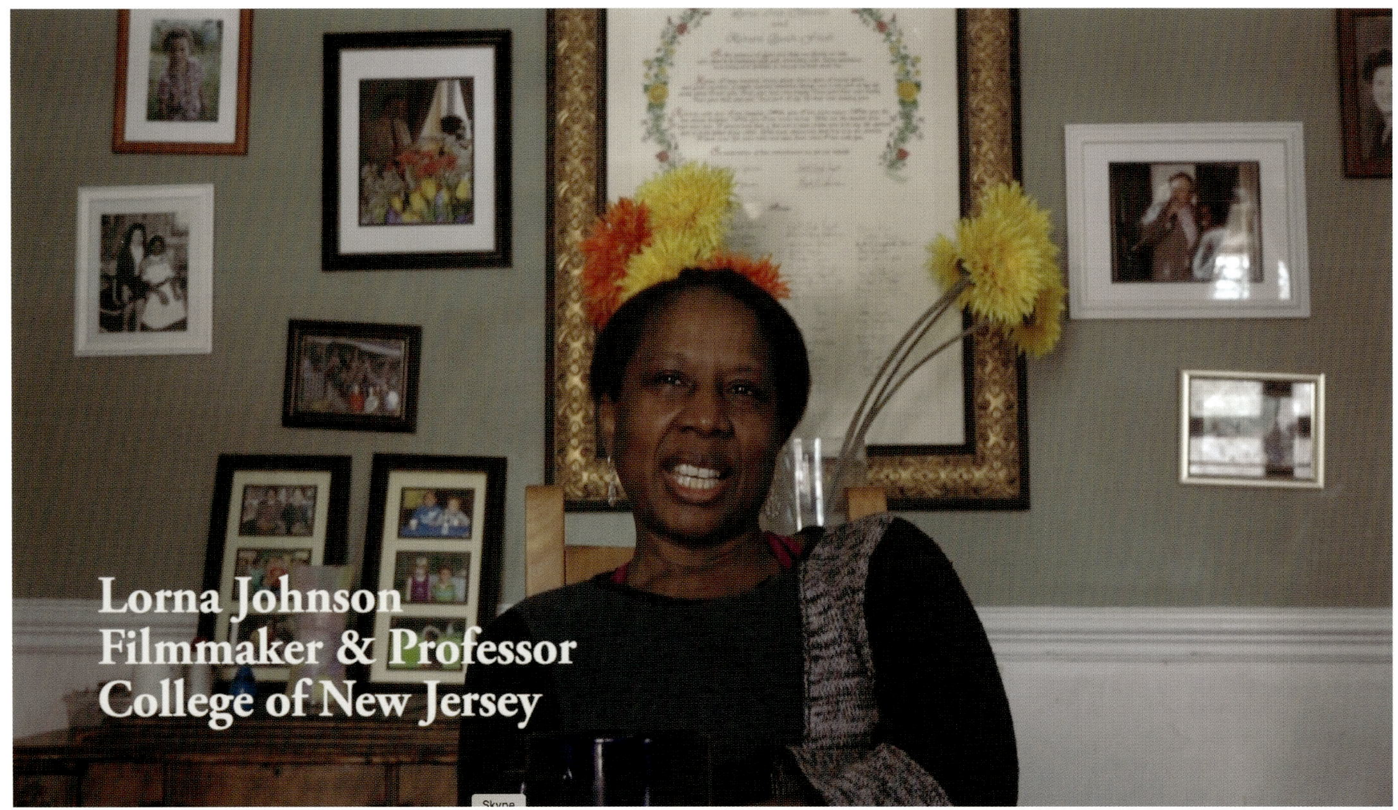

Charlie (off camera): It's hard to know if John and Noah's friendship will continue beyond a certain number of years. They could end up going in quite different directions, and the reason they get together once or twice a year is because of us. It's special for us.

Lorna Johnson-Frizell: I think so. I appreciated that you reached out. We did it the first time. I didn't necessarily know that we would continue doing it. It wasn't necessarily my first impulse. It wasn't. And then I started appreciating it more. Now it's like, "Wow!" I really, really appreciate it. I appreciate building relationships, and relationships that last through iteration of yourself. Those are challenging and beautiful. Right?

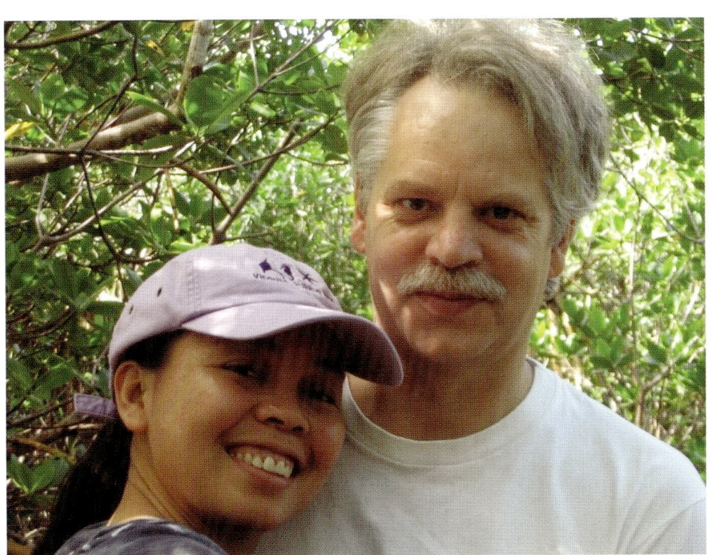 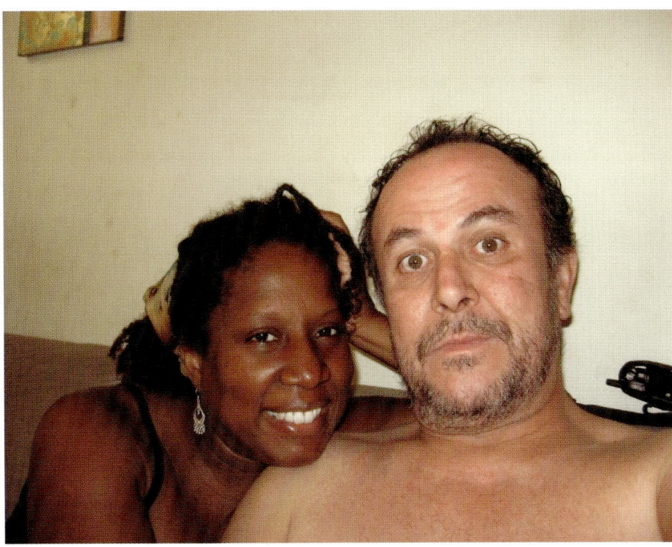

CM: Noah's mother Lorna and I had become friendly because of our shared interests in both documentary and African American cinema. Then I married your mom, a girl from the Philippine islands and Lorna, who came from another set of islands, married an Irish Catholic cabinetmaker from Philadelphia. And we had sons—you and Noah—only a few months apart.

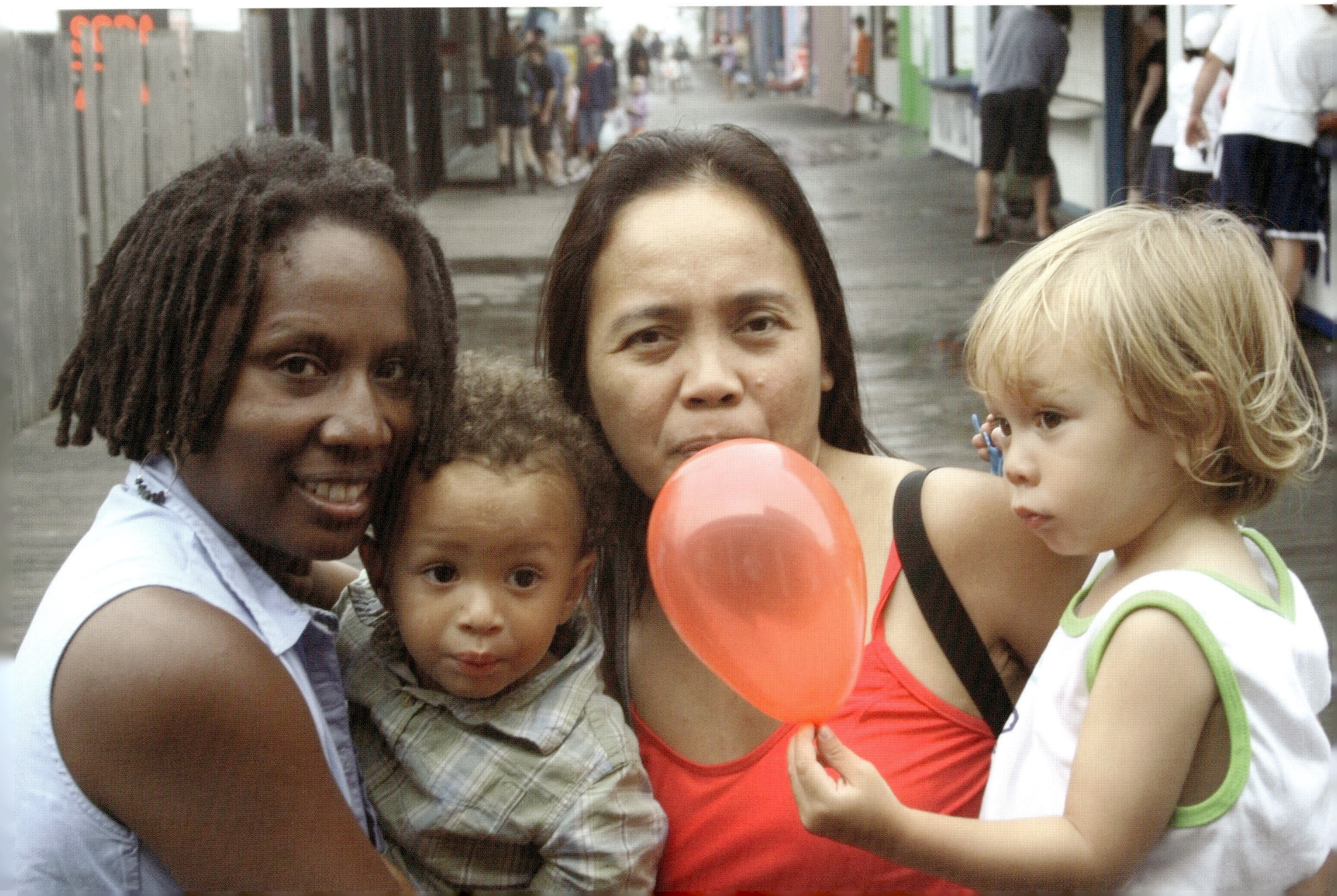

Lorna: I think photographs for me are probably very important because I don't have a very strong memory of people in my past, having lived in Kansas City, Missouri, and prior to that, Jamaica, and prior to that, England. The photographs jogged my memory of these places and these people. I don't have multiple relationships with people from those different eras. But I don't have that many photographs.

CM: So, which ones would she take if she could only take a handful?

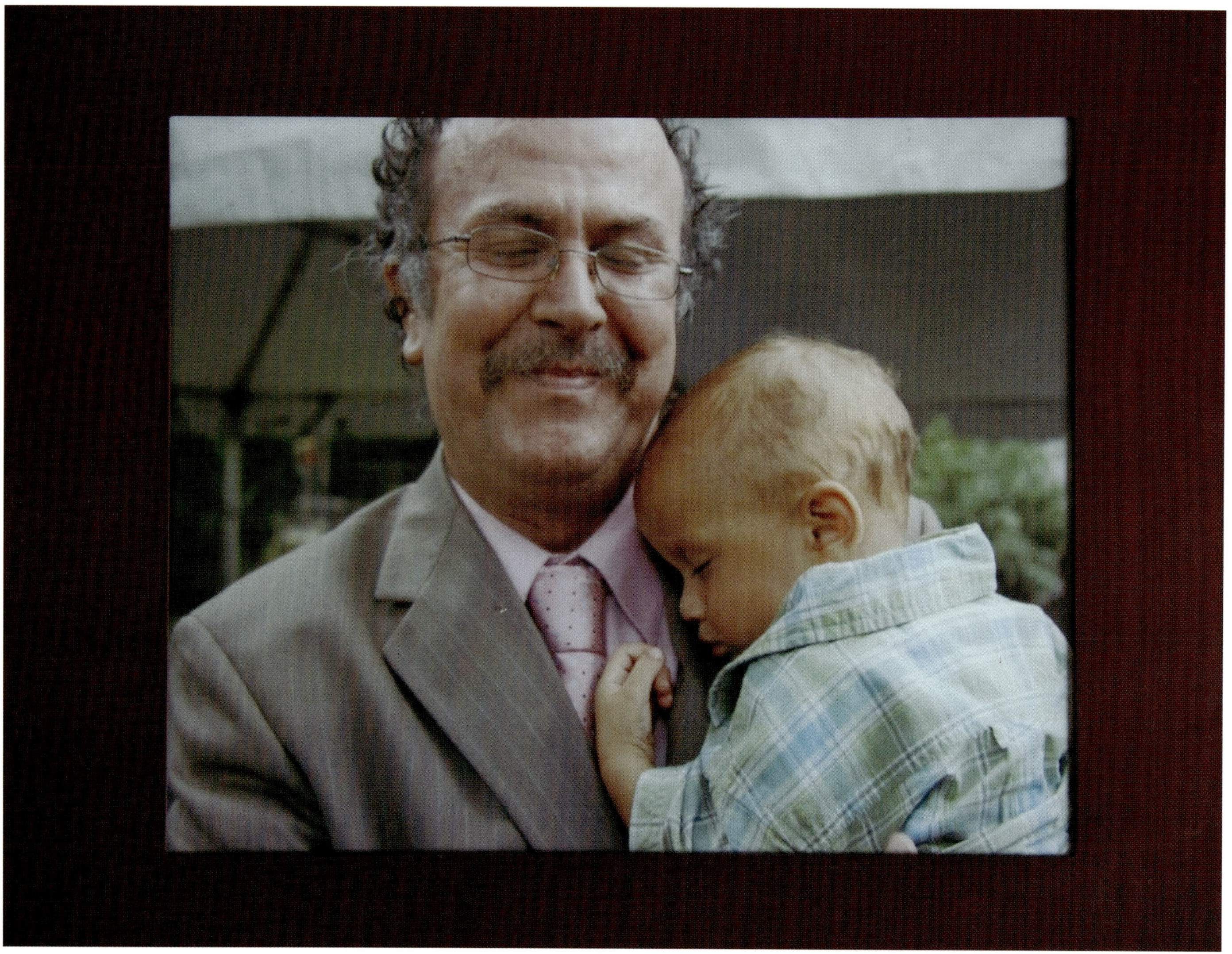

Lorna: Oh, that's a good one. All of Noah. There's no question. I think we have some very good photographs of Rich holding Noah. They're so full of love. They're so full. There's one photograph of Rich holding Noah at our wedding. It's just the expression on Rich's face. And then Noah's just collapsed. It's so ecstatic. That one is just perfect. It captures the melding of these two human beings, the big human being and the little human being, and it's just lovely.

For some reason, I don't do a lot of documentation. Rich does a lot more than I do.

Charlie: Huh. So, you do the video and he does the still?

Lorna: It's funny. I do the videos professionally. I don't do them for my life. I don't record just for fun.

Charlie: So, what about *About Love* then?

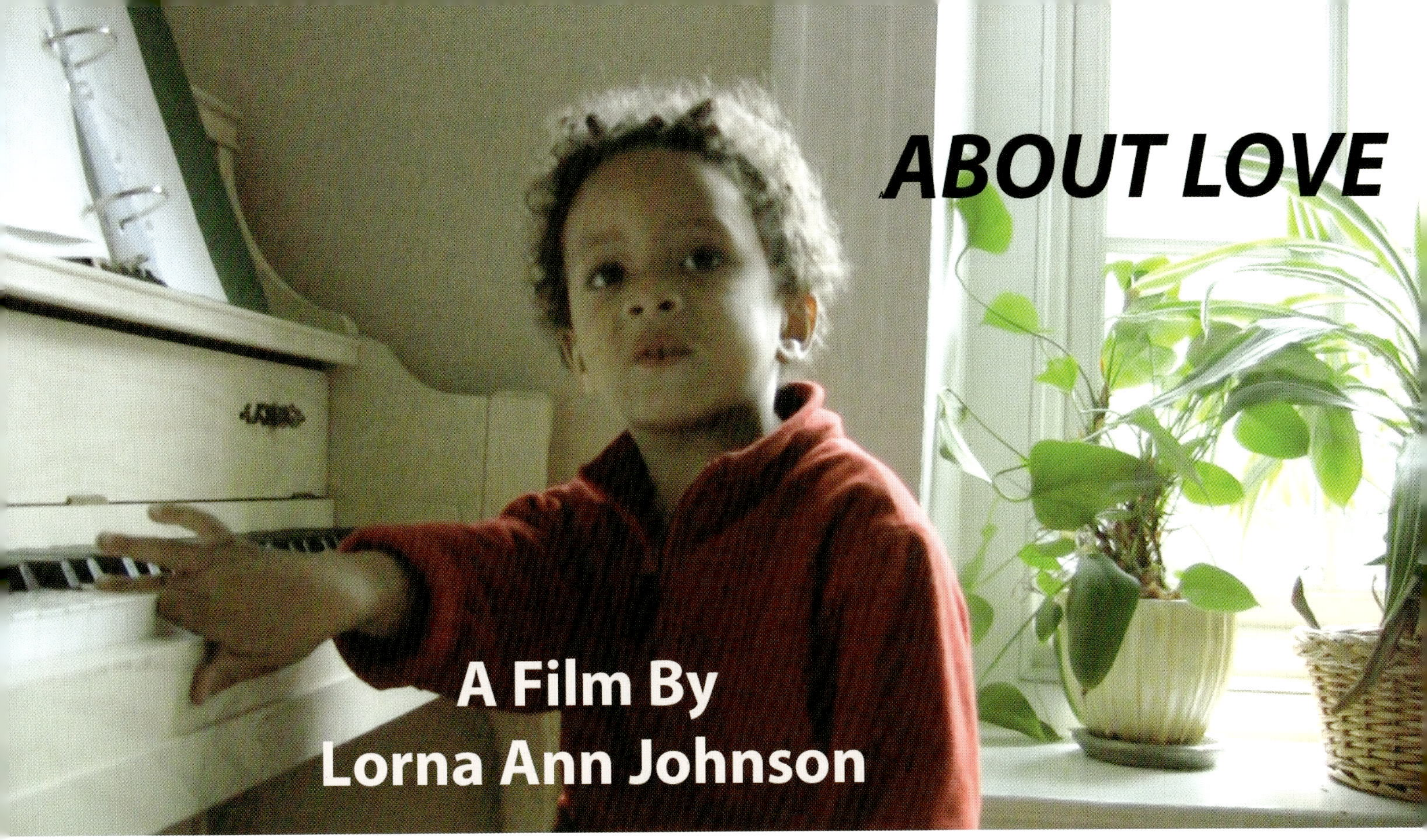

ABOUT LOVE

**A Film By
Lorna Ann Johnson**

CM: Lorna made her documentary *About Love* in 2013. After being turned down by several festivals, she began to rework it. This remarkable film currently survives only as fragments.

Lorna: Oh, God. That's a good one. I think I knew that I was doing that. Most of that was me recording because I knew that I was doing a film. I knew that I wanted to do a film. I didn't necessarily complete the film.

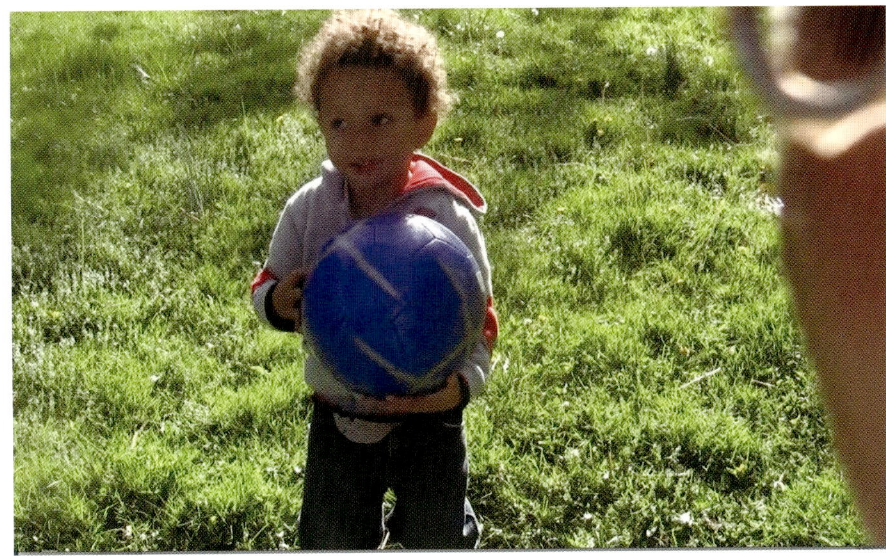

Scene #1 from *About Love*:

Lorna (voice over): Dear Noah, I started to think about love when you were born. Loving you was so easy and I wanted to hold on to it. So I decided to go on a journey. A journey to discover love.

Rich Frizell: I'm not sure. What is the question?

Lorna: How do you make love stay? Or, why doesn't love last forever?

Charlie: *About Love* and *For John Carlos* come from very similar impulses. [Note Bene: *For John Carlos* was the working title for *Our Family Album*.]

Lorna: Yea. I will finish that film. I don't know what it will be called but I will finish that film. Maybe I'll get back to it in the summer after this film, this new film.

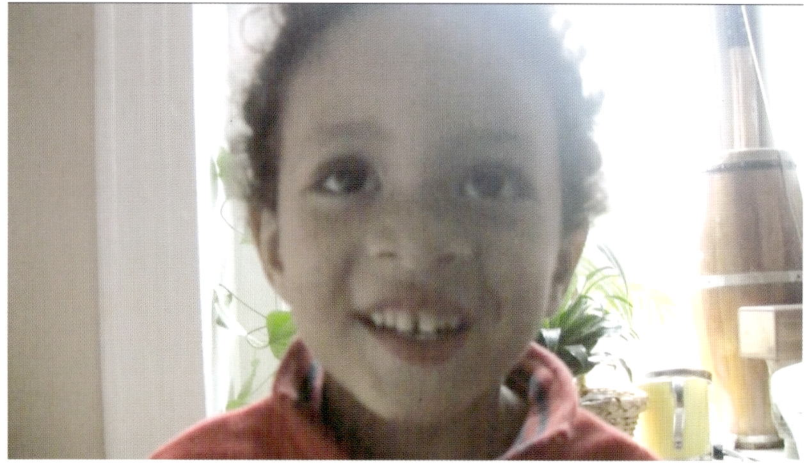

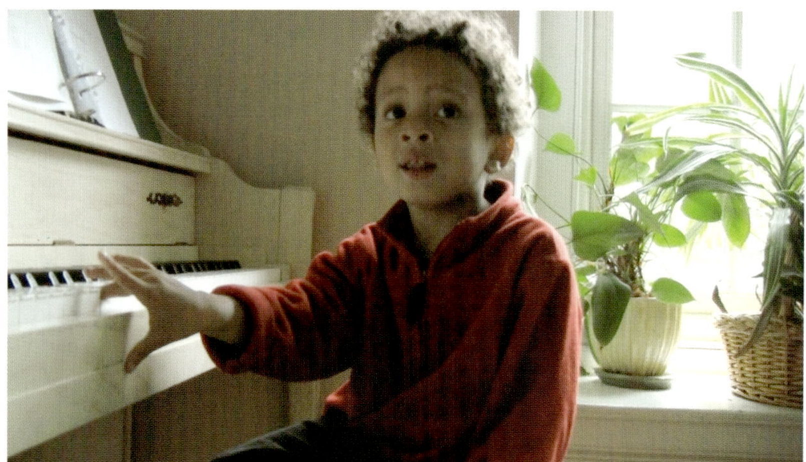

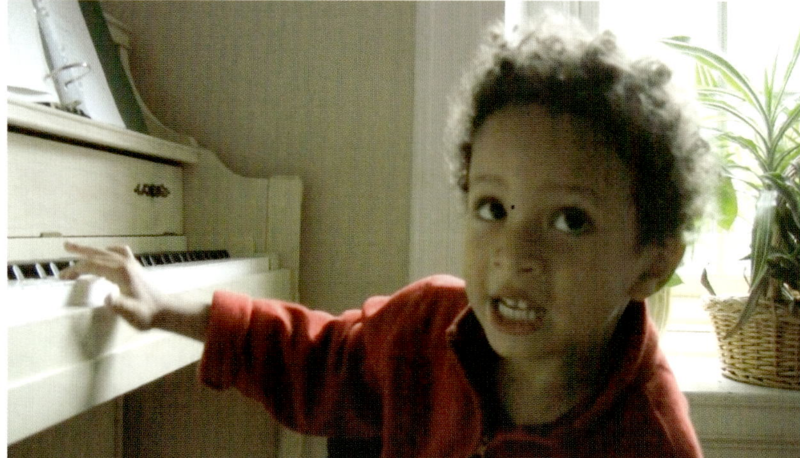

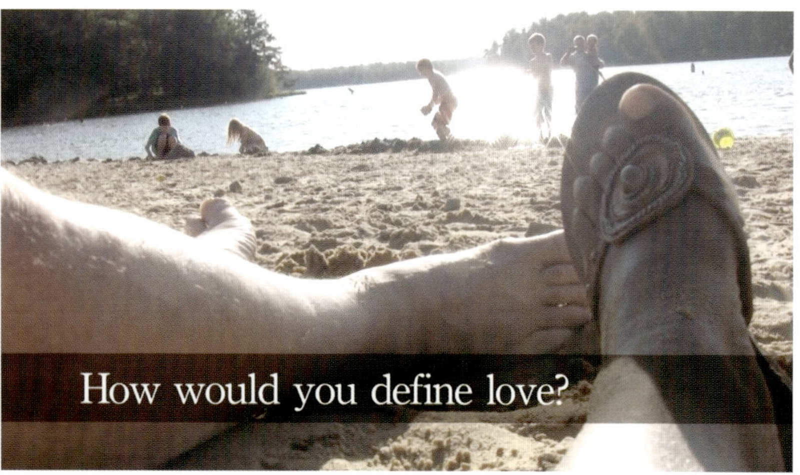

Noah is playing "Ode to Joy" on the piano through much of this scene.

Lorna: So, what is love?

Noah Frizell: Hugs and kisses.

Lorna: Really?

Noah: Yeah.

LJ: That's cool. Do you want more love?

Noah: Yes. Noah has more love. Don't you? You just gave me love.

Lorna: I did?

Noah: Yeah.

Lorna: What did I do?

Noah: You just kissed me. You just brightened me.

Lorna: I just what?

Noah: Brightened me.

Lorna: Brightened you?

Noah: Yeah.

Lorna: Really?

Noah: Yeah.

Lorna: Love brightens?

Noah: Yeah.

Scene #3 from *About Love*:

Lorna: How would you define love? Just say that is a dumb question.

Rich: [Laughs] It's the answer people have been looking for, for many generations. And I don't know that any of the great poets have gotten it right yet. It's selflessness.

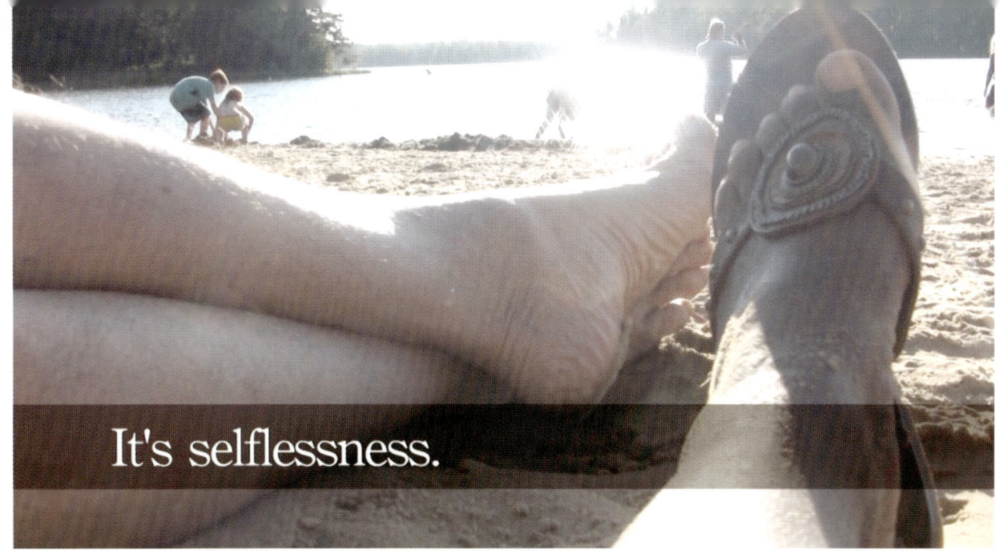

Lorna: What's selflessness?

Rich: Love. It is where the other person matters more. You know. That's why it's difficult.

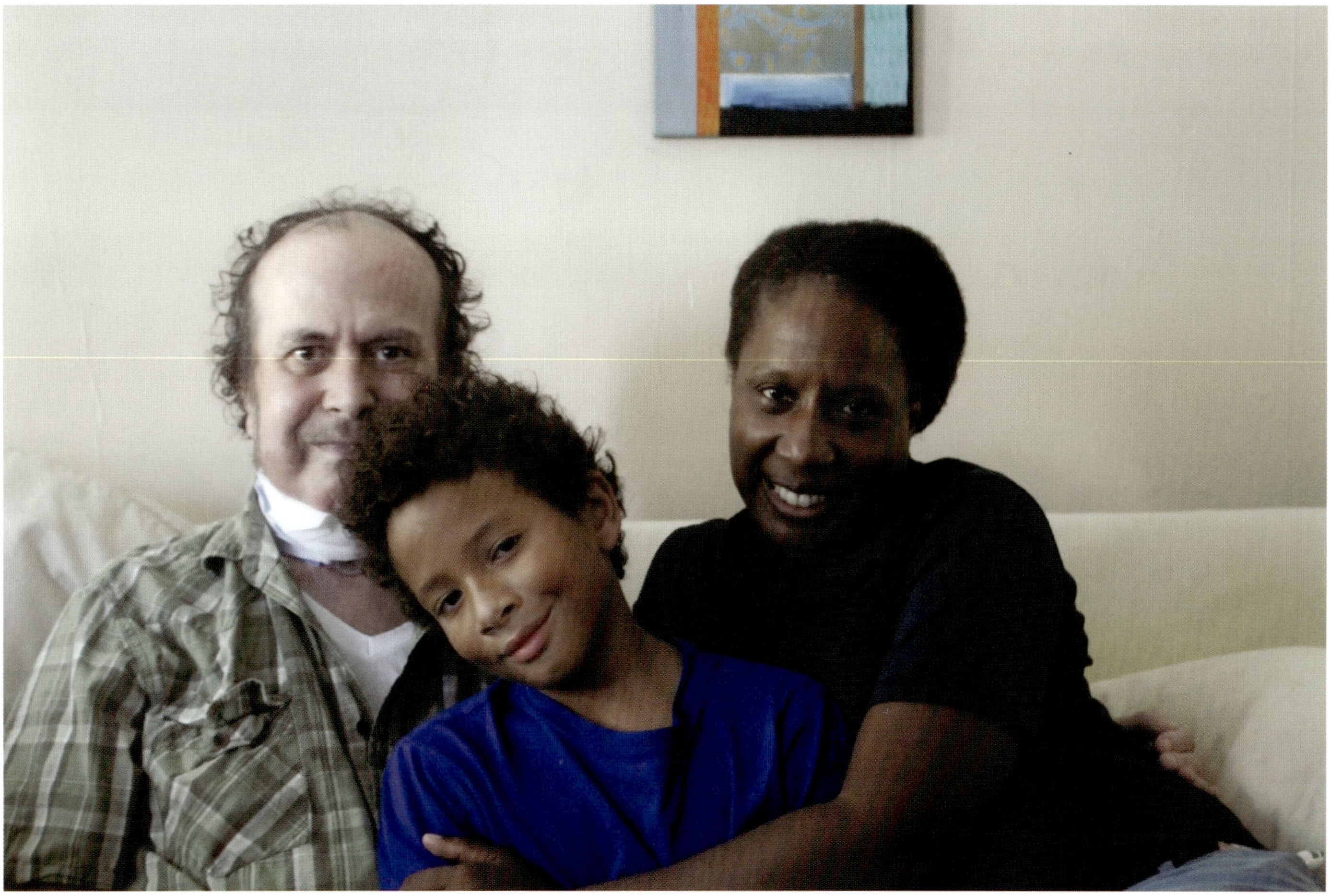

CM: Rich is now struggling with throat cancer, and I have come to realize that my frequent urgings for Lorna to work on *About Love* have been insensitive to the all-consuming demands on love that this ordeal requires. There is nothing left over for representation and reflection. Like my mother who stopped making her photo album when my father had his nervous breakdown.

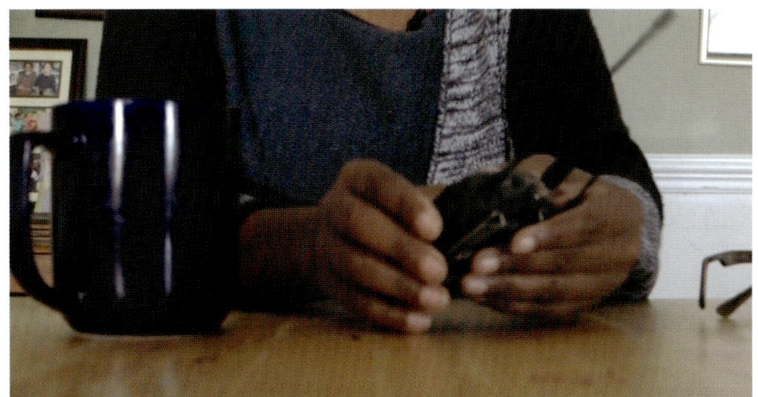

Lorna: Oh, God. Being on camera is like therapy. That's why it's difficult. Because you talk too much when you are on camera.

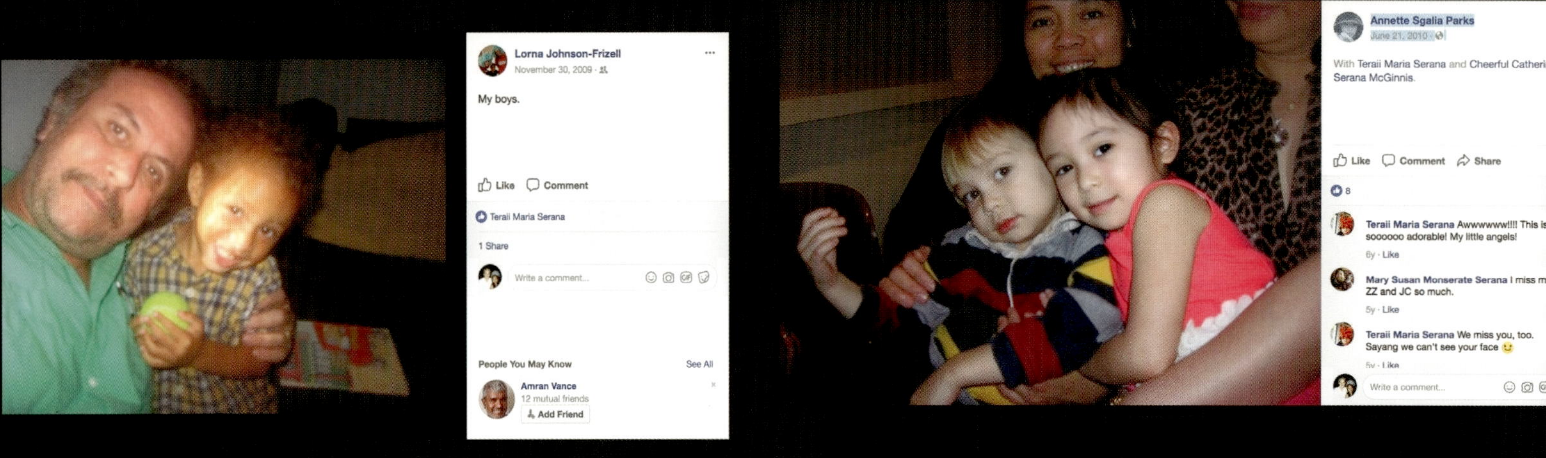

TS: You and Noah grew up in the age of Facebook. Two months after you were born, it became available to everyone.

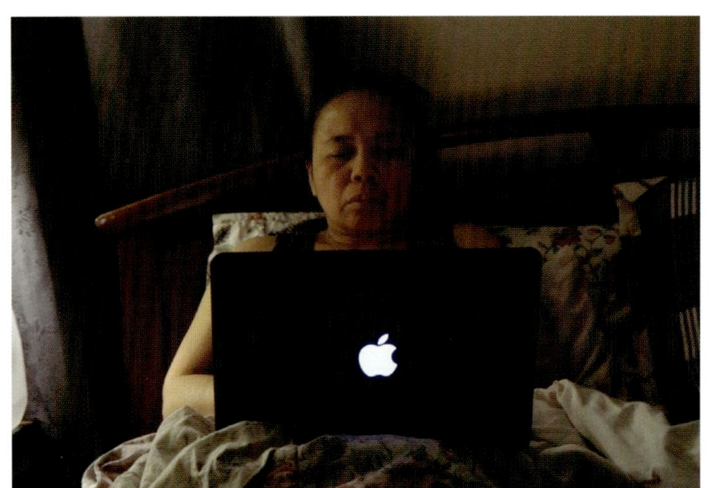

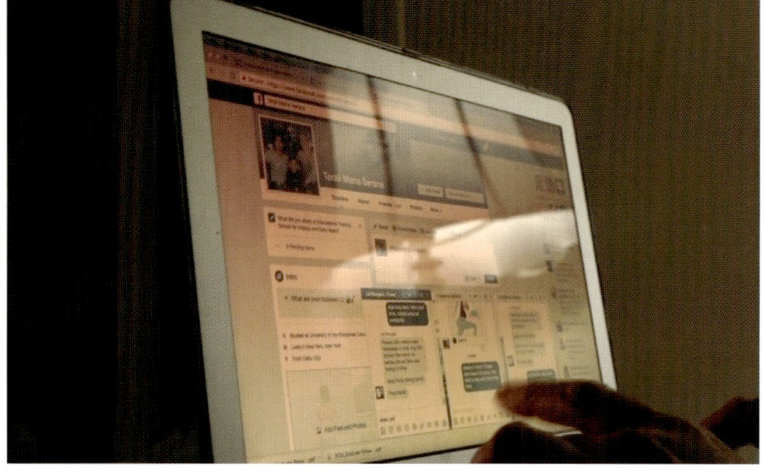

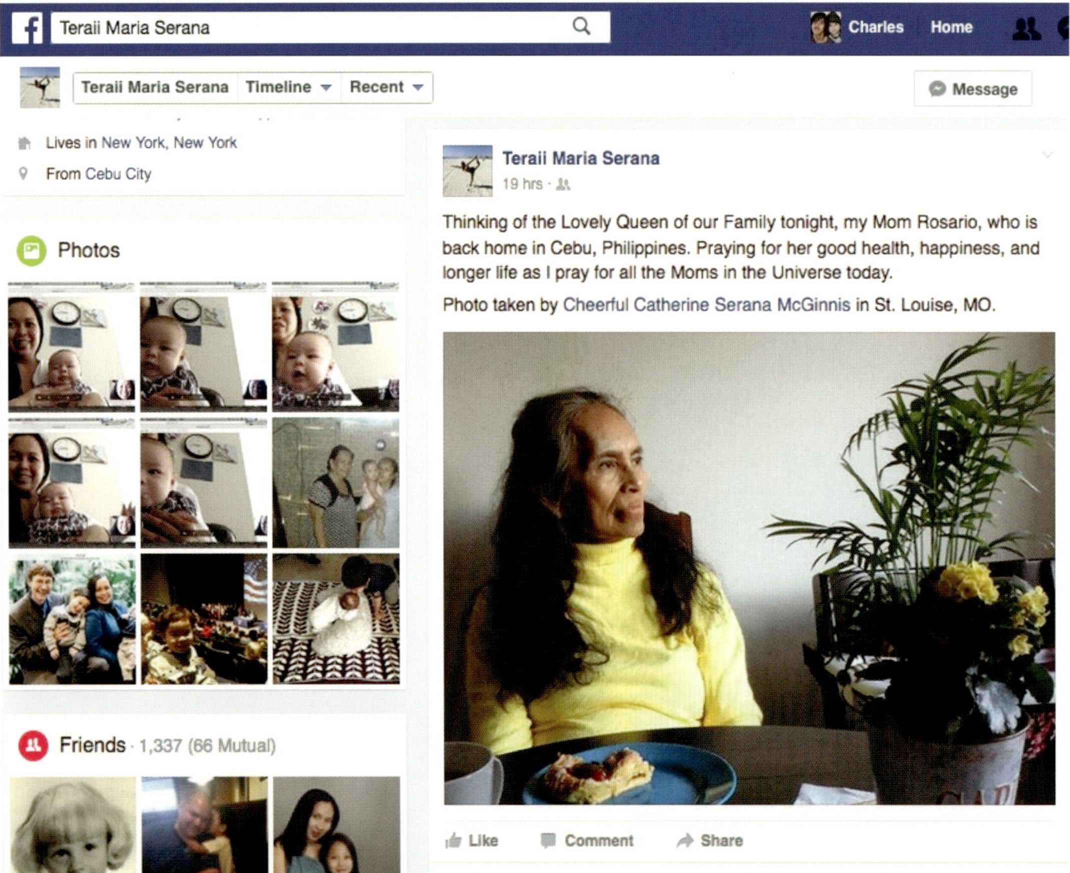

CM: With friends and family scattered about the world, your mom is always posting and messaging. In many respects her family album lives on the web. Photos of births, birthdays and everyday events. Lost photos are discovered and shared. Absent loved ones remain close.

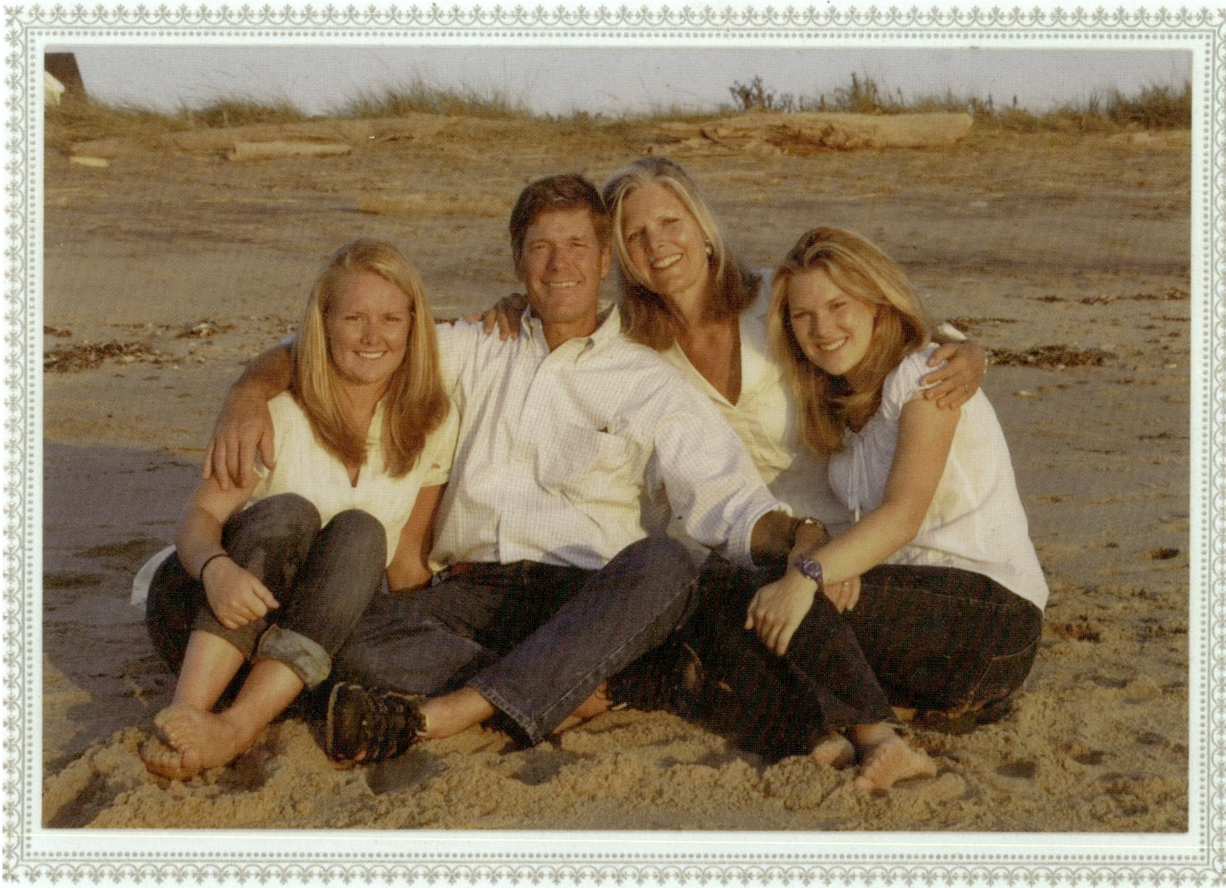

CM: The Musser side of the family stays away from Facebook. Its publicness and the absence of a concrete image unnerve them. Carefully composed family portraits for the annual Christmas card are still their preferred means of sharing family images with a wider, if still limited, circle of friends and acquaintances.

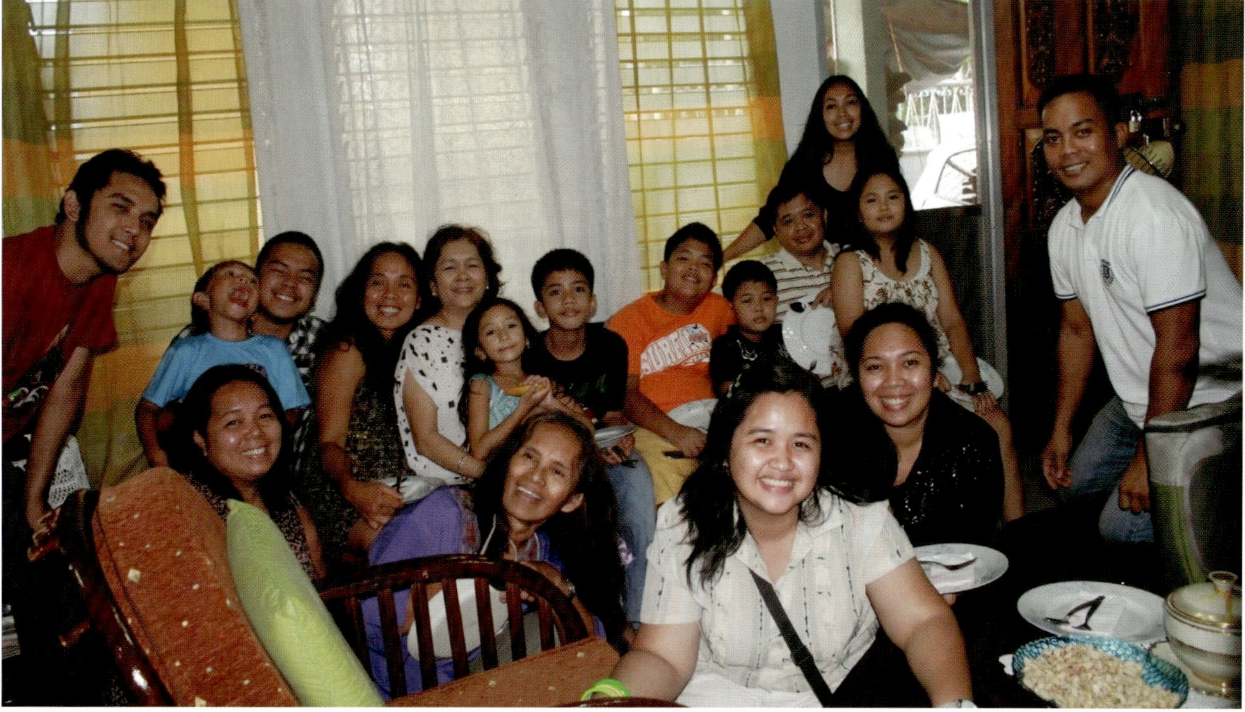

Threese: Facebook postings periodically document large gatherings of the clan. But sometimes we don't just read about them. We are there—as when we returned to the Philippines in the summer of 2013.

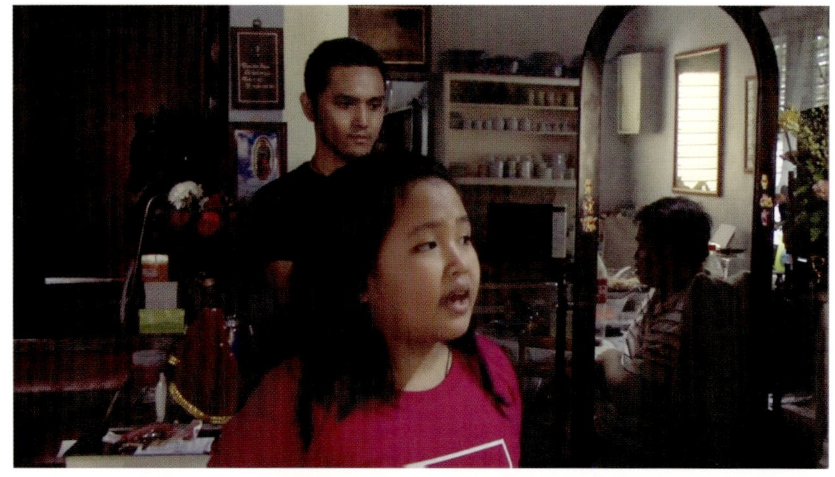

When an activity such as karaoke is central to a culture's mode of sociality, it is impossible to avoid. Almost by necessity, it becomes a motif. Here John Carlos gets a lesson in karaoke from his uncle and cousins. Threese's sister Anne is married to Rene Martel, and their three eldest children show the way.

John Carlos: Okay. You sing. She's singing!

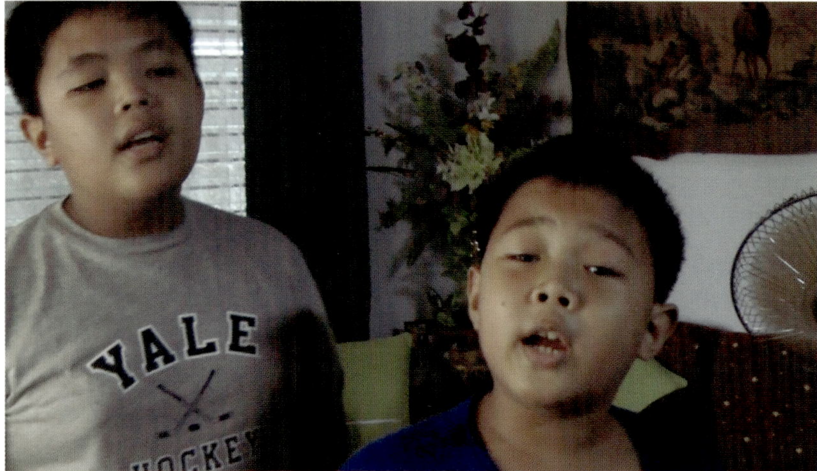

Lisenbelle Martel: Just give me a reason, just a little bit's enough. Just a second we're not broken just bent, and we can learn to love again.

Elian and Eleazar Martel: And being apart ain't easy on this love affair.

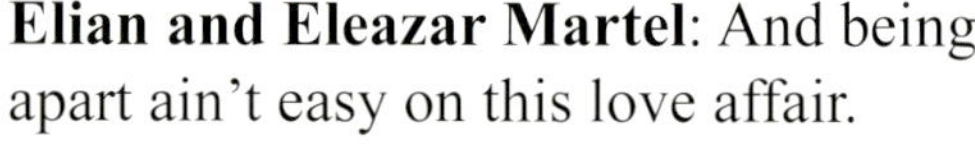

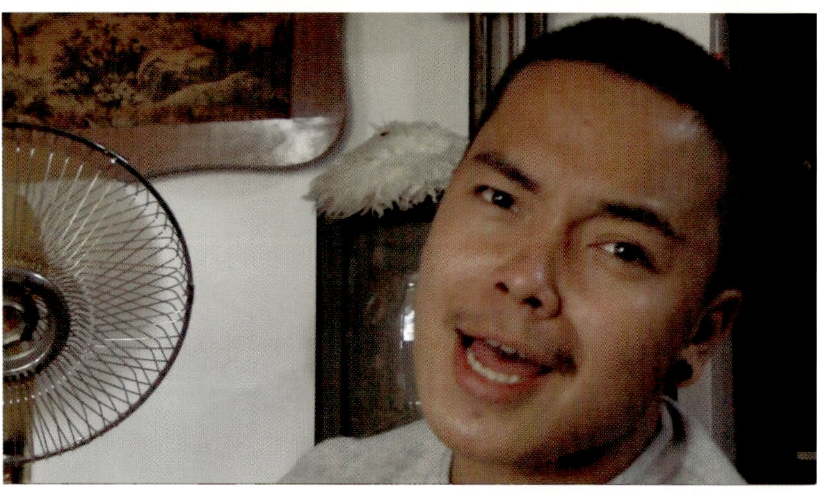

Matthan Serana: Pano makasaboy.
          (How to join in.)

Group: Of melodies pure and true, singing: "This is my message to you ou ou...."

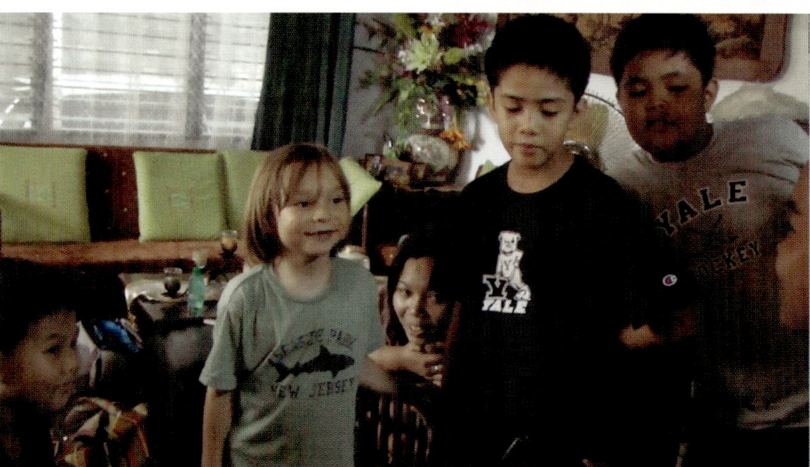

CM: You were six and we brought them t-shirts from the U.S.. You even got to spend time with Binhi. After eight years he barely remembered that your mom had been his mom.

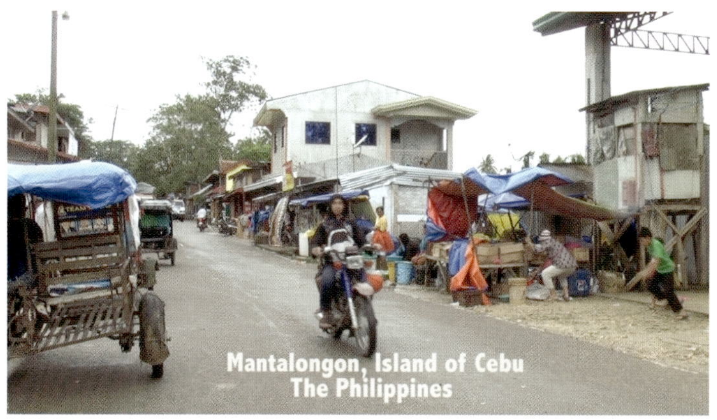

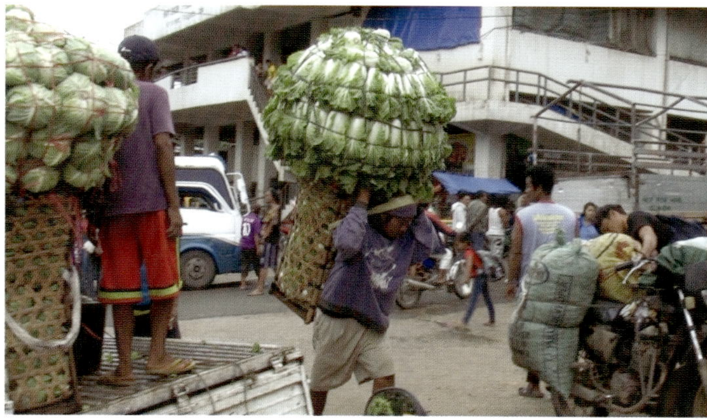

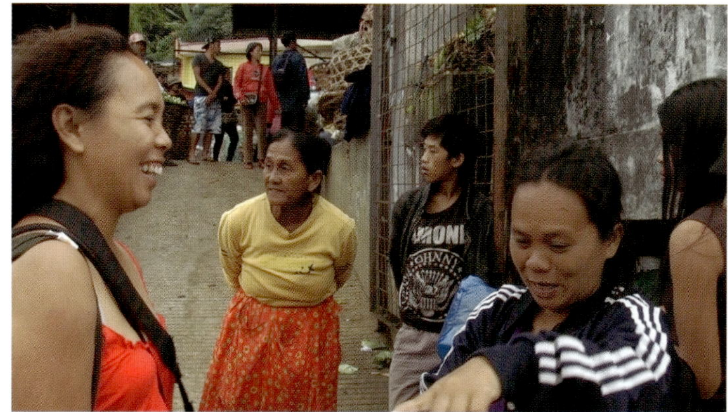

TS: We also visited relatives in the mountains of Cebu, where Mamay had grown up and I spent my summers. First, we had to reach the market town of Mantalongon.

CM: Your mom quickly ran into a cousin. It was a happy reunion, though we soon discovered that her husband had been killed by a bus, and she had to sell fish to make a living.

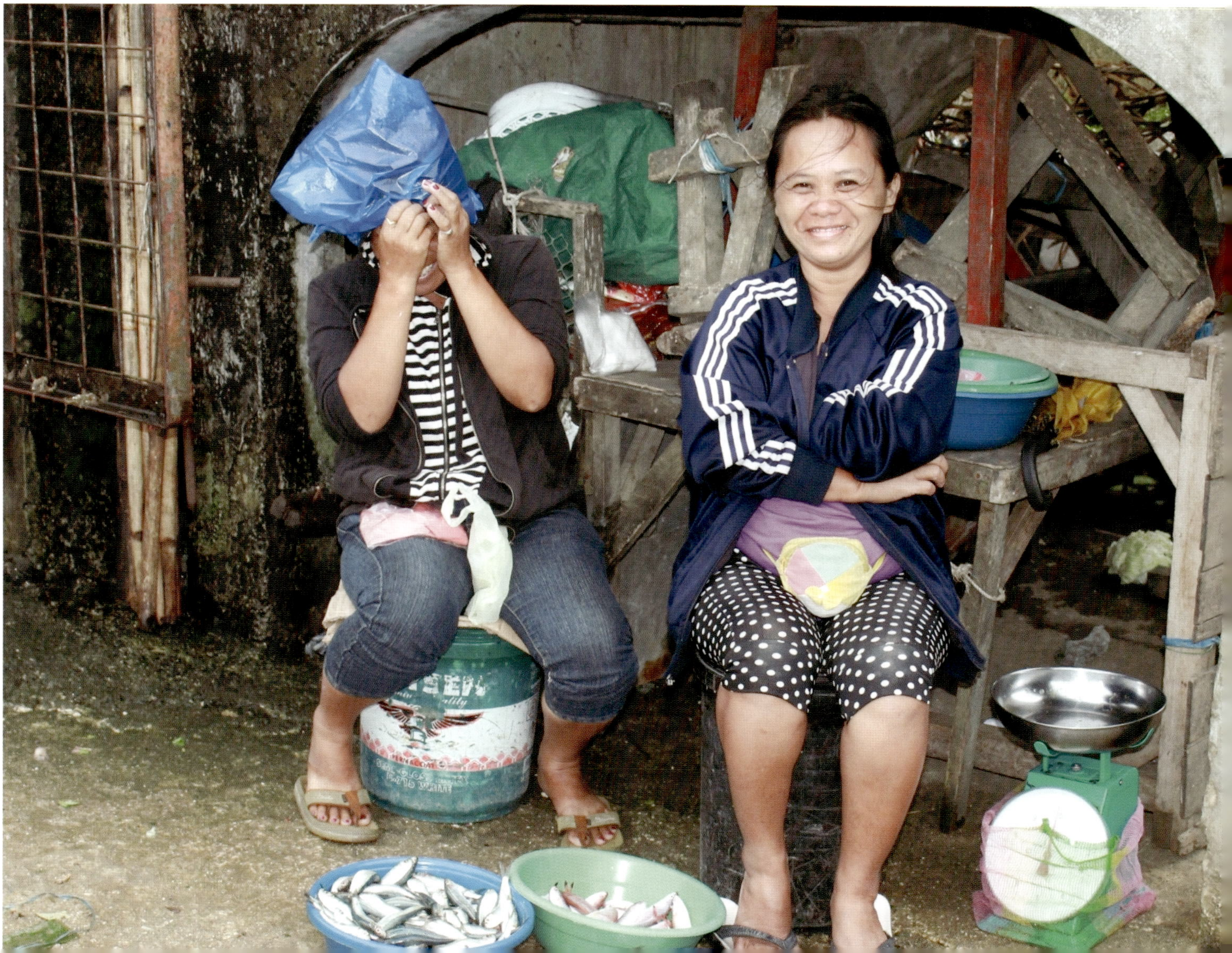

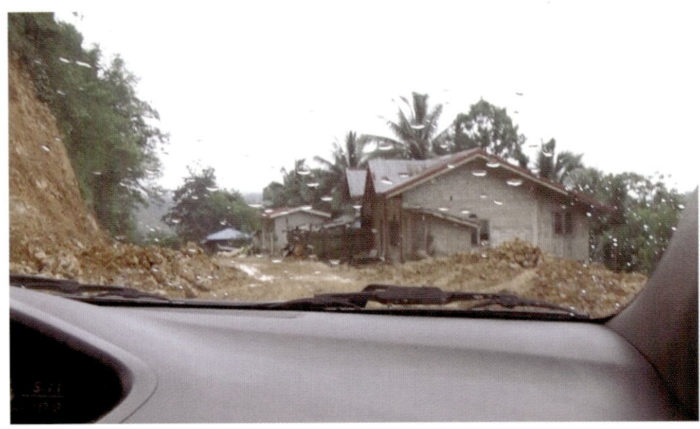
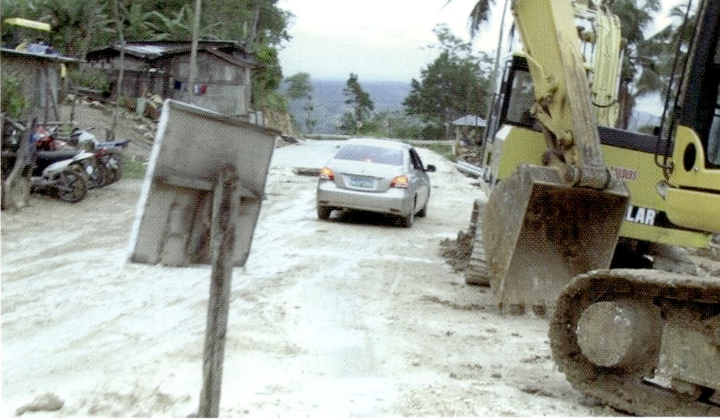

TS: The road to Manlapay is not always passable. Sections were being paved…but that doesn't stop the mud and rock slides.

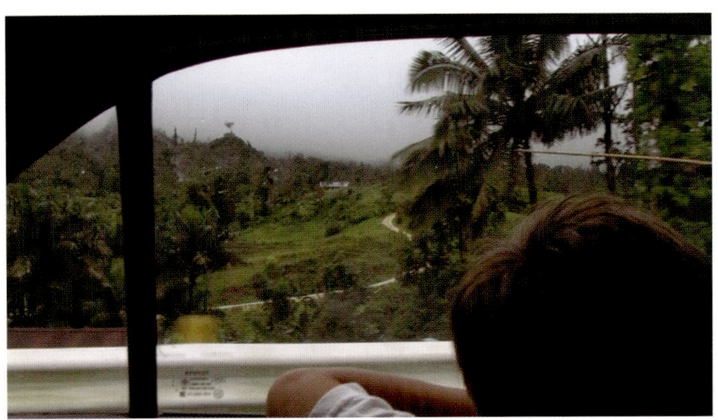
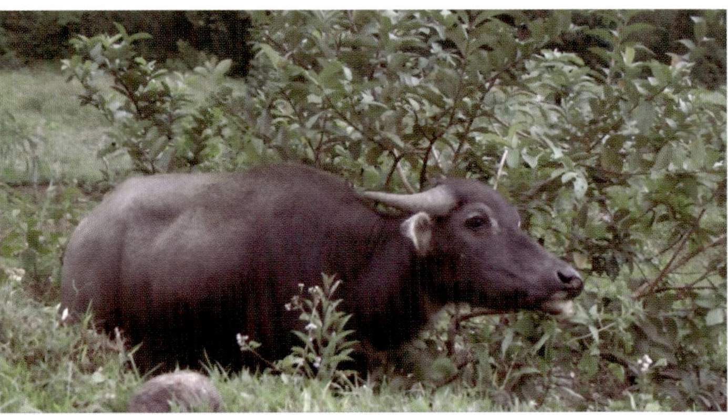

John Carlos: Hi, Carabao!

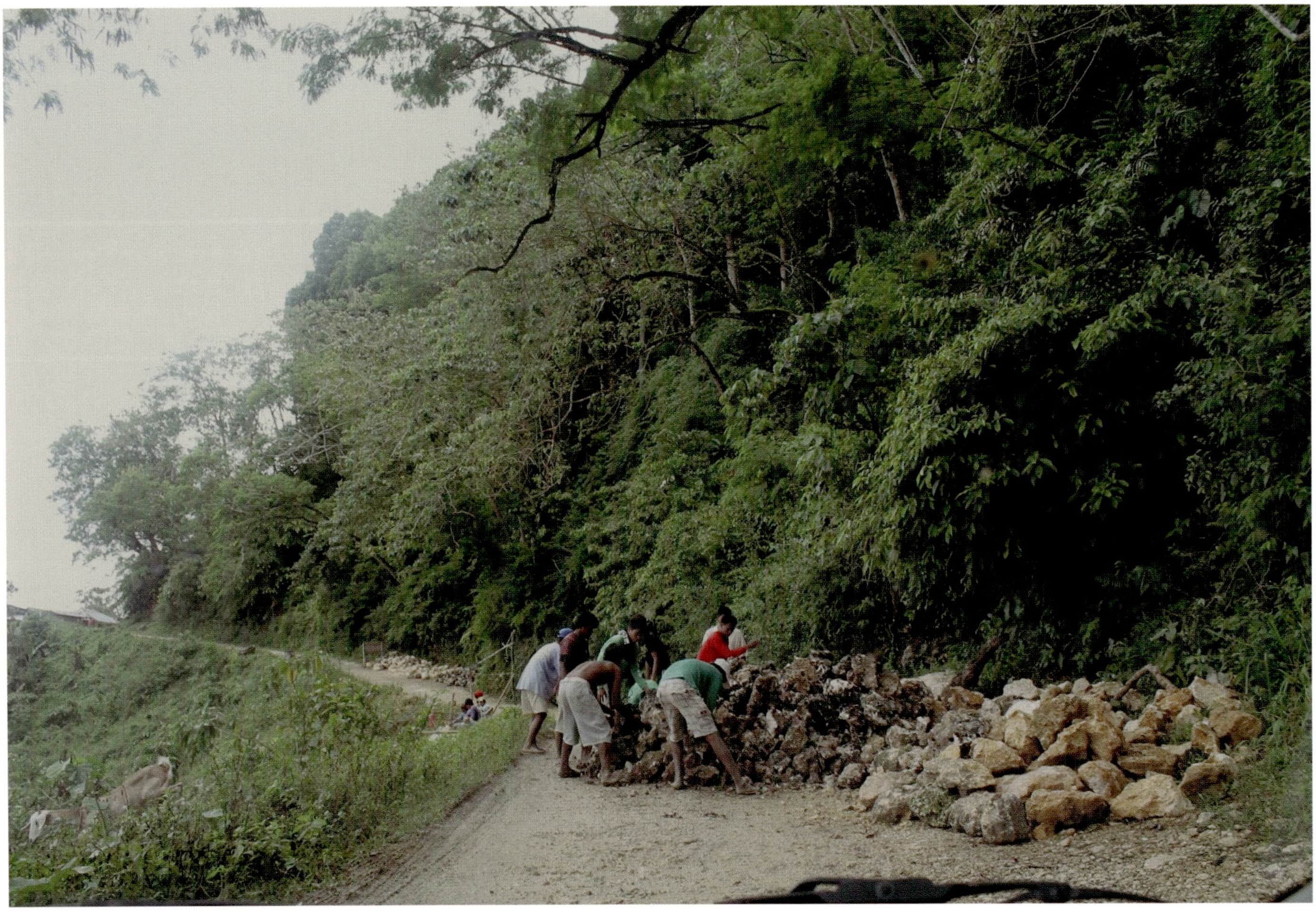

Manlapay is a barangay with a land area of 5.26 square kilometers. In 2008 it had 322 households and a population of 1,949. In 2015 its population was 2,152. Just about everyone living in Manlapay is related.

TS: We stayed in a house built by my aunt who was living in Texas.

CM: You went to school with your aunt and uncle who were your own age. If they weren't aunts and uncles, your classmates were second and third cousins. So was the teacher, even the principal.

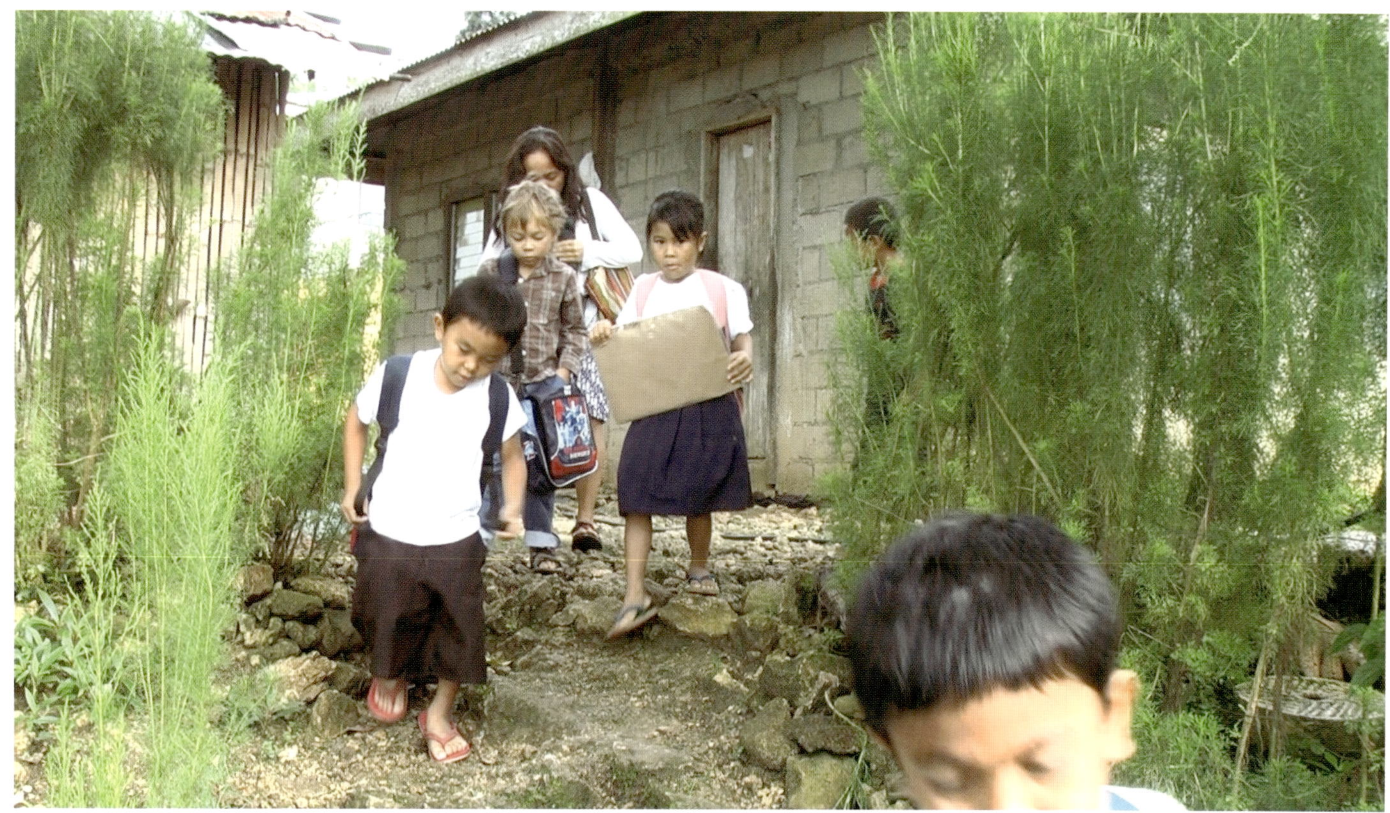

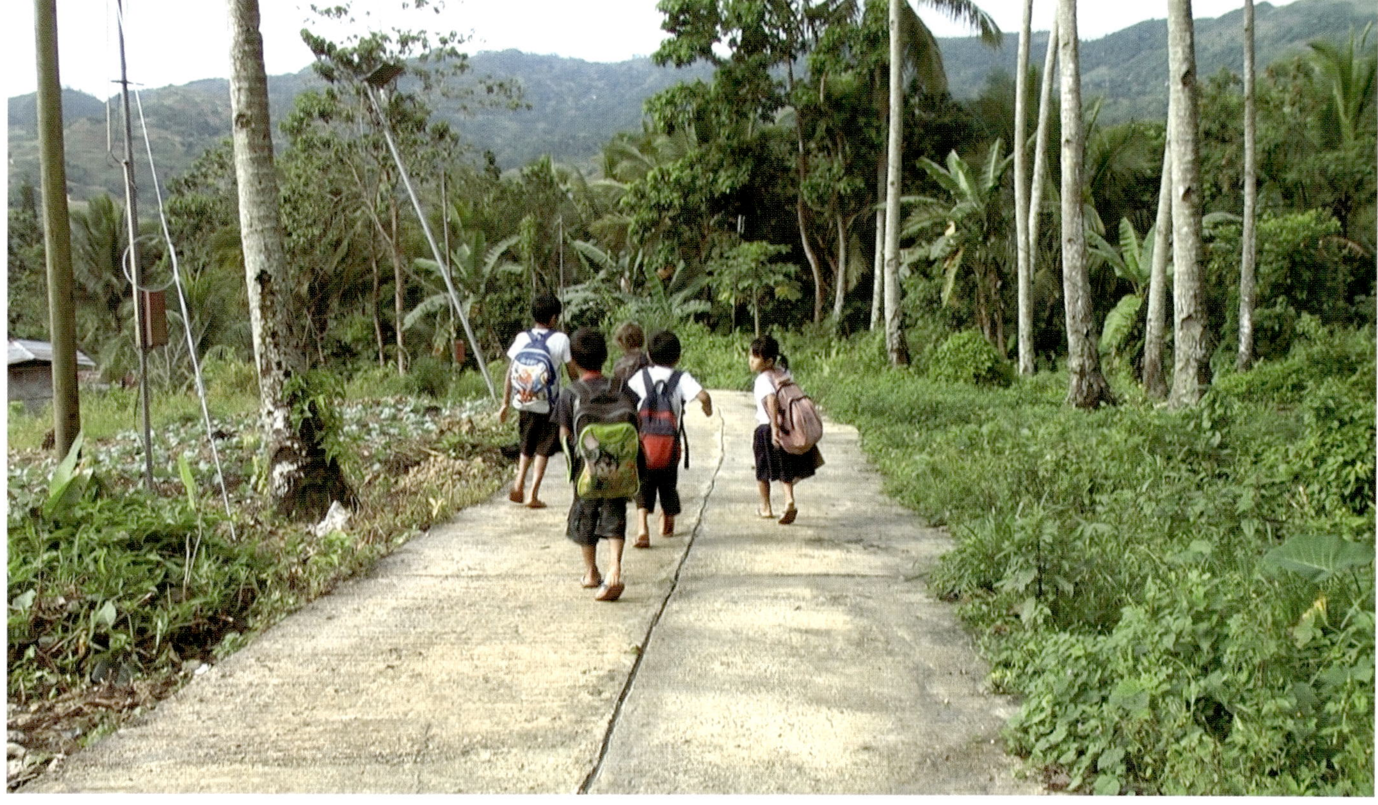

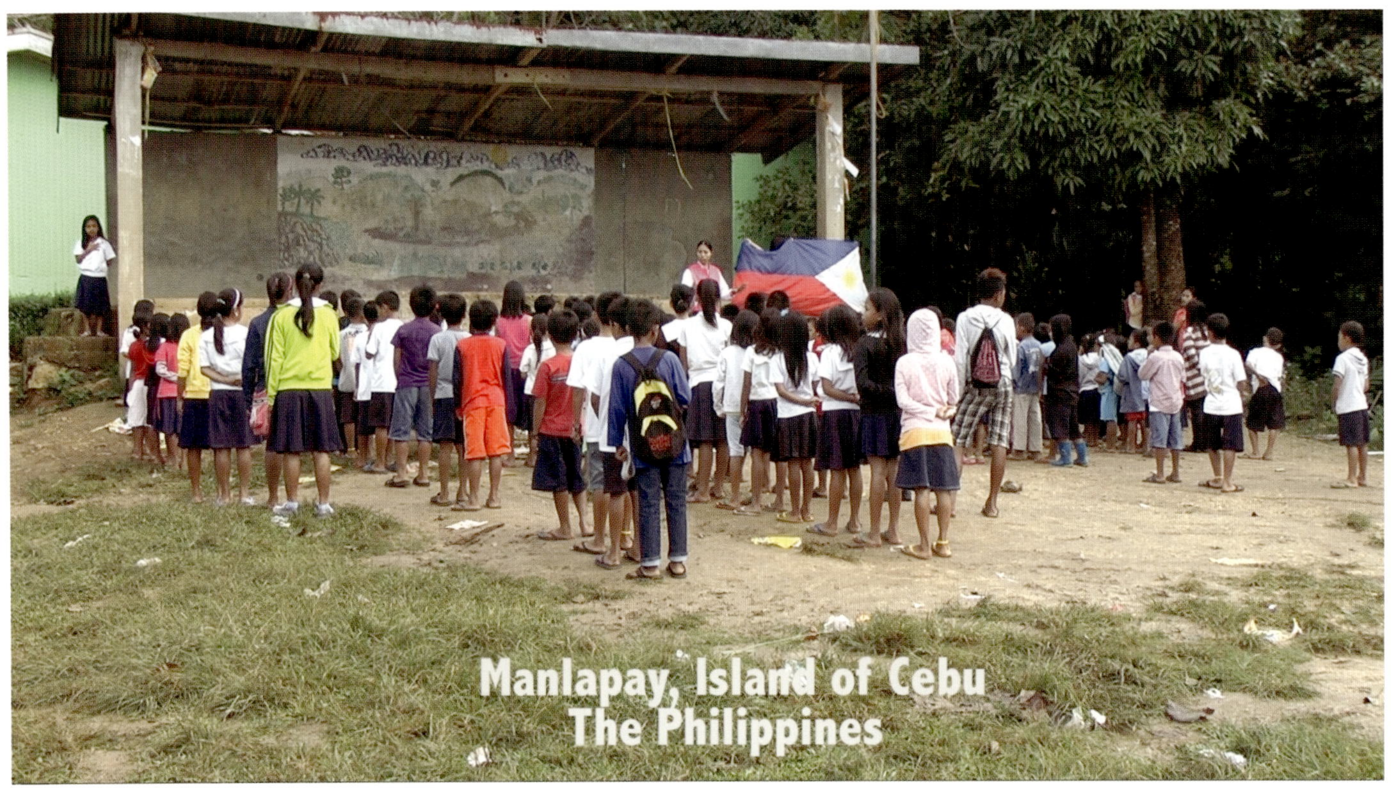

Students sing "Lupang Hinirang," the Philippine national anthem:

Bayang magiliw	Land of the morning
Perlas ng Silanganan,	Child of the sun returning
Alab ng puso,	With fervor burning
Sa dibdib mo'y buhay.	Thee do our souls adore.
Lupang Hinirang,	Land dear and holy
Duyan ka ng magiting,	Cradle of noble heroes
Sa manlulupig,	Ne'er shall invaders
Di ka pasisiil.	Trample thy sacred shores.

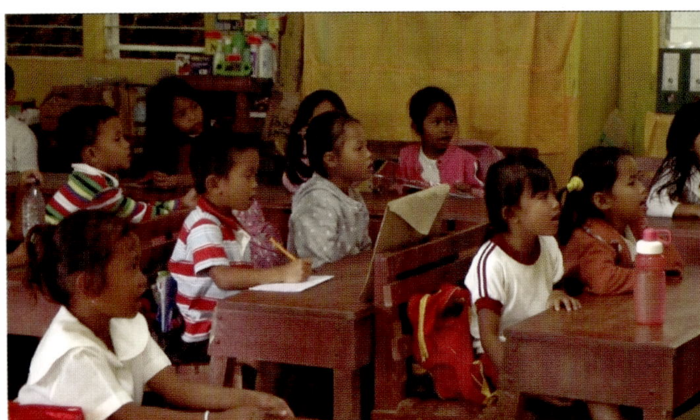
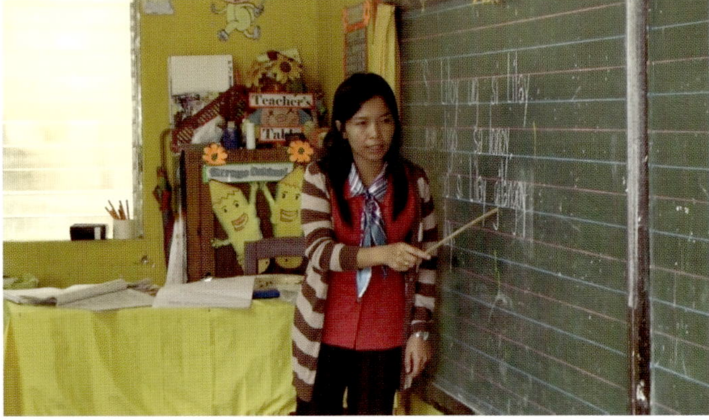

Children (reciting from the blackboard): Si Liloy ug si Lilay naligo sa lonoy. Nalunod si Lilay. Gilangoy ni Liloy. (Liloy and Lilay went swimming in the lake. Lilay was drowning. Liloy swam to her.)

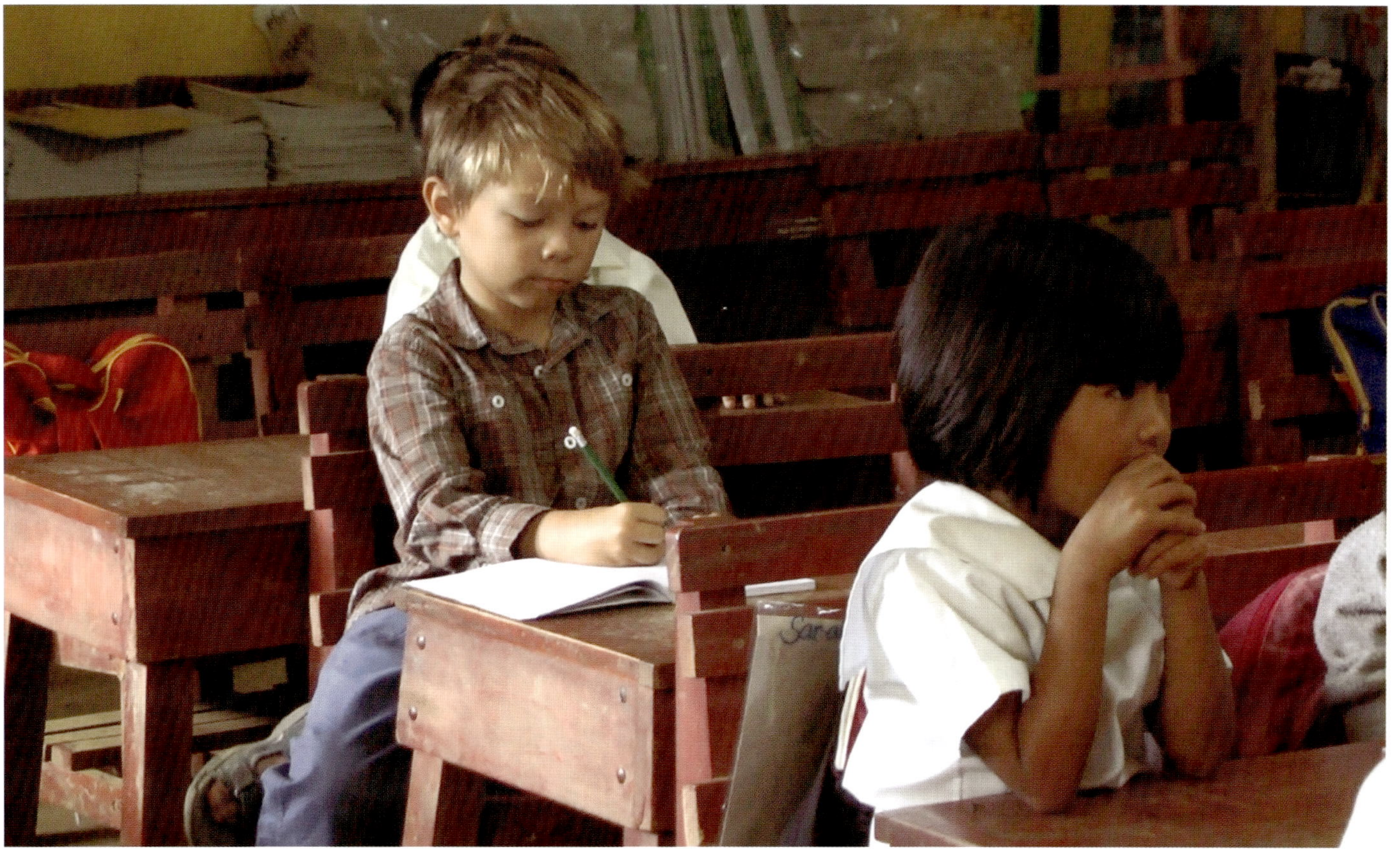

TS: We hoped you'd learn some Cebuano but it wasn't easy.

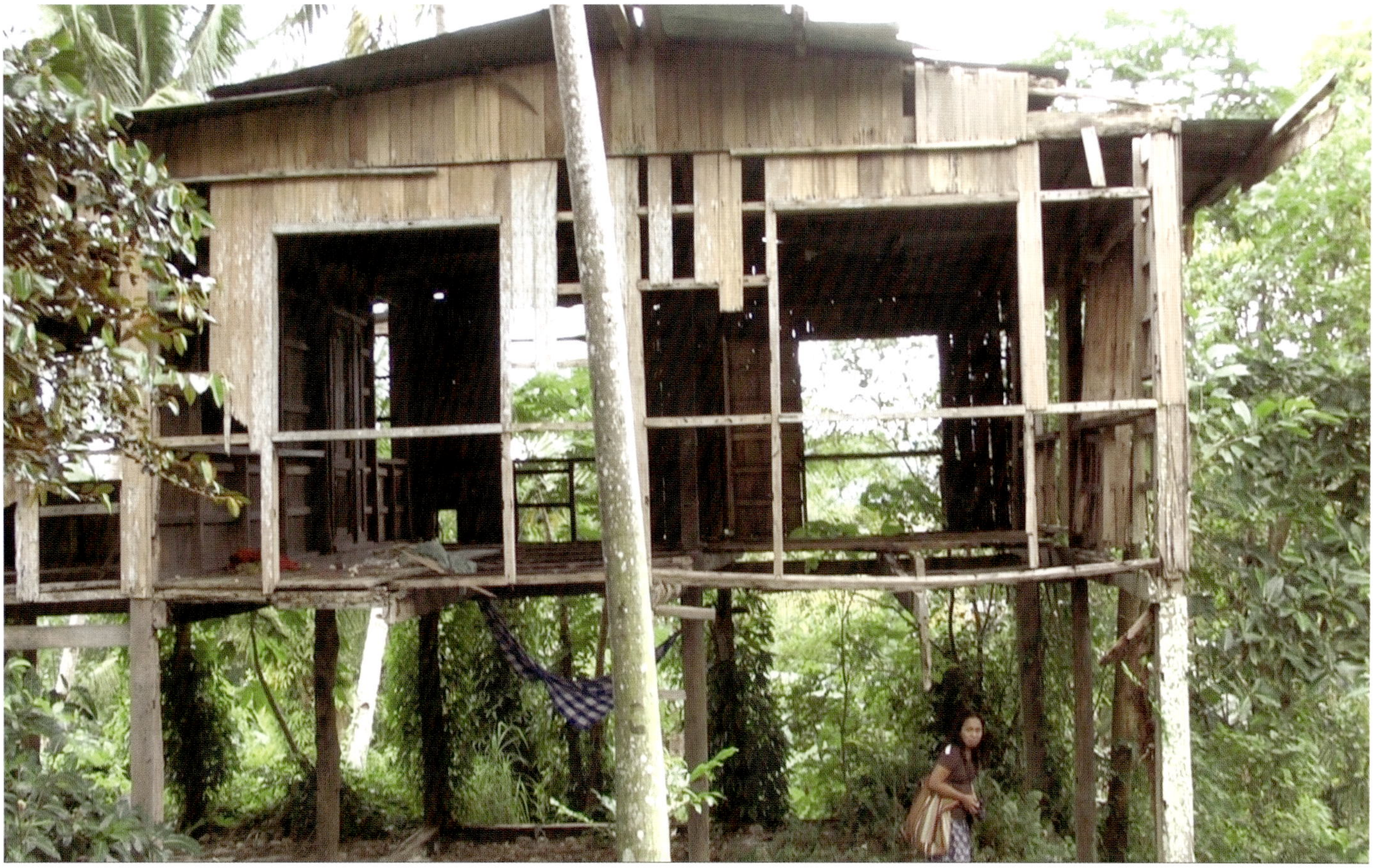

CM: We had our own educational projects. Your mom visited the abandoned house of her grandfather, where she had often stayed when she was a child.

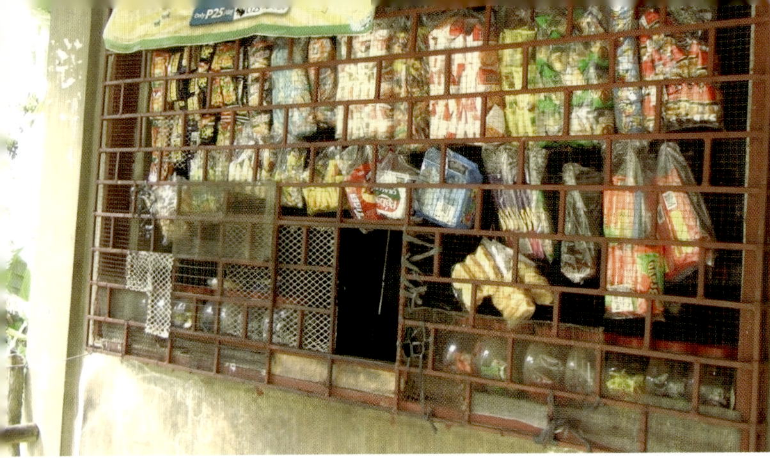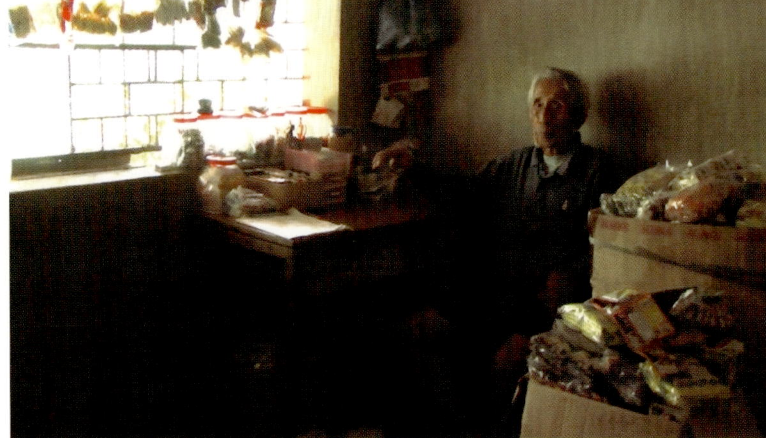

TS: We spent time with my mother's uncle, Victoriano Bejagan, who stills runs a family store. Later we interviewed him about our family's history.

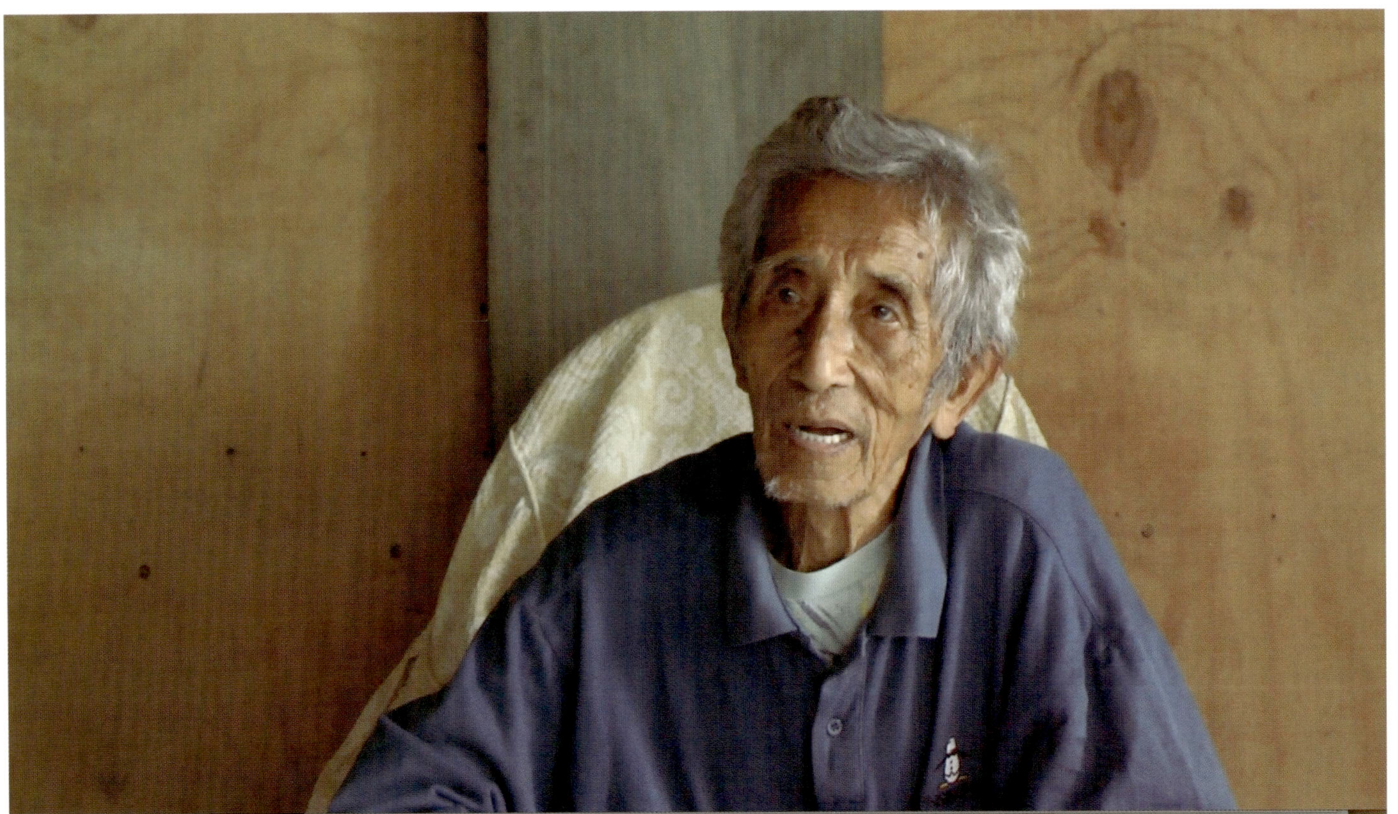

Victoriano Bejagan: My father's father, Longhino, was born out of wedlock. His father was a… Beltran. Because his mother was a Bejagan, he took his mother's maiden name.

Threese: So, he's a Beltran. Is that where the Hispanic part of the Bejagan came from?

Victoriano: Yes.

Threese: Because you all have Spanish features. So, would you know if that Beltran was a Spanish soldier or what?

Victoriano: I don't really know what he was. You know, all we do is inherit these stories.

Threese: So the Bejagans were really Beltrans?

Victoriano: Yes. And on my mother Anastasia's side, they descended from the Lumayags. They were also Spanish.

Threese: But what made them Spanish? "Lumayag" is a Filipino name [meaning "sailor"].

Victoriano: Oh, no, they came from Spain.

Threese: So possibly, "Lumayag" was their adoptive Filipino name?

Victoriano: We were told that the Lumayags first came to the Philippines with Magellan.
…..

Victoriano: About our life growing up here. I remember well the time your grandmother Pisya gave birth to your mother.

Threese: Why?

Victoriano: I admonished the pregnant Pisya to stop traveling because she was ready to pop out anytime and give birth on the road. And so, indeed, it happened. She gave birth on the road.

Threese: Where was she going?

Victoriano: She was coming home from Dalaguete.

Threese: So she came from Dalaguete. Walking?

Victoriano: Yes, walking. There was no transportation. So she gave birth in Ablayan.

Threese: Was it day or night?

Victoriano: Daytime. Your mother was born by the hemp plantation.
……

Victoriano: When your uncle Mory got married, Lola Pisya traveled to the city to buy a wedding cake as a present.

Threese: Ahh. Wedding cake.

Victoriano: Yes. A wedding cake. But her trip ended in an accident in Naga. She died. The coal truck on which she was riding was totaled and [Lola Pisya] was buried under the coal.

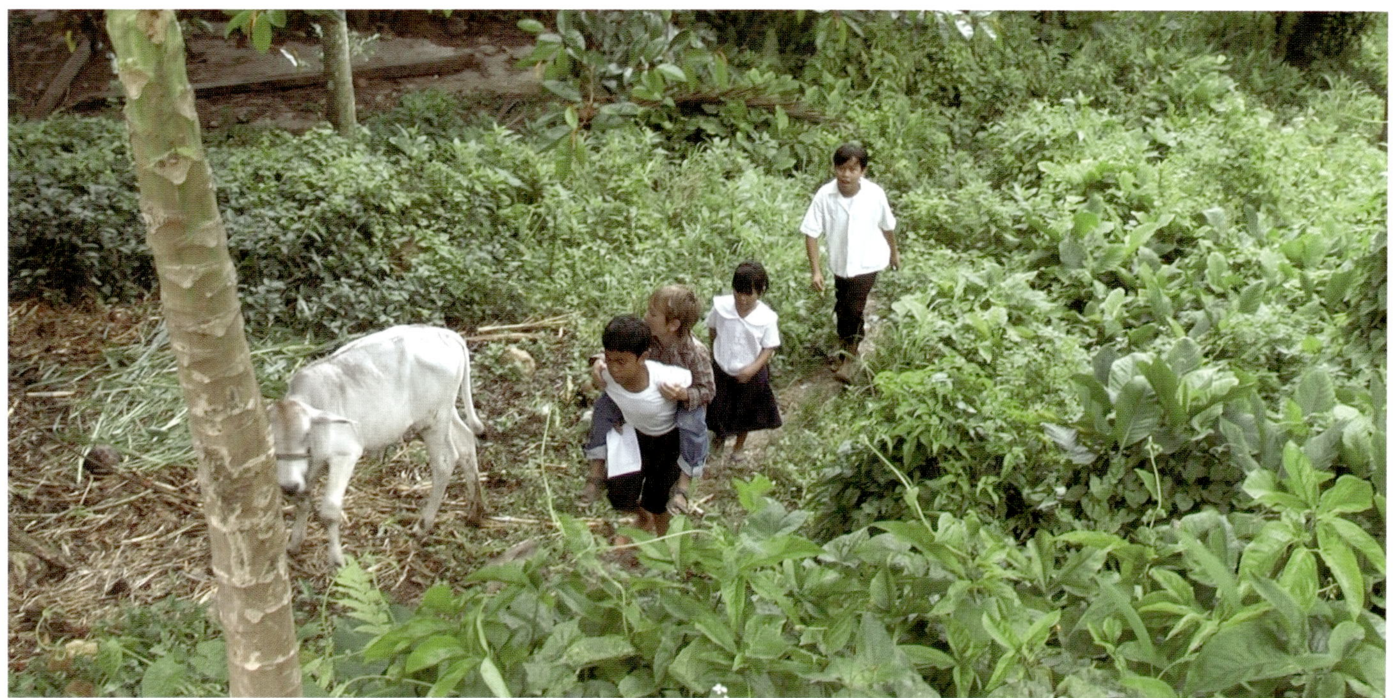

Threese: John, what is that? Why aren't you walking?… It's a baby cow.

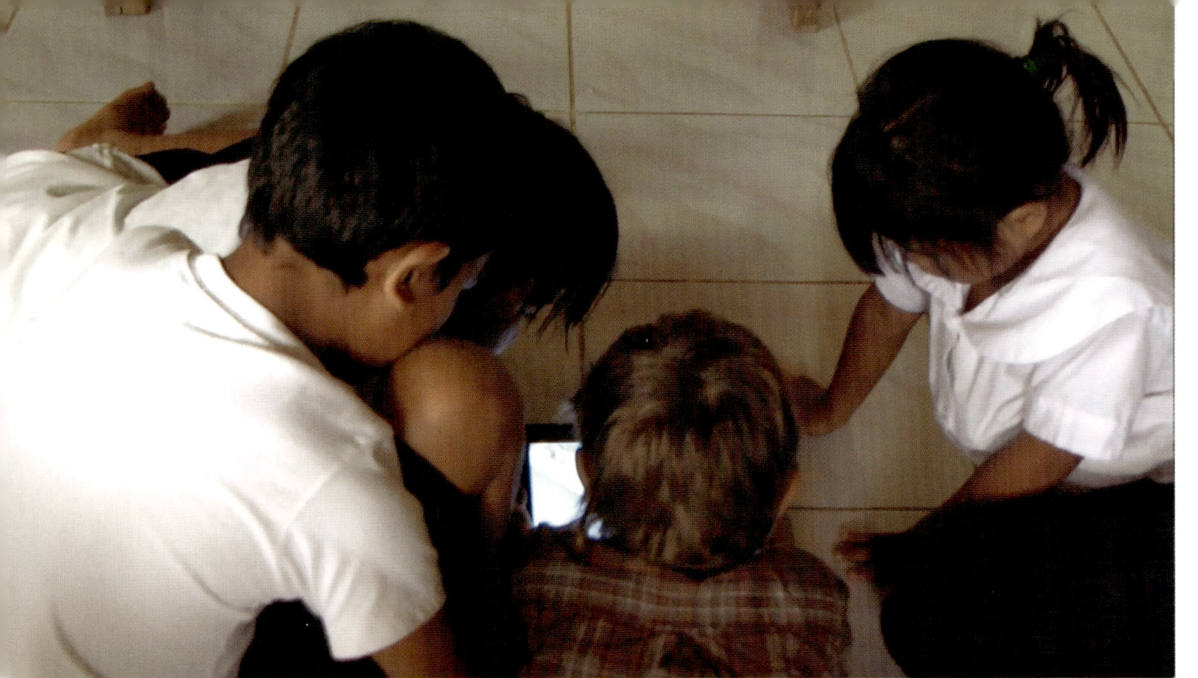

CM: You were making friends but language and culture were barriers.

Charlie: John Carlos, why don't you show them the farm [a game John Carlos often played in the U.S.].

John Carlos: What farm? They already know the farm. They are bored with the farm.

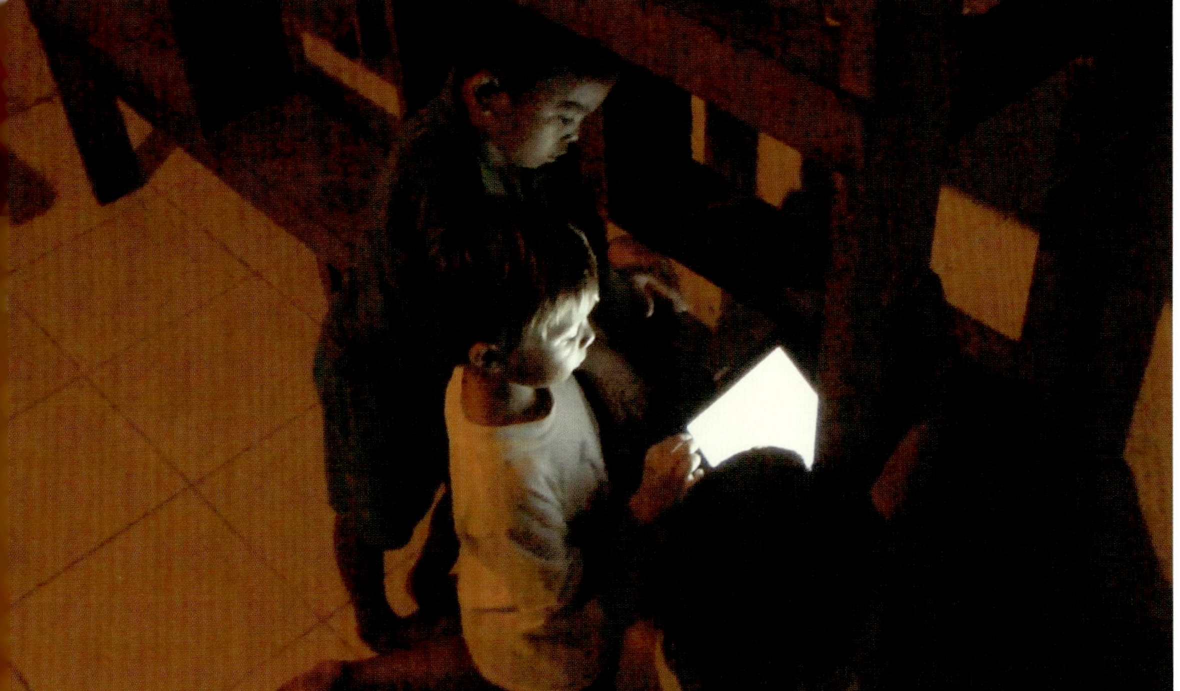

When we first arrived in Manlapay, John Carlos was immediately embraced by his cousins/classmates. Although we sometimes found it difficult to watch the awkwardness of their interactions, intervening only seemed to make it worse. Patience was required. Within a few weeks John Carlos seemingly understood what his friends were saying. The nature of their play changed, even with the iPad. But the iPad was often forgotten as they chased each other around a pole and then played various children's games.

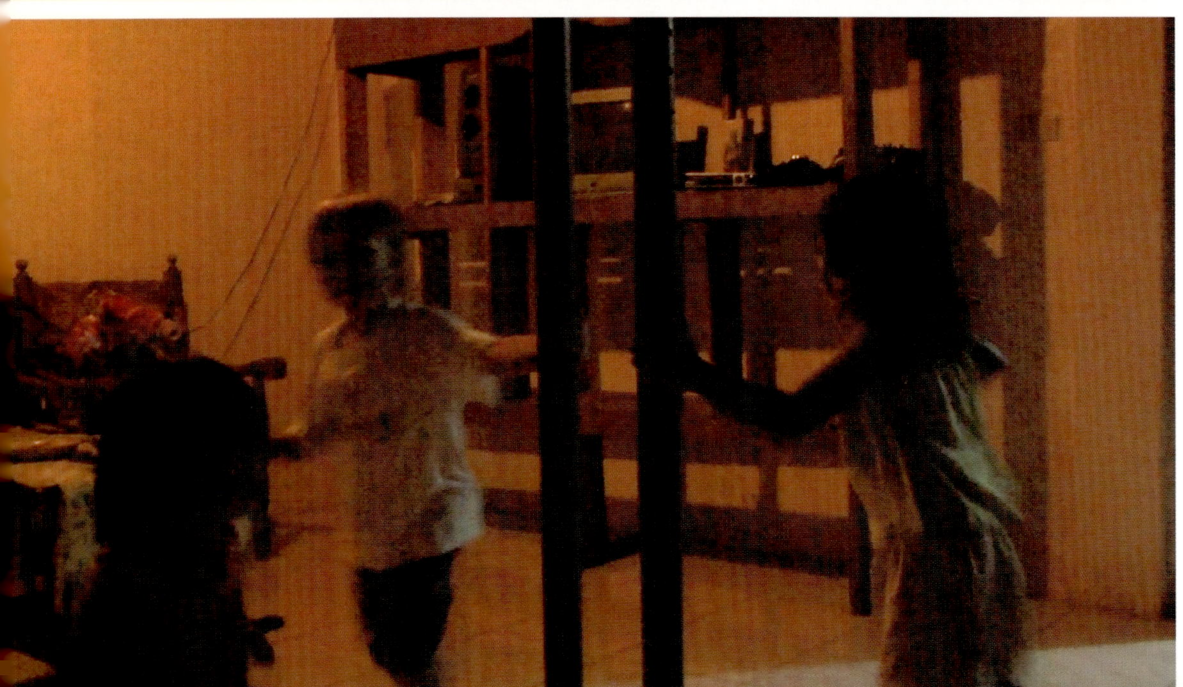

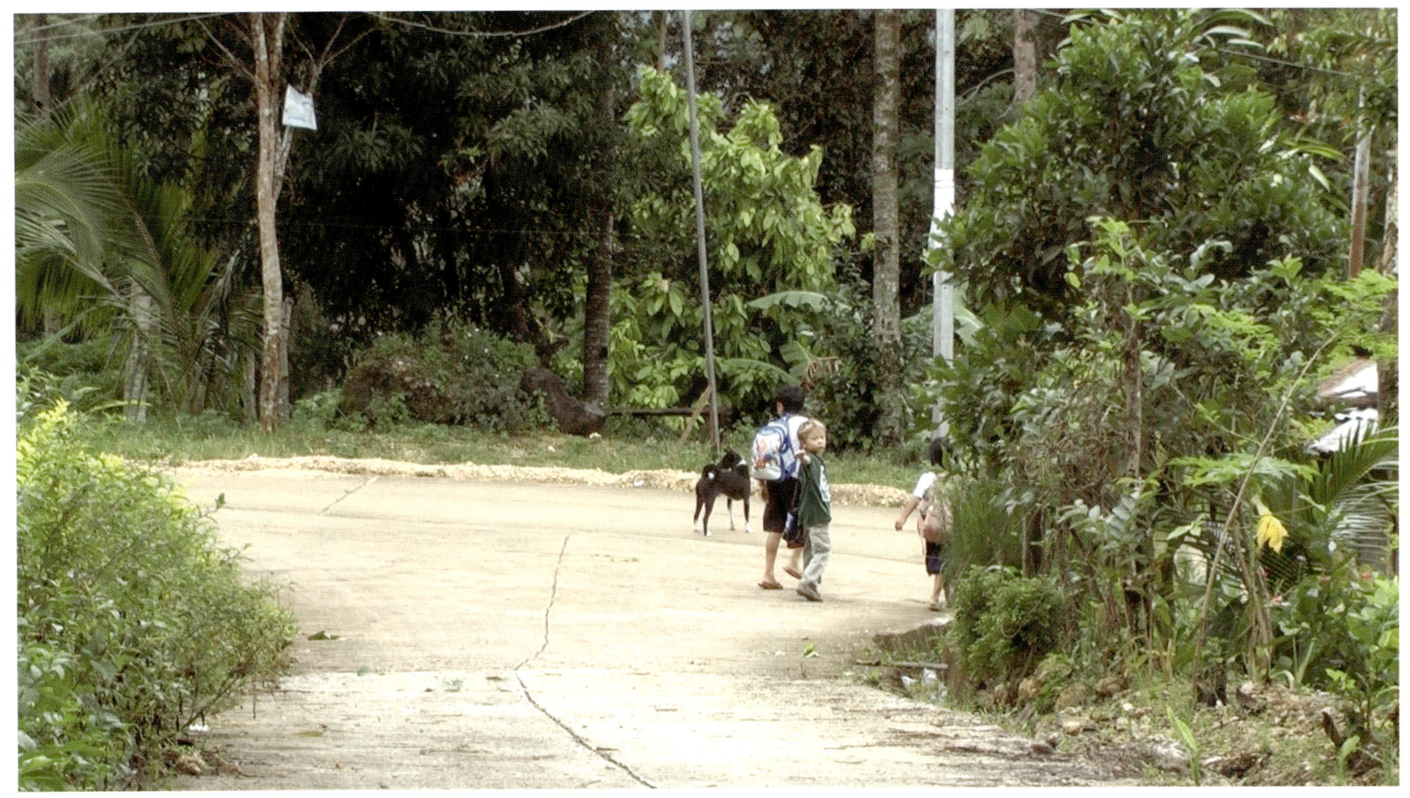

Threese: Keep going. You're late. Hurry. Hurry.

CM: It makes me want to make a family album entitled *John Carlos in Manlapay*, in which school pictures are always family photographs.

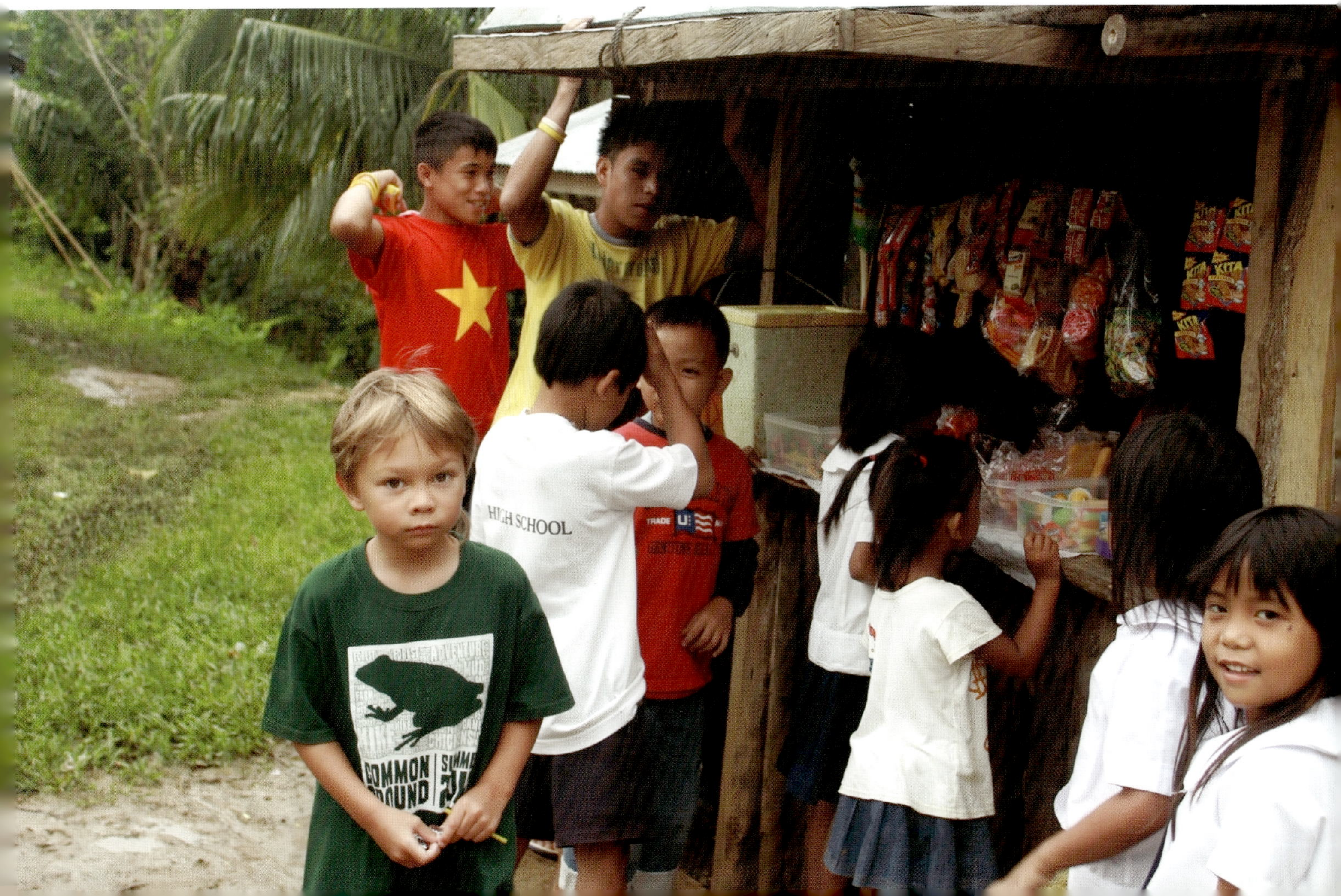

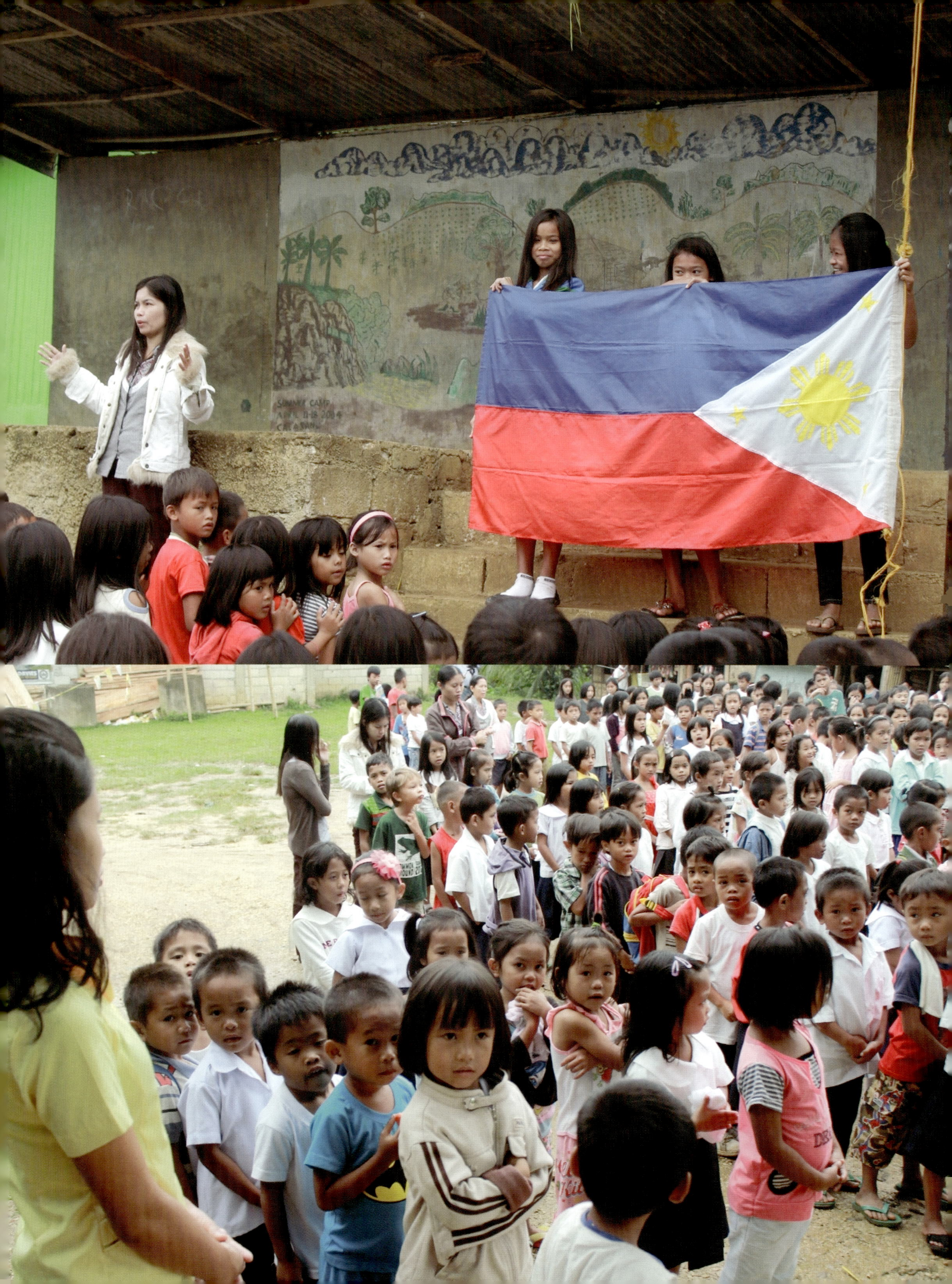

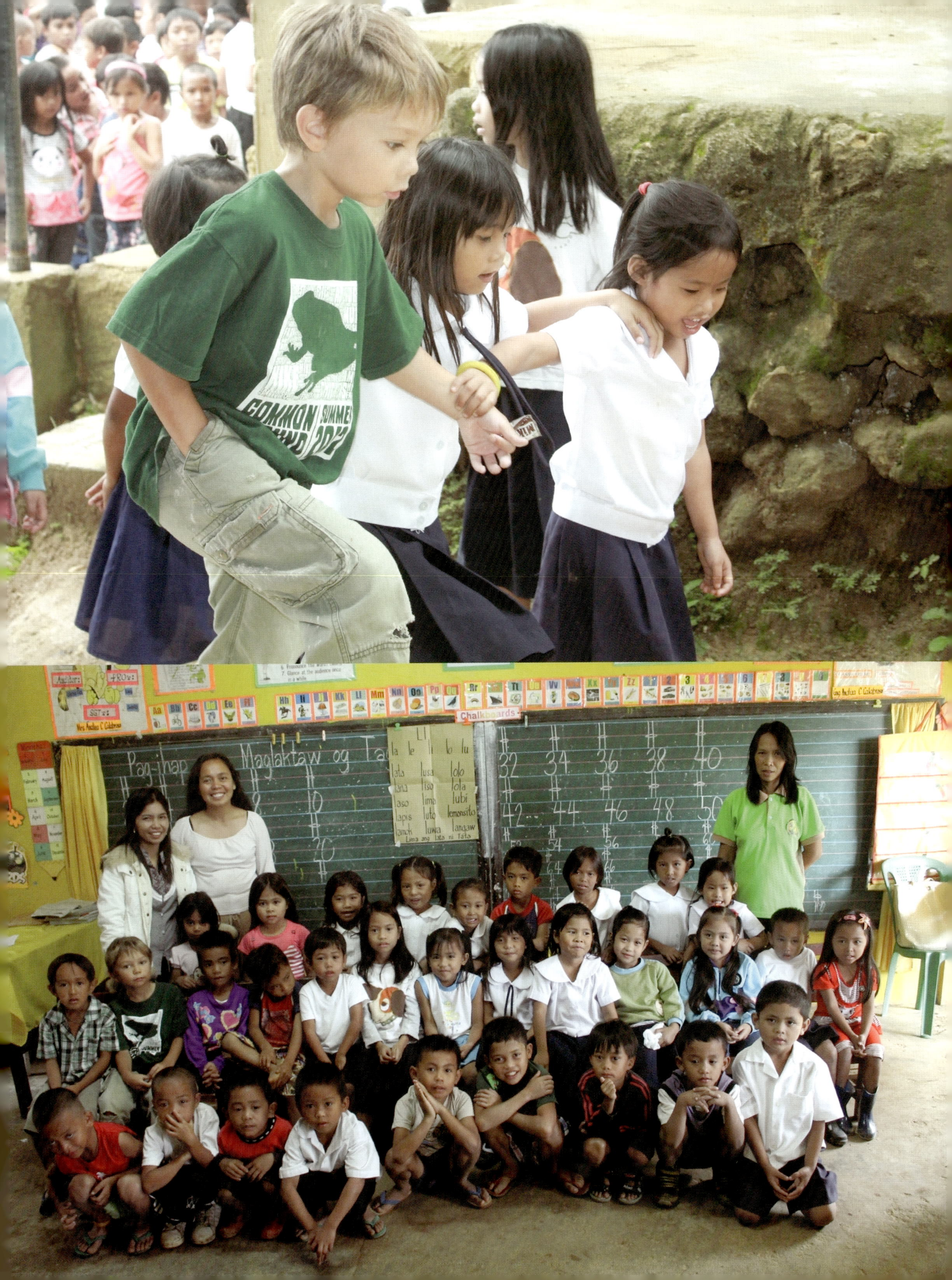

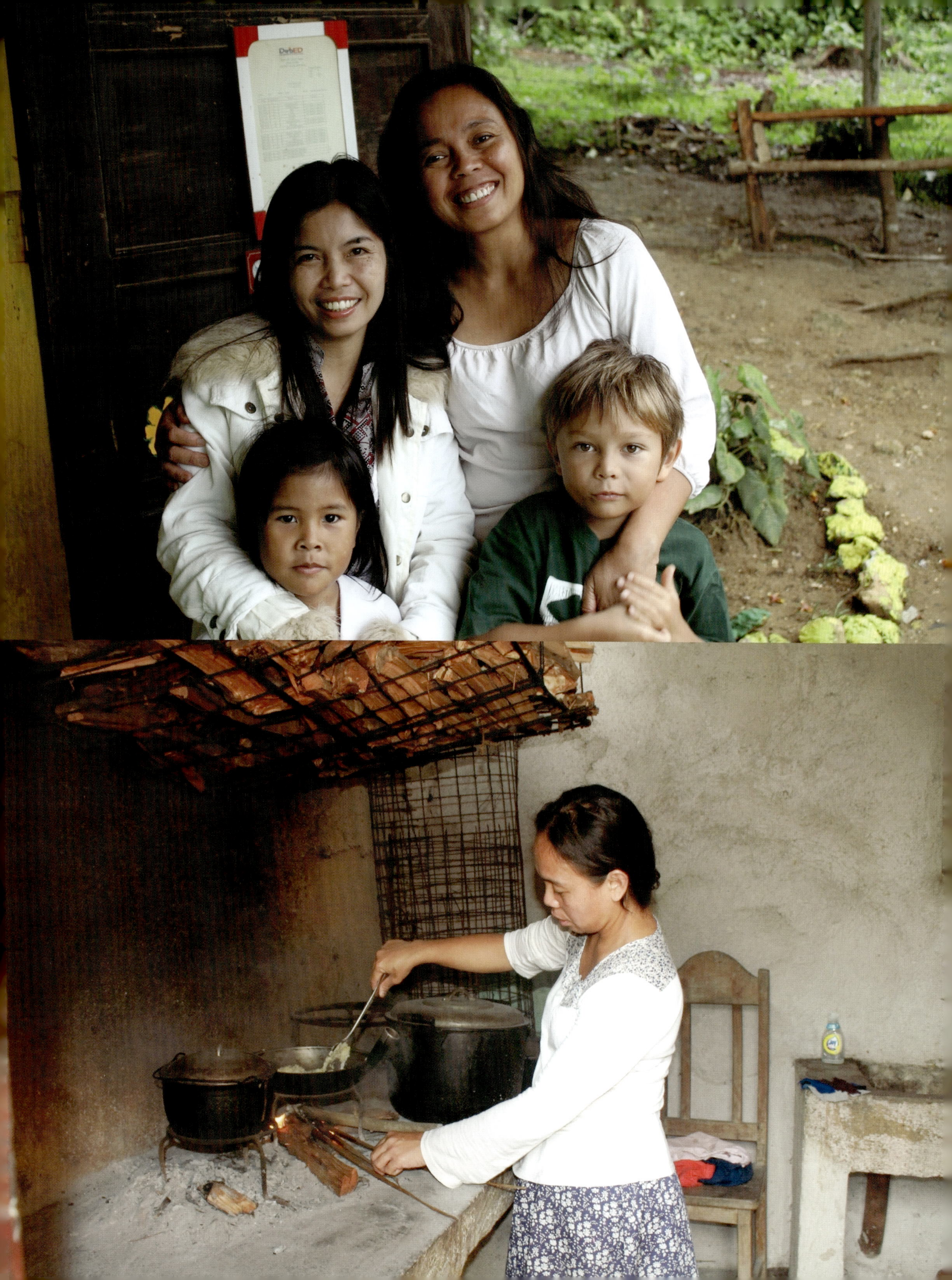

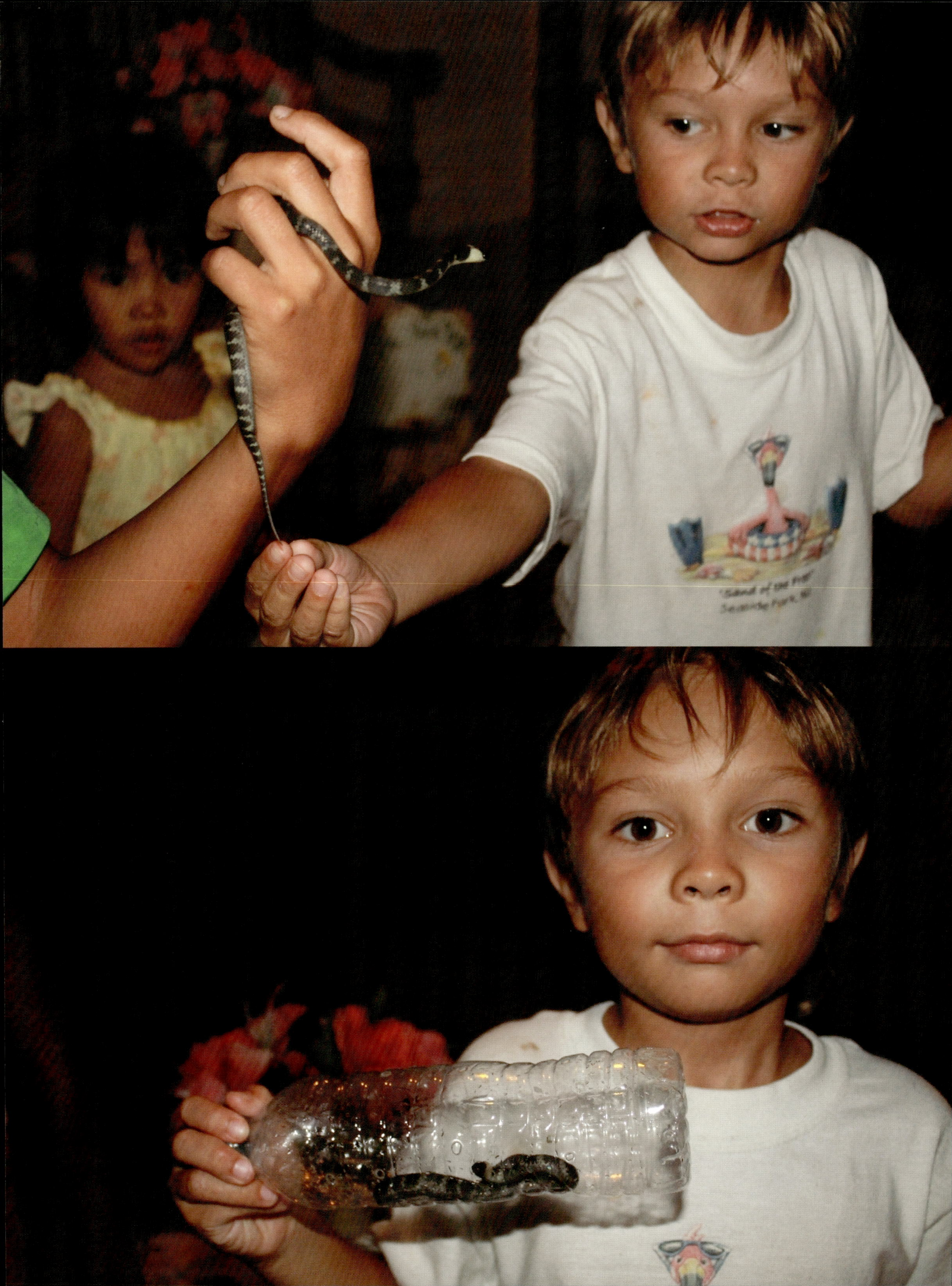

Because everyone in Manlapay is related, when a relative dies the entire town attends the funeral. Services take place at Our Lady of Consolation Parish, where music and song are manifestations of this communal experiences. For this reason, it seemed an appropriate audio accompaniment to these images.

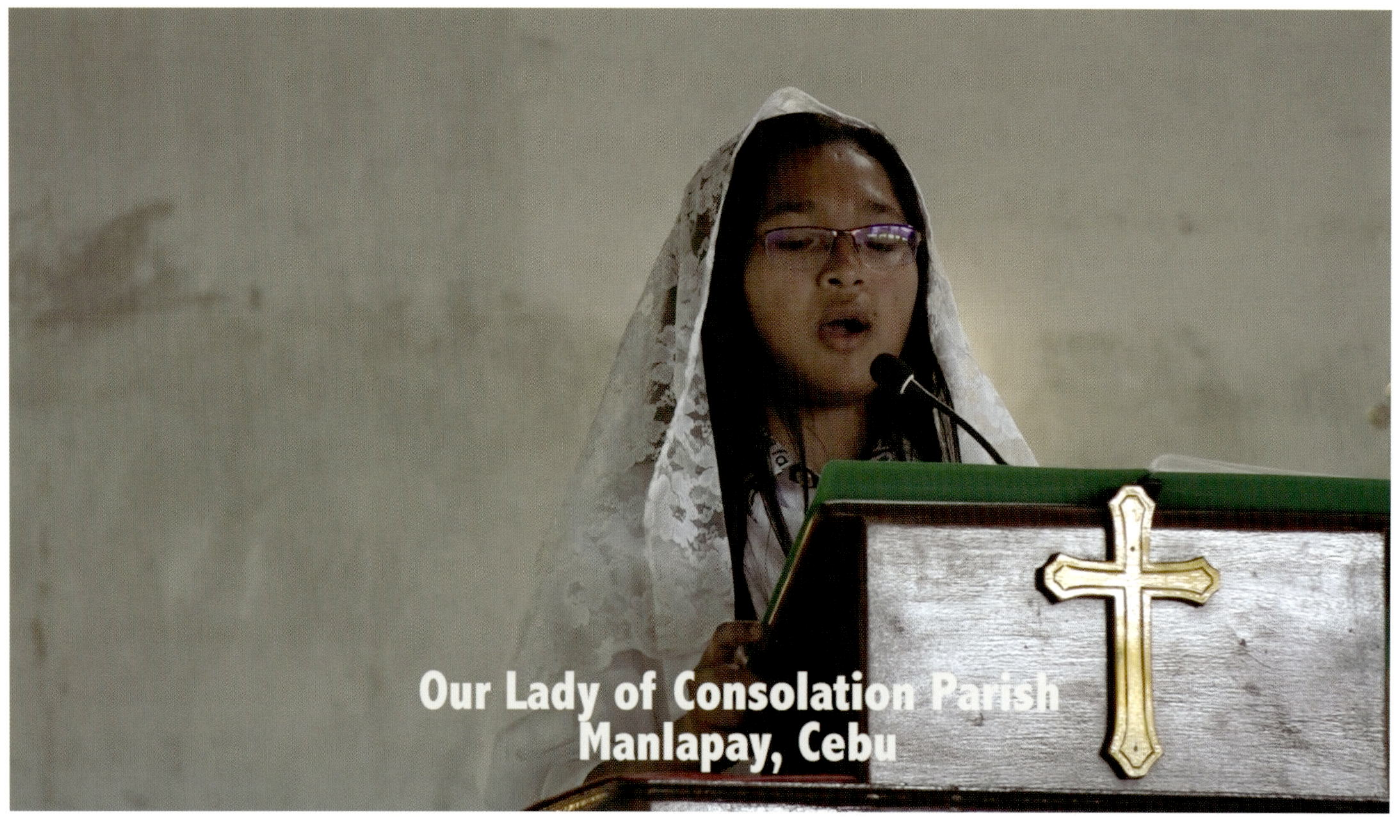

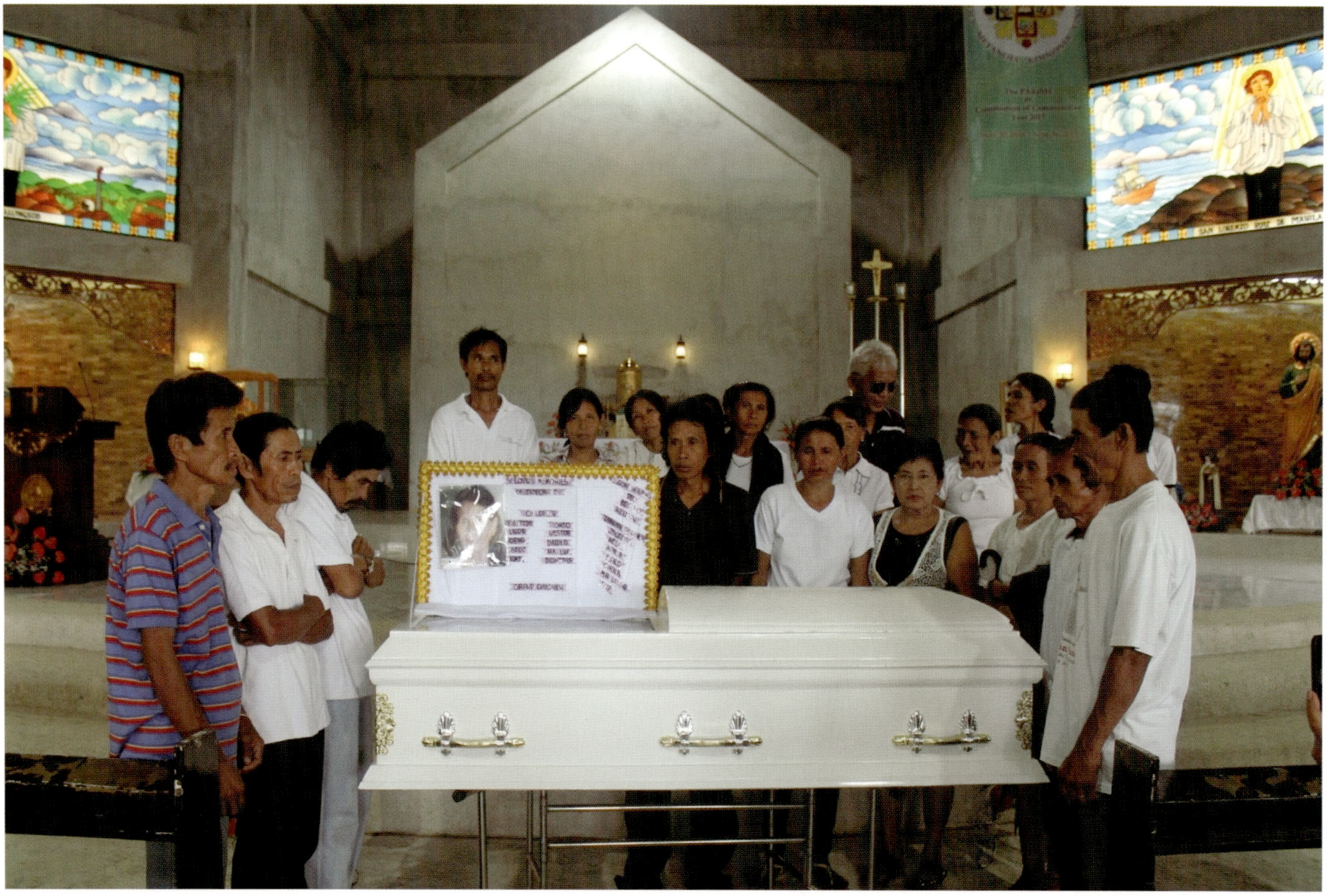

In a world in which all the residents of a barangay are relatives, and schoolmates are typically cousins, categories collapse; the school yearbook does double duty as an annual installment of the family album. This insularity comes with serious problems; having a high school sweetheart is often fraught. The opprobrium around cousins marrying cousins is intense even as exceptions abound. This made me think of other situations where photo albums that document a group or way of life are also family albums. In particular, there is the National Fairground Archive, founded by Vanessa Toulmin. The archive gathers together photographs and broadsides that reveal a way of life on the British fairground. Yet these images of carney culture are also images of an extended family.

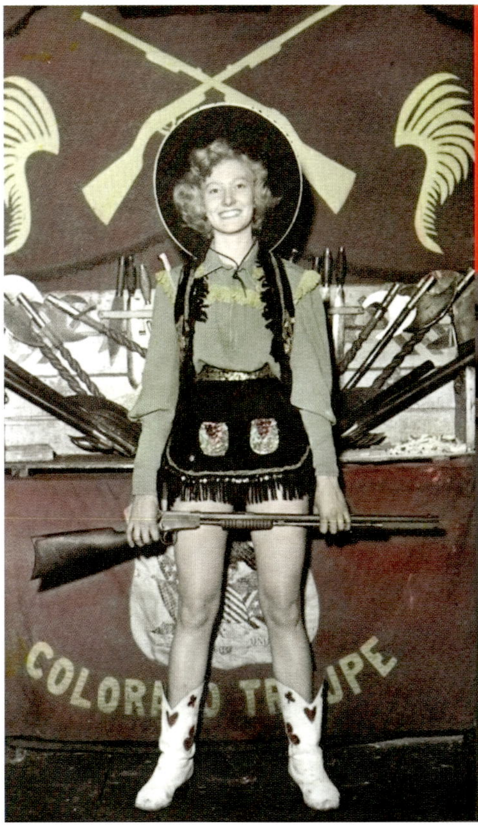

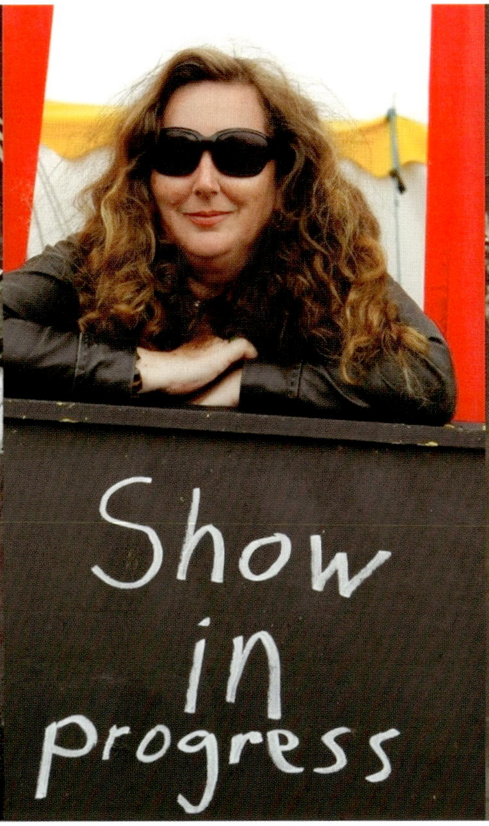

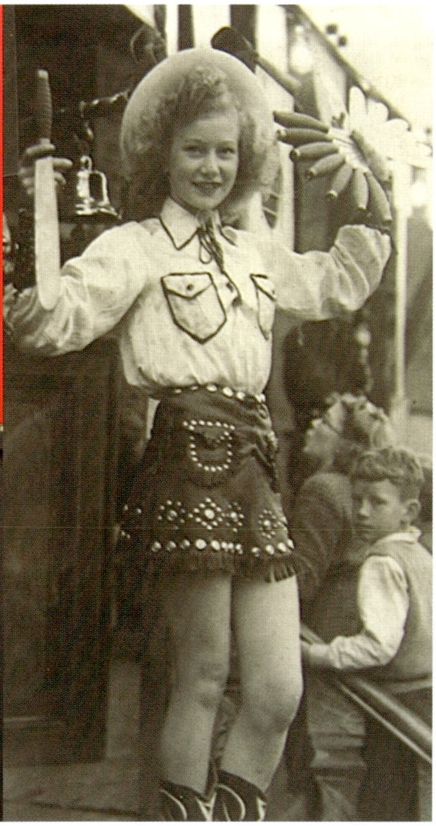

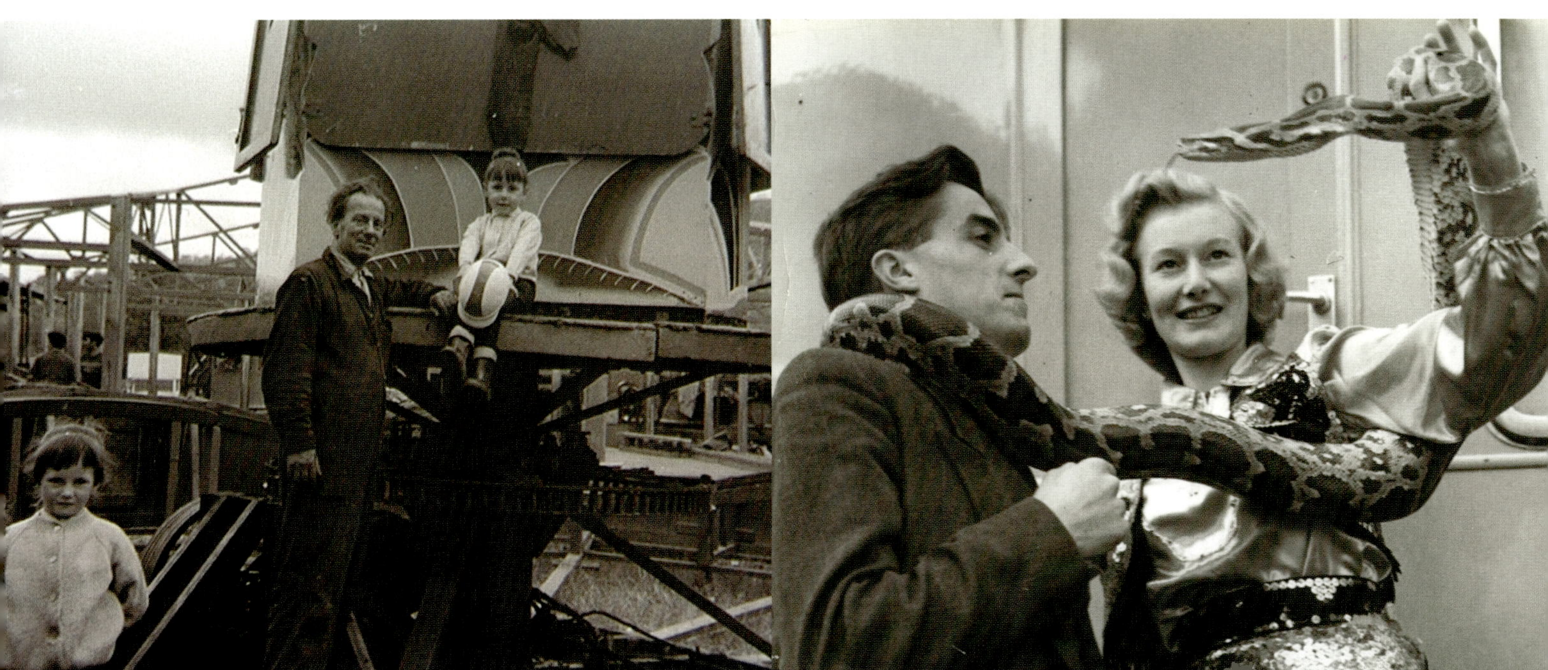

CM: Likewise, England's National Fairground Archive has a collection of photographs that constitute one massive family album. It was founded by Vanessa Toulmin, my fellow scholar of early cinema. Vanessa grew up on the fairground, where any given family was somehow related to every other carney family.

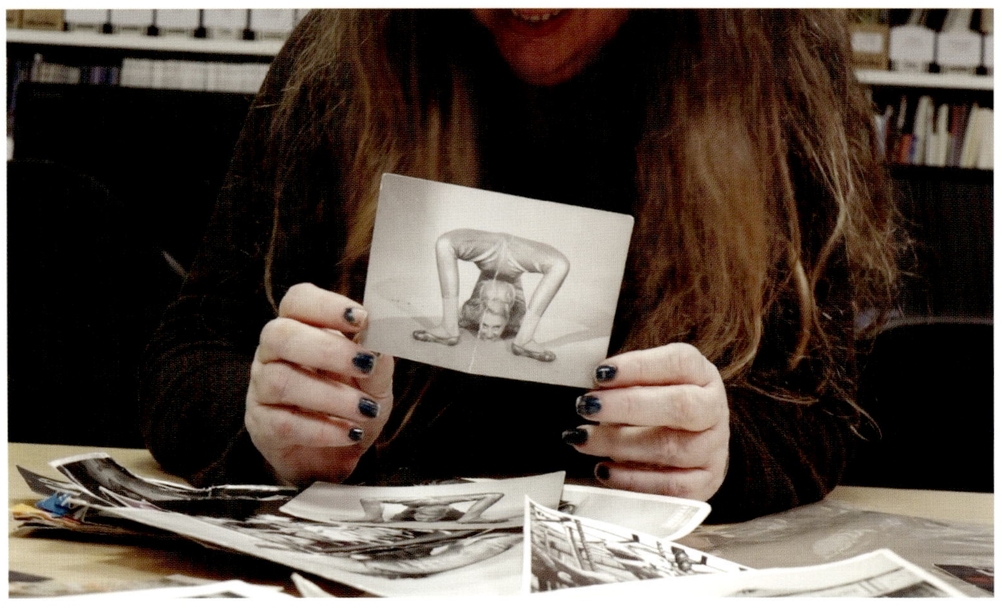

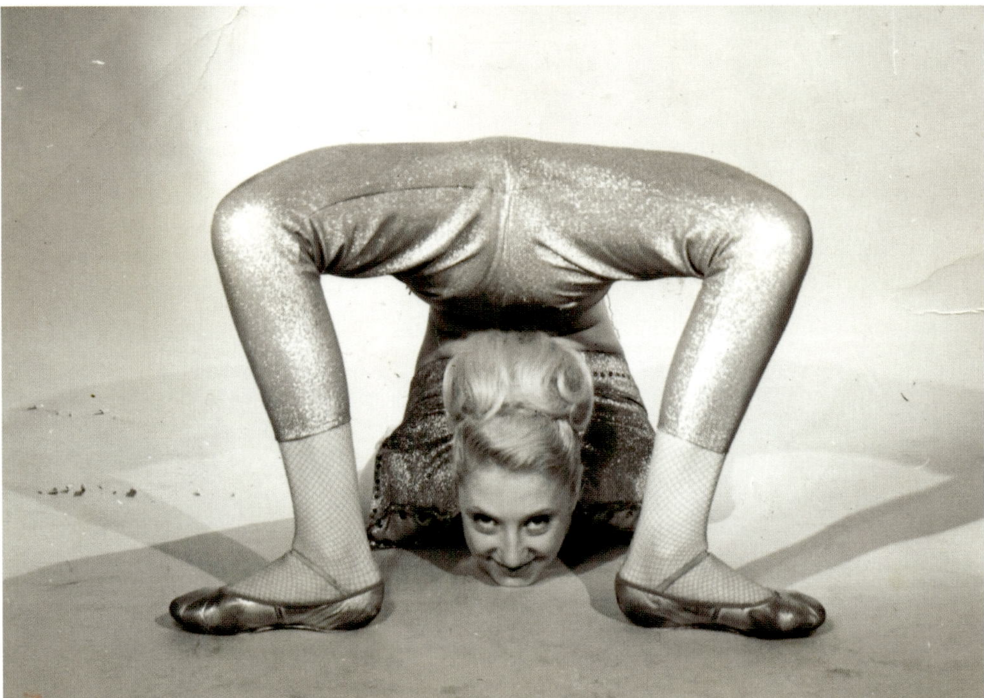

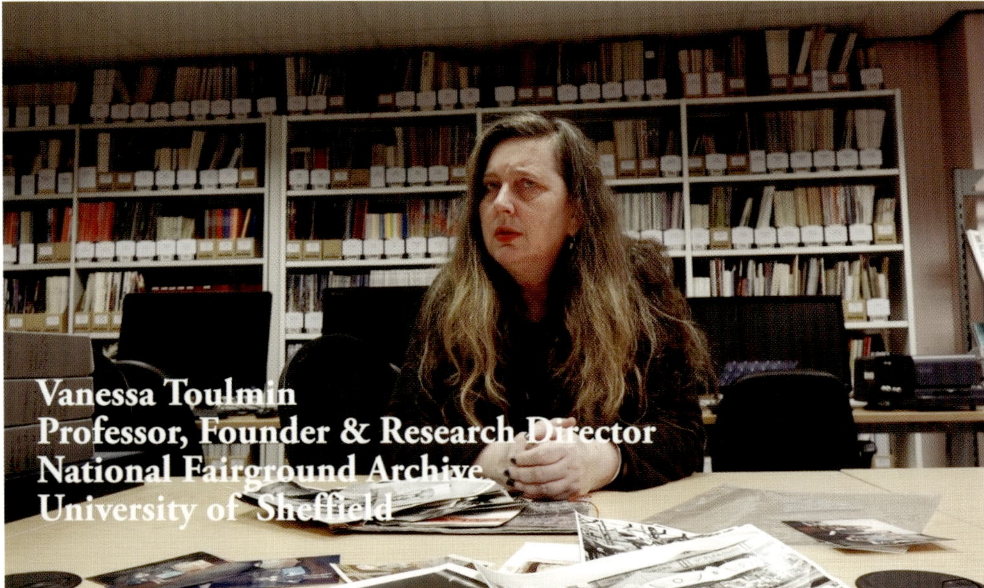

Vanessa Toulmin
Professor, Founder & Research Director
National Fairground Archive,
University of Sheffield

Vanessa Toulmin:
This is my Auntie Brenda, who is my mother's younger sister. And that's when she was in the Moulin Rouge. She was a variety act, a speciality act. My favorite photograph of her is, it's actually on my business card with her doing the crab, which is a very famous contortion routine. I use that picture when I am in difficult positions, which as a university academic could be quite often. These are my own family copies but I've put copies in the archive.

We're five generations on the fairground, which is not a lot by showpeople's standards. Most show people are seven or eight generations.

So, when I set up the archive in 1994 I didn't want it to be about my family. It's about the family that is the show family. But I named it National Fairground Archive because of what was on the birth certificate of traveling show people, which is "No Fixed Abode." They will say "Where are you born?" And it will say, "N. F. A." –No Fixed Abode. That's why I called it the National Fairground Archive. So, it was neither national, neither a fairground nor an archive, but I wanted to call it that because of the No Fixed Abode. So, obviously, now it's changed. I no longer run it. It is now the National Fairground and Circus Archive, but to me it will always be No Fixed Abode.

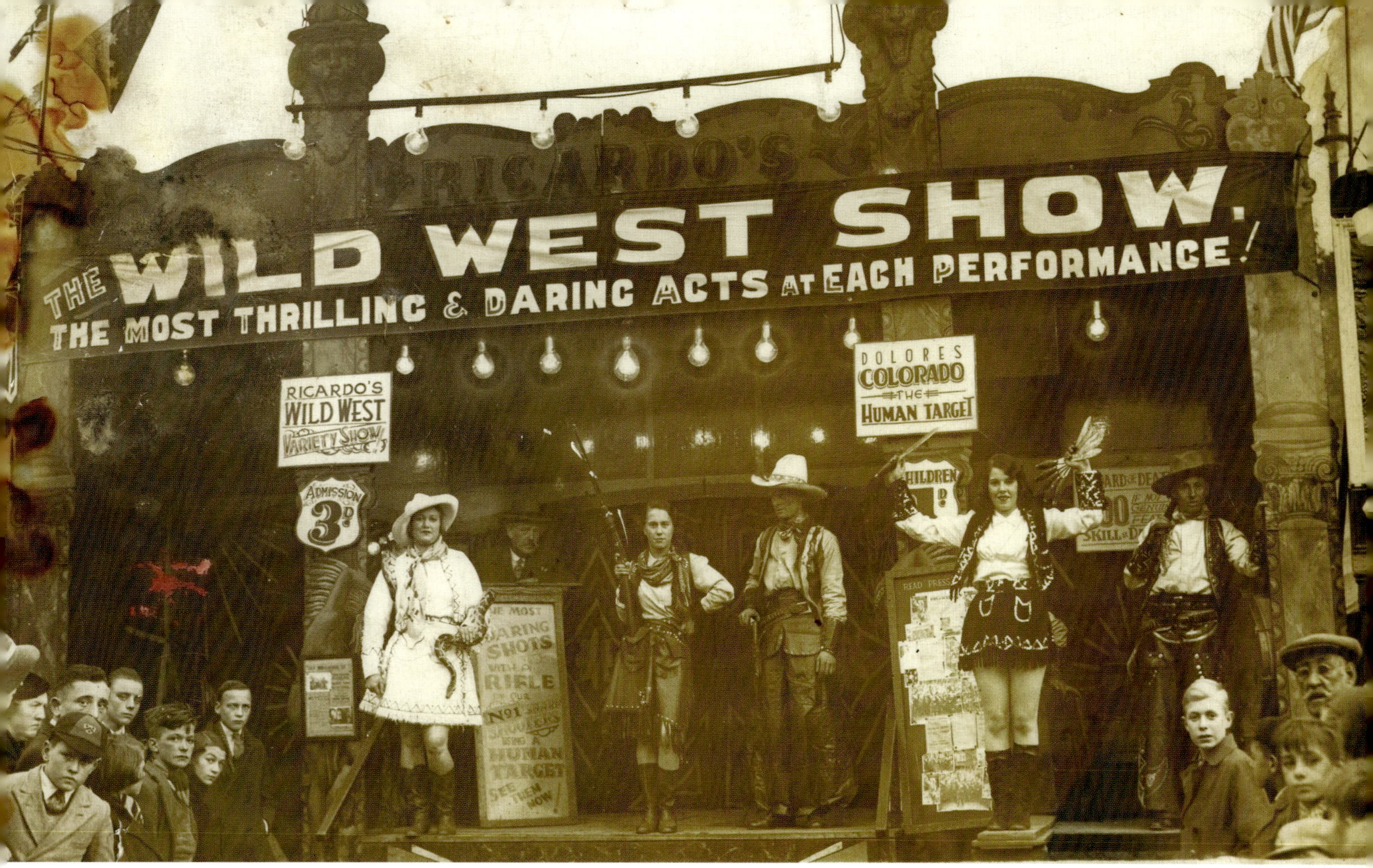

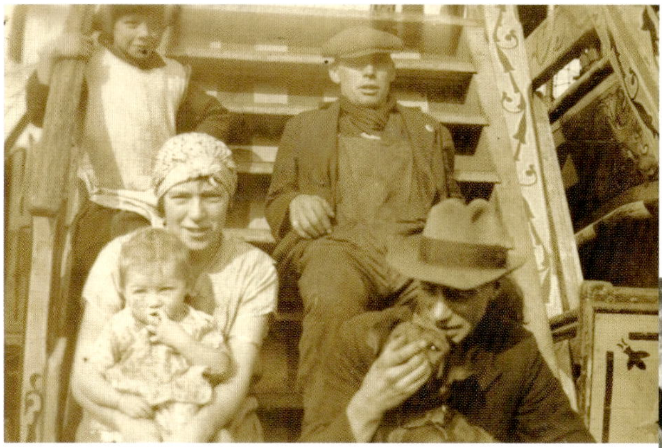

Vanessa: So, it is a collection relating to a group of show people who are connected through kinship, or family, or business, or through shared lifestyles of over 150 years. And that's really my extended family.

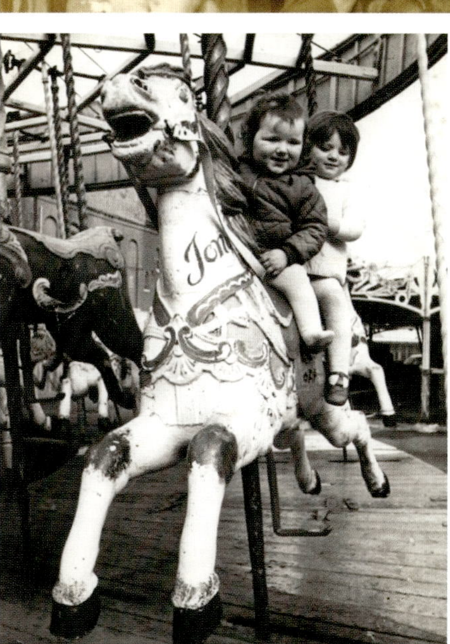

Vanessa Toulmin as baby (left).

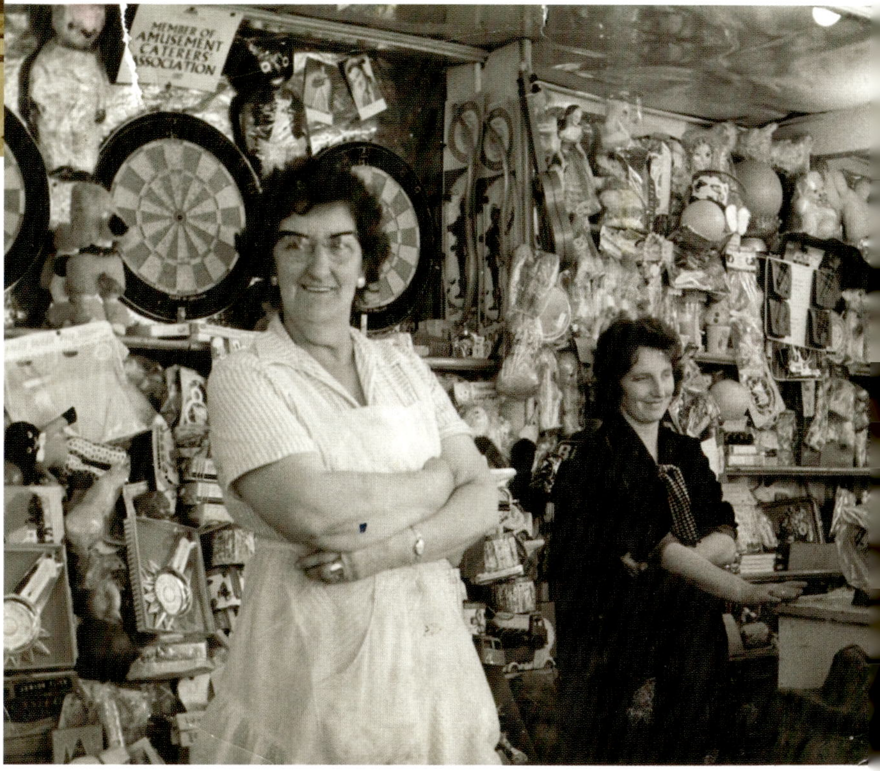

Her grand-mother and mother (right).

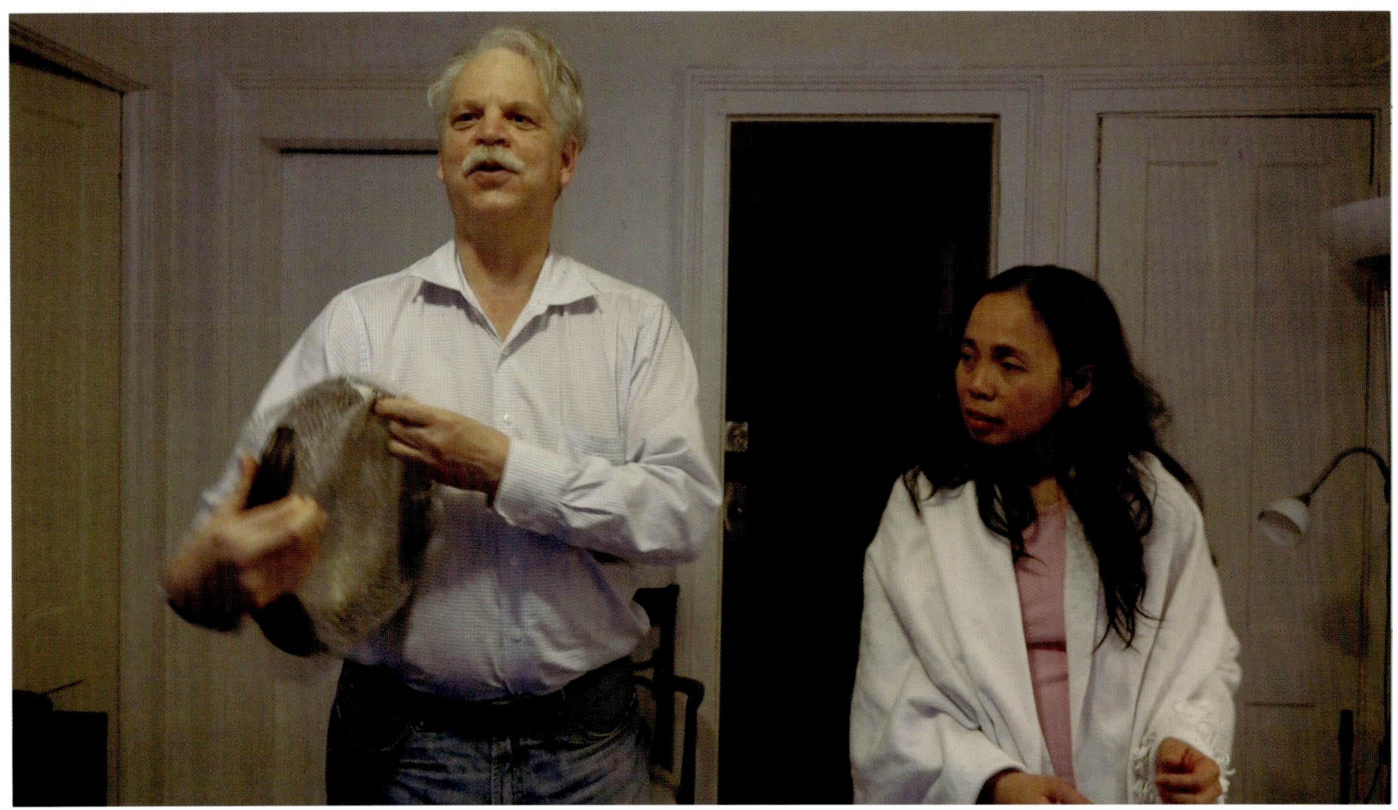

Charlie: So I was given this [photograph] at a certain point by my aunt because this goes to the oldest male Musser in the male line. So, my grandfather, my father… me. Right?

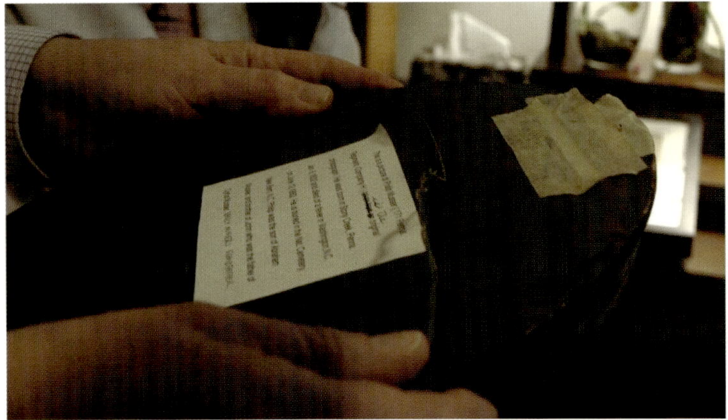

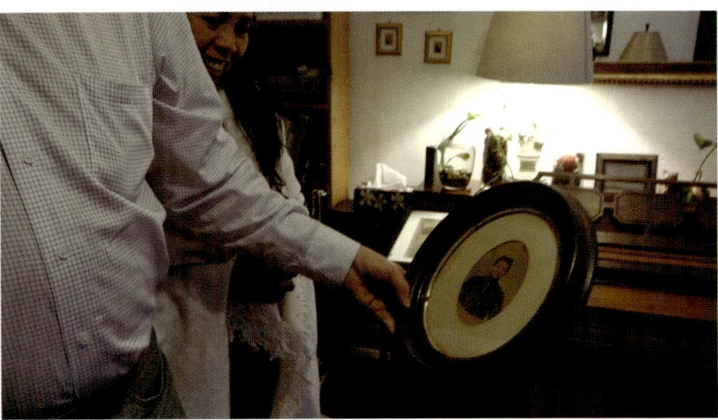

Charlie: [Reading text on the back of the frame] It says, "This is a picture of Philip Musser, of the 171st Pennsylvania regiment, Company H. He was born in Stoney Creek, Pennsylvania, Jan 6th, 1832 and died of fever in Washington, North Carolina on June 12th, 1863. He is buried in the national cemetery in New Bern, North Carolina. Philip was the son of Abraham Musser and brother of John, who was the father of Cyrus Musser." Cyrus Musser is my great grandfather.

So I was given this as the male heir after I got married. And then I had a daughter and then I got a divorce, and they took it back to give to my second cousin John Musser because he just got married and they were sure that he would have a son. But, in fact, he had two daughters. When we had John Carlos, my aunt was actually in the hospital. She was dying. And I put John Carlos in her arms and said I want my photograph back.

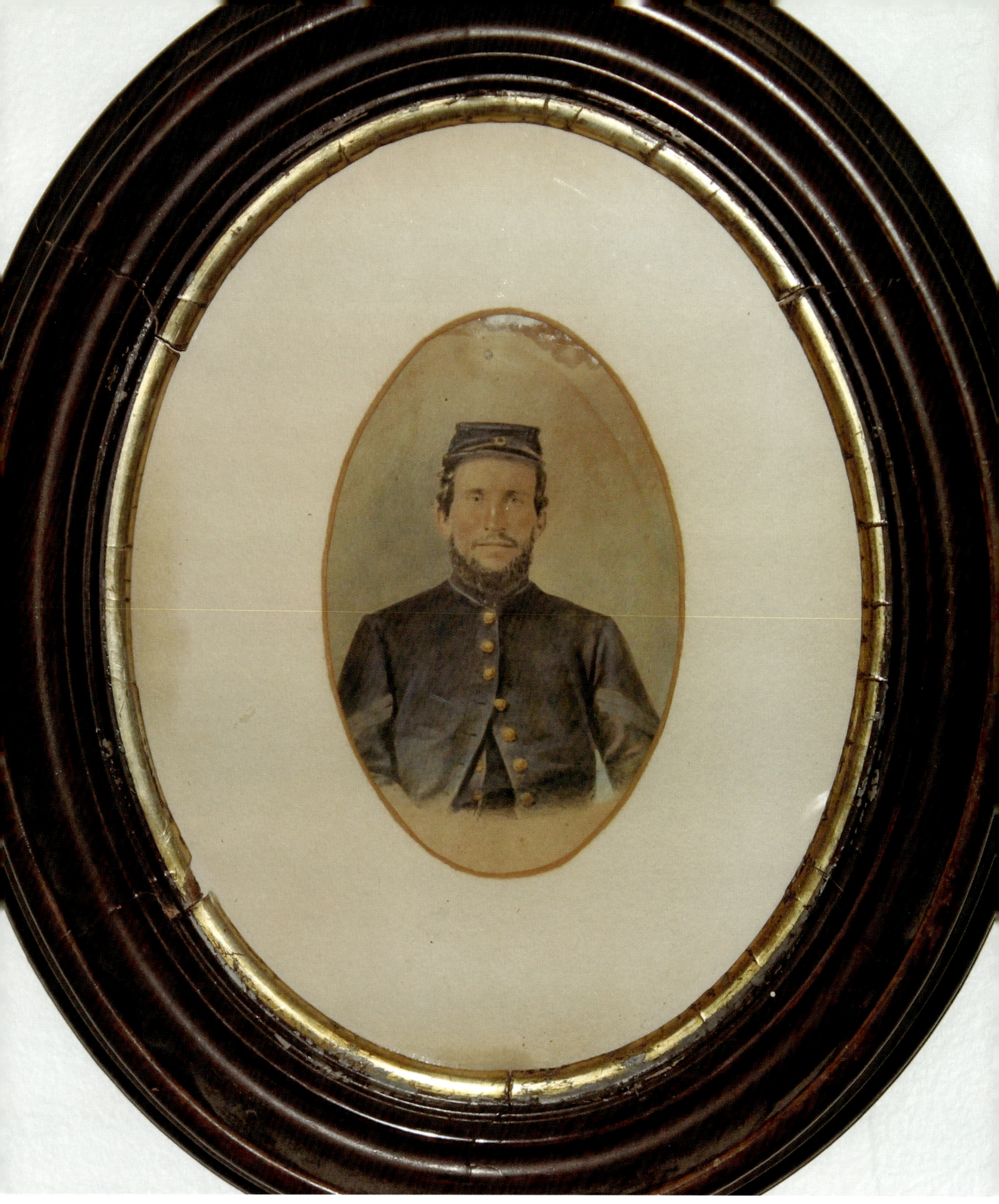

Charlie: When they took it away from me it was like, "You have failed. You have not done what you are supposed to do. And don't you forget it." On the other hand, what if John Carlos had been a girl? Then I might not have been able to reclaim this.

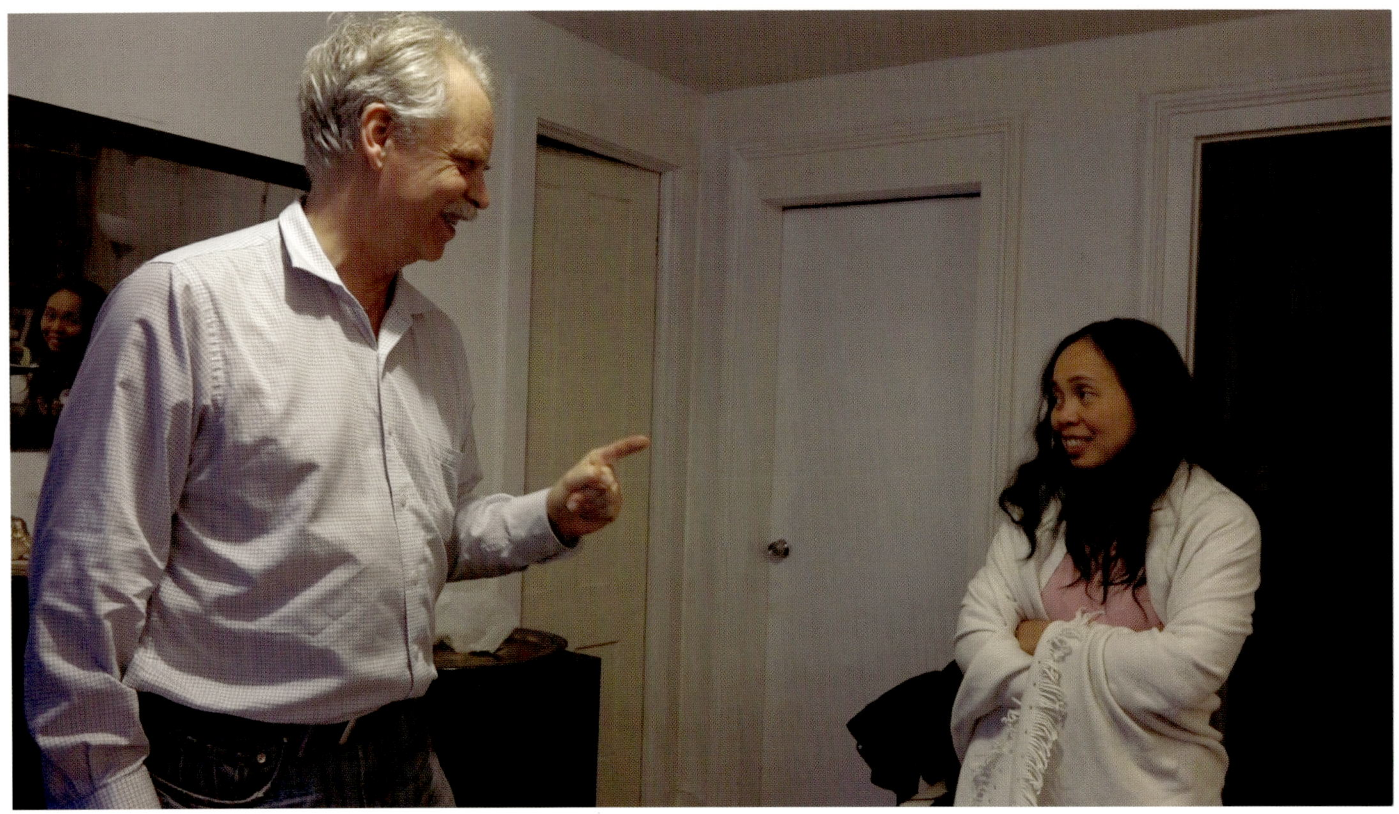

Threese: So, she took it away from John and gave it to you?

Charlie: No. It never got to John because he still had to prove himself. But it was taken back from me, and she held on to it in trust.

Threese: Alright. So, funny.

The ways in which parents (or an aunt) encourage their children to reproduce—and renew the family album, so to speak—are worthy of a monographic study. In our family it was always clear that certain items such as silverware went to the daughters (or nieces). Other possessions were to be handed on to sons or nephews. Moreover, the older generation is always looking ahead. After all, they do not want family heirlooms to end up in a flea market. I had had Philip Musser's portrait for a number of years, but my aunt felt it had become time to think of its long-term future. Obviously, such a situation can become fraught. John Carlos is the only great-great-great grandson of Philip's brother, John Musser, who bears Musser as his last name.

My Aunt Nancy must have had many conversations with her cousin Virginia "Ginger" Musser about what to do with Philip Musser's photograph. They were very close, and Ginger would have looked out for the interests of her nephew and my second cousin John Musser. Much later, I discovered that my aunt had made a somewhat sleazy reproduction of Philip Musser's portrait, which she had no doubt intended to give me as a kind of consolation prize. What the photograph means to those who have held it in trust has doubtlessly varied. If it testifies to those principles for which Philip gave his life, then which principles? Justice? The end of slavery? Racial equality? A better world? Since the specifics of Philip's beliefs are unknown, I can only look directly into his eyes and reflect on what they are for me.

In making Our Family Album *I became intrigued by the recurrence of certain types of images. The one of me, John Carlos and Threese on the following page, taken in Moalboal, Cebu Province, recalls the one of my parents and me when I was about the same age. This is a classic image of parents with their first born, but these two also quietly announce: here is the heir apparent of Philip Musser's portrait. Photographs are perhaps the only things that have been successfully passed down to me from my great-great grandfather, John Musser.*

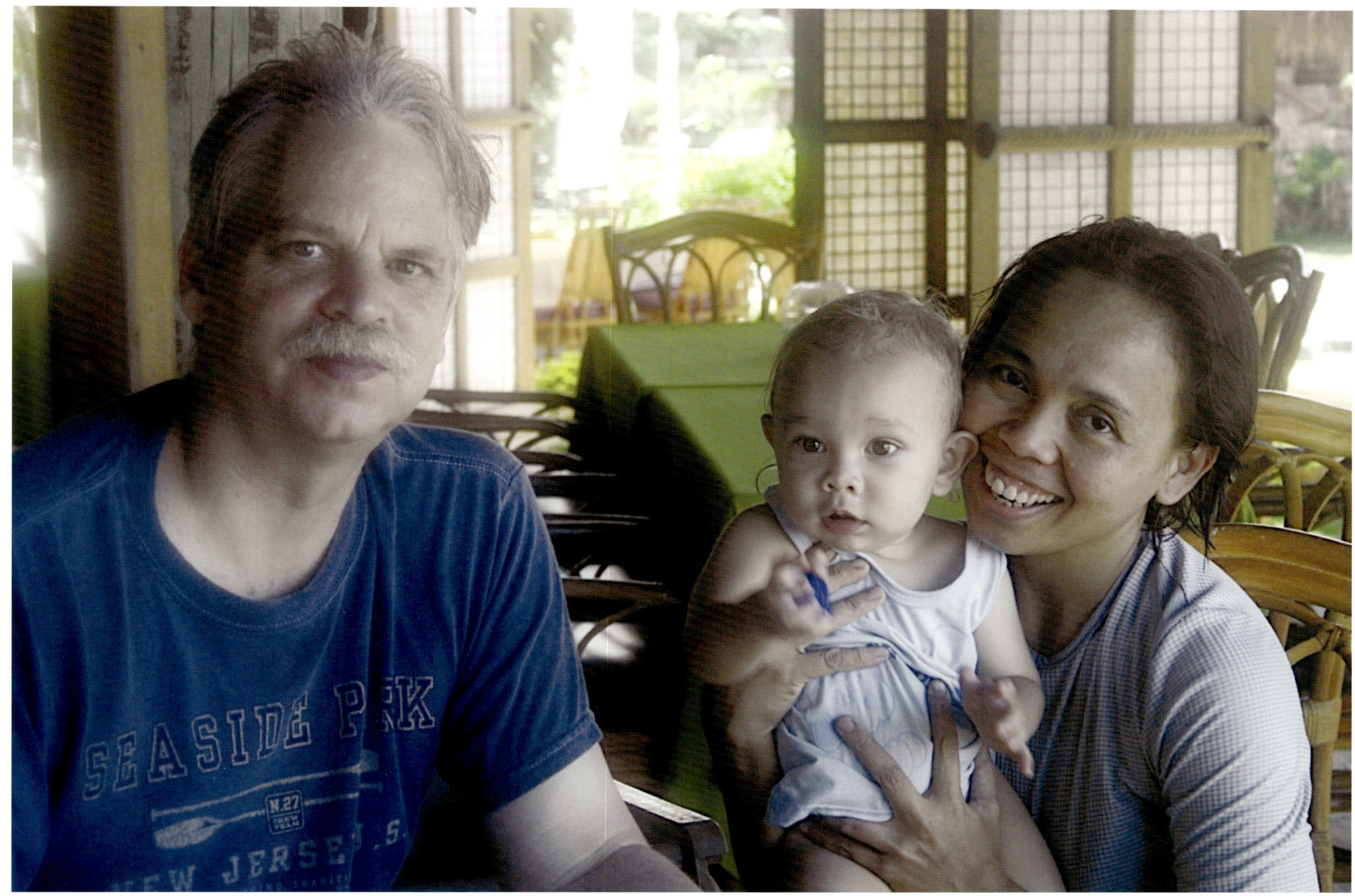

Most Americans don't even realize that the Philippines was a colony of the United States for 50 years. It is a remarkable instance of historical amnesia. A critical moment in the history of our two countries was the brutal Philippine-American War of 1899-1902. The local population had essentially achieved its independence from Spain, only to suffer a brutal war of re-colonization by the Americans—a military power which often left "burned-out villages and horribly mutilated bodies" in its wake. This war provided source material for a group of highly sanitized and romanticized filmed reenactments made by the Edison Manufacturing Company, which had previously produced The May Irwin Kiss. *Nick Deocampo uses these films as a starting point to explore some of the complexities of this relationship.*

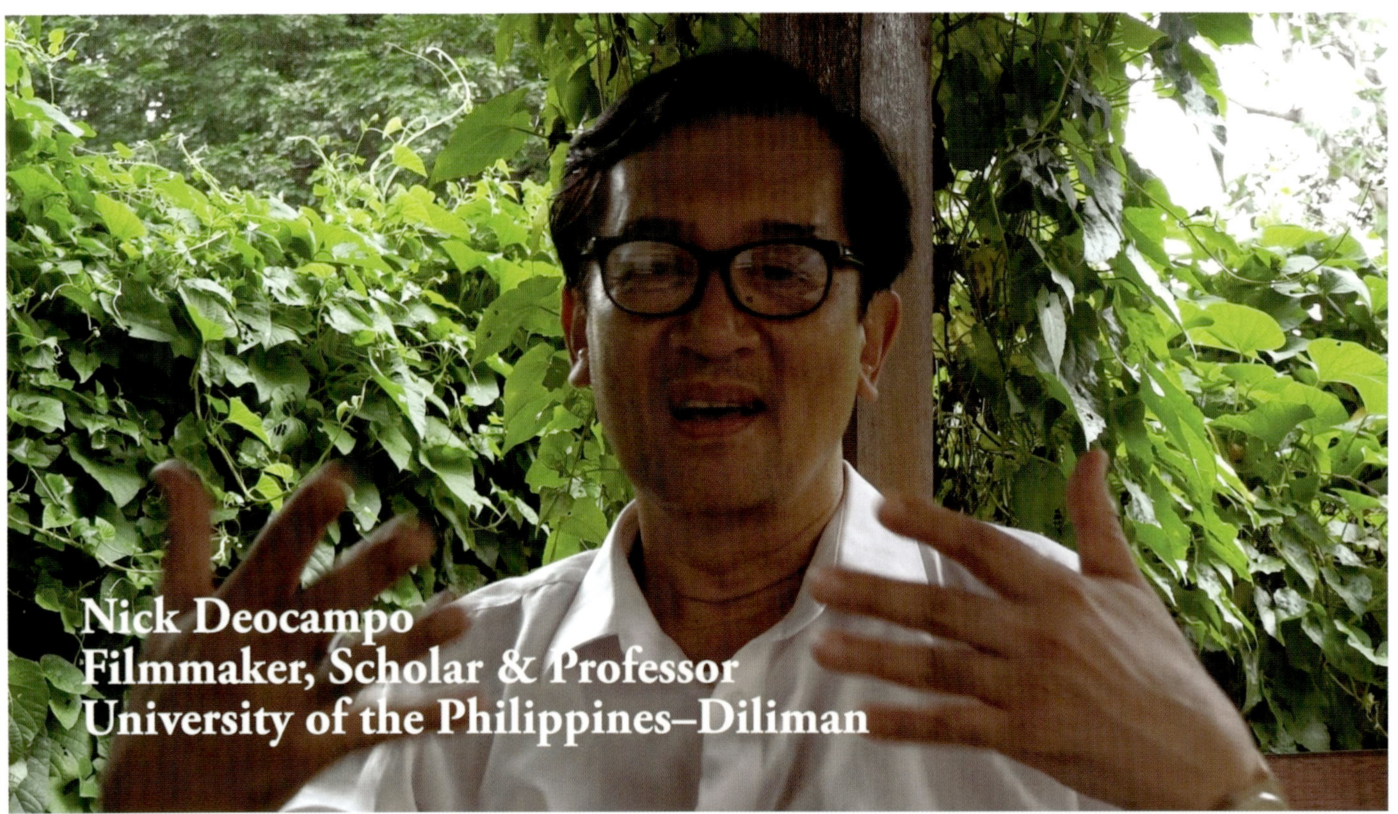

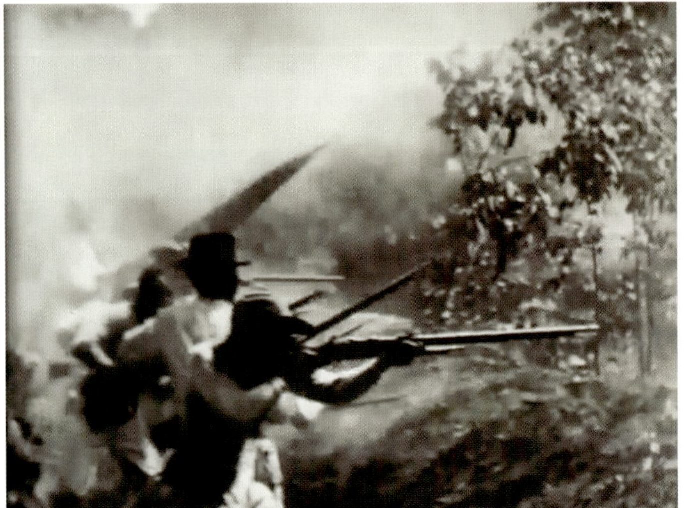

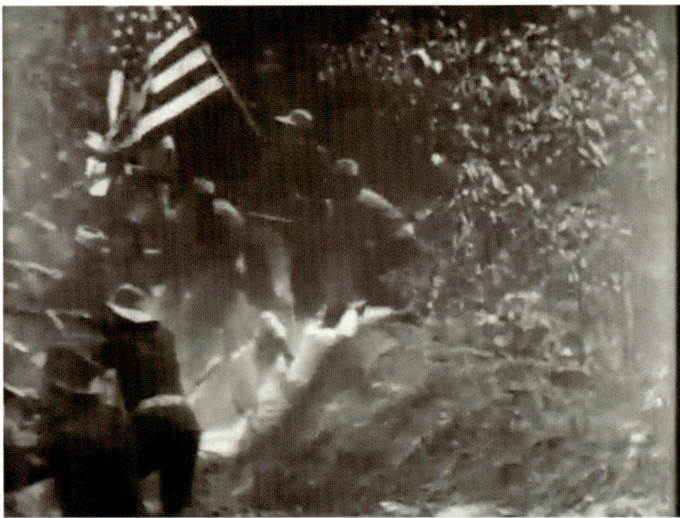

Nick Deocampo: The initial encounter between Americans and Filipinos was really a traumatic one and it resulted in war. The Edison films were actually the testaments to this traumatic encounter. The subject matter is war. The erasure is complete and totalizing. They are defeated, the natives—meaning the Filipinos, who are not even Filipinos because they are being acted out by African Americans. So, there is this double denial of identity and personality.

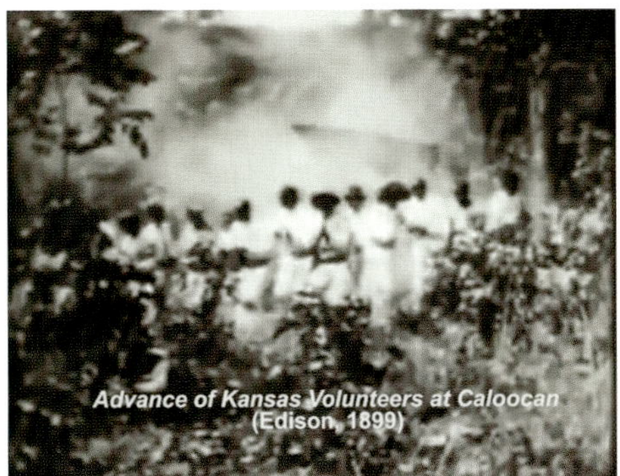

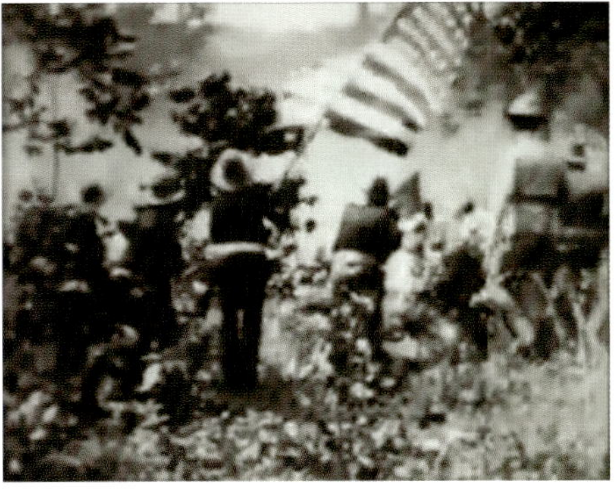

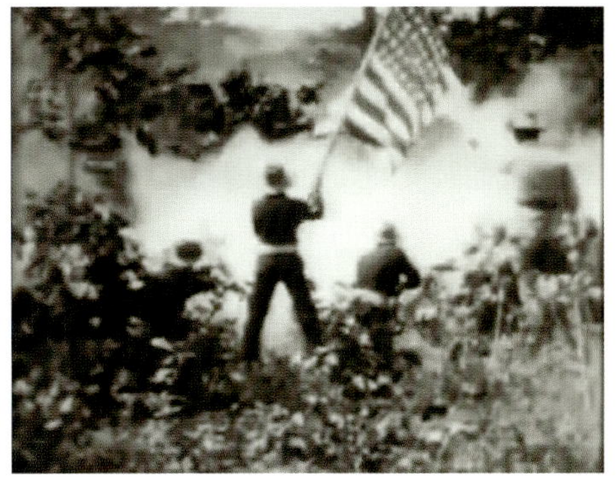

Nick: The Filipinos whom you see in *Advance of Kansas Volunteers at Caloocan,* dominate the entire cinematic screen at the beginning of that less than a minute-long film. At the very end of that one-shot, one-scene film we get a total reversal of who gets to own the cinematic screen—and that is the flag waving Americans. They invade the shot, coming from the position of the camera, so that the I meaning capital I, letter I meaning. the subjective "I" of the eye of the camera is very apparently that of an imperialist onlooker. Reified by that camera that is pointed towards the very narrative that unfolds in less than a minute. So the trauma is overwhelming and horrifying for someone like me who is very sensitive to the readings of these narratives.

That was the beginning of the relationship. It was a shaky, rocky relationship between two people. But can nothing redeem that? A relationship between an American and, let's say, a Filipina, going into the sacred ritual of marriage, I think is very redeeming.

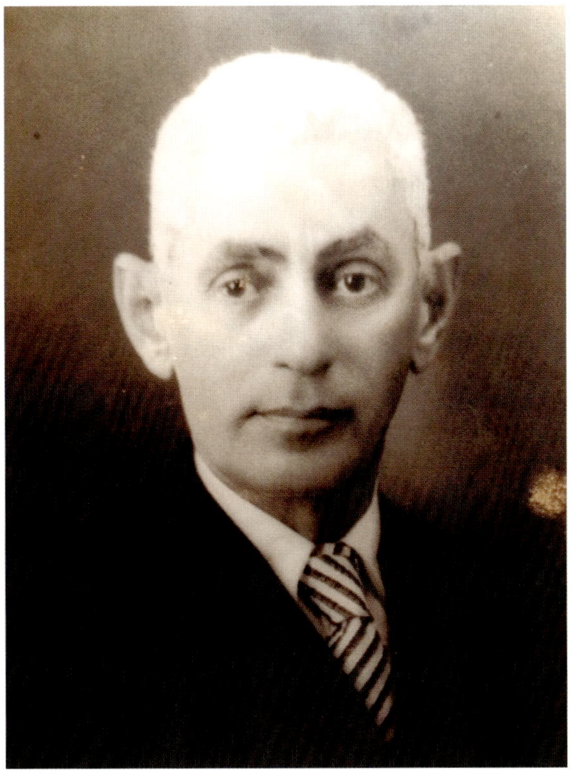

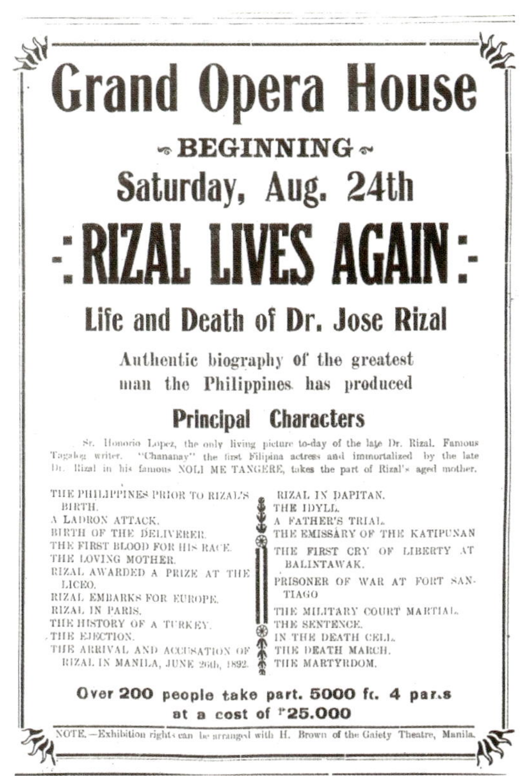

Grand Opera House

⚬ BEGINNING ⚬

Saturday, Aug. 24th

∹ RIZAL LIVES AGAIN ∹

Life and Death of Dr. Jose Rizal

Authentic biography of the greatest
man the Philippines. has produced

Principal Characters

Sr. Honorio Lopez, the only living picture to-day of the late Dr. Rizal. Famous Tagalog writer. "Chananay" the first Filipina actress and immortalized by the late Dr. Rizal in his famous NOLI ME TANGERE, takes the part of Rizal's aged mother.

THE PHILIPPINES PRIOR TO RIZAL'S BIRTH.
A LADRON ATTACK.
BIRTH OF THE DELIVERER.
THE FIRST BLOOD FOR HIS RACE.
THE LOVING MOTHER.
RIZAL AWARDED A PRIZE AT THE LICEO.
RIZAL EMBARKS FOR EUROPE.
RIZAL IN PARIS.
THE HISTORY OF A TURKEY.
THE EJECTION.
THE ARRIVAL AND ACCUSATION OF RIZAL IN MANILA, JUNE 26th, 1892.
RIZAL IN DAPITAN.
THE IDYLL.
A FATHER'S TRIAL.
THE EMISSARY OF THE KATIPUNAN
THE FIRST CRY OF LIBERTY AT BALINTAWAK.
PRISONER OF WAR AT FORT SANTIAGO
THE MILITARY COURT MARTIAL.
THE SENTENCE.
IN THE DEATH CELL.
THE DEATH MARCH.
THE MARTYRDOM.

**Over 200 people take part. 5000 ft. 4 par.s
at a cost of ₱25.000**

NOTE.—Exhibition rights can be arranged with H. Brown of the Gaiety Theatre, Manila.

CM: Our situation reminds me of Edward Meyer Gross, who came to the Philippines in 1902 as an army nurse, just as the war ended. In Manila he met and married Titay Molina, a star of the Zarzuela Theater—the Sarah Bernhardt of her country. Not unlike Bernhardt who was making early feature films such as *Queen Elizabeth*, Gross and Molina together made the first feature films in the Philippines. They began in 1912 with *The Life and Death of Dr. Jose Rizal*—an historical drama focusing on the national hero who had died fighting for independence. Molina played Rizal's lover, who mourns his death and then flees into the mountains to fight the Spanish forces.

Nick: These are two opposing things. One is the trauma caused by war. The other is the love that can be generated between people. So those are the two extremes. In between we can find cinema. Which is a cultural bond between us two. It was a heritage we got from a colonial experience, but the significant thing is what did we make out of it. Within the century, when Hollywood dominated our consciousness and our way of life in this country, we turned cinema which is otherwise foreign, colonial, international into something which is native. We made a national culture out of cinema. What do you make of that? Between war and love is desire brought about by cinema.

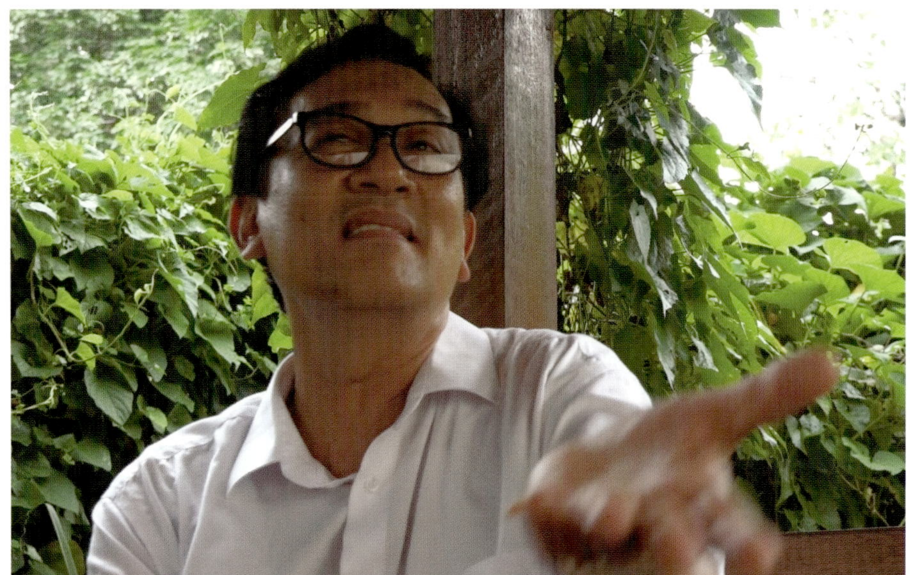

Nick: Pardon me but I am still the kind of person…people will laugh at me, but I am still fantasizing I can find my male lover somewhere out there. Are you out there? And, you know, the American fantasy is there. Why not?

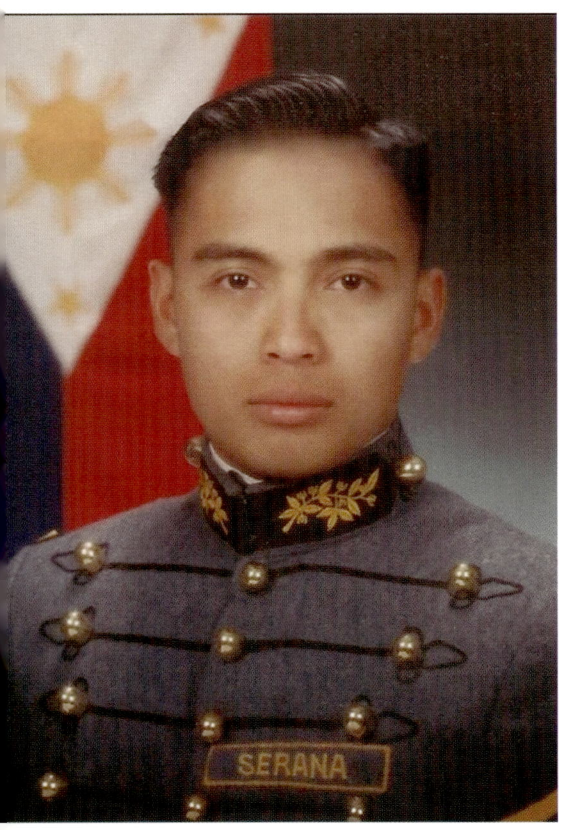

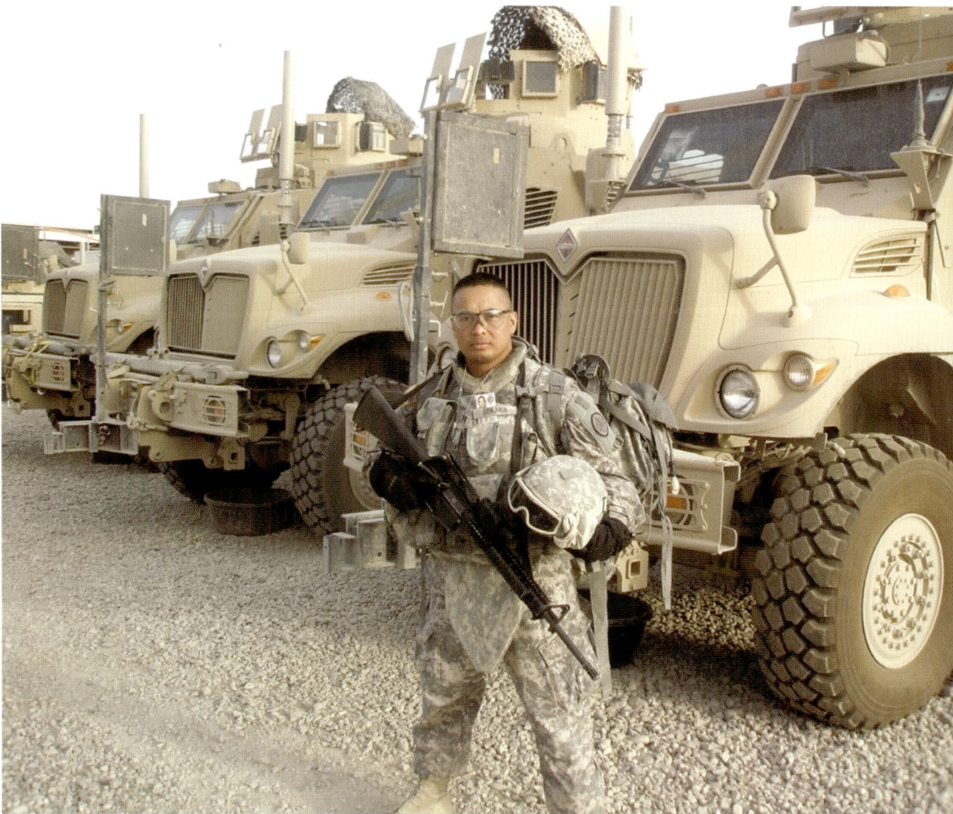

TS: Your Tito Dada also embraced the American fantasy. After serving as an officer in the Armed Forces of the Philippines he later became an enlisted man in the U.S. Army. In the process, he brought Binhi, age six, to the U.S. as his son.

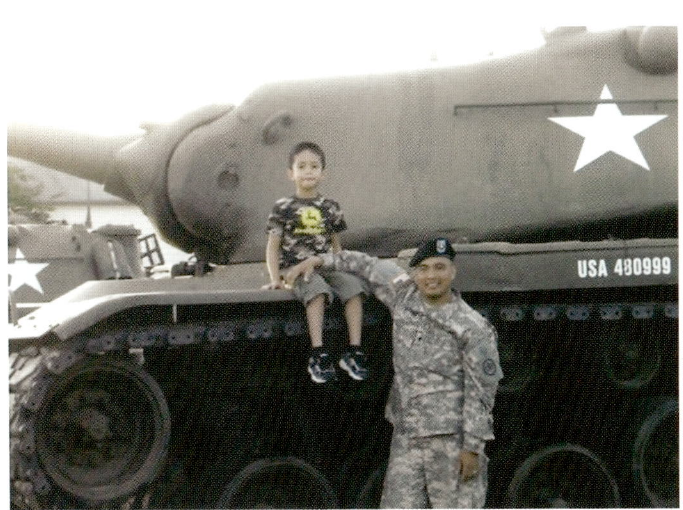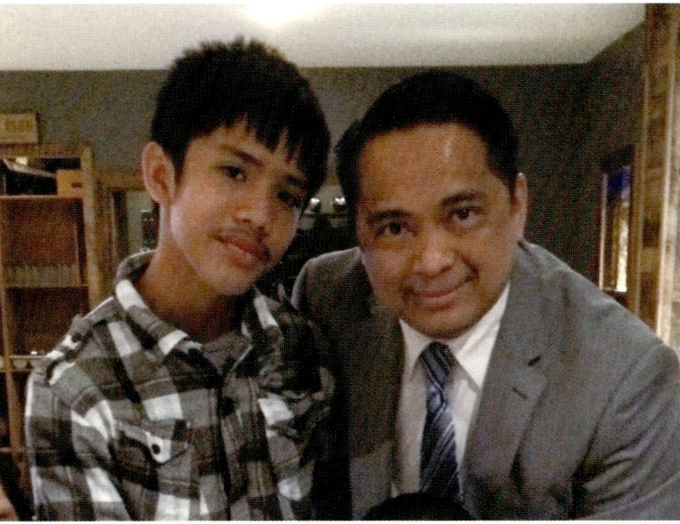

CM: But as he prepared to go to Iraq he sent Binhi back to the Philippines. Your uncle was eventually discharged, struggling with Post Traumatic Stress Disorder and other maladies. Binhi only came back to the U.S. six years later. Photos and Facebook postings can be deceptive: Theirs was a rocky relationship.

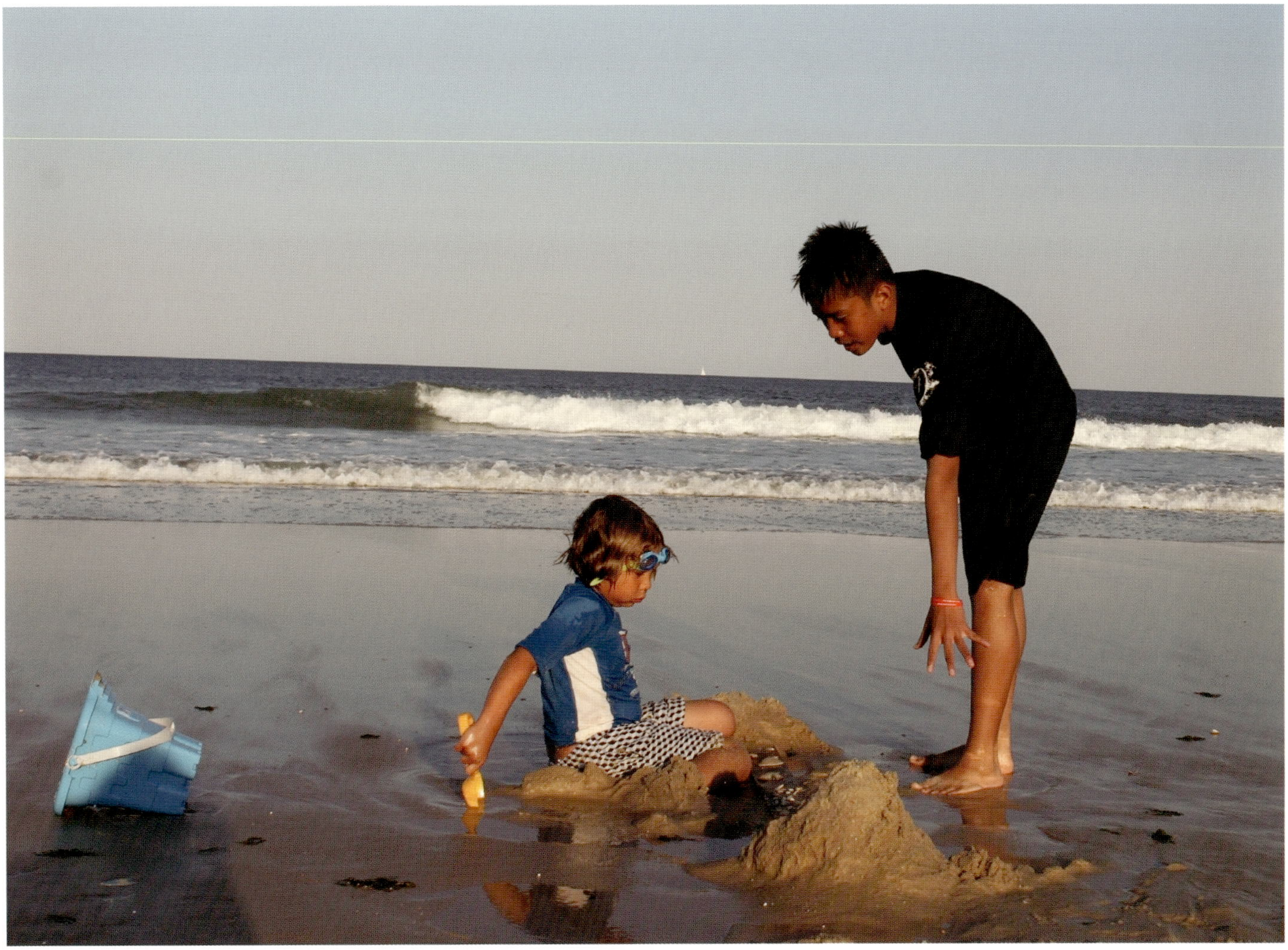

TS: So, when Binhi joined us at the Jersey shore it was a relief for both of them. Yet he just made our vacation that much better. After all, you had always wanted a brother. For several years, in fact, you had had an imaginary younger brother. It was an amusing flight of imagination, except that it got me into trouble a couple of times when you proudly told strangers that he had been left at home—alone.

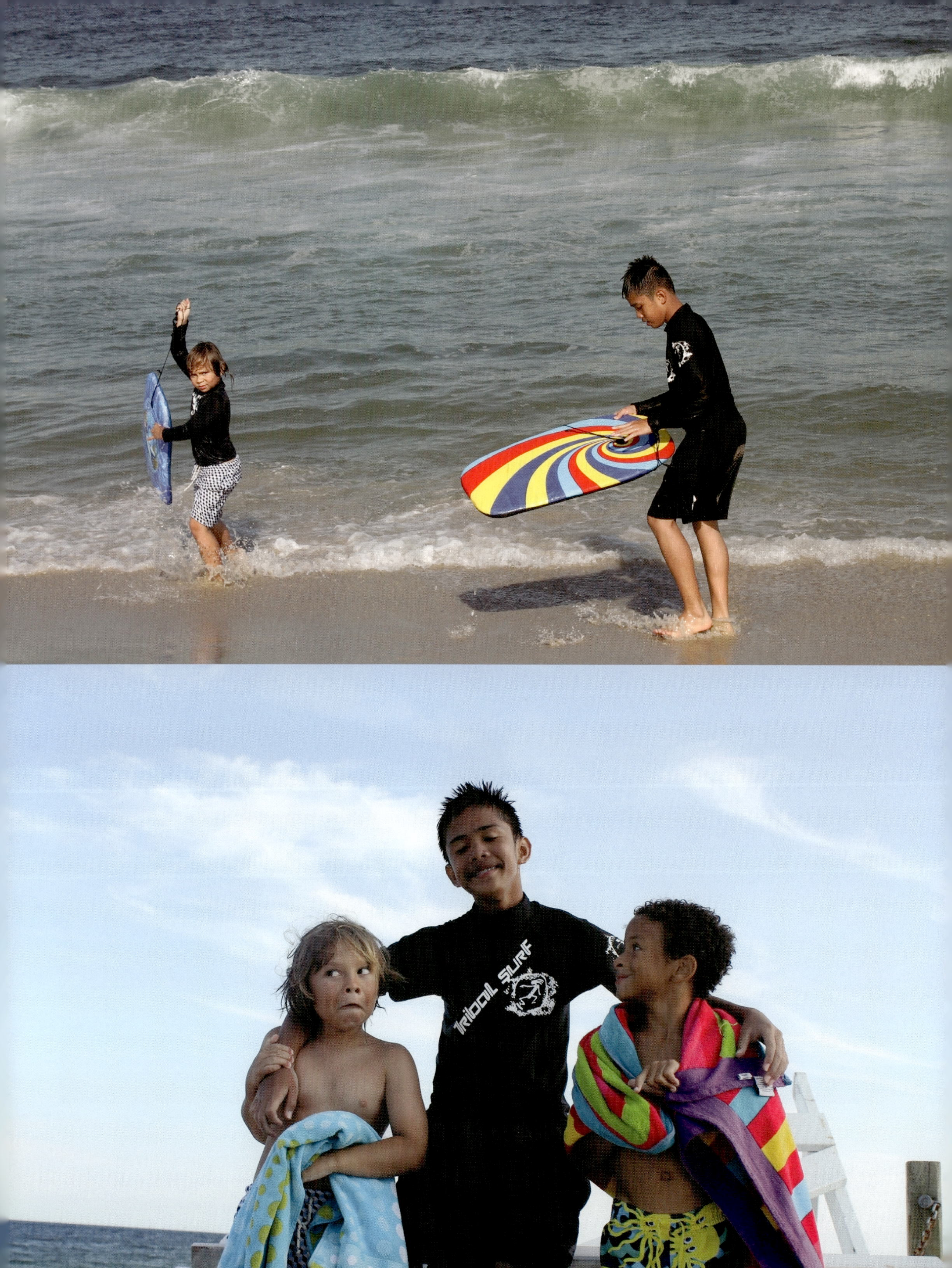

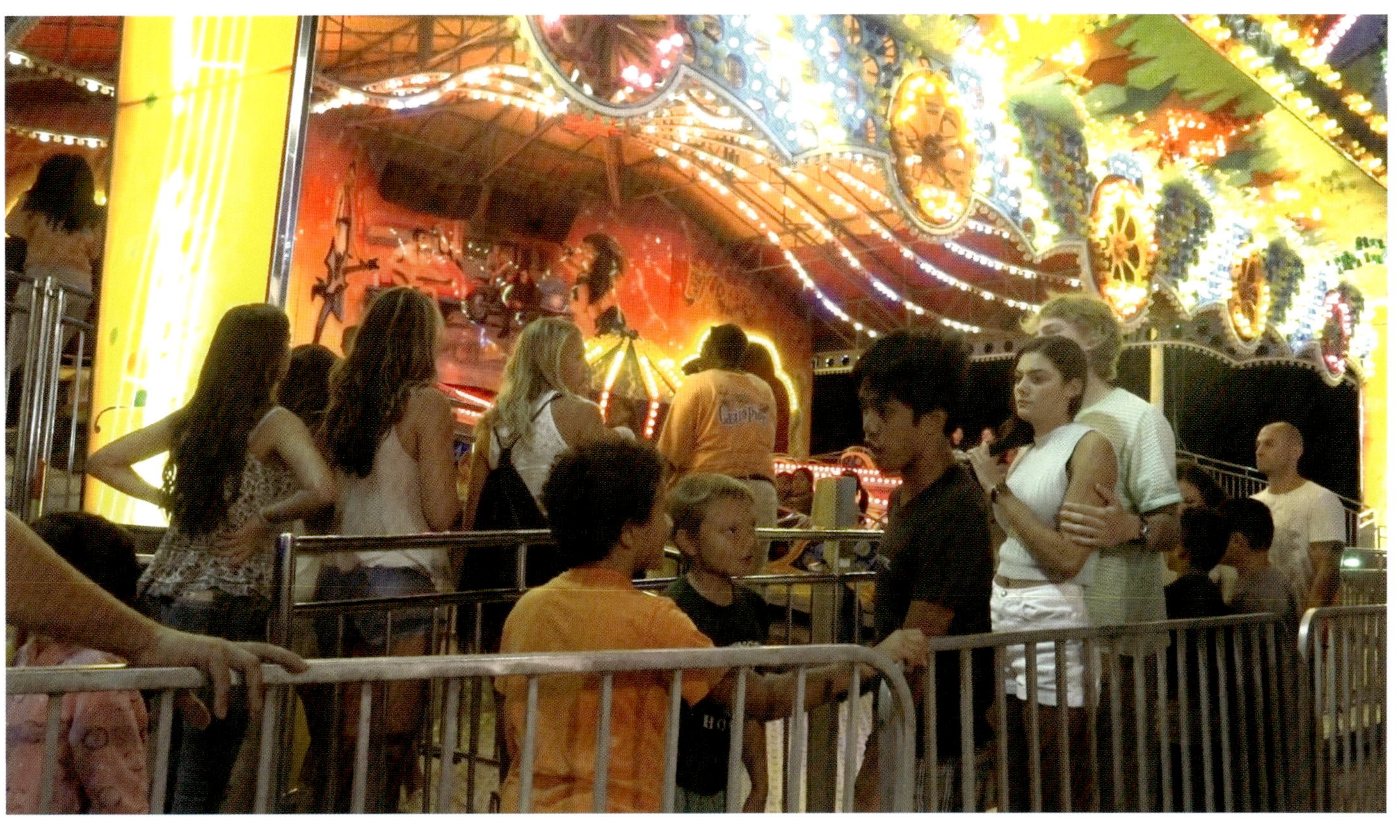

TS: Binhi joined us again the following summer.

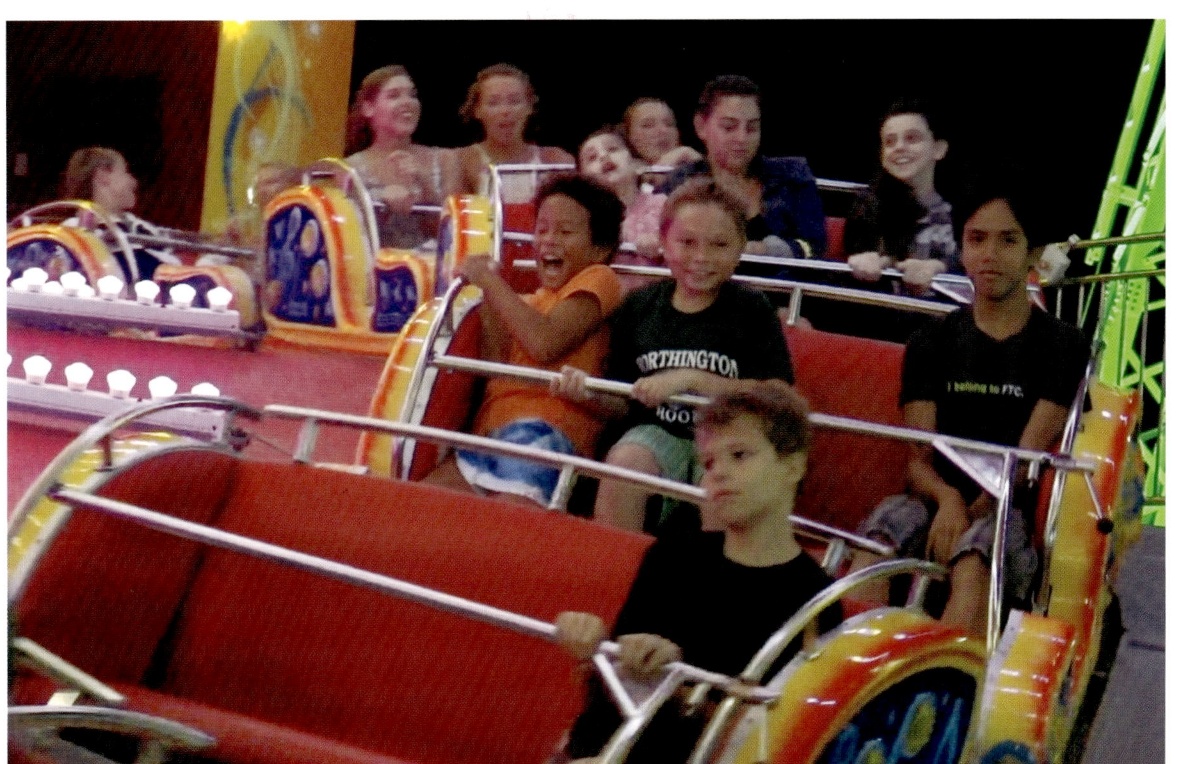

Binhi Serana: You know, I rode that six times already. Six times in my life. So, if you put me there again, I'm just going to fall asleep.

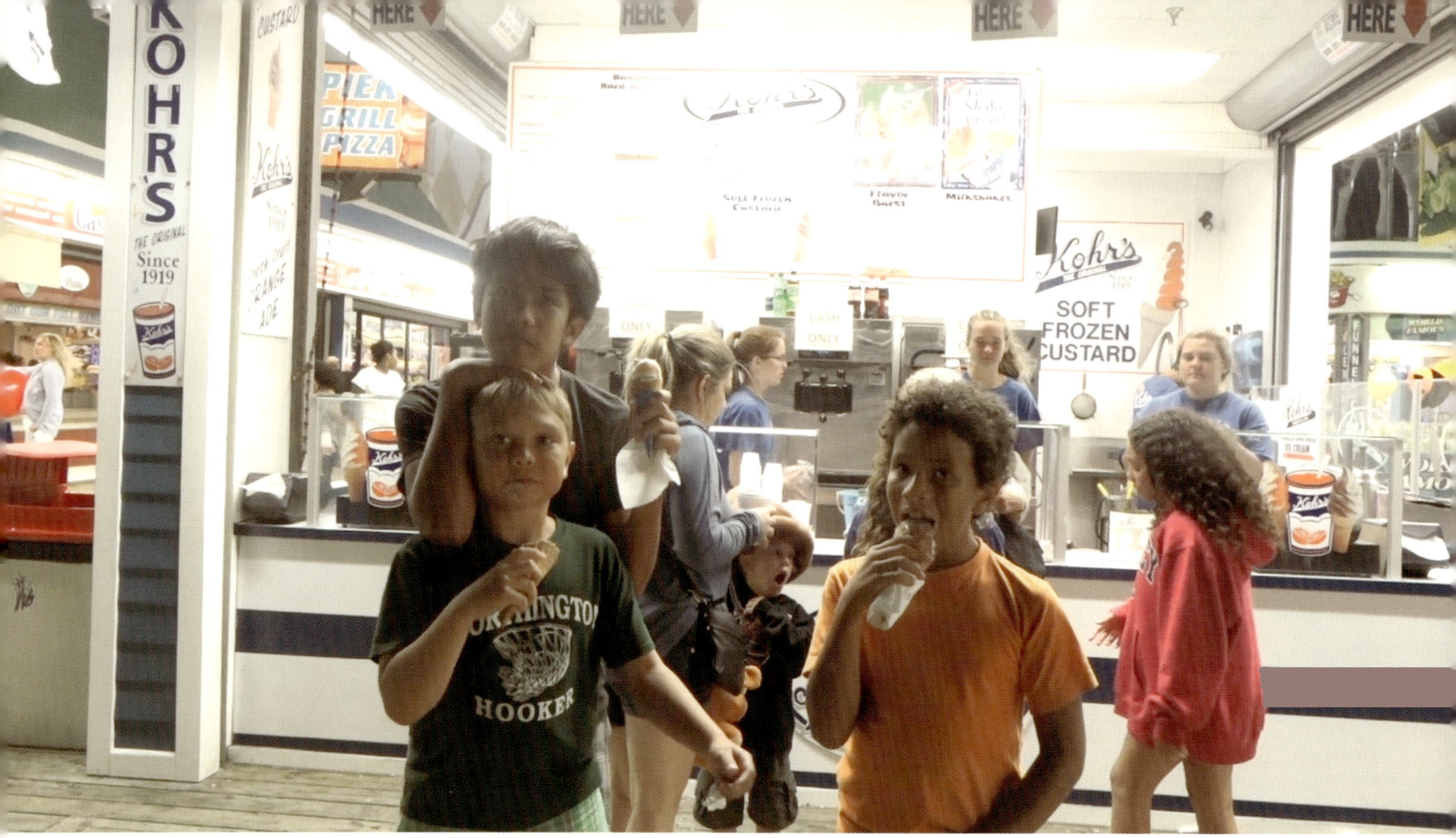

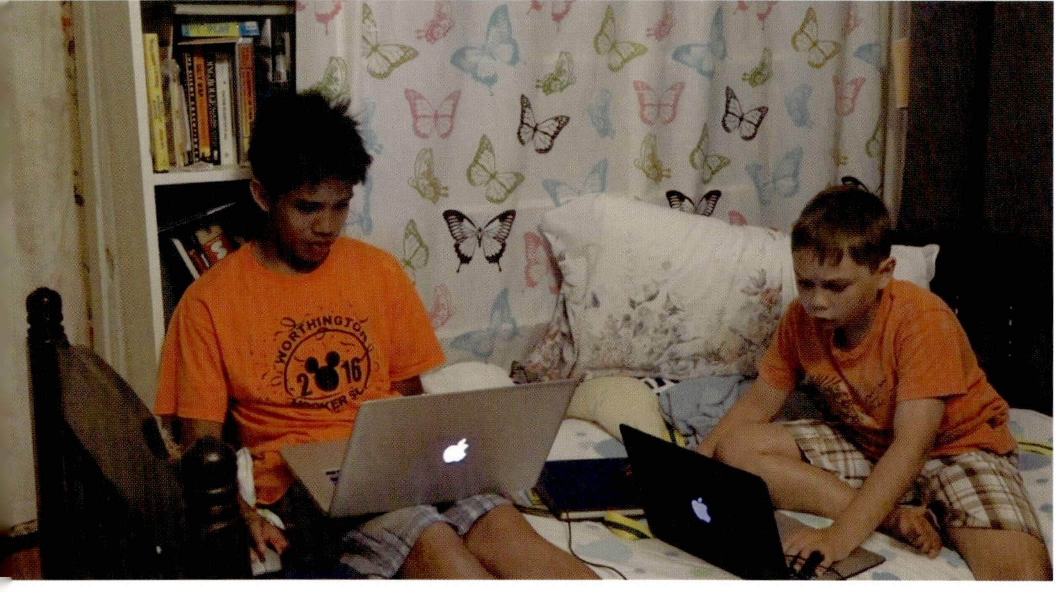

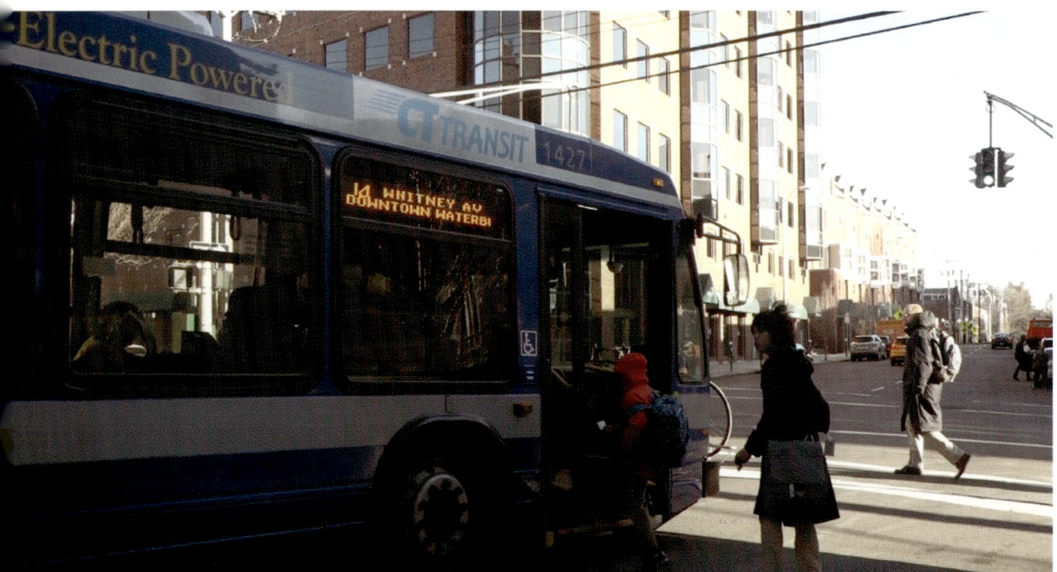

John Carlos: This is hilarious, Who grenaded you?

Bihni: No one grenaded me yet.

John Carlos: Yes, I saw an explosion.

Binhi: Not me!

TS: With your Tito Dada preparing to send Binhi back to the Philippines yet again, we intervened. And so Binhi became your full-time brother. The two of you even went to school together on the bus.

Charlie: Okay, guys. Have a good day!

John Carlos: I love you Dad.

Bringing Binhi back into our family was a step towards repairing a spiritual wound that I had created some eight years earlier, when Threese came to the United States and we left him behind. At first, I had managed to be blind to the offence, but its severity had become steadily more apparent over time.

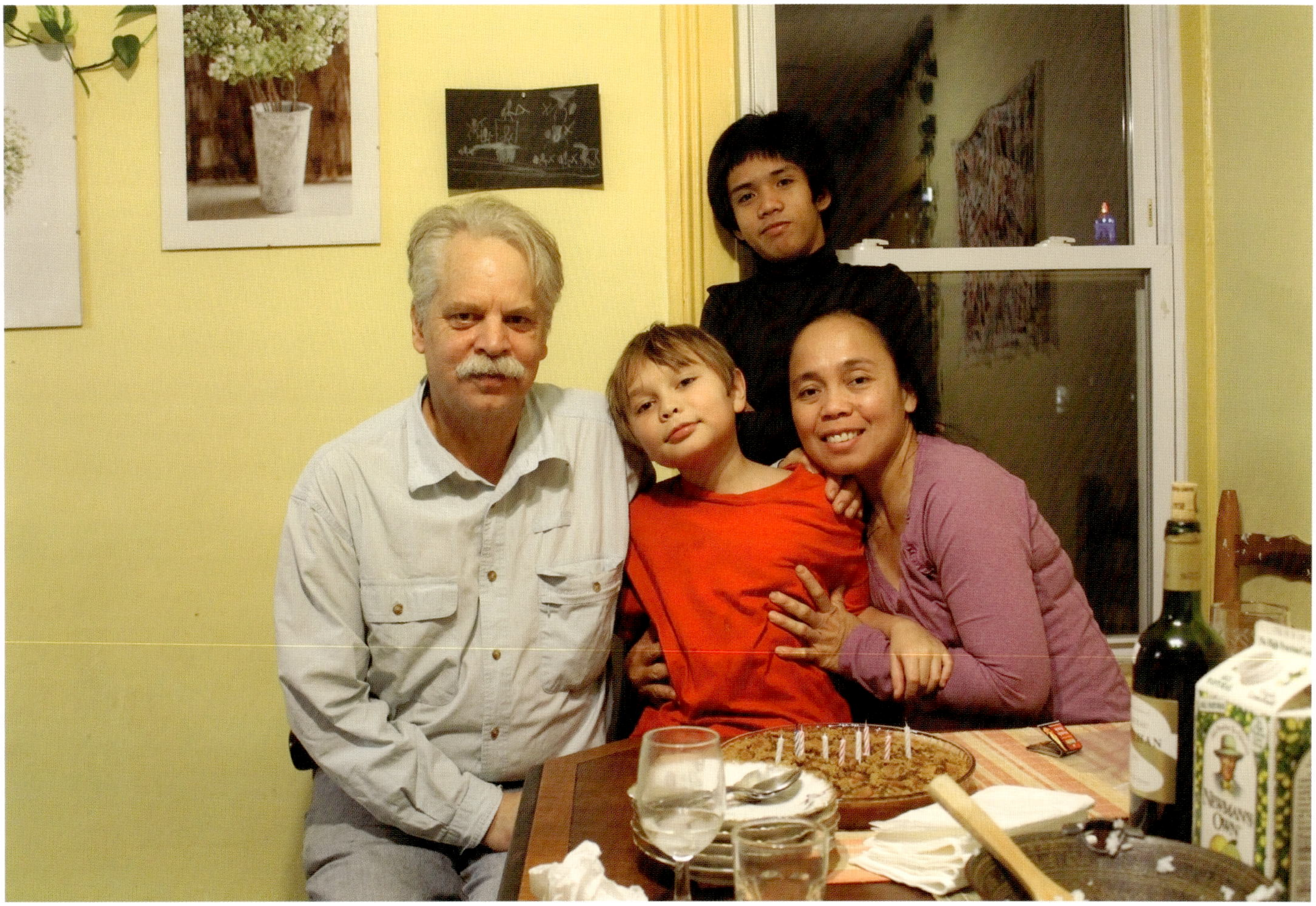

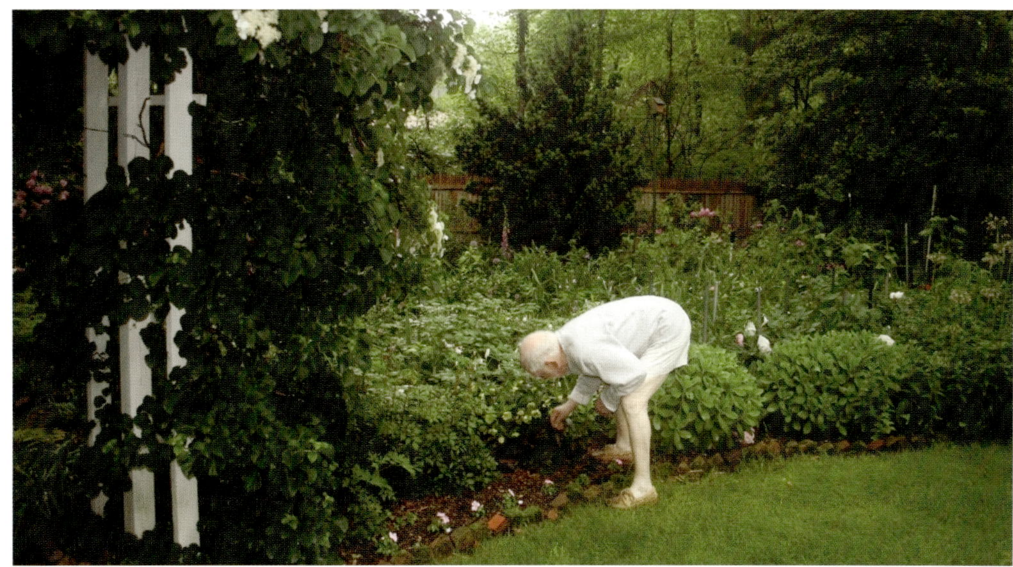

Growing up I spent part of every summer with my Aunt Nancy and Uncle Ferd. I always felt more in tune with their way of life than that of my parents. For instance, my Aunt ate blueberry pie for breakfast whenever she felt like it! Later, when my mother moved to South Carolina with her new husband, Hannah and I (later with Threese and John Carlos) spent our summer vacations and family holidays with them.

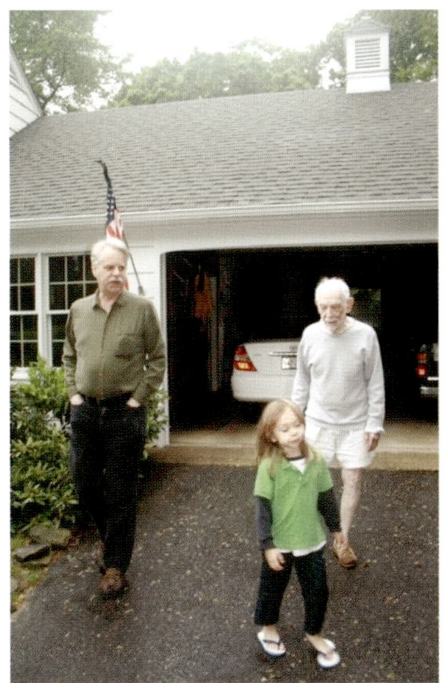

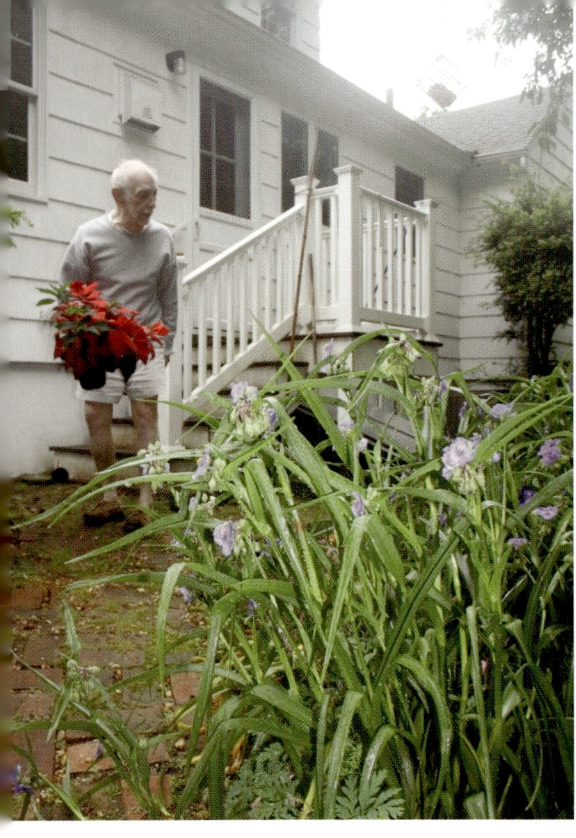

CM: I always associate the Jersey shore with my Aunt Nancy and Uncle Ferd. They did not have children but they did have the most beautiful garden. After she died he kept it going for quite a few years. But two years ago he got seriously ill. That scared him and he decided to move into a retirement community.

Charlie: I just remember when there was the service for Aunt Nancy a whole bunch of photographs were put out.

Ferd Klebold: That's right, Charlie. They're all gone. Every one of them.

Charlie: And you don't know where they went?

Uncle Ferd: They went in the trash. Nancy says get rid of all this junk.

Charlie: Really?

Uncle Ferd: Yeah. So.

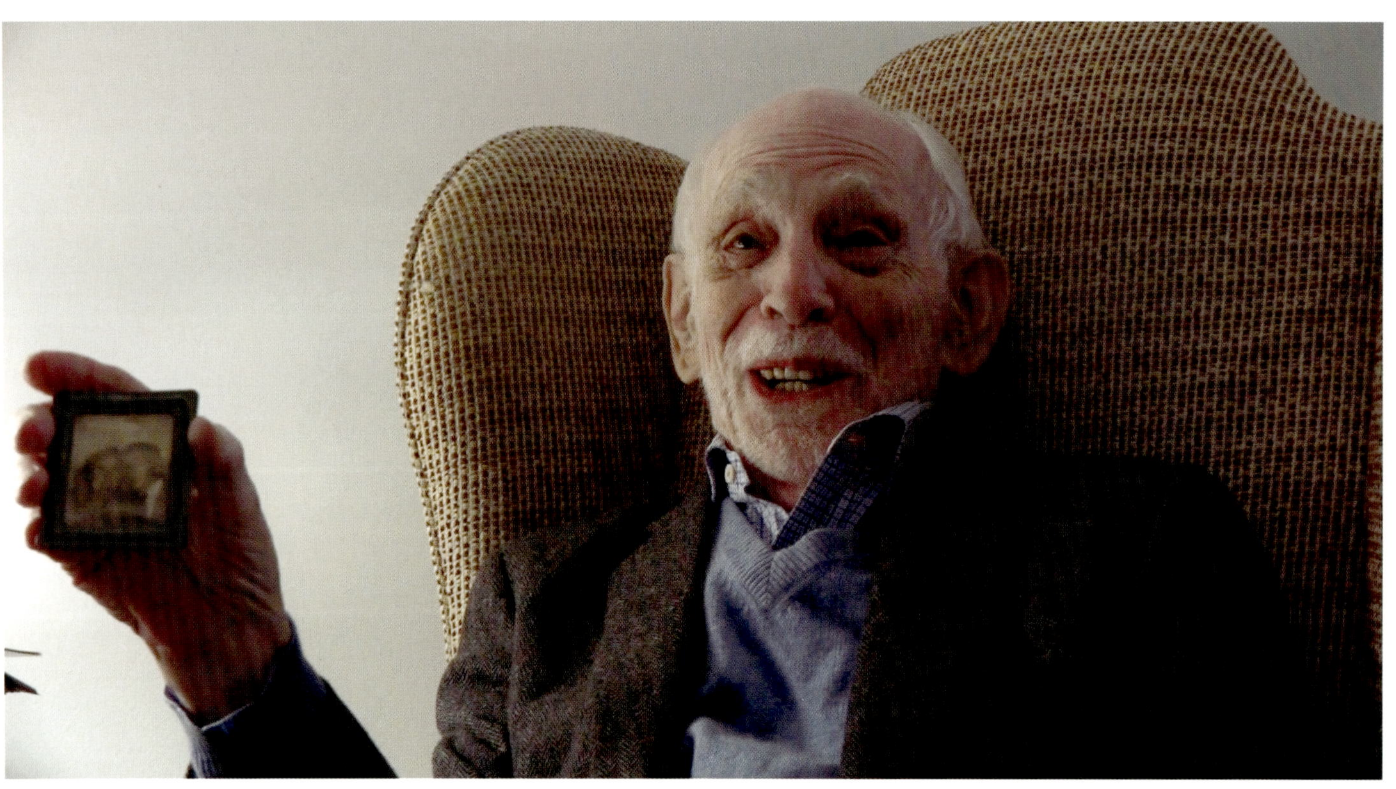

Charlie: So you only have a couple left.

Uncle Ferd: Only have a couple left. I think I have one, of us, taken up at the boardwalk. One of those boardwalk things where we had to put in 50 cents or something like that. We were on a date up at the boardwalk and that is the way you had to dress in those days. A tie on, Charlie, and a white shirt. That's a sport's jacket I wore in high school.

Charlie: Oh, really.

Uncle Ferd: That's how old it is, Charlie.

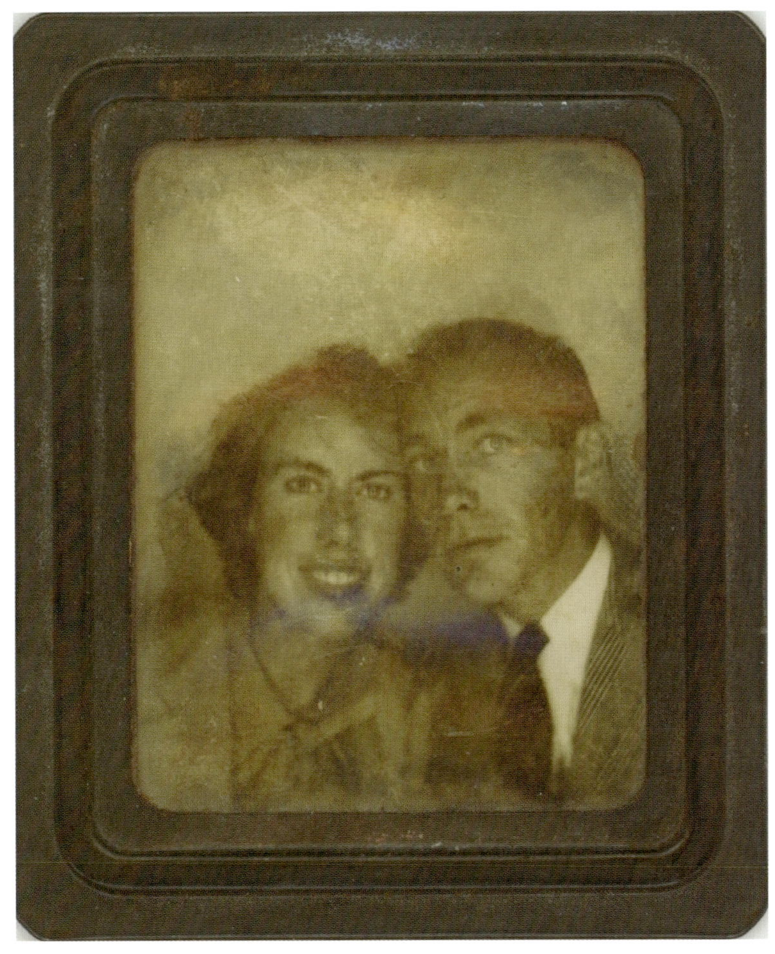

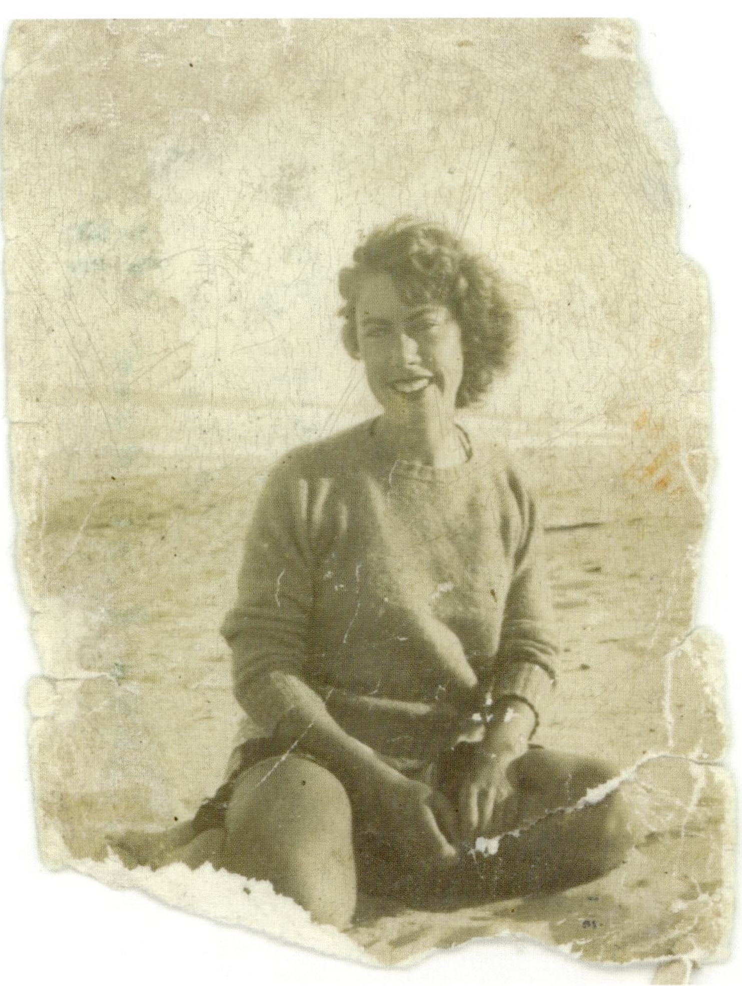

CM: Somehow, their first photo together has survived. Is it the last image you let go of? It reminds me of the first one that your mom and I arranged to have taken. Clowning around. Having fun. Not too serious but somehow knowing that it might be important.

Uncle Ferd: Family stories I can help you with, Charlie, but photographs, I don't have any.

Charlie: So how did you meet my aunt?

Uncle Ferd: Chief Brown of Seaside Park came over to the house and says, "I am looking for a reliable person to be a policeman. The main reason I want you is to drive the two women lifeguards to work every day, and bring them home for lunch and then pick them up again, take them back to work, and pick them up at 5 o'clock." Nancy was one of them. So, I'm driving her home. This is about the fourth or fifth time. I asked, "How would you like to go down to Island Beach and eat a couple of steaks and clams?" And she says, "Island Beach. I haven't been down there in years. Mr. Williamson used to take us down there." And she said, "Yes, that would be nice." I asked what time I should come and she said, "Come over around 5:30." And I came over to the house, and she wasn't ready. There was this man standing there. He looked like he had just got out of college. And he said, "What do you want?" And I said, "I am here to pick Nancy up." So, she came down the stairs and said, "Hi, Walter. What are you doing here?" And he said, "Well, where are you going?" "I'm going out on a date." He says, "How can you go out on a date when you're engaged to me?" I didn't know what I was getting into. Nancy says to Walter, "You go home, Walter, I'm going out on a date with him. We're going down to Island Beach." And we went.

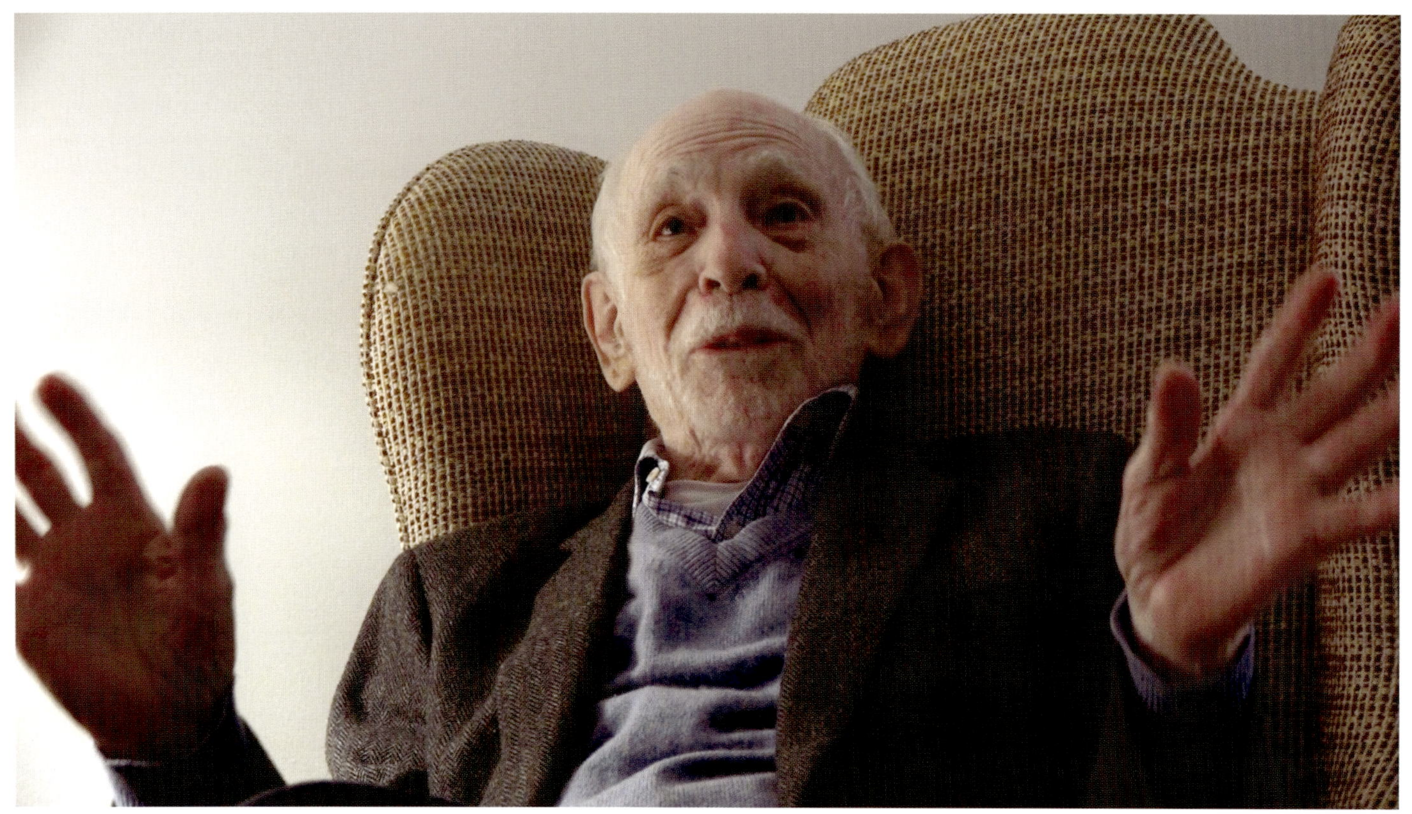

Uncle Ferd: That was it, Charlie. That was in 1947.

Charlie: And then it took a year before you took that photograph at the Heights.

Uncle Ferd: Up at the boardwalk. Yeah.

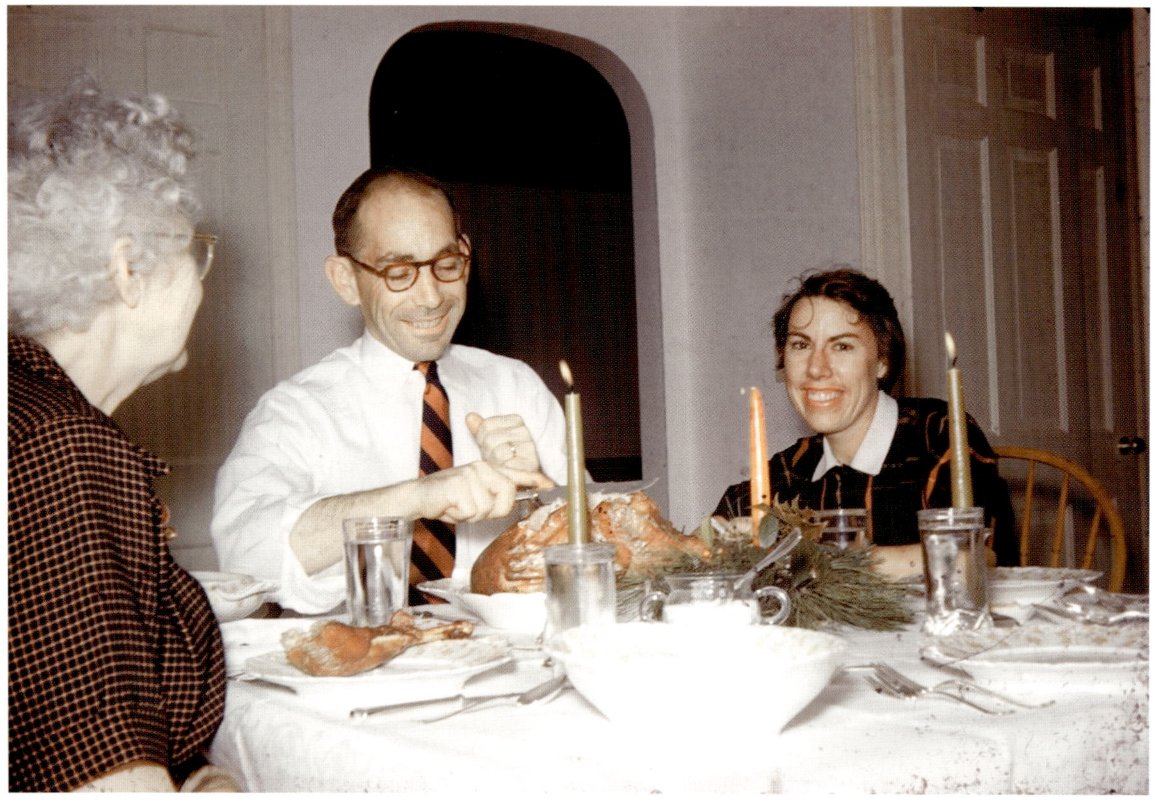

CM: For many years Uncle Ferd and Aunt Nancy were my surrogate parents, and I was happy to find a couple of images of them, like this one of Thanksgiving with my grandmother.

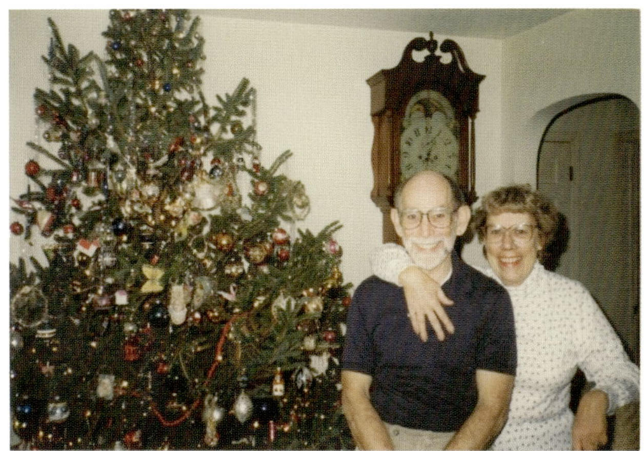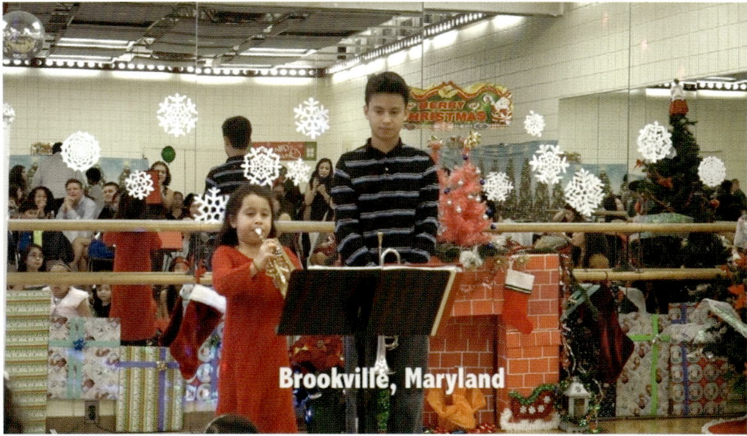

When we were no longer able to visit Aunt Nancy and Uncle Ferd on holidays we began to attend an annual Filipino American Family Christmas Party in Brookville, Maryland. It was started by Threese's best friend, and we quickly felt right at home. Here were our counterparts—families just like ours!

TS: We've been going to the Filipino American Christmas Party for as long as you can remember. It's organized by the Filipina wives, and the husbands just come along for the ride.

CM: This year your mom was master of ceremonies.

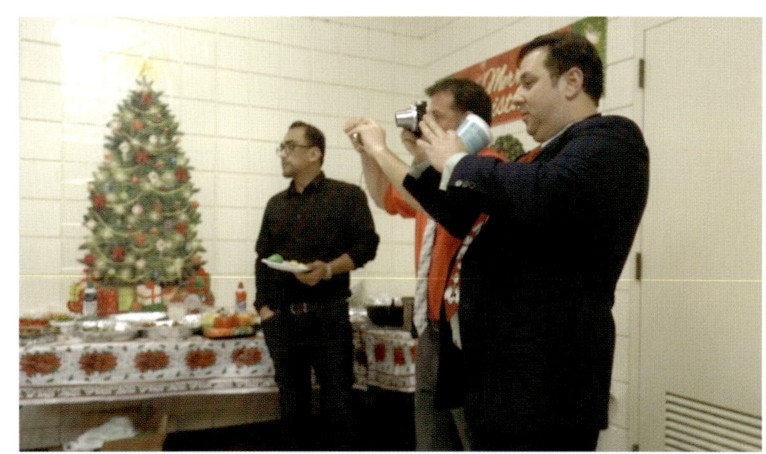

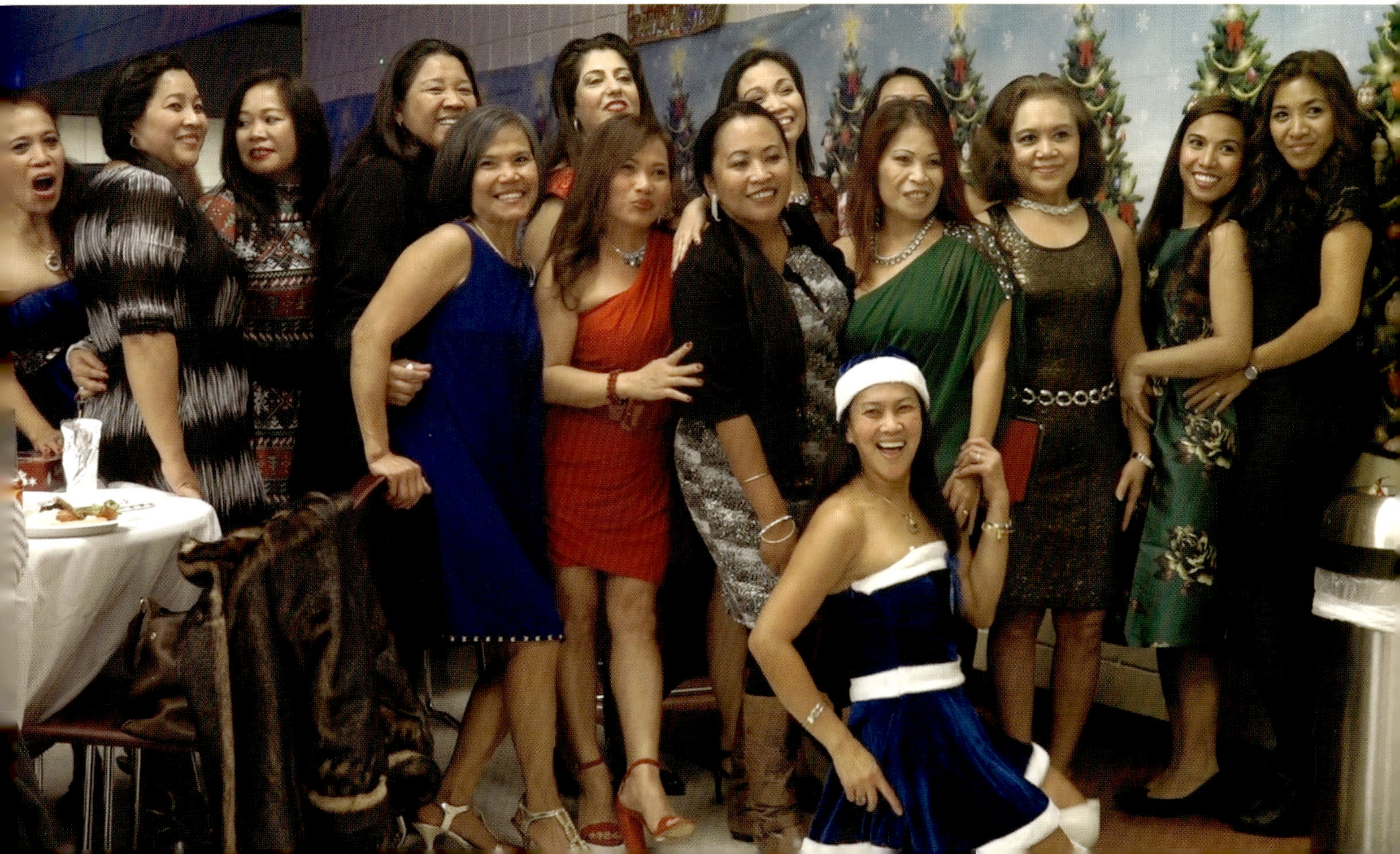

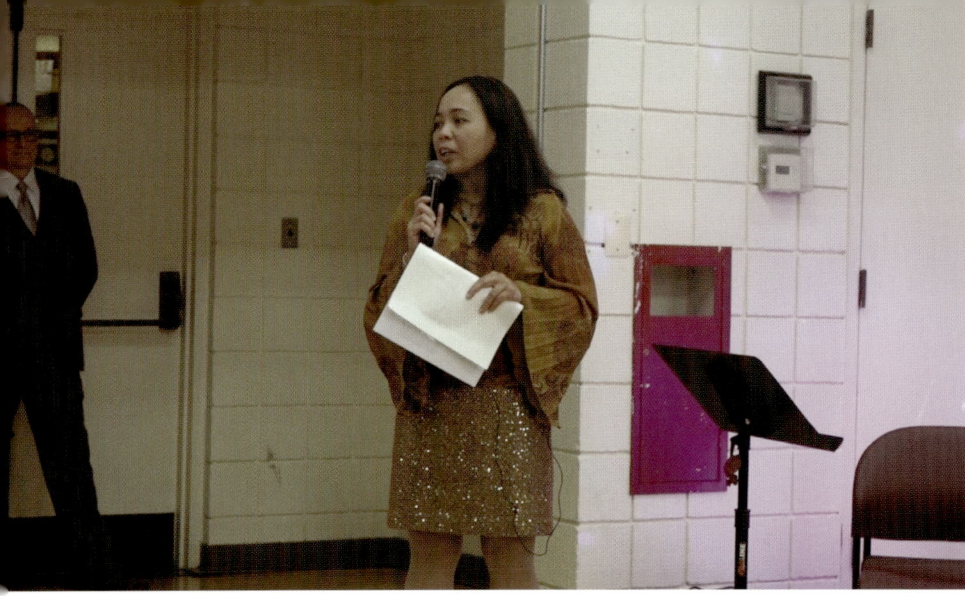

Threese: So, the moms are pretty talented. I am pretty sure the dads, too. But this is the time for the moms to shine. And we are going to start with Lei Marie. Let's give her a big round of applause.

Lei Marie dances to "Jingle Bell Rock," Jennifer Hodzic sings "Have Yourself a Merry Little Christmas," her daughter sings "Sounds of Silence," and John Carlos sings "The Wren Song."

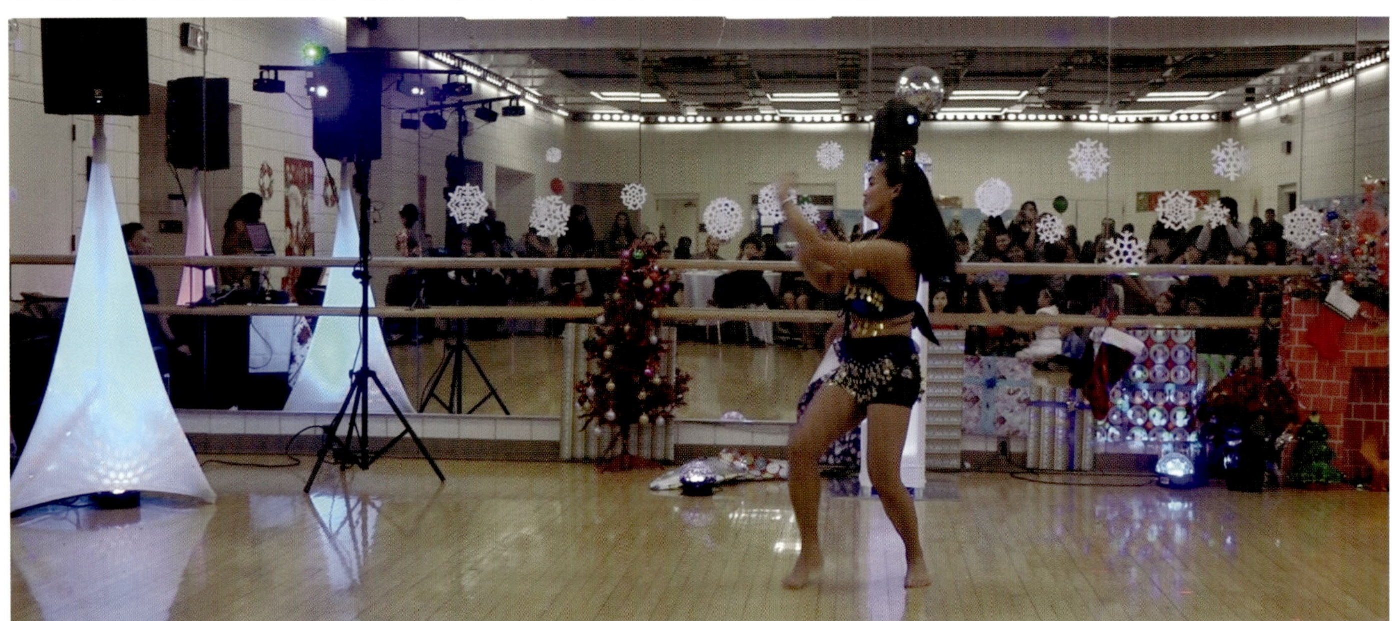

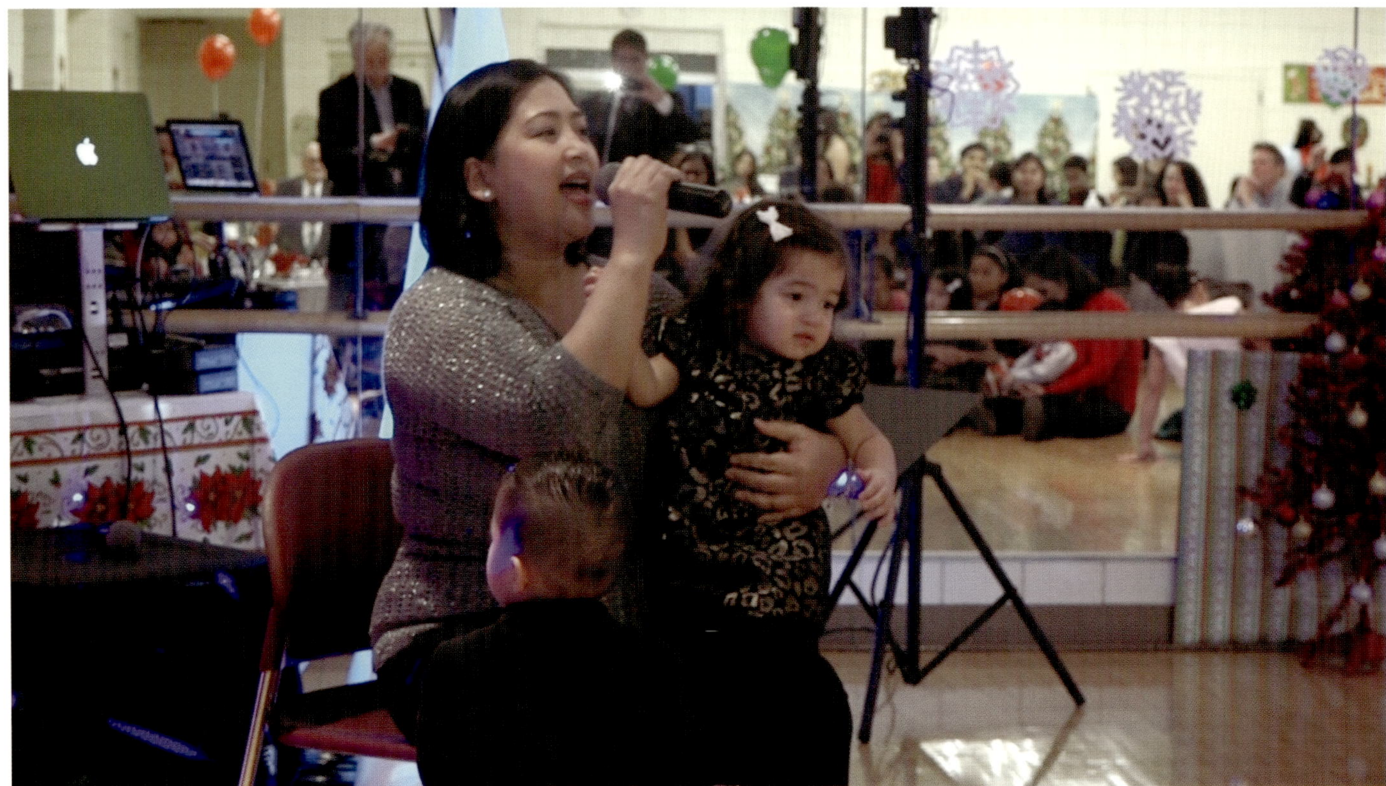

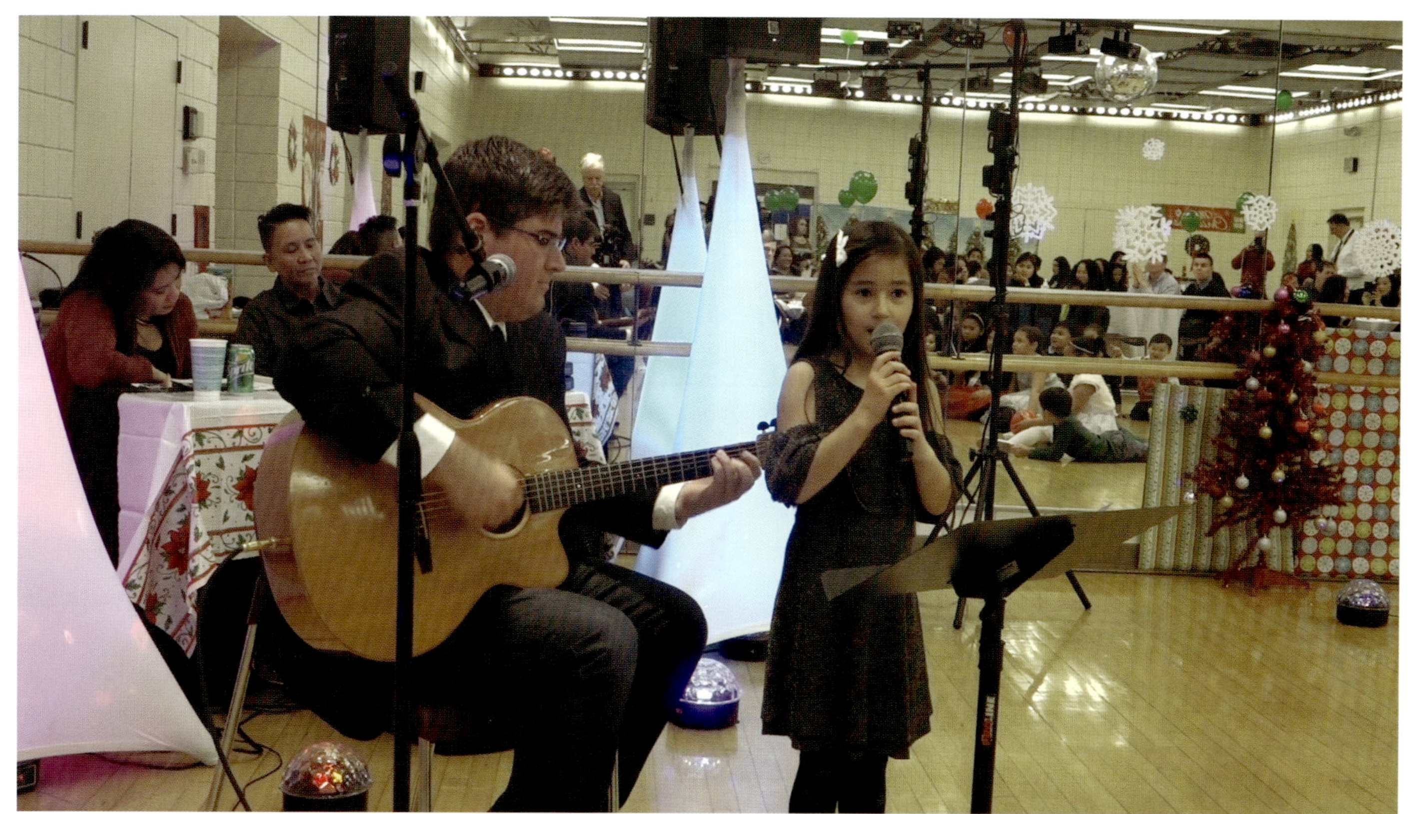

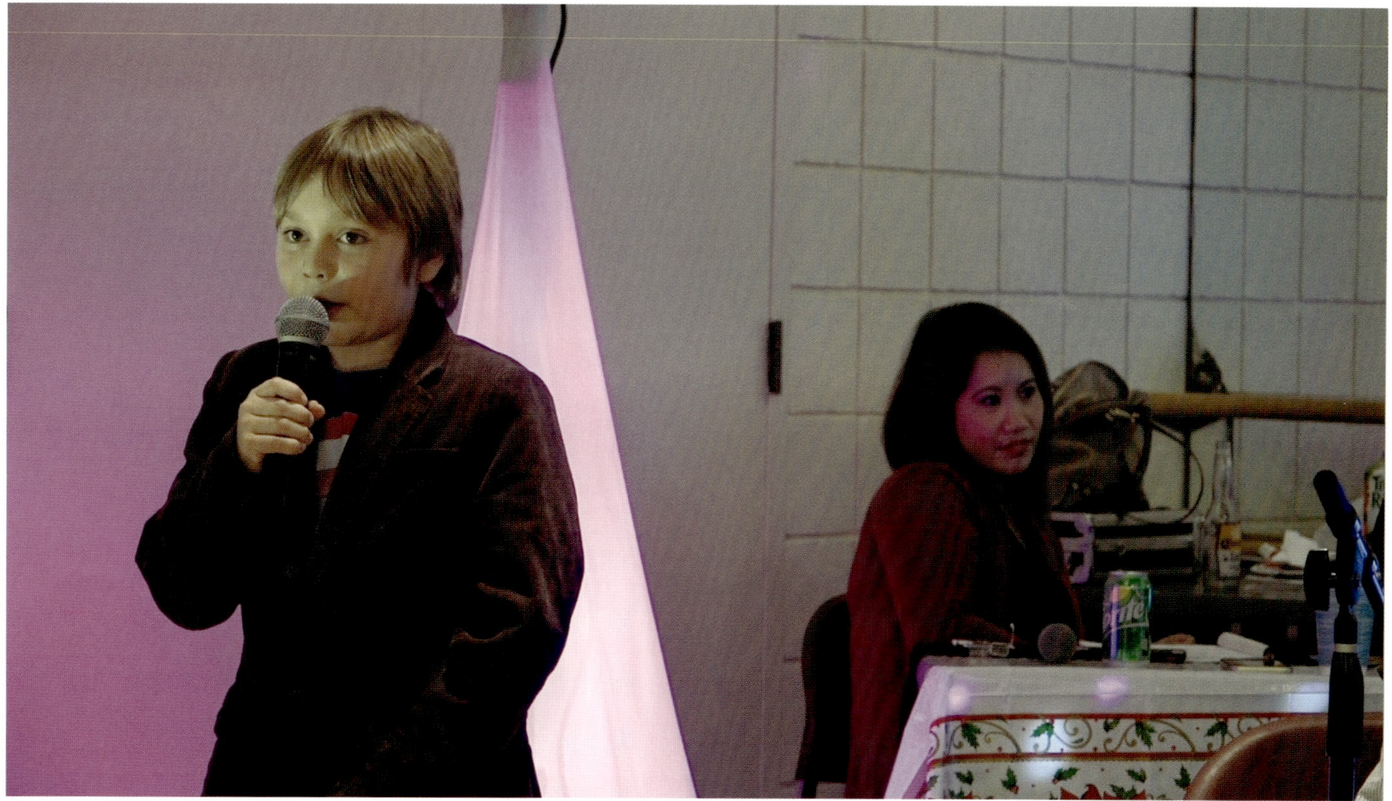

December 17, 2016. We had already filmed this Filipino American Christmas party several times for an unfinished film entitled Visa Wives. *It was good practice for everyone. We had become just two of the group's many photographer/filmmakers. I knew what was likely to happen and what I needed to do to prepare. John Carlos sang with a confidence that showed off his Filipino roots. Afterwards I put down my video camera and took some photos of family friends, which I later cut to the music of John Carlos singing.*

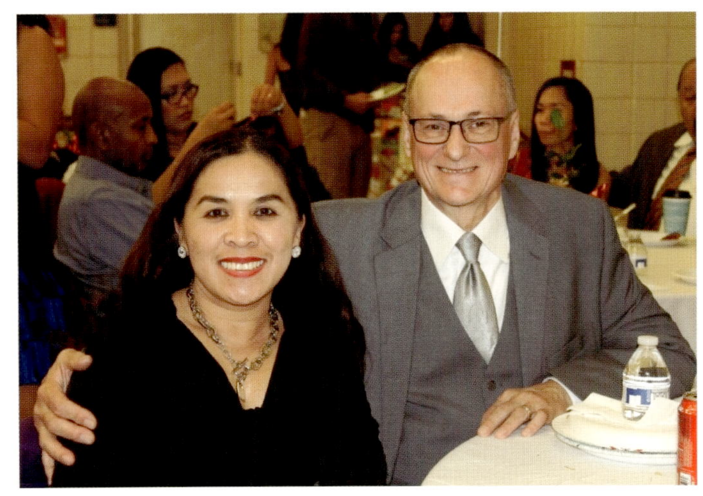
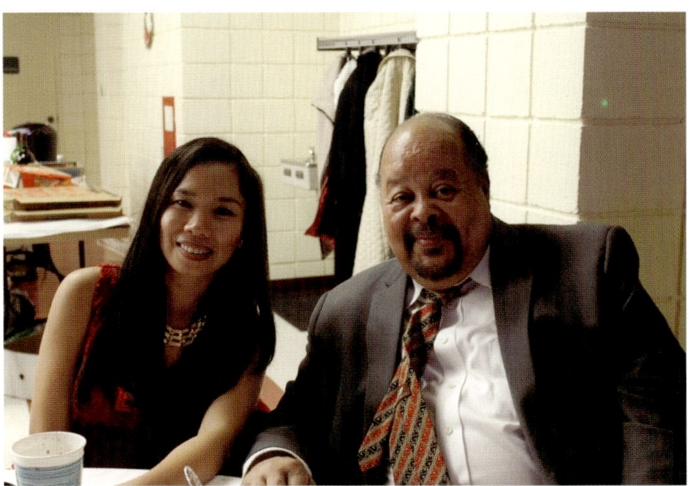
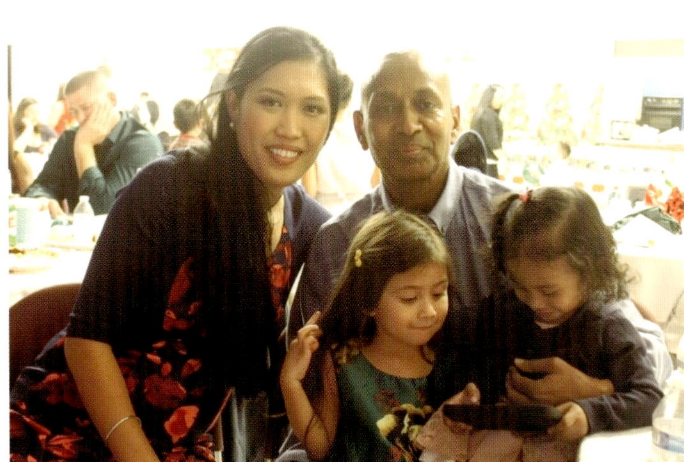
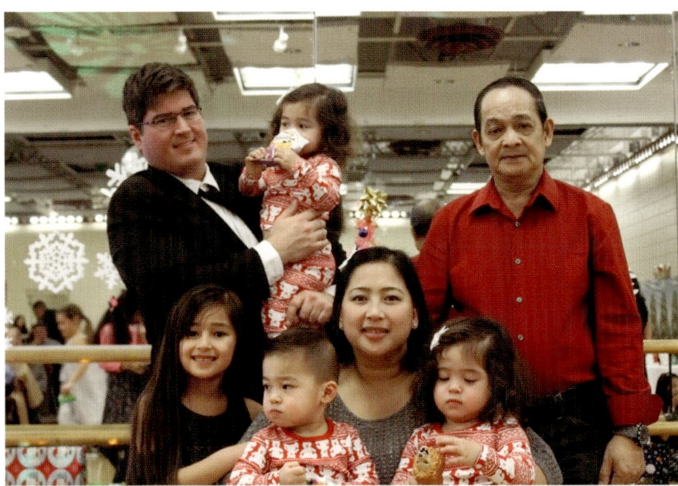

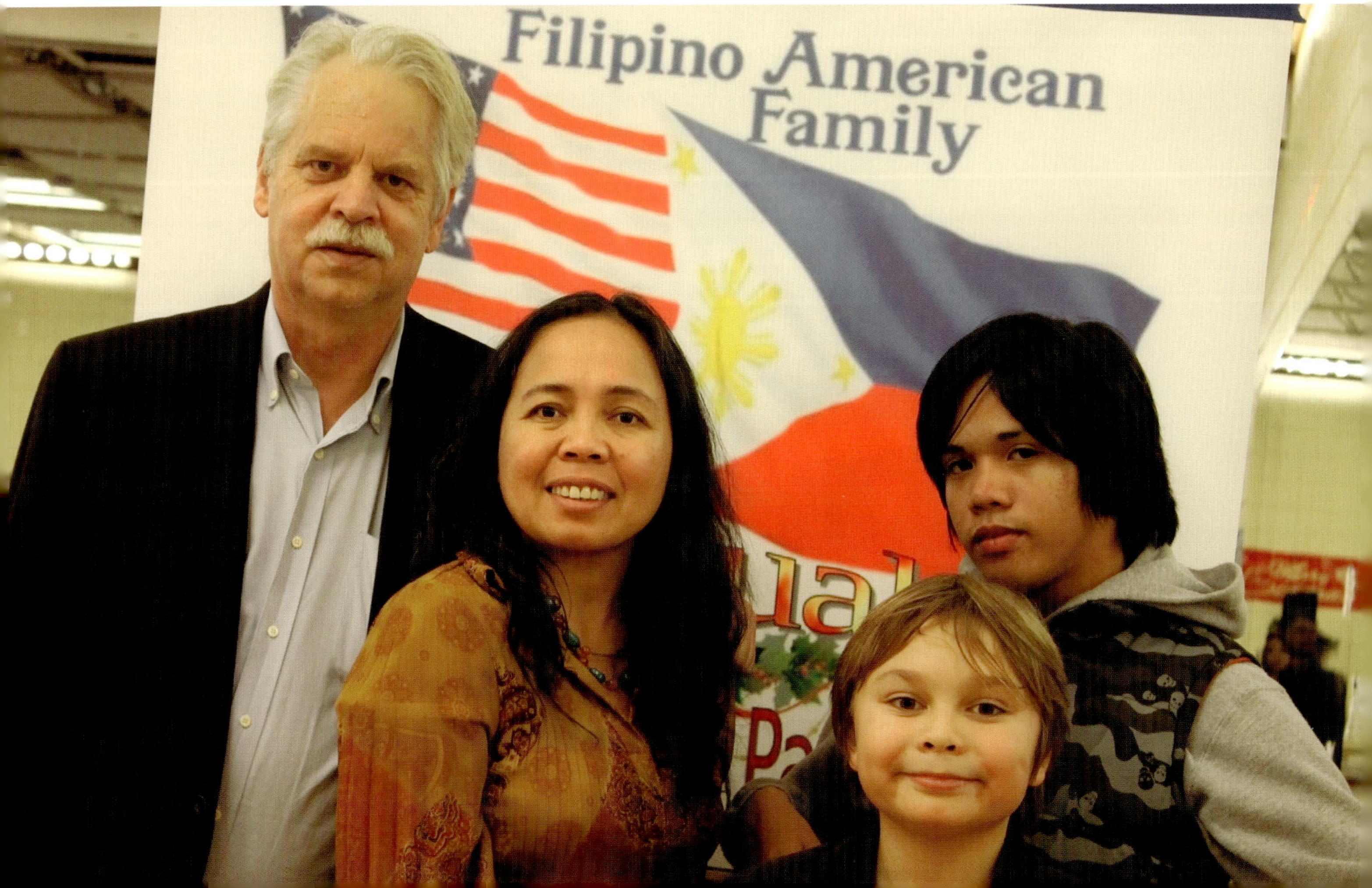

Filipino American
Family

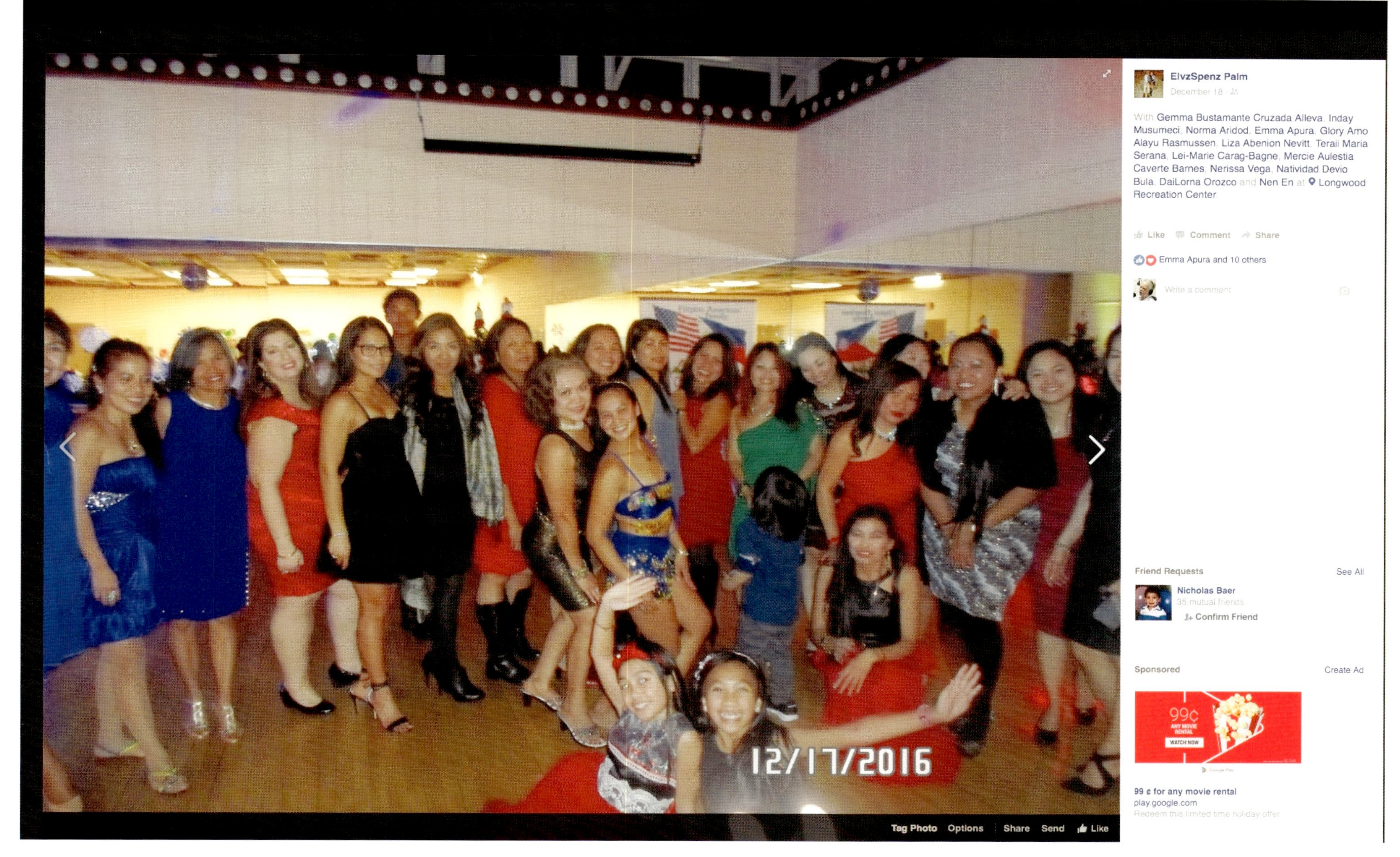

12/17/2016
Tag Photo   Options   Share   Send   Like
ElvzSpenz Palm
December 18
With Gemma Bustamante Cruzada Alleva, Inday Musumeci, Norma Aridod, Emma Apura, Glory Amo Alayu Rasmussen, Liza Abenion Nevitt, Teraii Maria Serana, Lei-Marie Carag-Bagne, Mercie Aulestia Caverte Barnes, Nerissa Vega, Natividad Devio Bula, DaiLorna Orozco and Nen En at Longwood Recreation Center
Like   Comment   Share
Emma Apura and 10 others
Write a comment
Friend Requests   See All
Nicholas Baer
35 mutual friends
Confirm Friend
Sponsored   Create Ad
99¢ ANY MOVIE RENTAL   WATCH NOW
99 ¢ for any movie rental
play.google.com
Redeem this limited time holiday offer

December 24, 2016. Religion can play a divisive role in families as well as in the world more generally. Working in the New York film industry, I had picked up my share of Yiddish expressions. Without realizing it, I was passing for Jewish. Or at least my colleague Bob Sklar somehow thought that I was a nice Jewish boy and introduced me to Hannah's mom on that basis. When our marriage didn't work out, religion emerged as a fault line, with Hannah and her mom on one side while I was on the other (I had eventually been outed as a WASP). The situation was frustrating to be sure, but the perpetuation of that division with the next generation was even more distressing: Hannah's brothers on her mother's side were likewise Jewish, while John Carlos was not. Or so we thought. In truth, it was John Carlos who put the pieces of the puzzle together and launched us on an unexpected journey of recuperation and discovery.

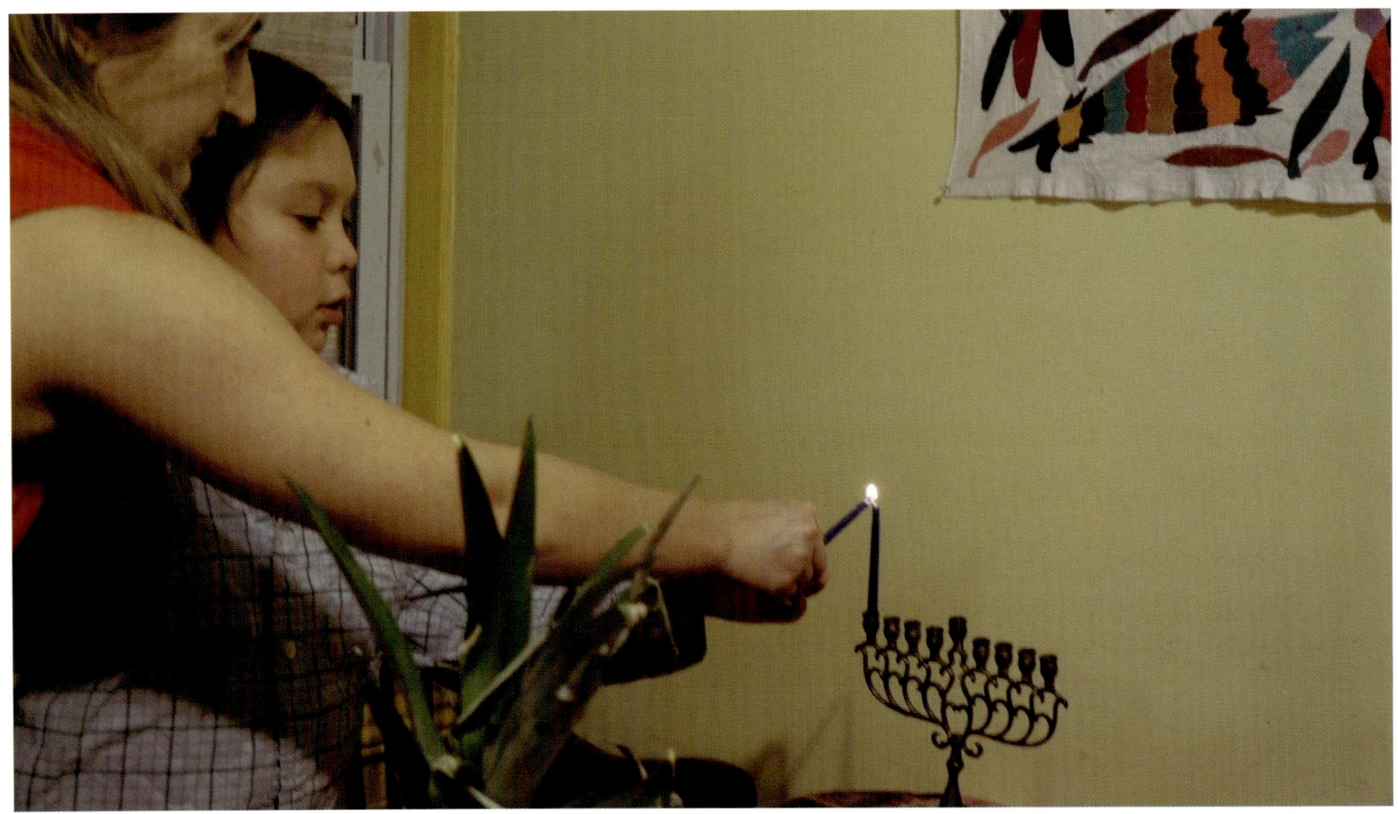

CM: When Hannah's mom and I went our separate ways I insisted on holding on to the menorah, which I had bought so we could all celebrate Hanukkah. For many years it sat in a cabinet. But then… last year, when your sister Hannah didn't show up for a visit you got very upset. In tears, you cried, "Doesn't she know I am Jewish?" But if you were going to give any substance to that claim, it seemed time for you to mark some Jewish holidays and learn some Hebrew prayers.

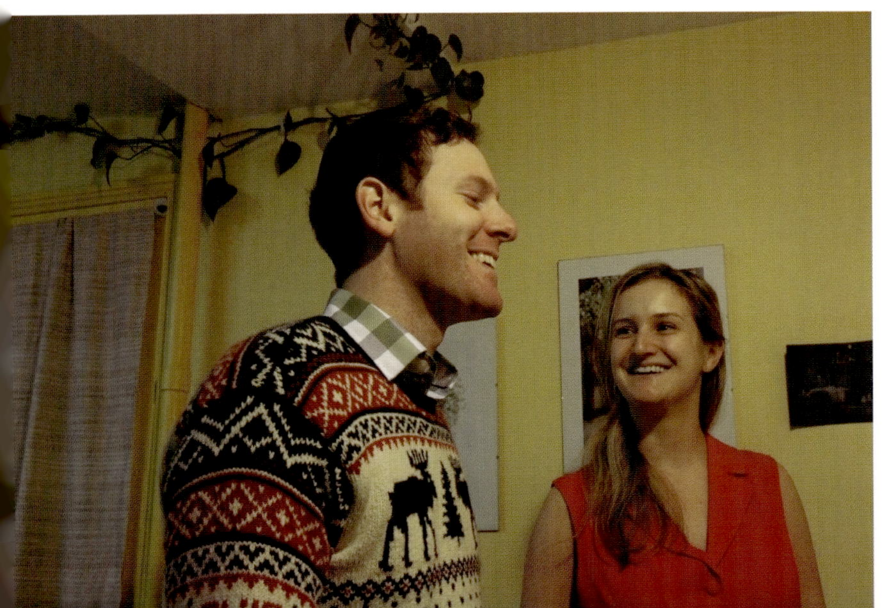

Masha Shpolberg: Do you want to hold [the candle] with me? We can do it together. We can light this one. There we go. And now we have three blessings that we say, and the first blessing says, "We thank God for the light to light the lights of the Hanukkah candles." …You can say the first part of the blessing because it is always the same: "Baruch atah Adonai."

Masha and Josh Glick sing "Baruch atah Adonai" with John Carlos (off screen).

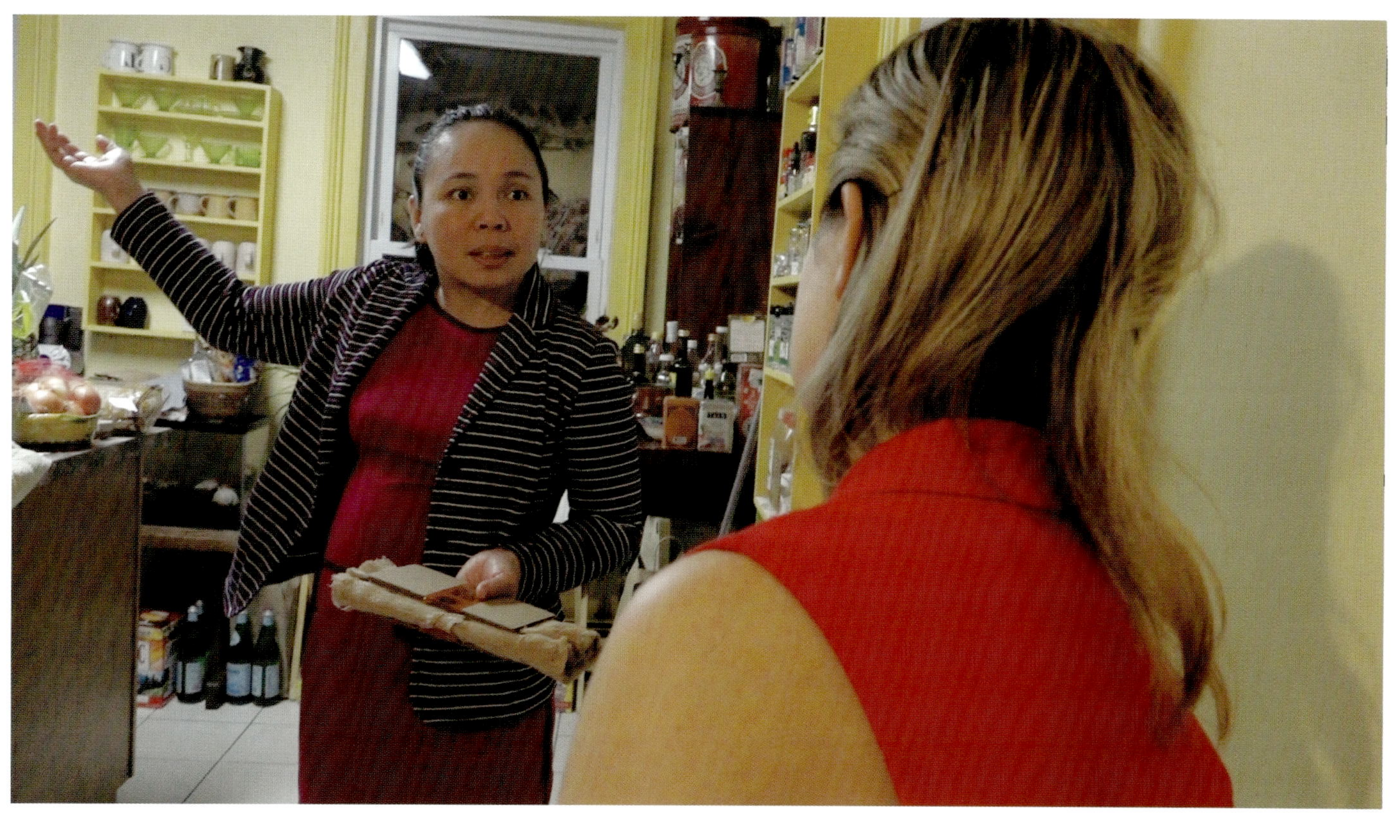

Threese: Because I was like, No, it can't be. But then my mom's story started to make sense. Because why would they go to the mountains? It's so far away.

Masha: It was this old secret…

Threese: Yeah. But he has this prayer that he prays, and he has this thing on his head. And my mother was talking about this book that—She said she can't read the letters. It looks like some kind of hieroglyphics or Japanese writing, but Mom doesn't really know about this because she can't read. And she was told we're not supposed to tell that we're Jewish because Christ was killed by the Jews or something?

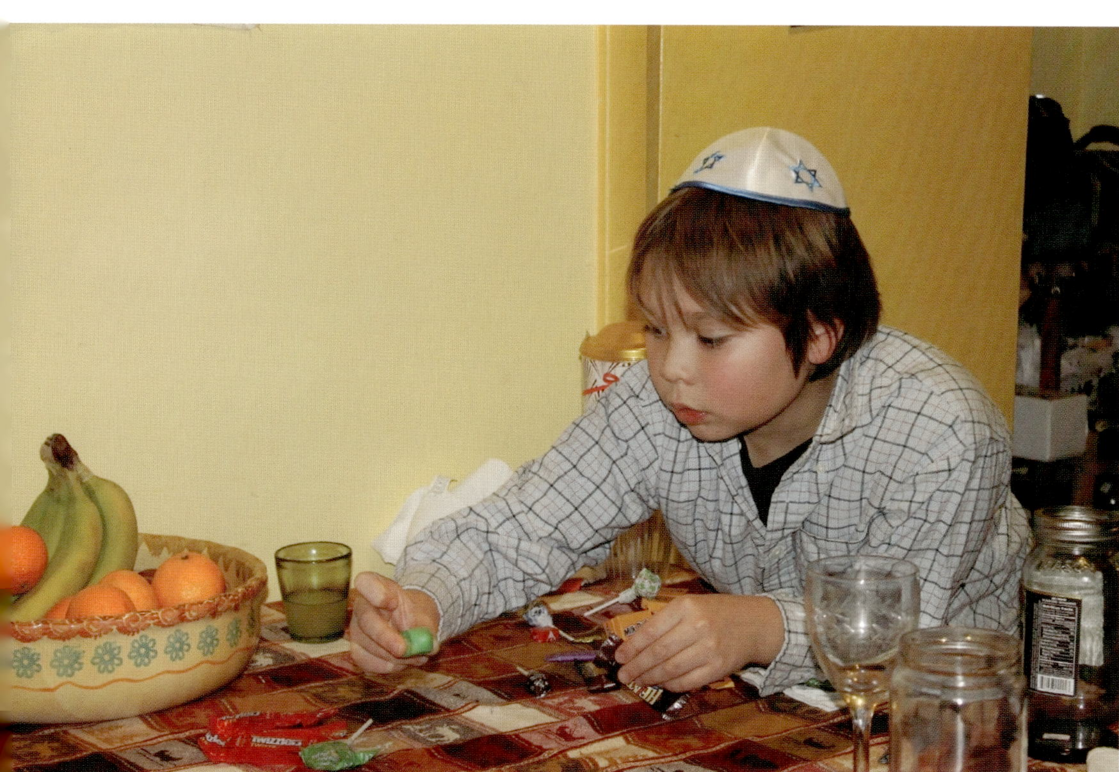

Masha: That makes sense. It's the usual explanation.

Threese: So, we can't really because Catholics they are going to actually…

Masha: Does she remember any holidays?

Threese: No, they were very Catholic…

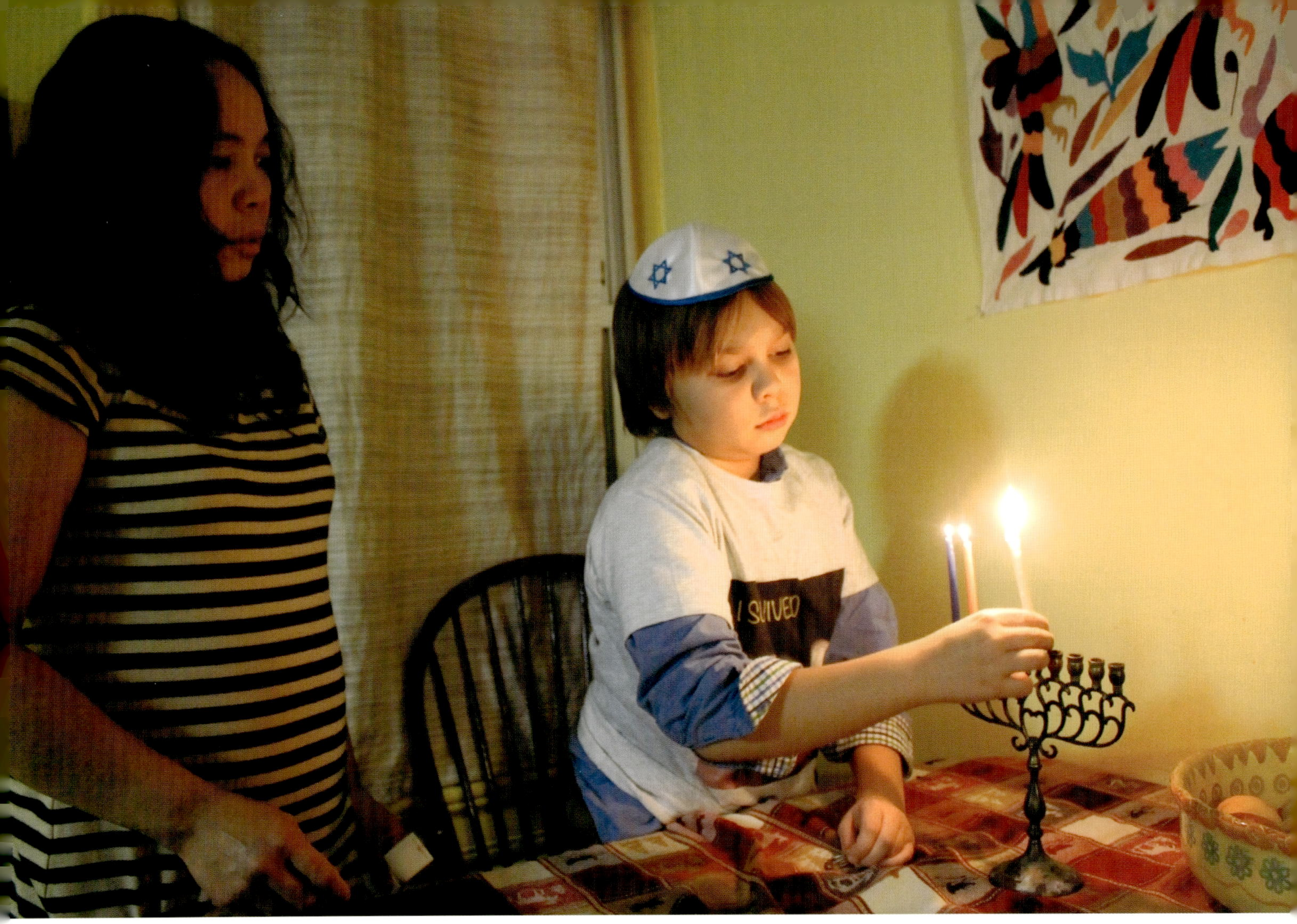

CM: So we need to return to the Philippines not only to search out family photographs in the attics of your mother's relatives, but to try to find out more about this story.

TS: Some roots are not always so easily traced in photographs.

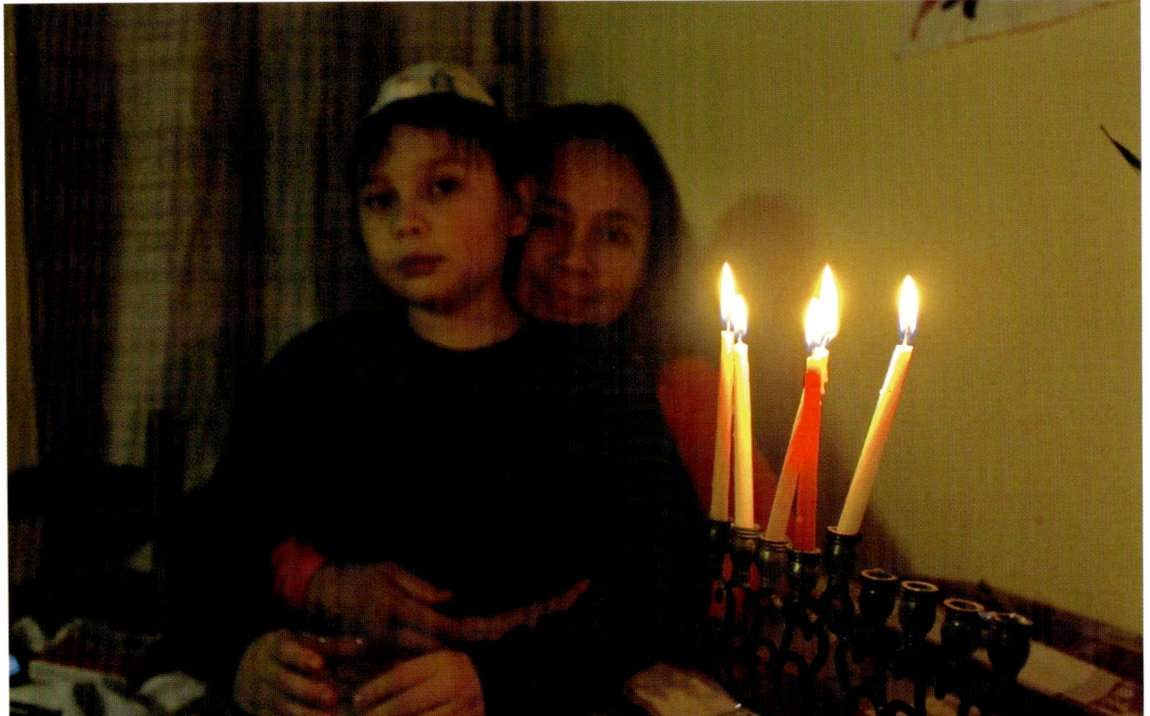

CM: The Mussers also faced religious persecution. Anabaptists—later known as Mennonites—they suffered expulsion, confiscation of property, and prison. Fleeing Bern, Switzerland, they went first to Germany and then to Lancaster, Pennsylvania. Hans or John Musser arrived in the early 1700s and our family tree has had a lot of John Mussers ever since.

Early Musser Immigrants to Lancaster County

```
1-Peter Moser (A) b. Jan 1671, Biglen, Bern, Switzerland, c. 4 Feb 1671, Biglen,
  Bern, Switzerland, bur. After 1731, Ittlingen, Baden, Germany
 +Unknown
|--2-Peter Moser (B) b. Abt 1692, d. After 1747, Ittlingen, Germany
|  +Unknown
|  |--3-Peter Musser (C) b. Abt 1725, Switzerland, d. 1794, Hempfield Twp,
|  |   Lancaster Co, Pennsylvania
|  |--3-Jacob Musser (D) b. Abt 1726, d. 1788, Strassburg Twp, Lancaster Co,
|  |   Pennsylvania
|  |--3-Henry Musser (E) b. 1730, d. 13 Mar 1805, Brecknock Twp, Lancaster Co,
|  |   Pennsylvania, bur. Pine Grove Cemetery
|--2-Joseph (Jost) Mosser (F)  b. 1693, Illtingen, Germany, d. 1761, Lampeter Twp,
|   Lancaster Co, Pennsylvania
|  +Unknown
|--2-John (Hans) Musser (G) b. 1695, Ittlingen, Germany, d. Apr 1752, Lancaster Borough,
|   Lancaster Co, Pennsylvania, bur. Musser Family Cemetery, Manor Twp,
|   Lancaster Co, Pennsylvania
|  +Unknown
|--2-Catharina Moser b. Abt 1697, Ittlingen, Germany
|--2-Magdalena Moser b. Abt 1704, Ittlingen, Germany
|--2-Christian Mosser b. 1705, Ittlingen, Germany, d. 1741, Lancaster Co,
|   Pennsylvania
|  +Unknown
|--2-Barbara Moser b. Abt 1707, Ittlingen, Germany
```

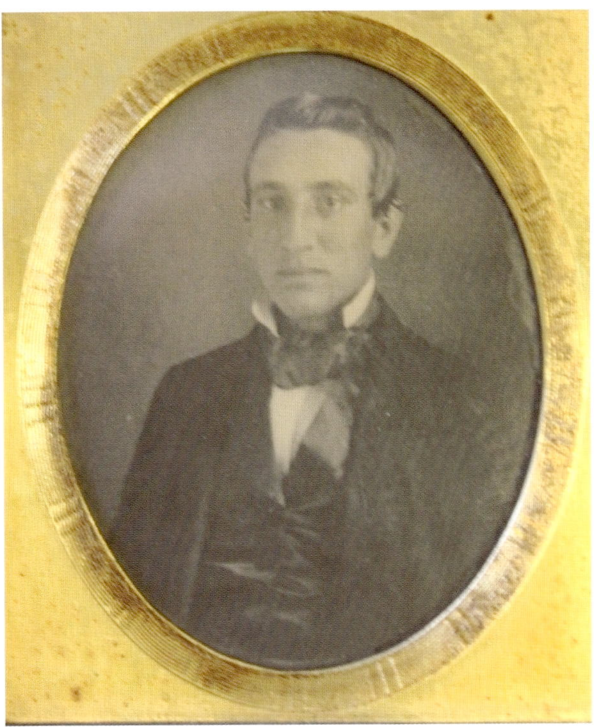
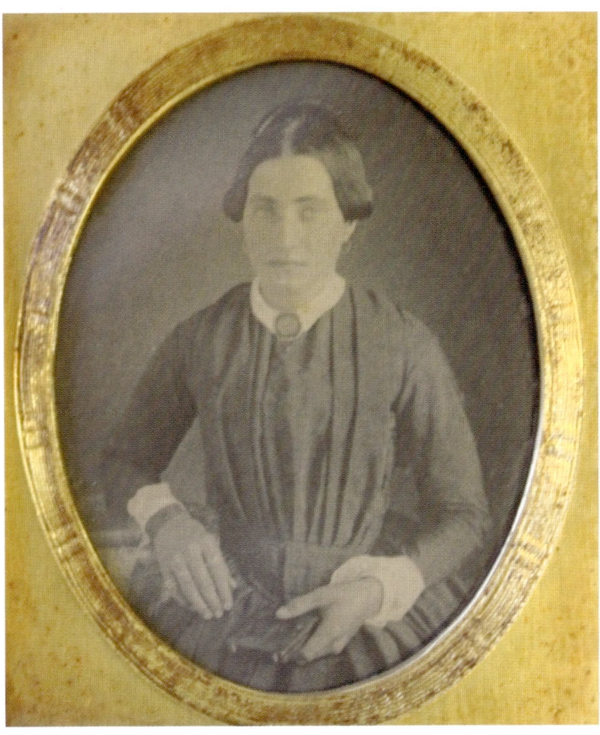

CM: This seems to be the oldest photo of a John Musser—a tintype from the early 1860s. This John worked for Joseph Brubaker, a blacksmith, married his daughter Rose Ann, and took over the business. Their son Cyrus became a minister and editor of the *Reformed Church Messenger*.

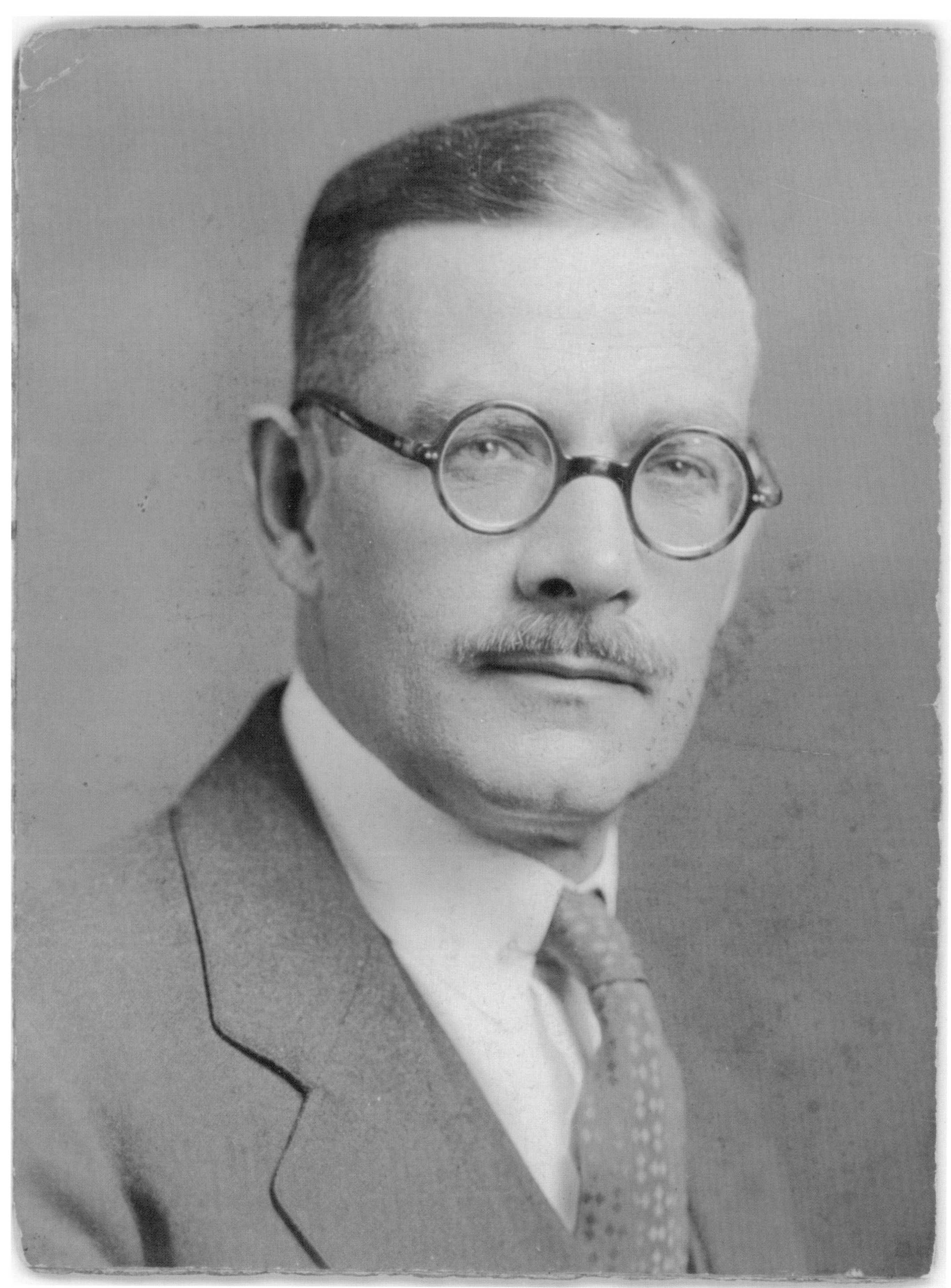

CM: His son, John Musser, left religion behind and became a professor and chair of the History Department at NYU.

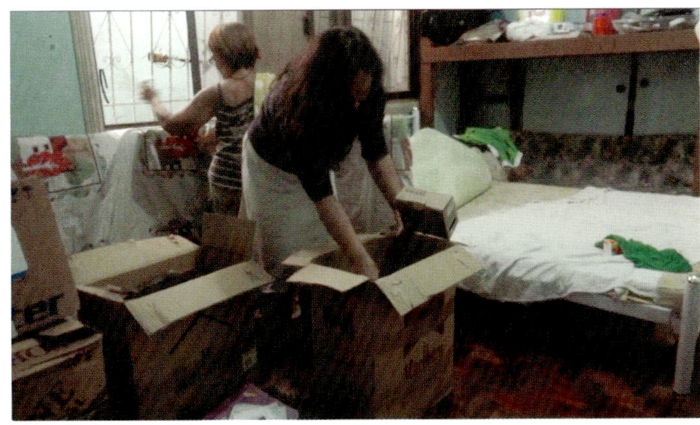 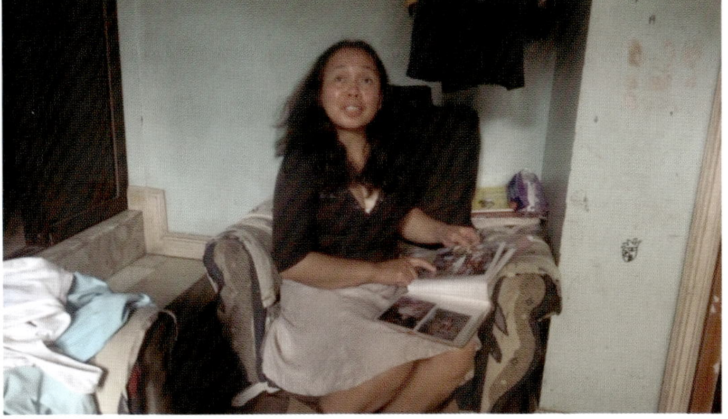

TS: The family album is a misnomer. Photos are stored away in decomposing boxes and mixed up with various papers. There are dozens of albums, scattered about. Some had not been opened for decades,

Threese: These are Keith's pictures.

CM: Your mom and I scavenged for family photographs at your Tito Dada's house in Manila.

Threese: A picture of when we got married!

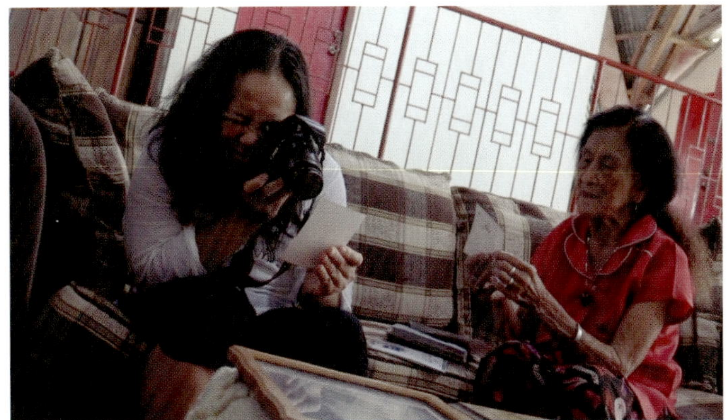 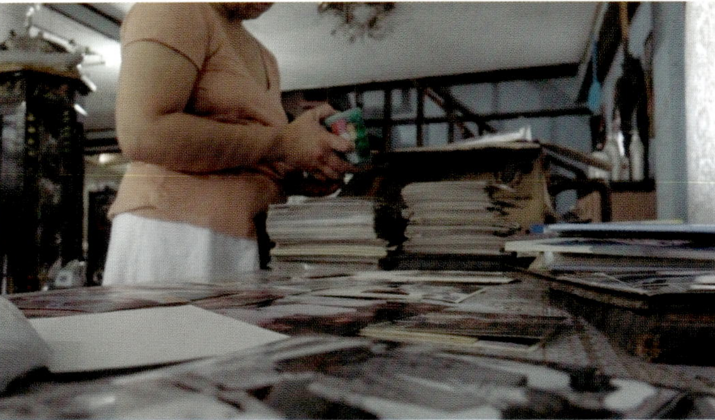

TS: We visited aunts in Manlapay…and raided the Serana archive in Cebu.

CM: For many years I thought there was only a single tattered photo of your mother as a baby—labeled "Threese at Five months." In fact, there are dozens.

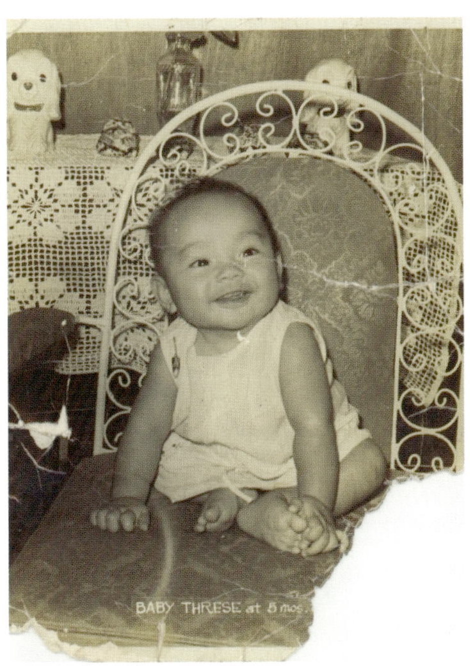

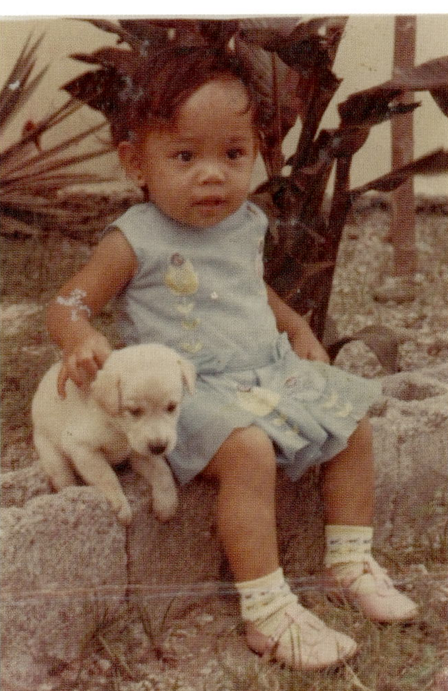 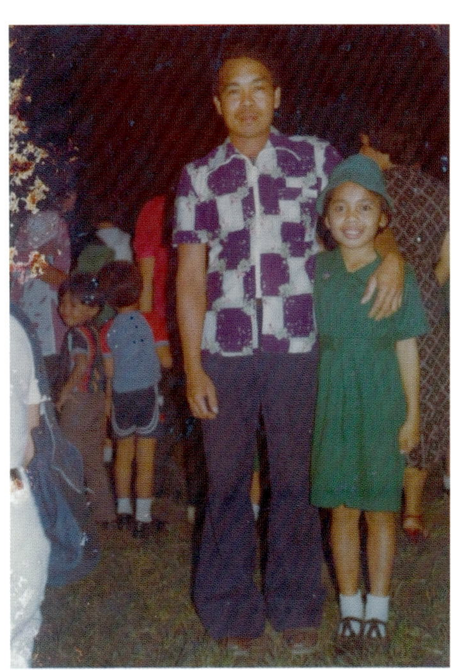

Threese: They definitely love to take pictures as you can see. Wow?… So, this is me.

CM: There are quite a few of your brother Binhi as well.

TS: And though we looked hard, we never found a good quality copy of the ubiquitous Serana family portrait.

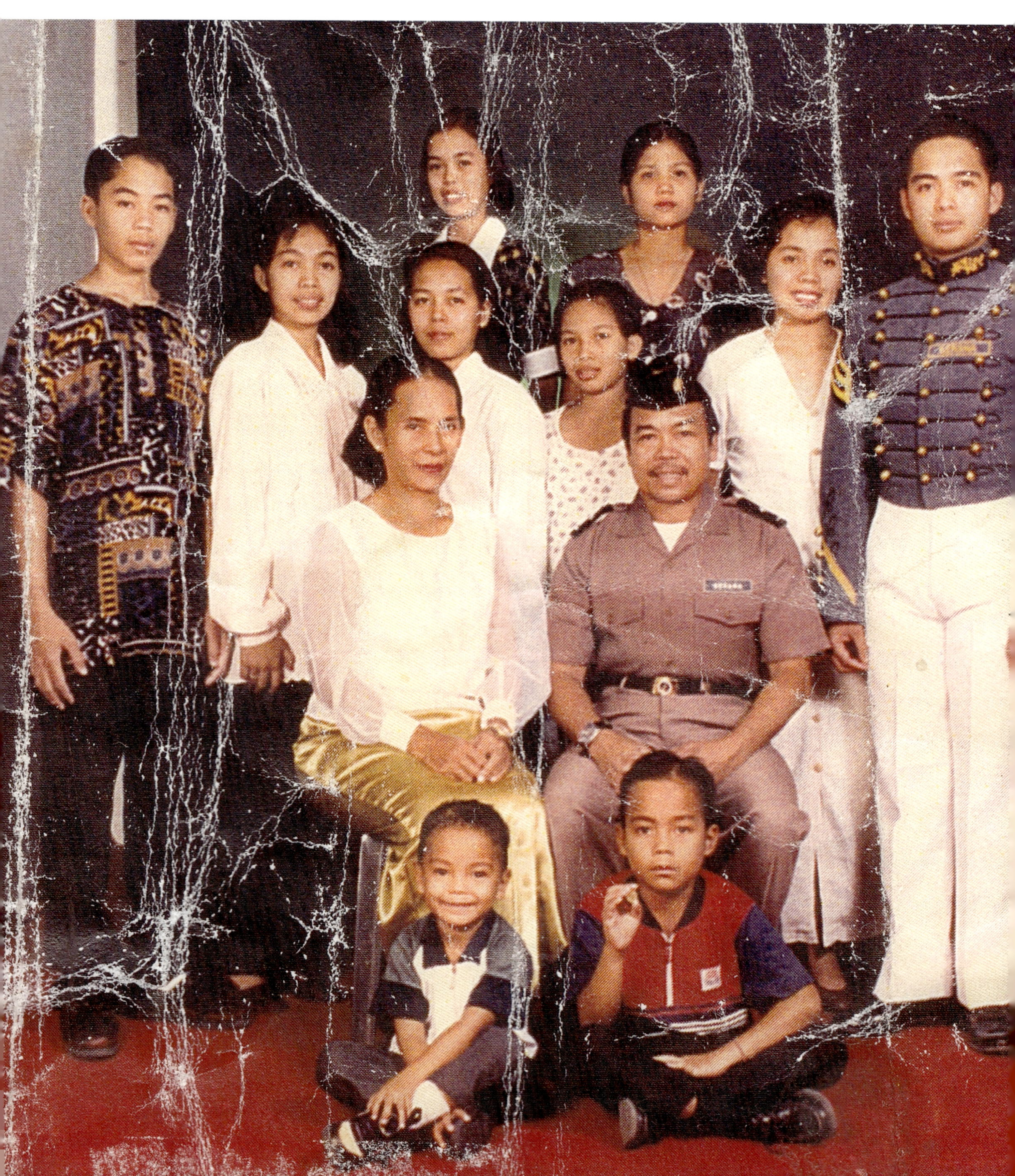

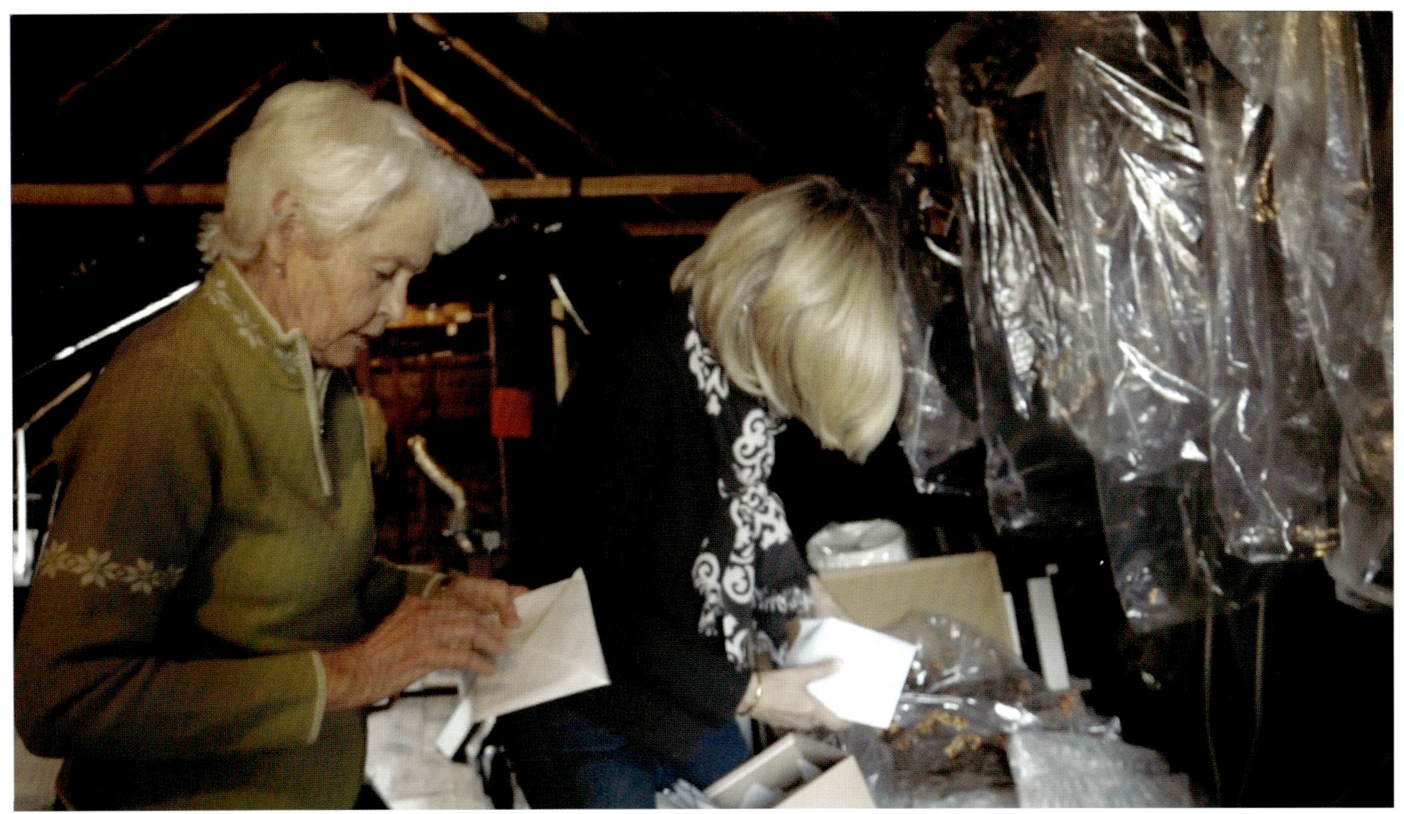

CM: The Musser side was somewhat easier. My mother had sent her family album to my office through the mail—uninsured! And in the months before her death my Aunt Nancy apparently gathered and organized Musser family photos and put them in a box, which we found in my sister's attic. She saved many photos of her father, John Musser.

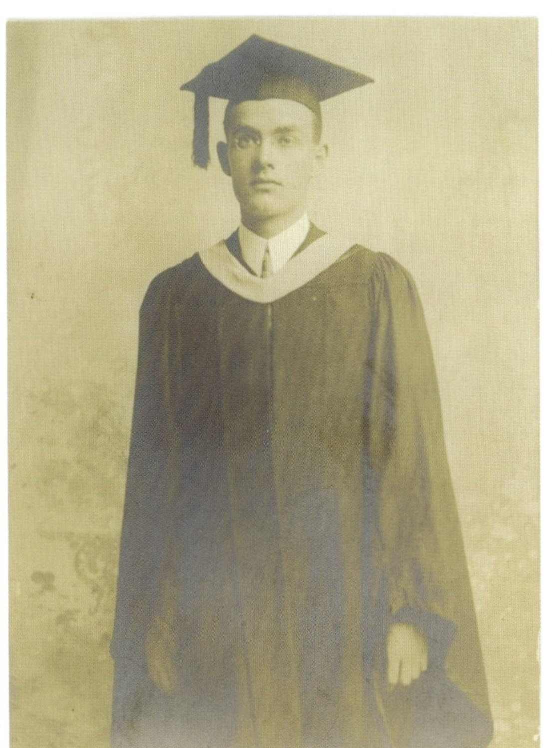

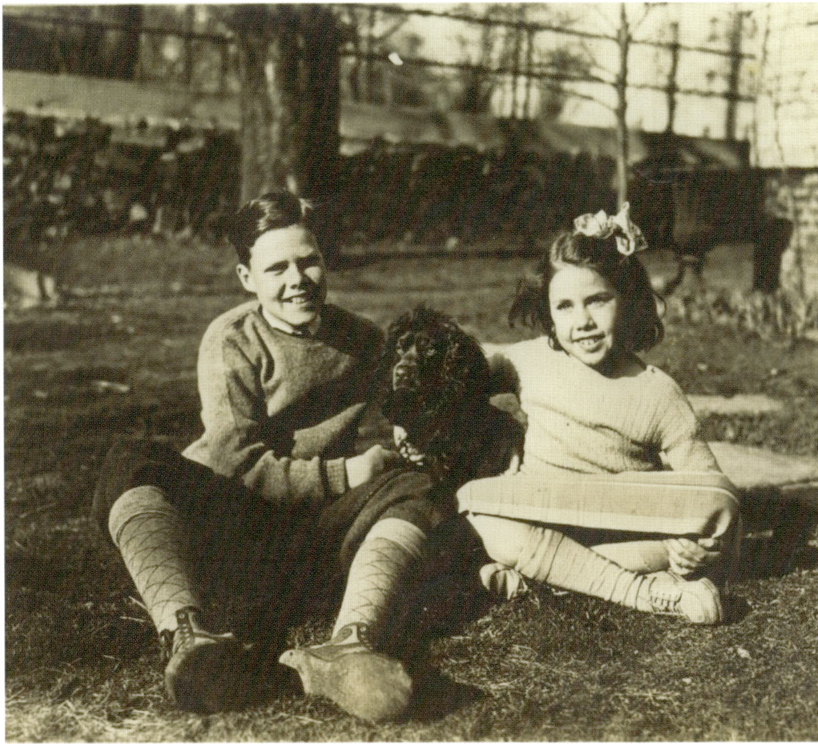

Mom: This has got to be your grandfather Musser [in cap and gown].

Jane: This has to be Dad, right? Who is that? Dad and Aunt Nancy?

Mom: Yes. Oh, that's adorable. Look at the knickers. Two of Mrs. Musser's Dead End Kids.

TS: It's sobering to think that a modest envelope of images so easily contains an individual's lifespan.

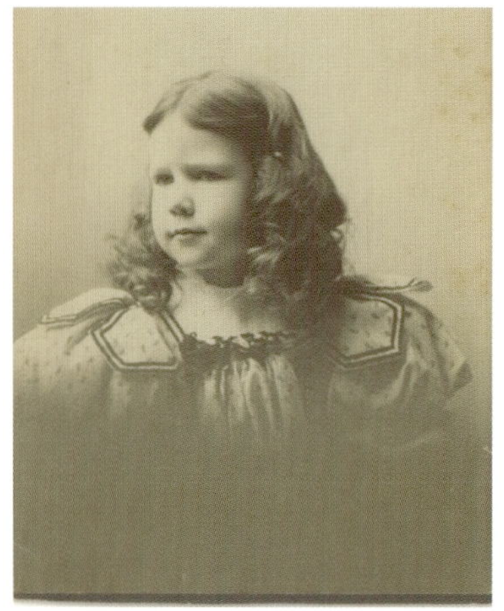

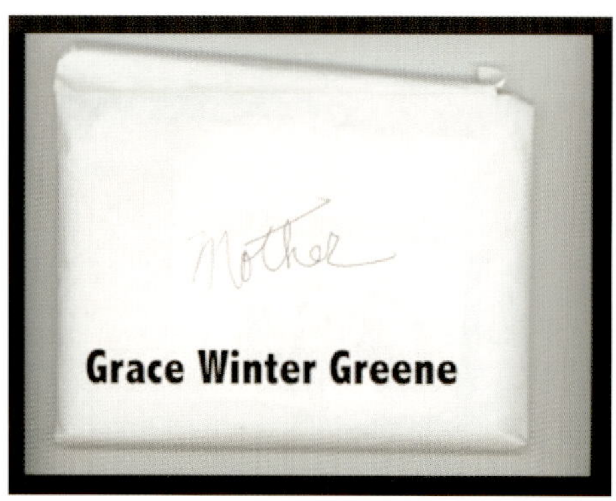

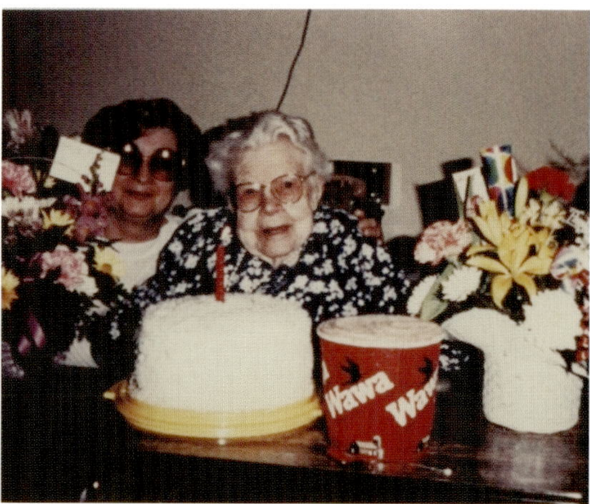

CM: And what about the photos that do not belong in the family album?

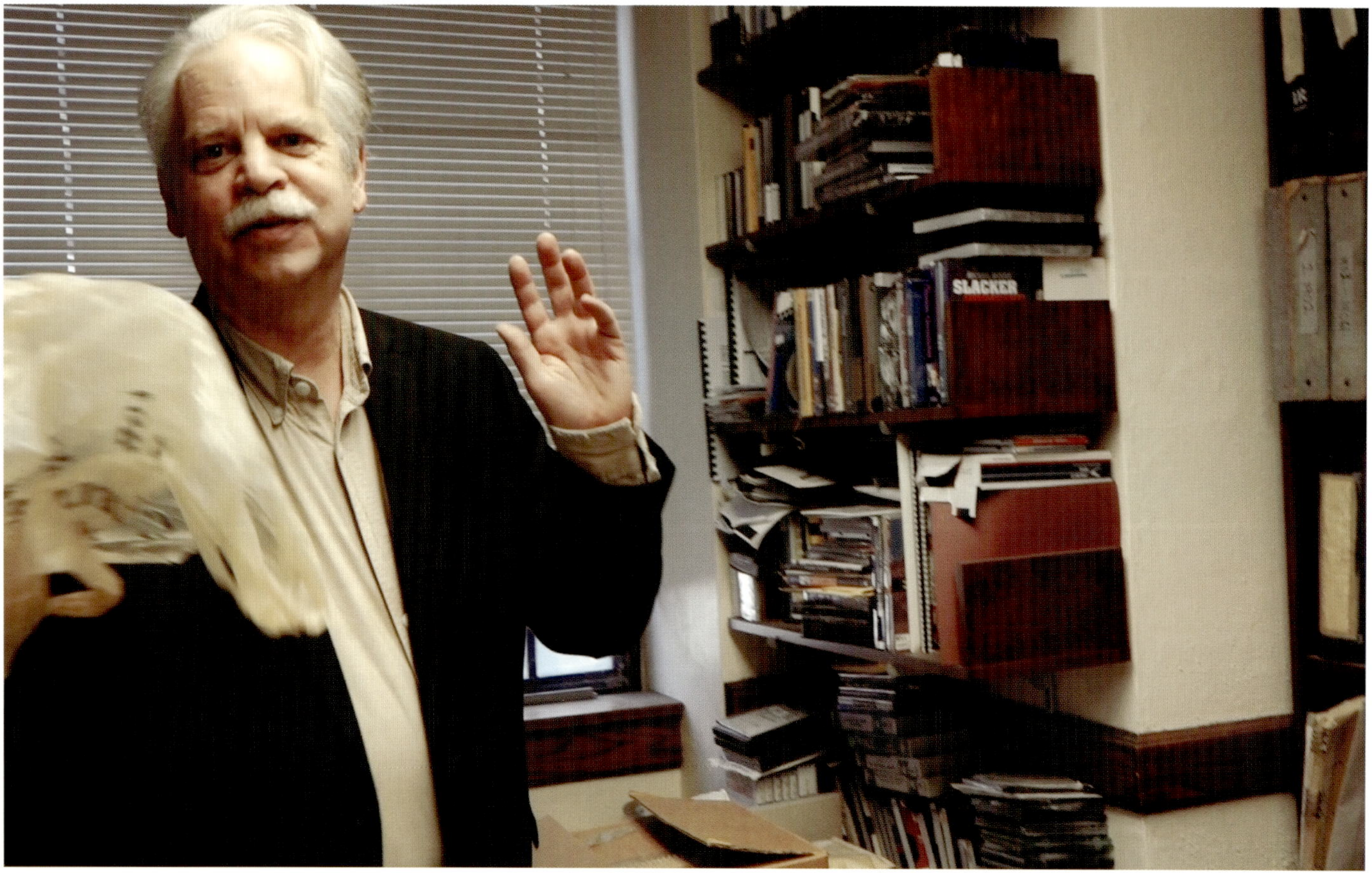

Charlie: This bag is what actually sat here on my desk for four or five years. My daughter Hannah came up one day and handed these to me. She said, "My mom was putting together the family album, and these are the discards." And the reason they were the discards is because I appear in them.

So, here's some…. Some of these are really nice. But they are also, either from when they arrived or otherwise, a little messed up. Hannah with my father when he was sick—that's great. This is like typical, right?

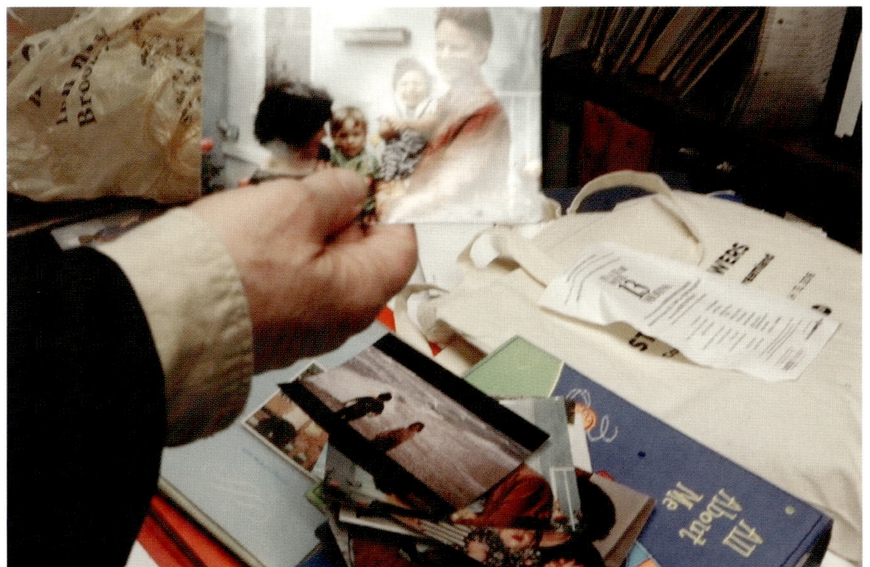

Charlie: Here's me with Hannah, her mom and Hannah's cousin. Definitely not something that she probably wanted in her album. And then there are some that are actually great, like one of my aunt and grandmother. I hadn't really looked at these. Some of these are when I was young and cute. Hannah with a cousin on my side. A lot of these are things that did not fit in her family album because they were too much Musser.

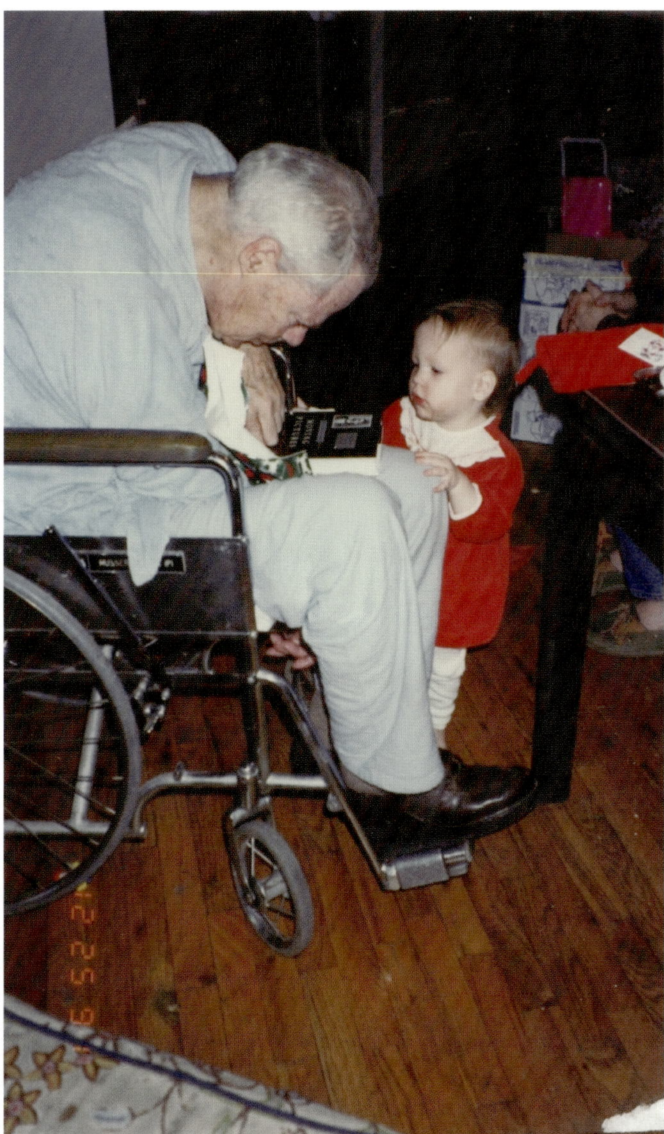

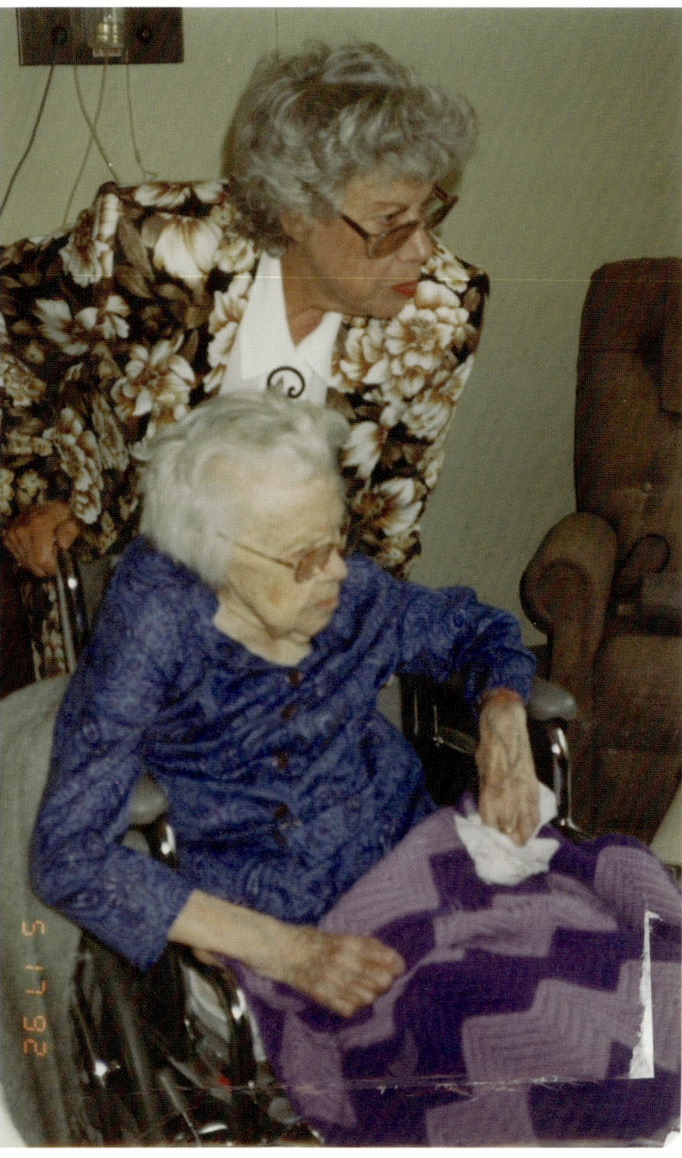

CM: Of course, our family photo archive contains similar problems. We have numerous snapshots of you with your sister Hannah and her college sweetheart, but they've become awkward reminders of their too youthful commitment. And lurking in my old address book are images of an ex-girlfriend, taken at the Jersey Shore.

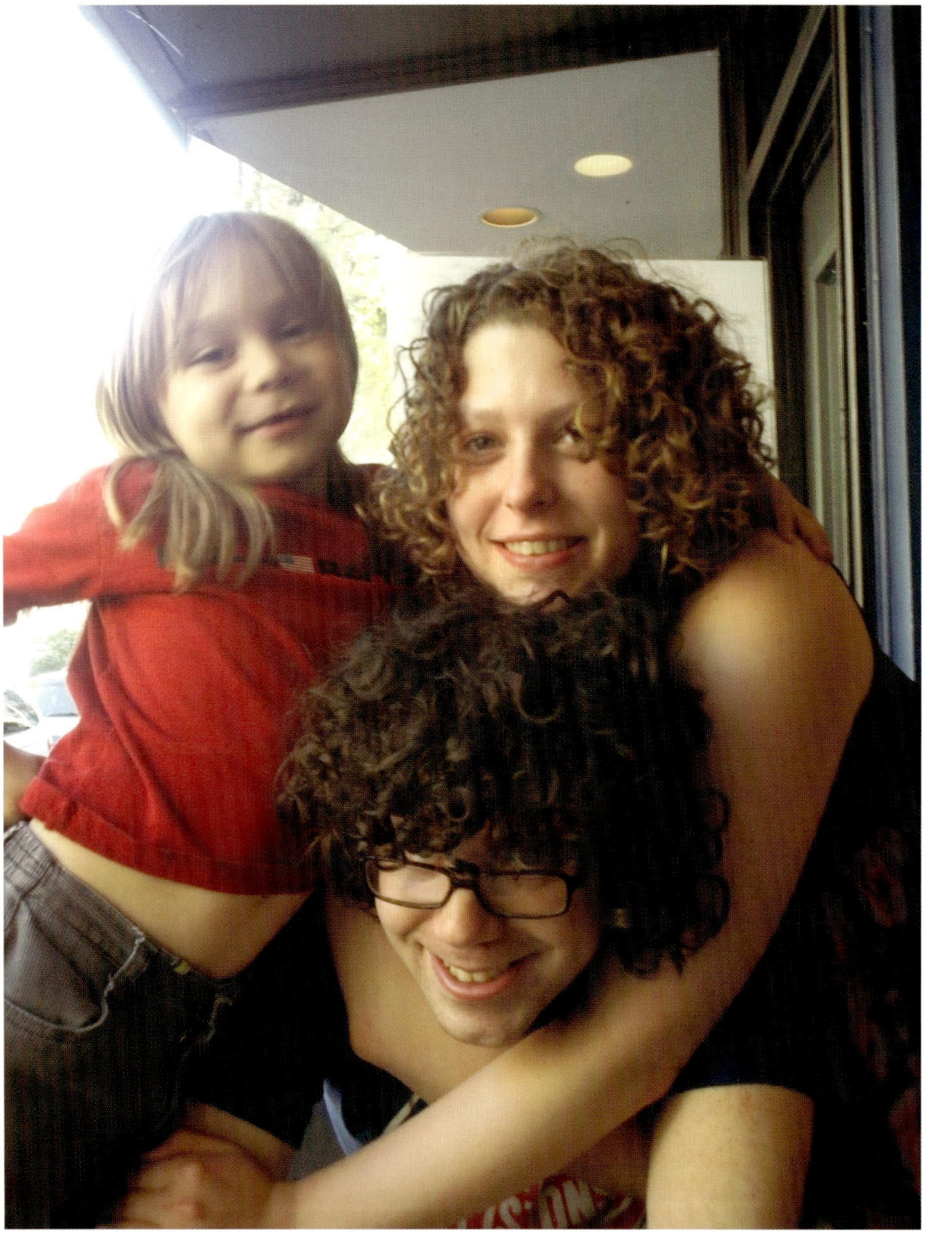

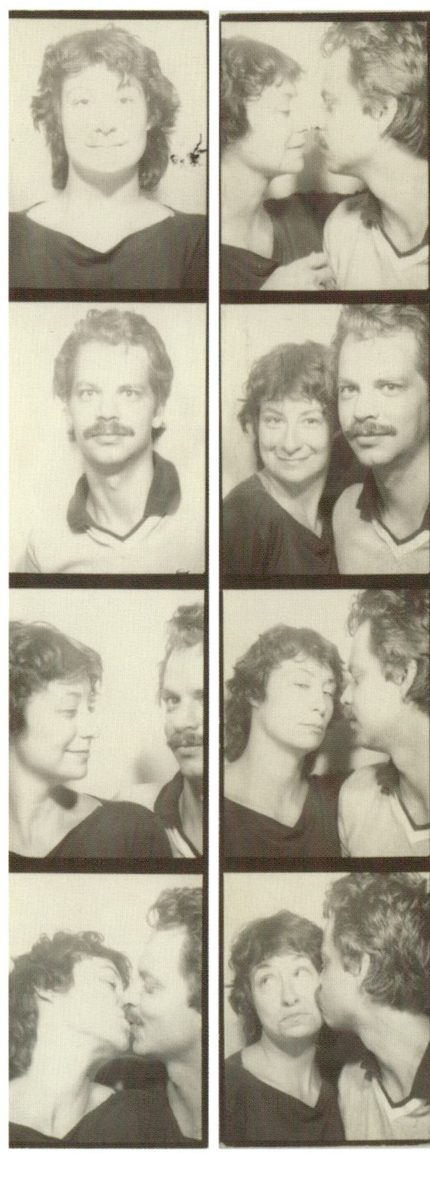

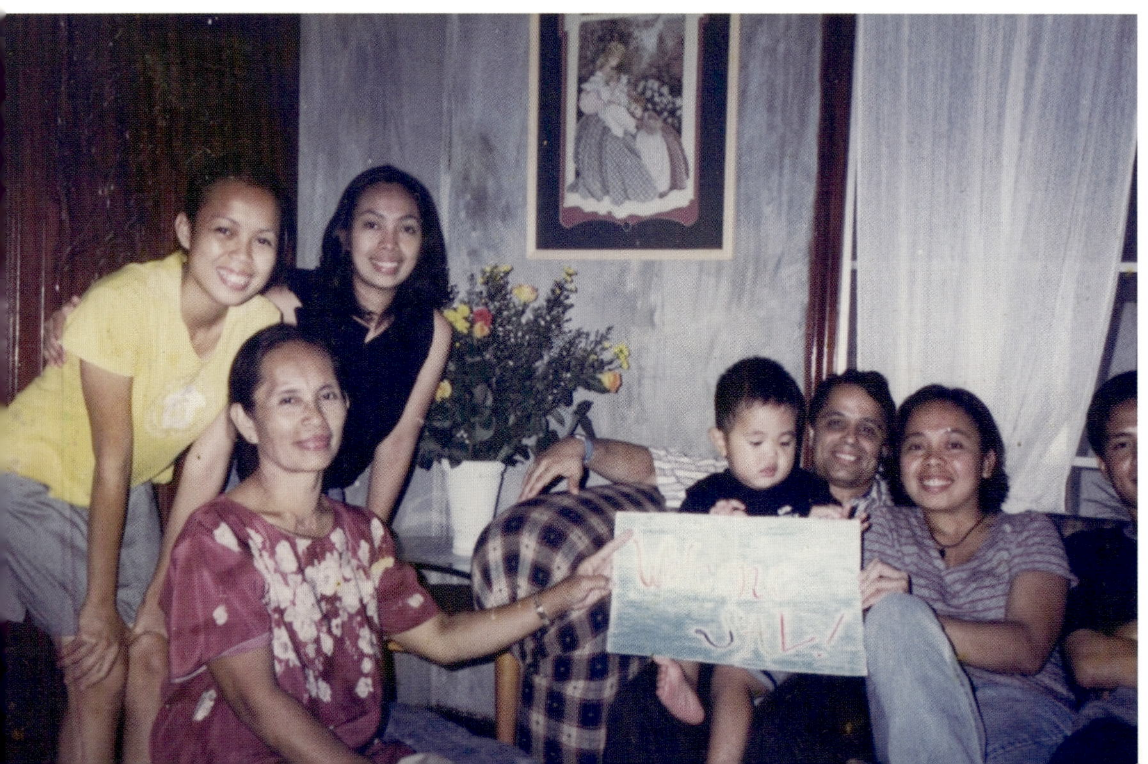

CM: The Serana archive contains snapshots of your mom's old boyfriends, too.

TS: There's a certain etiquette to the construction of a family album, which we seem to be momentarily violating. So let's change the subject.

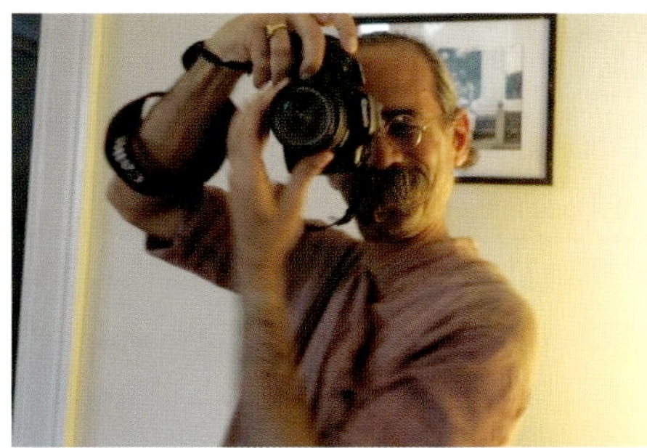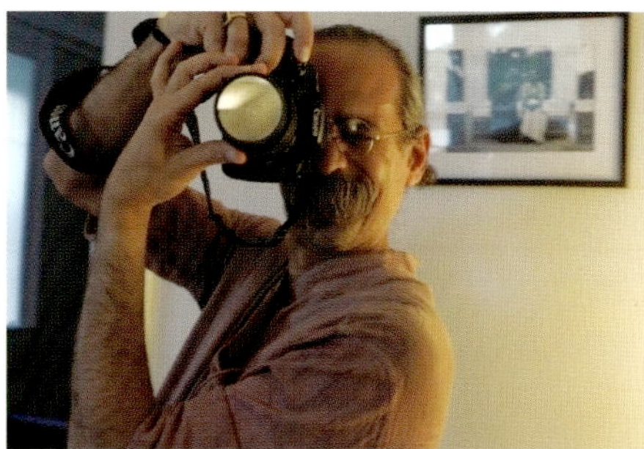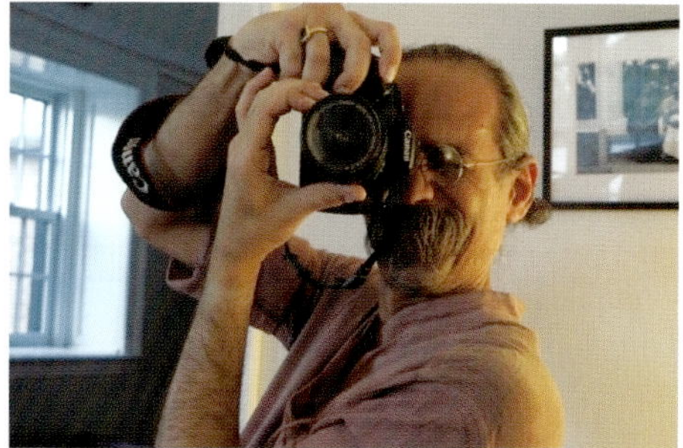

CM: One year Ashish and I taught Documentary Film Workshop together. We consistently offered conflicting advice to our bemused and sometimes frustrated students. So naturally we became the best of friends. As did our families.

TS: We ate dinners together, and their daughter Iravati was your reading buddy. Now, after ten years, they were suddenly leaving. And so we recorded our last supper together.

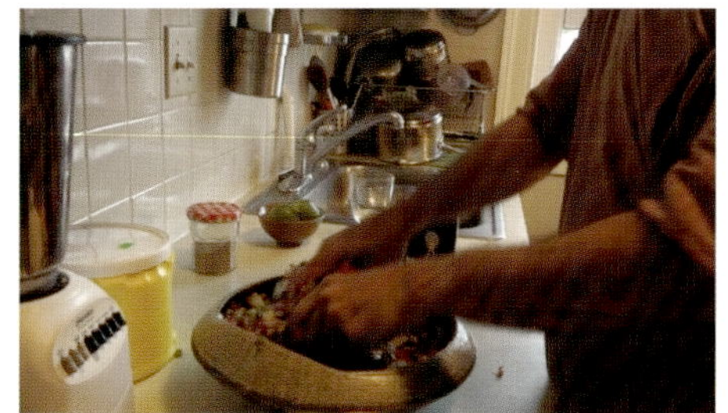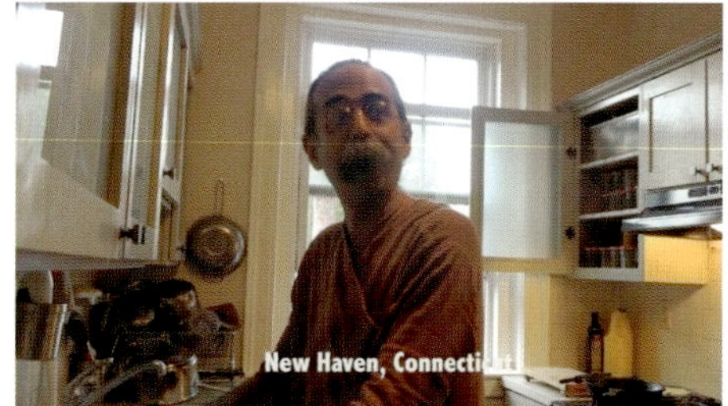

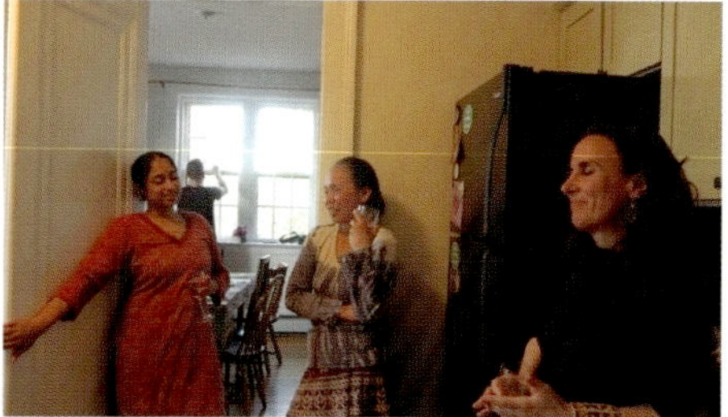

Ashish Chada: I think eating with hands is absolutely an ontological experience.

Ashwini Deo: A what experience?

Ashish: An ontological, Heideggerian experience.

Ashwini: An ontological? Heideggerian? Experience?

Dana Blanc: I don't know about these things.

Ashwini: Yeah.

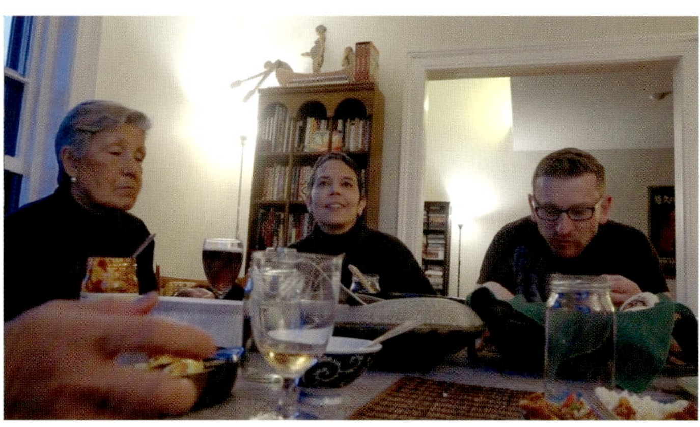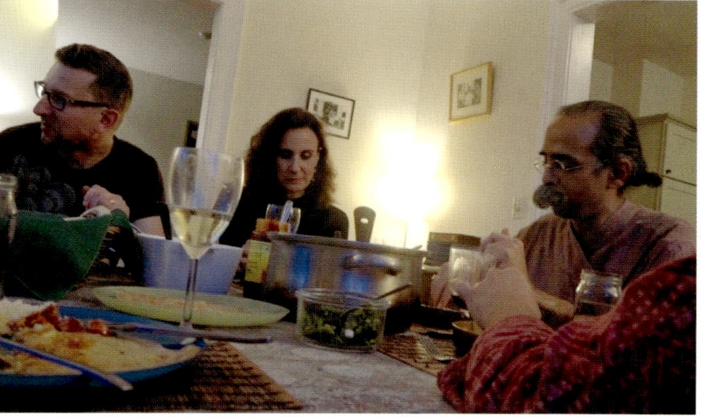

Maria Pinango: I was pulled out of bed because this was the last supper. "This is the last supper. We have to come."

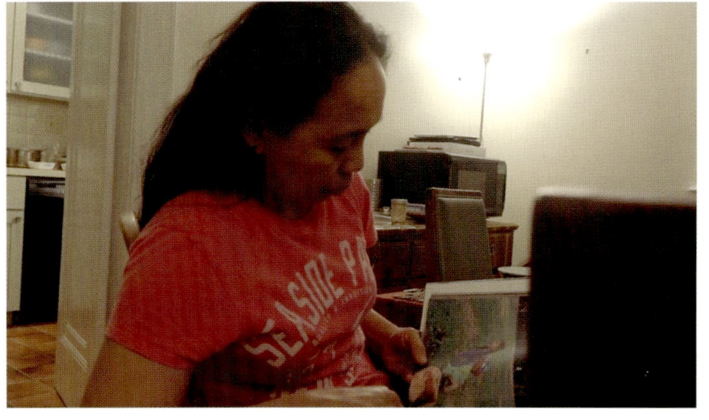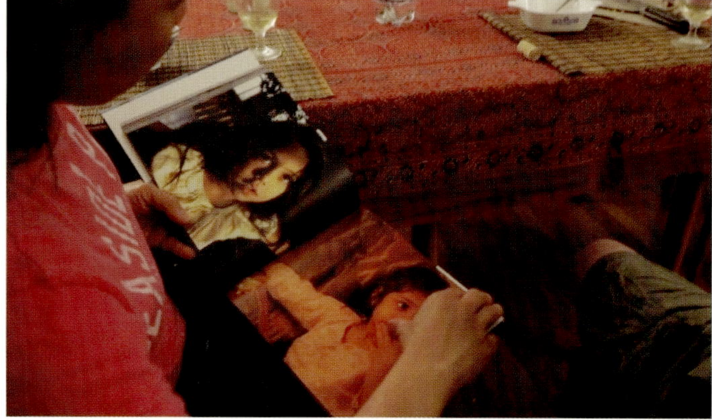

CM: In a moment of nostalgia for what we were in the process of losing, Ashish broke out some photo albums. And I came back the next day to talk to him about them.

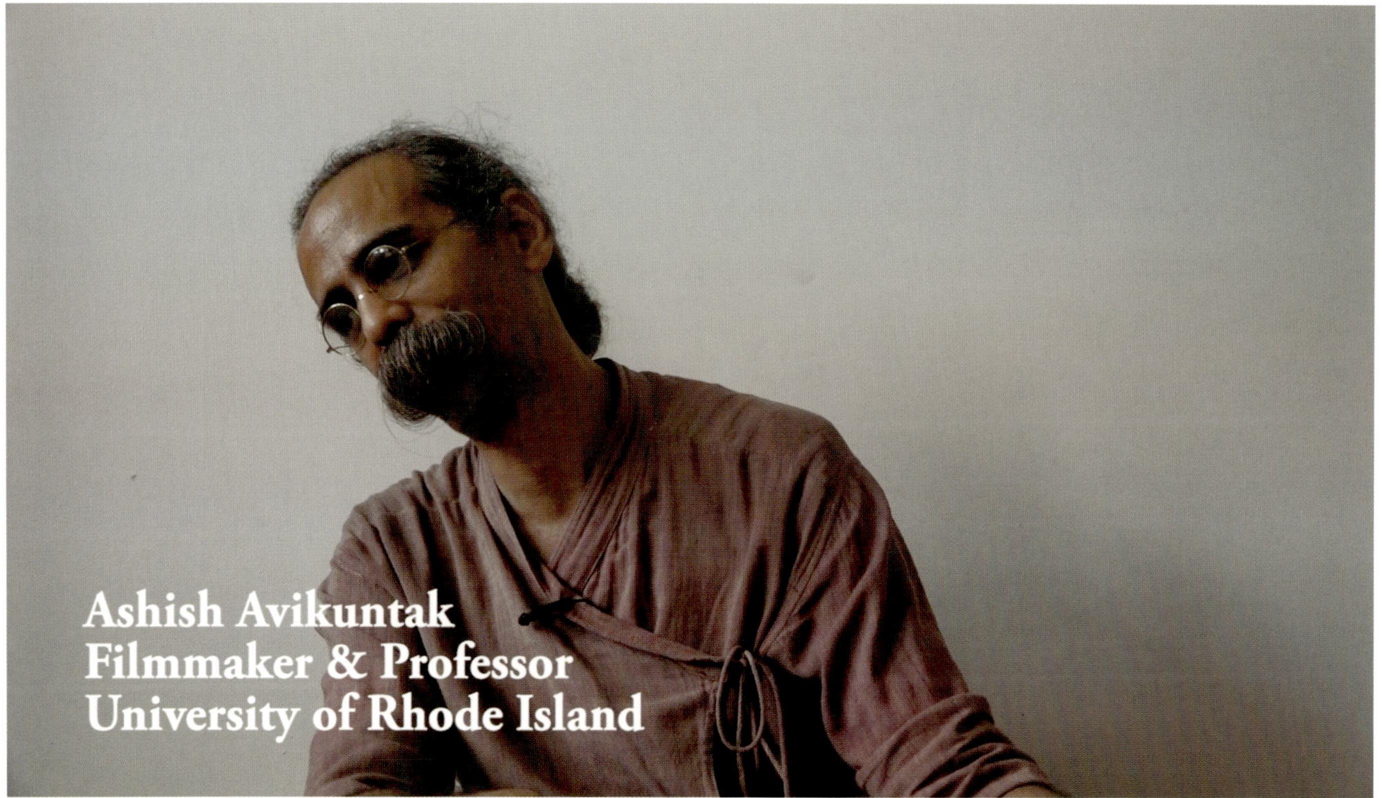

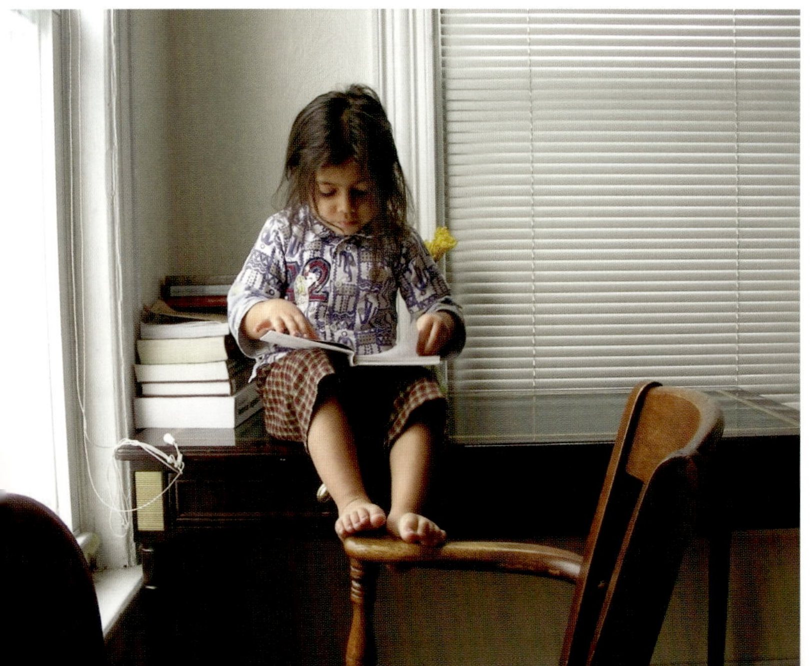

Ashish: The two books that you saw were a gift for Iravati on her 11th birthday. It's just that I have been taking so many pictures of her. I really feel strongly for the materiality of the photographic image. Not the digital, where you open your laptop and there are thousands and thousands of pictures. I really like the materiality. I have so much photographic work of family, of being together, that I think I can make multiple books. And I have always consumed a lot of photographs in the book form so to be able to produce a book… an album or something I really, really like. And it's not just on Iravati. I have done it on my own works. I have made books of my film works.

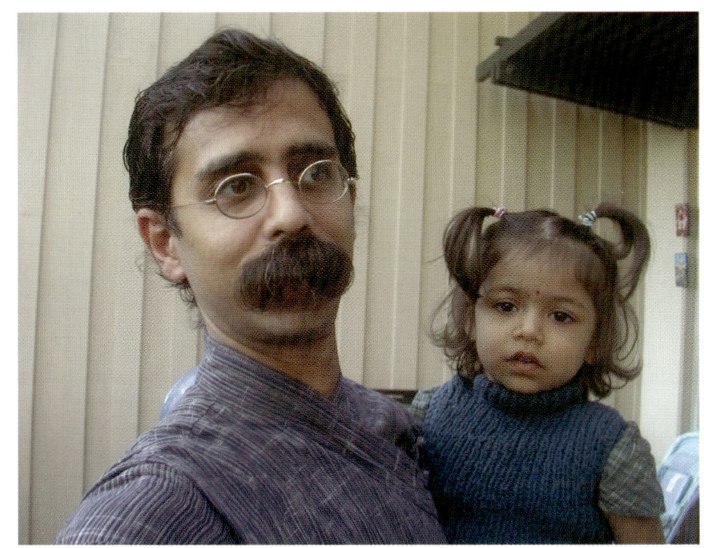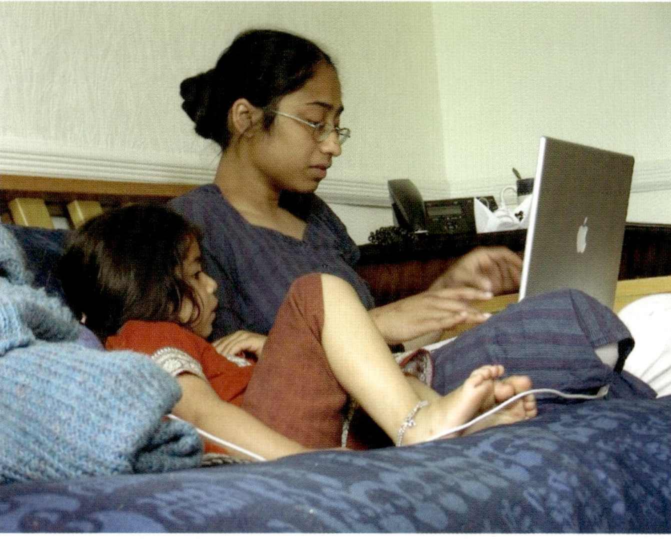

Ashish: More than the album, I think of it as an artist's book. And the good thing is this is the only one that exists, so it's not mass produced. It's almost like a work of art—an object of art. There is always the fetish of the singular object in this book form. All of this creates an aura. It is a mechanical object but it just exists as one piece. So, we came to this house in the summer, exactly around this time, end of May 2007. And I leave today. So it's been a very interesting journey these last nine years. It's had a lot of ups and a lot of downs, both in terms of the family, in terms of life.

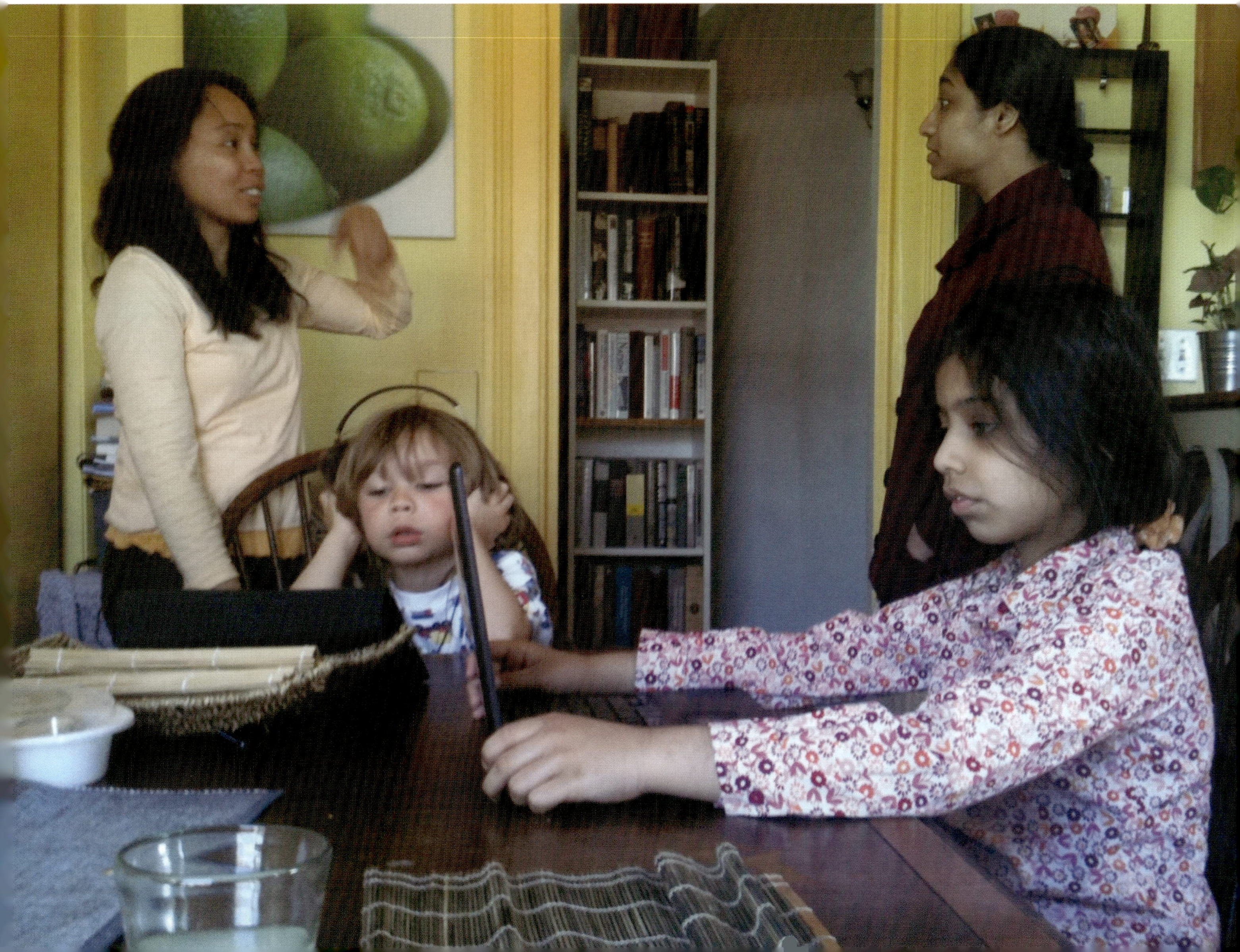

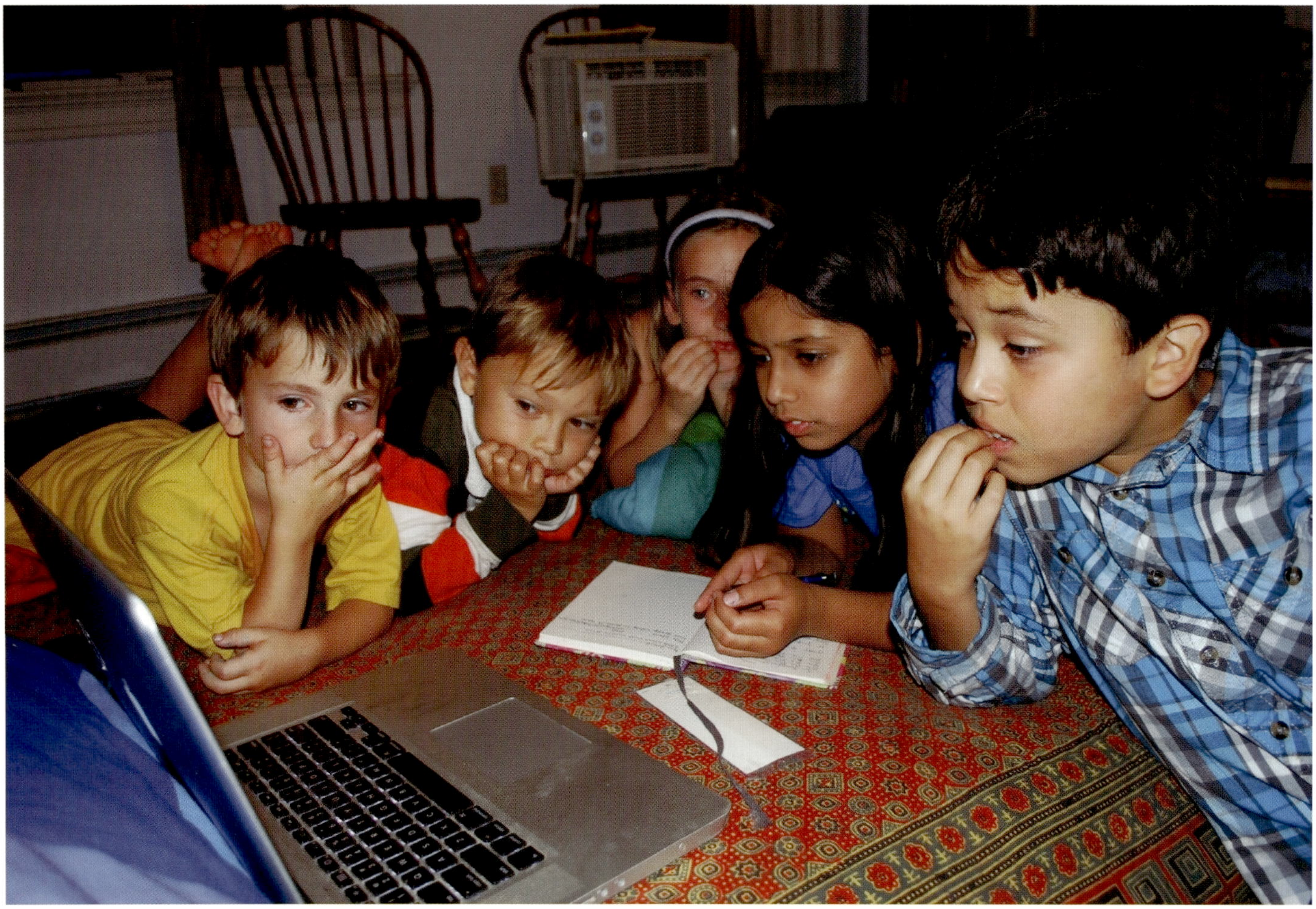

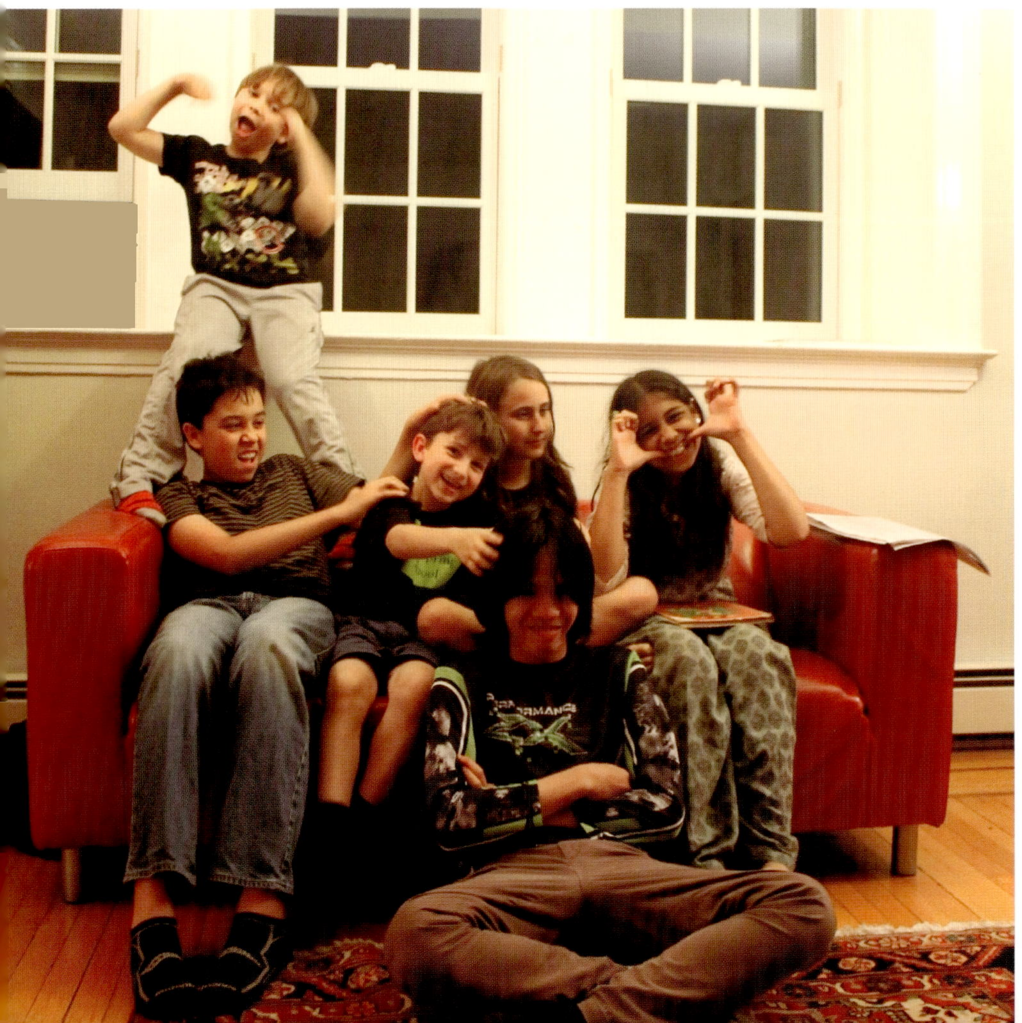

Ashish: Since I spoke to you yesterday I'm thinking I should make another book, which should be Iravati in New Haven, which would document these nine years of her. And through her it's my life, Ashwini's life, this house. So probably when I meet you next time you'll see that book— *Iravati in New Haven*. Yeah.

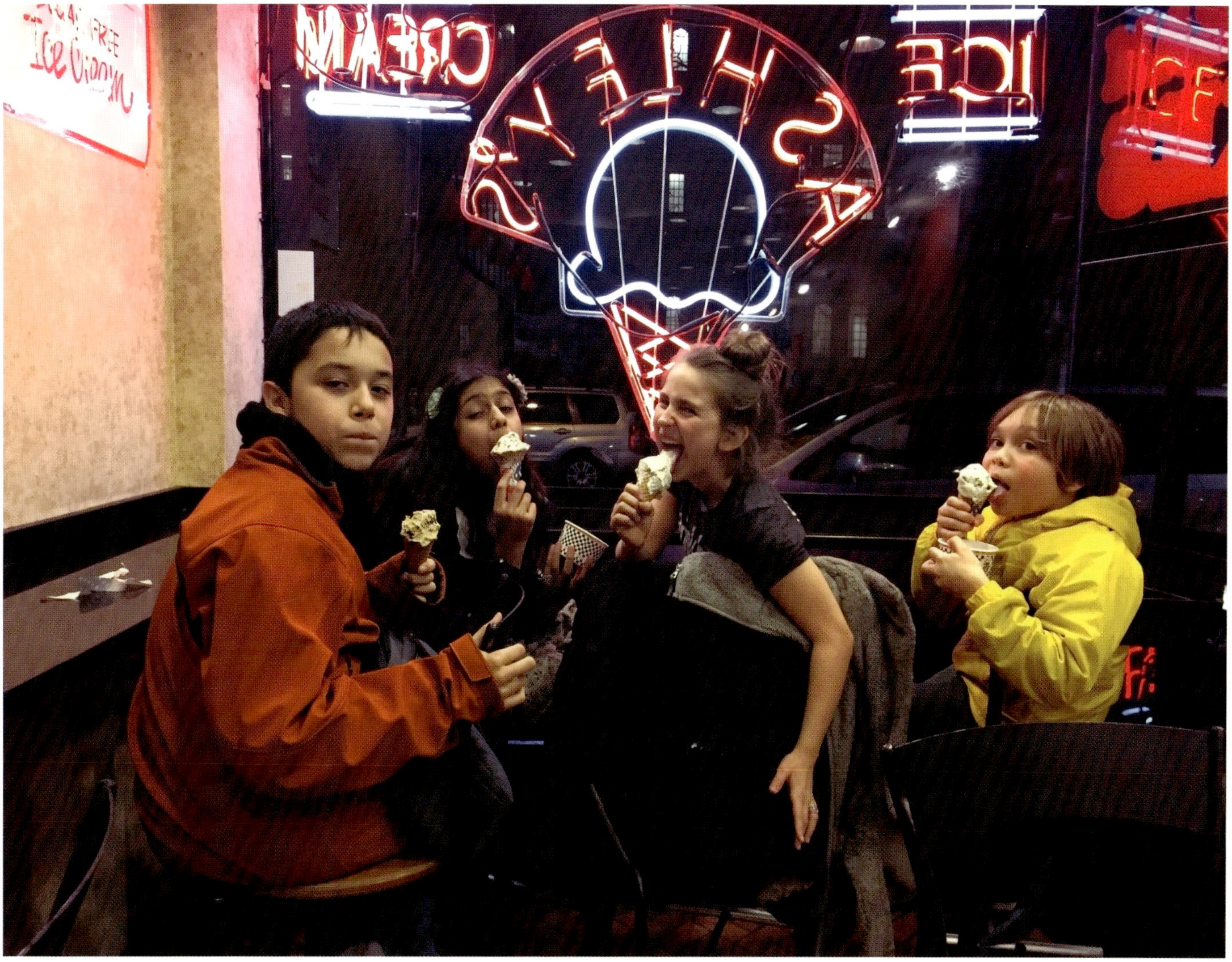

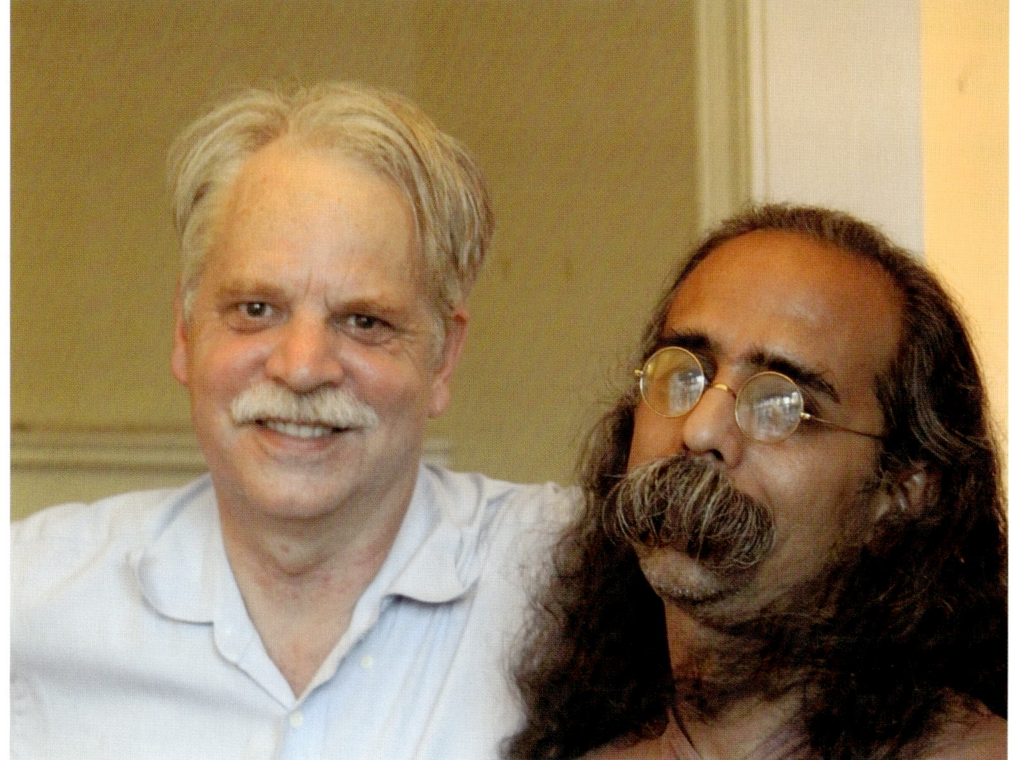

CM: Looking at these images many months later reduces me to tears. The sense of loss is simply over-powering. Would it have been better not to have taken them at all? Or should I have put them away for many years until I could appreciate them for what we had more than what we lost?

Ashish: I think I am very deeply attached to the photographic image. So deeply melancholic and nostalgic.

It had been four years since we had last visited the Philippines—the longest period of our absence. Binhi stayed behind to work as a camp counselor in New Haven and make some money (he would join us in the Philippines the following year—2018). We needed to finish shooting our documentary, but it soon became clear, even before we got there, that we had stayed away too long. The Serana family—or that part of it still in the Philippines—was in a state of crisis. Corrupt real estate speculators were threatening to take away the family's home in Cebu City. Threese's mother, Mamay, had been bouncing from one untenable situation to the next. The stress was affecting everyone. Threese's brother Chaumet Jethruvine ("Bunbun") Serana had become so depressed that he killed himself two weeks before we arrived.

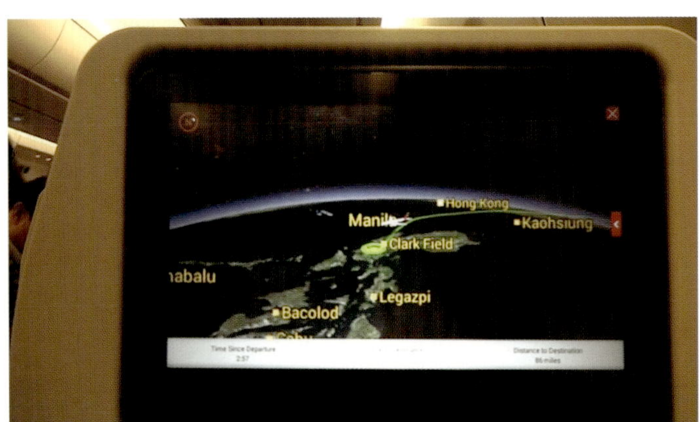

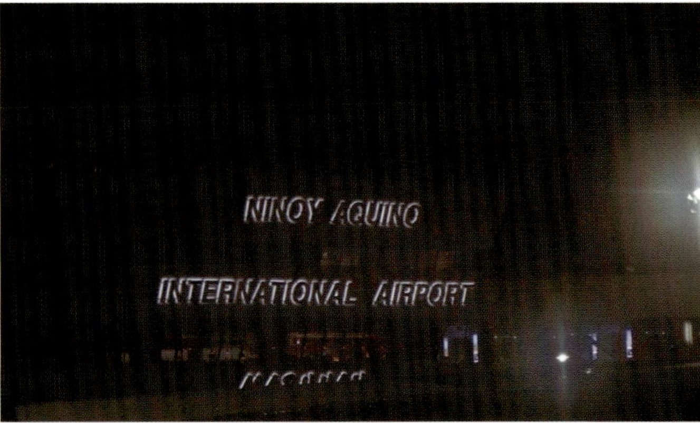

TS: When flying back and forth between New York and Manila we never have to reset our watches. The two cities are literally at opposite ends of the earth.

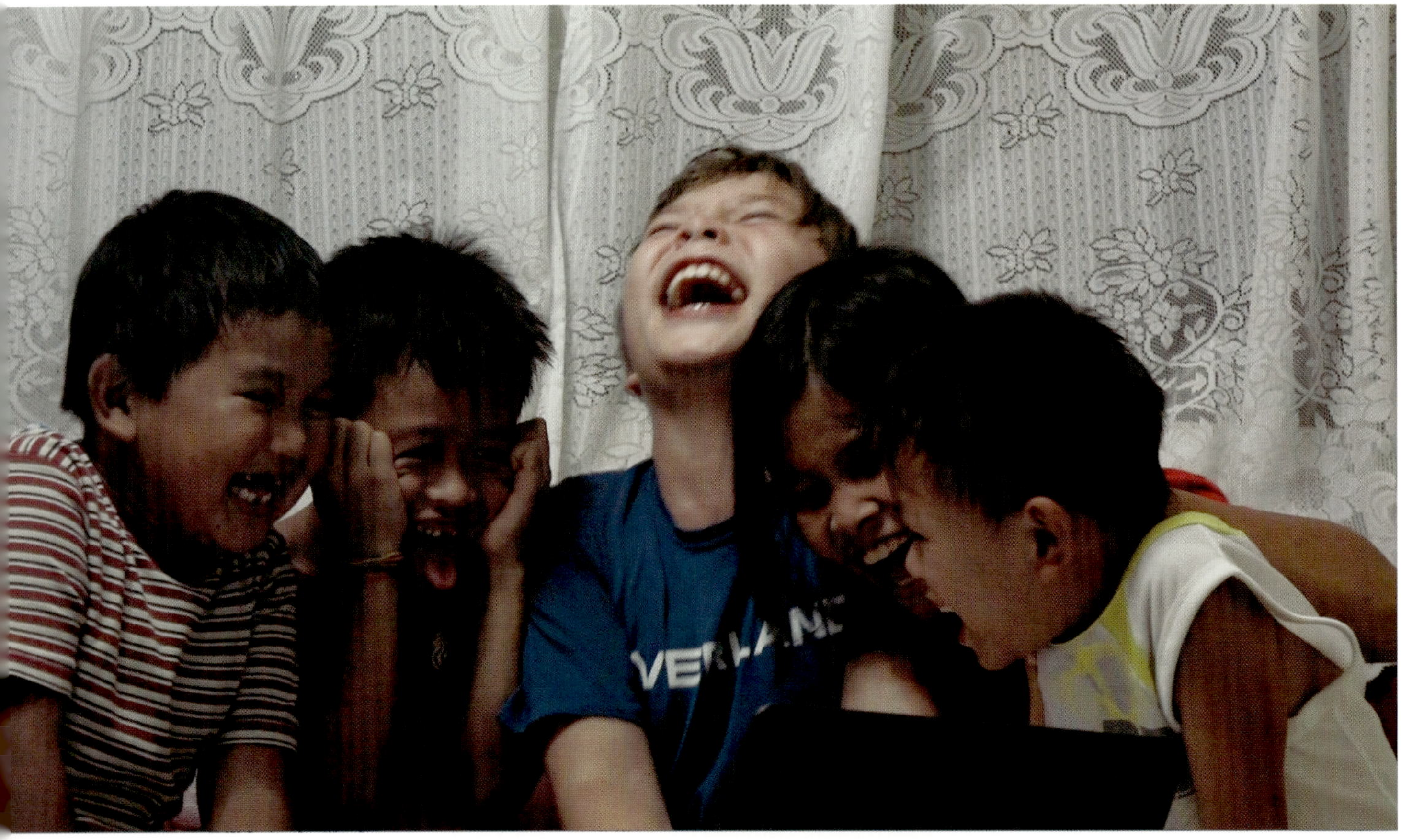

CM: When you were ten we again returned to the Philippines—to track down stories and photographs, and so you could reconnect with your relatives in Cebu and Manlapay.

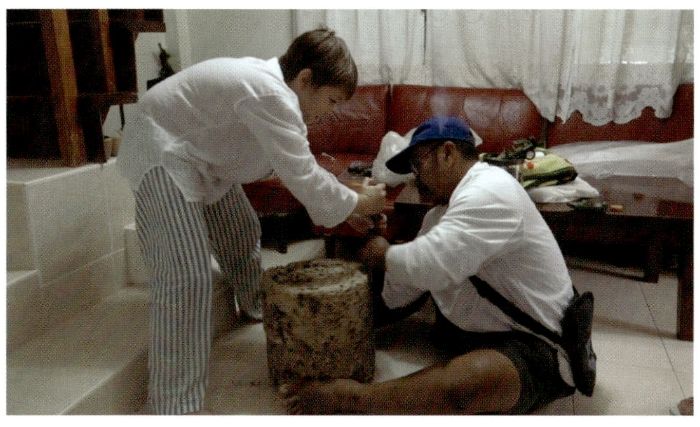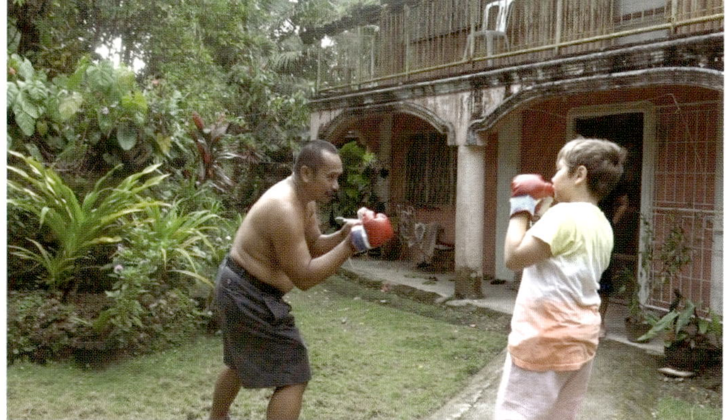

John Carlos: I can do it, I can do it.

TS: My uncle, Papa Jojo, taught you how they milled corn in the old days. And how it could make you strong so you could become a boxer like "Manny" Pacquiao.

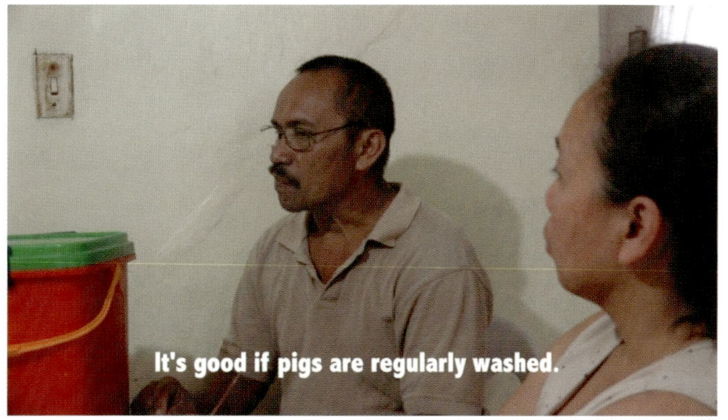

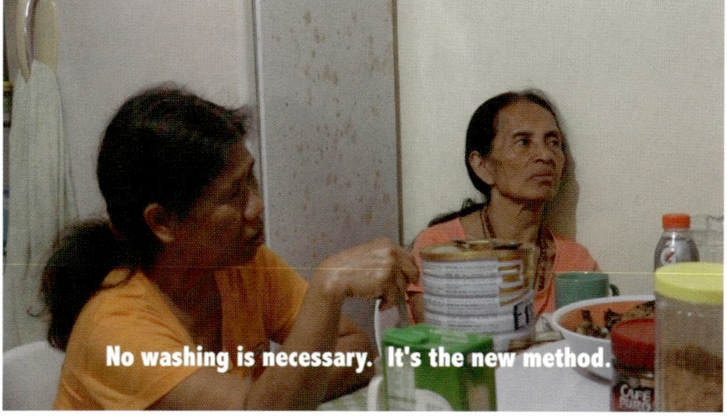

CM: Your grandmother Mamay was also returning to Manlapay. Suffering from early Alzheimer's, she felt more comfortable living in the familiar town of her youth. Her brother, Papa Jojo, who is in the piggery business, was becoming part of the support network that your mom was setting up.

Rosario "Mamay" Serana: It's good if pigs are regularly washed.

Juan "Papa Jojo" Dicdiquin: No washing is necessary. It's the new method.

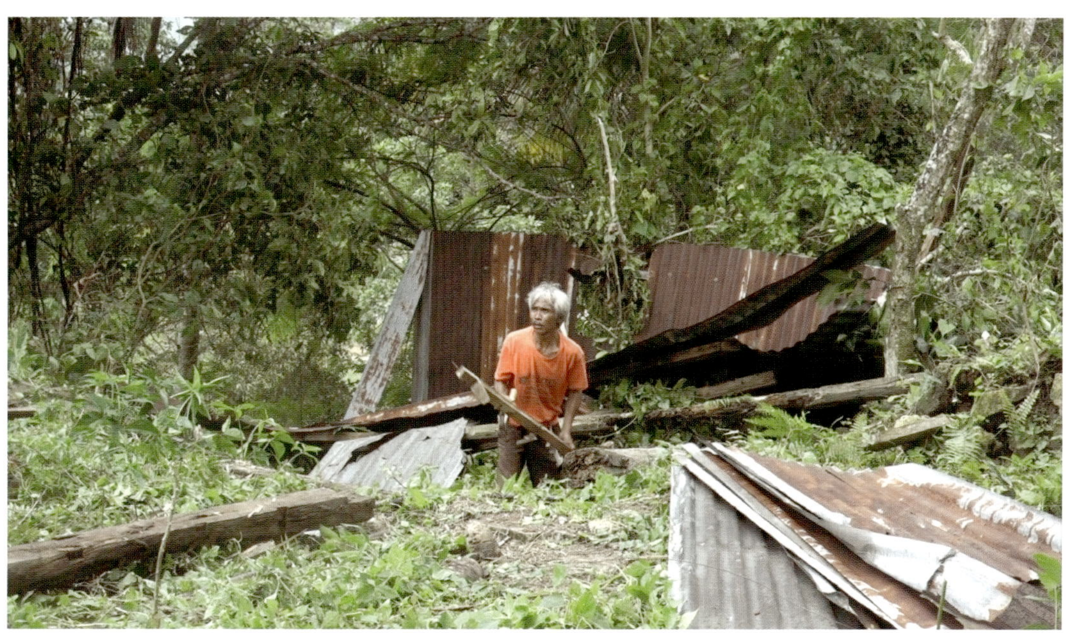

TS: As part of this arrangement, Mamay insisted that we tear down the abandoned home in which she had grown up. It was giving her nightmares.

Threese: We'll make this into small benches.

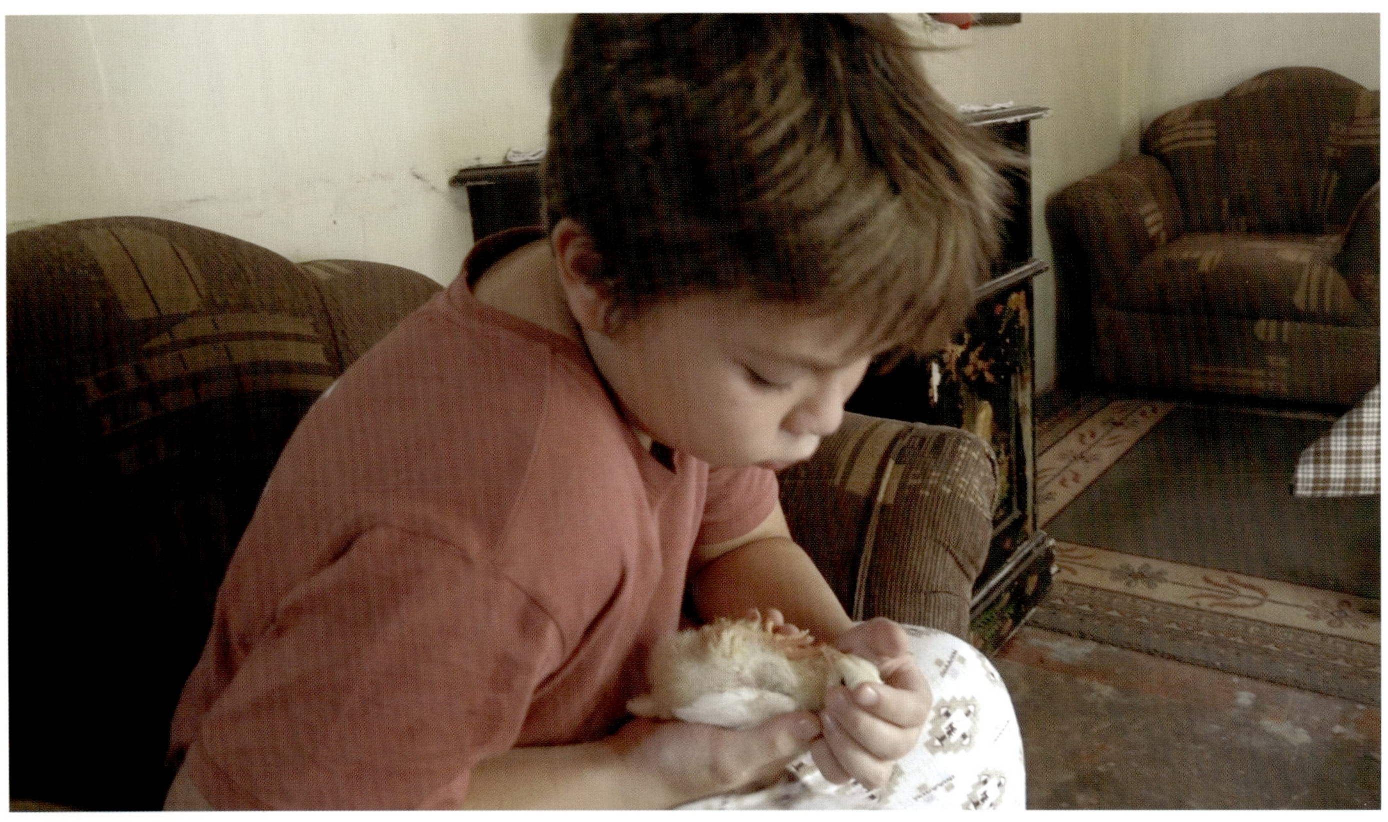

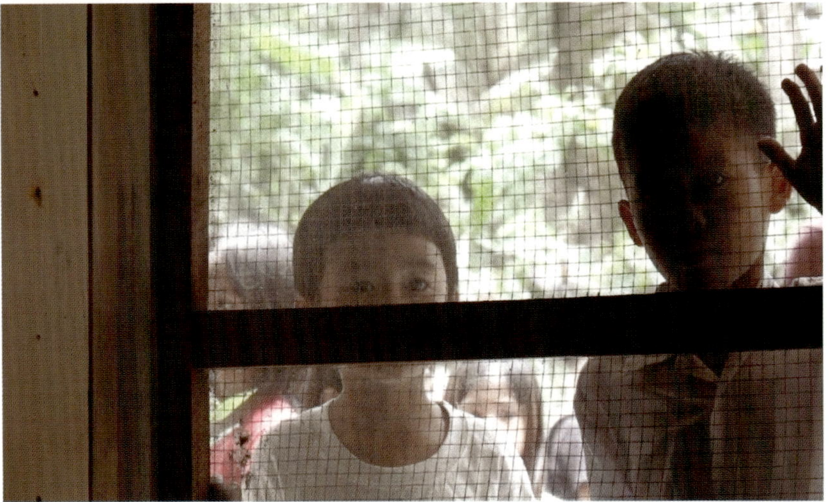

CM: You were promised a baby goat but given a fledgling chicken to raise instead.

TS: Knowing so little Cebuano, you didn't want to go back to school, but your old classmates camped out in the front yard until you agreed to go with them. Indeed, our yard became their playground.

CM: As the daily rituals of play neared their end your mom took some group photographs. These gatherings had now been marked, memorialized. But the images were not meant to be quickly shared. There is no Internet or cell phone service in Manlapay. And no handy photo shops.

TS: Rather, they have been stored away until a time when your friends have become adults working in distant cities and nations. Then, perhaps, we will circulate a few of these images on social media, evoking happy memories of a fleeting summer spent with an American cousin.

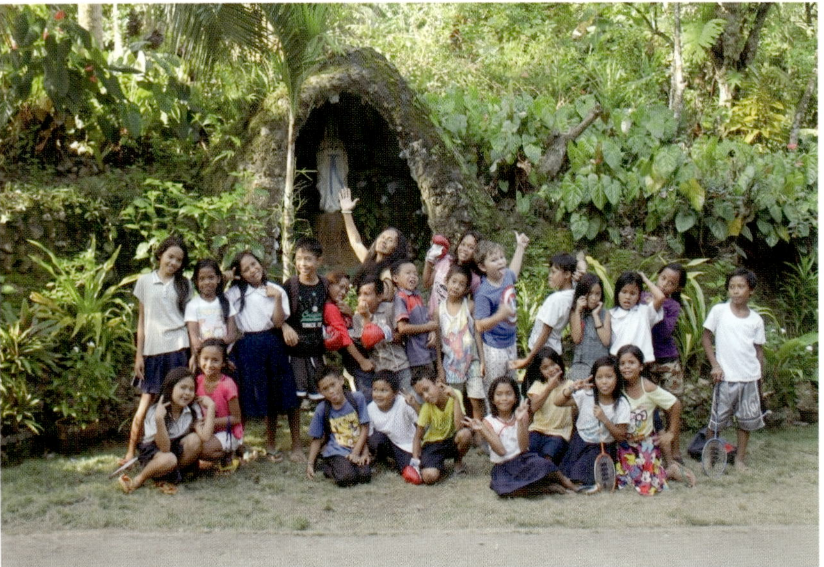

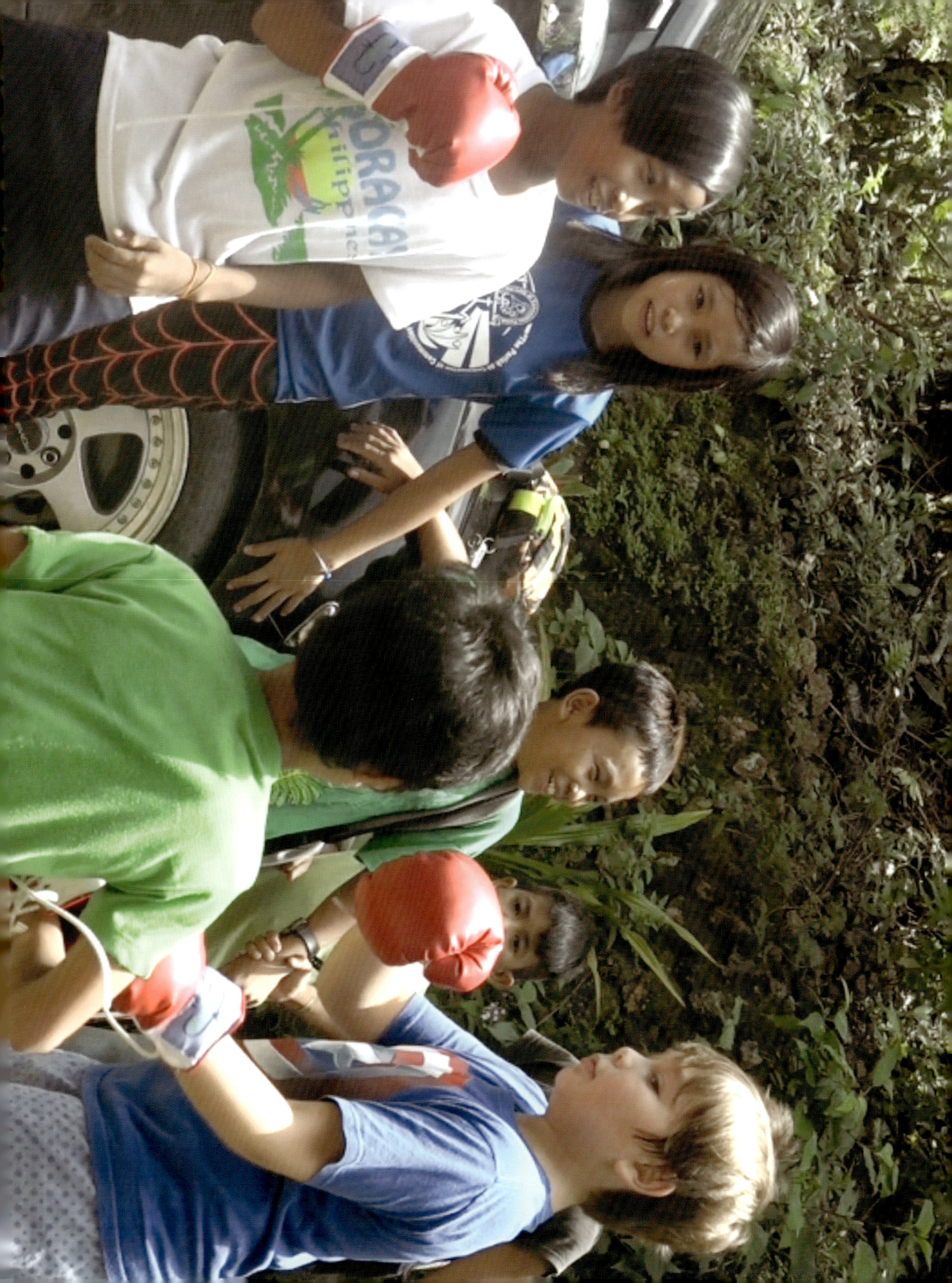

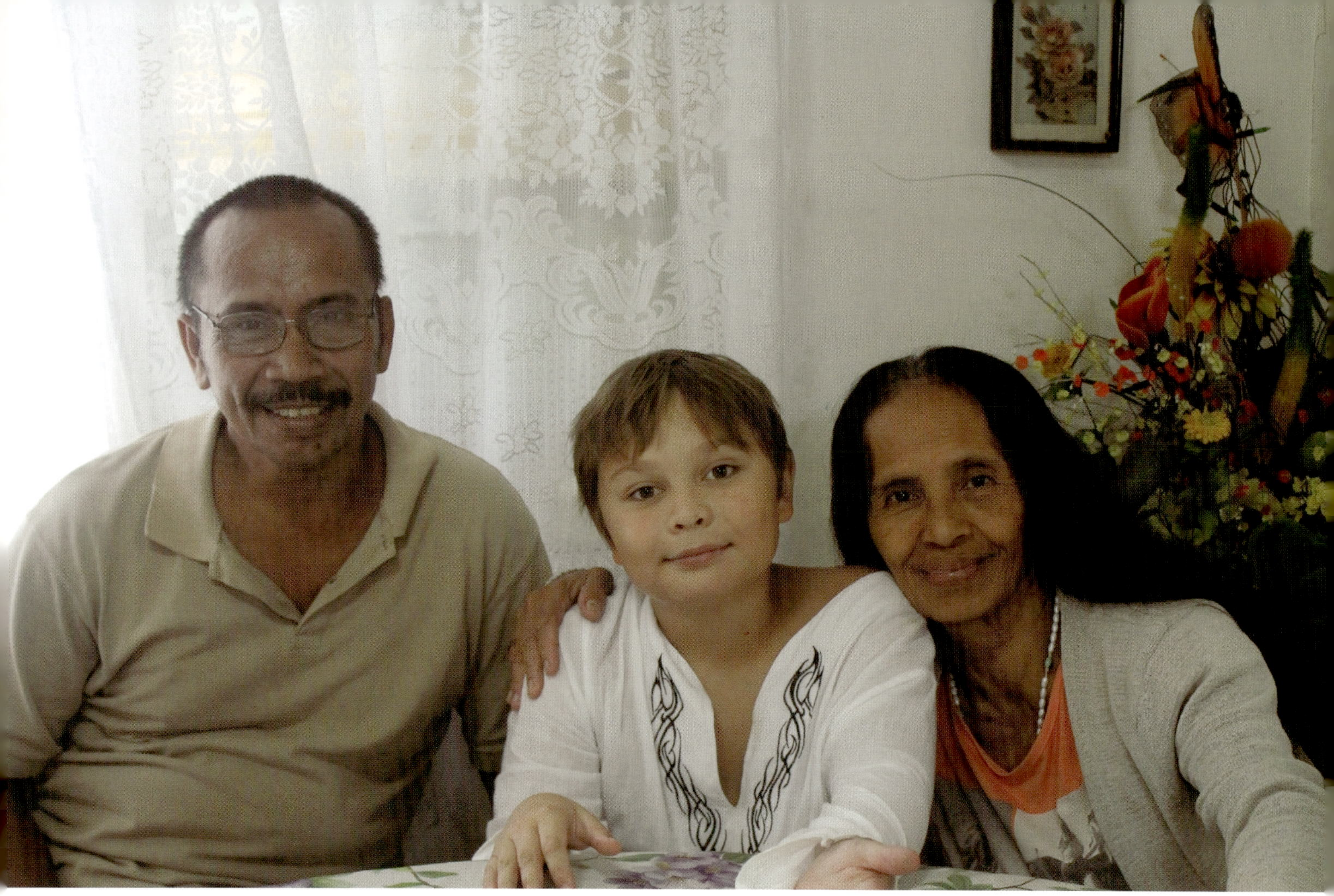

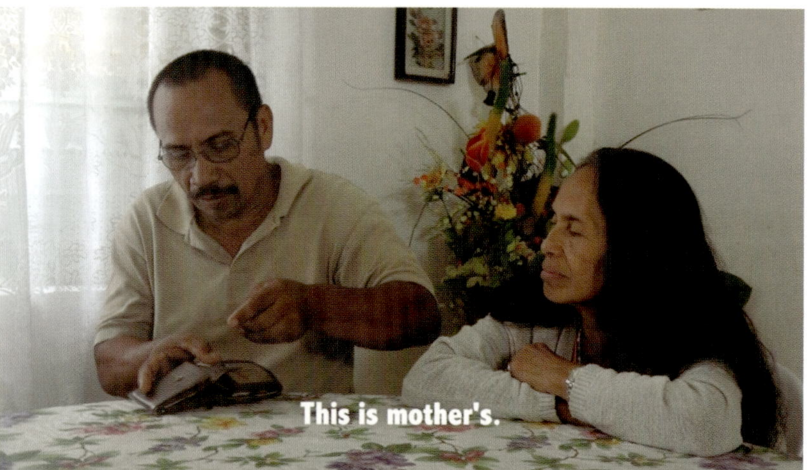

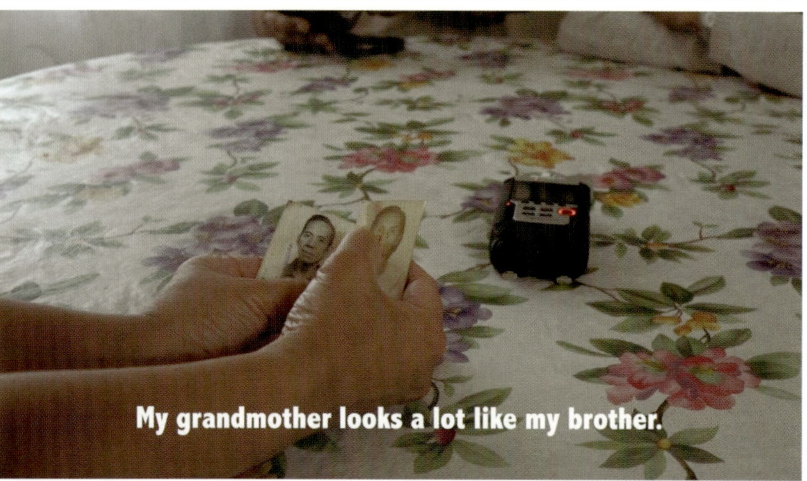

CM: Your mother and I were spending much of the summer searching for photographs of her grandparents, which might have escaped the Cebu floods. When interviewing Mamay's brother we encountered unanticipated success.

Papa Jojo: I have a picture of Father and Mother with me.

Threese: Which picture is that?

Papa Jojo: Only Father's.

Mamay: Let's copy and enlarge them.

Papa Jojo: This is Mother's.

Threese: This is my grandmother.

Mamay: I am glad you have the photographs.

Papa Jojo: It's from a long time ago.

Threese: My grandmother looks a lot like my brother, Jid.

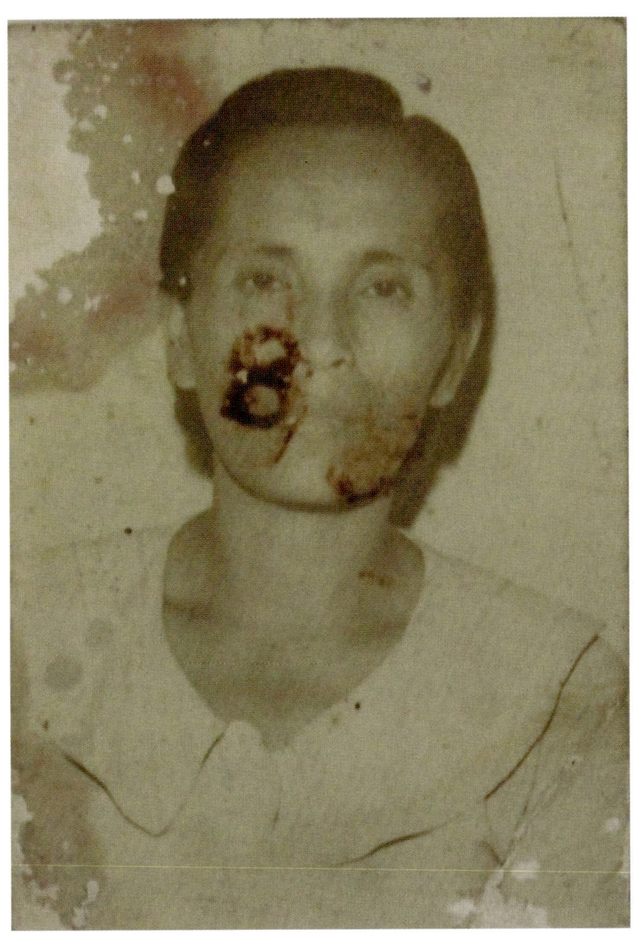

CM: So this is the woman who gave birth to your grandmother on the road to Manlapay and later died under an overturned coal truck.

Threese: Our search for the family's Jewish roots proved more elusive. We asked about the old Jewish prayer book that started it all.

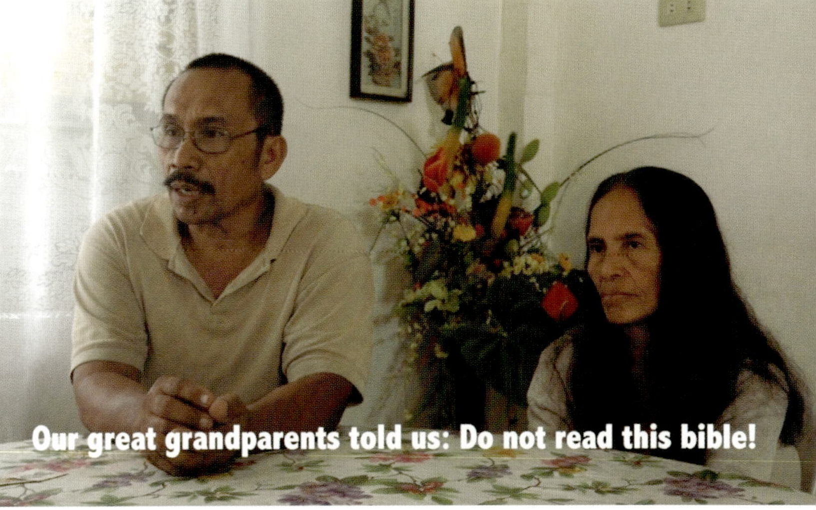

Papa Jojo: The way it was back then, our great grandparents told us, "Do not to read this bible!" Because we cannot understand the text. It would drive us crazy. The words were in Greek or Latin. We cannot understand what the words in the bible say because it has not yet been translated into Tagalog, English or Visayan. We were forbidden from reading the book. Only my great grandfather Ambrosio could read it.

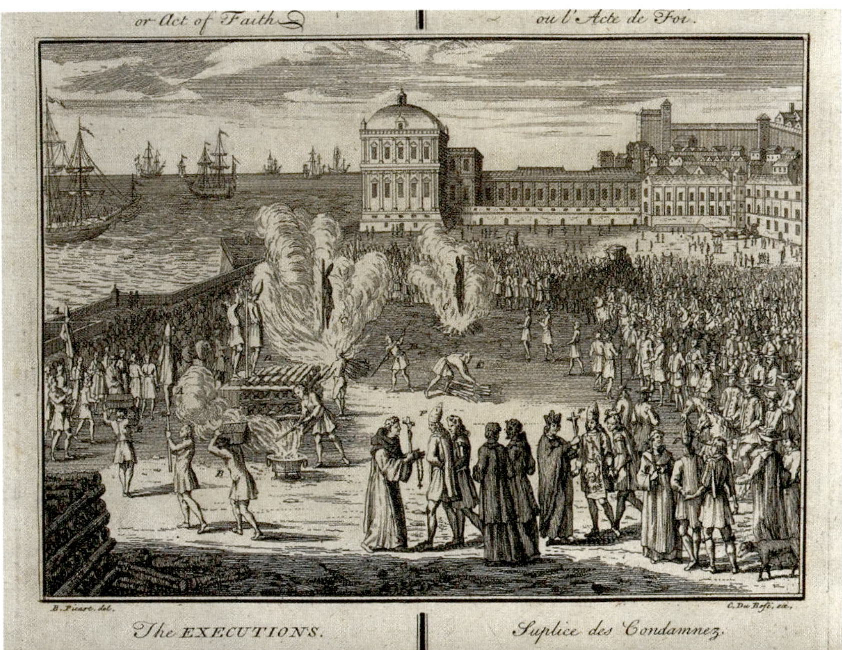

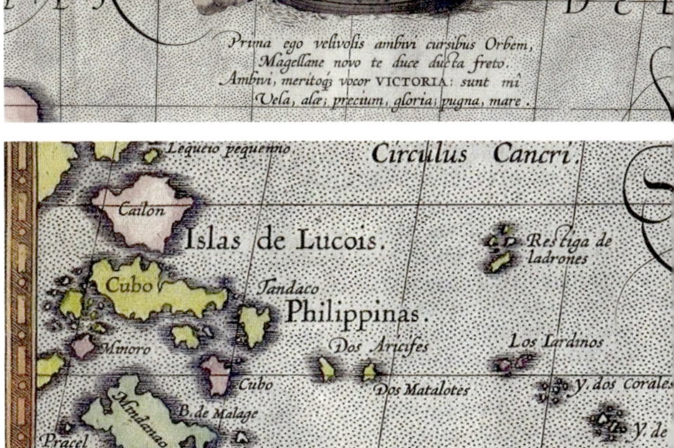

TS: Your dad gave me an article about two Filipino Conversos, named Jorge and Domingo Rodriquez. Caught practicing their Jewish religion, they were sent to Mexico and burned at the stake.

CM: After reading the piece your mom wept for a long time: The Rodriguez are part of her family tree. Was the ancestor who claimed to be one of Magellan's sailors a Jew who decided it was safer to stay in Cebu than return to Spain and its inquisition?

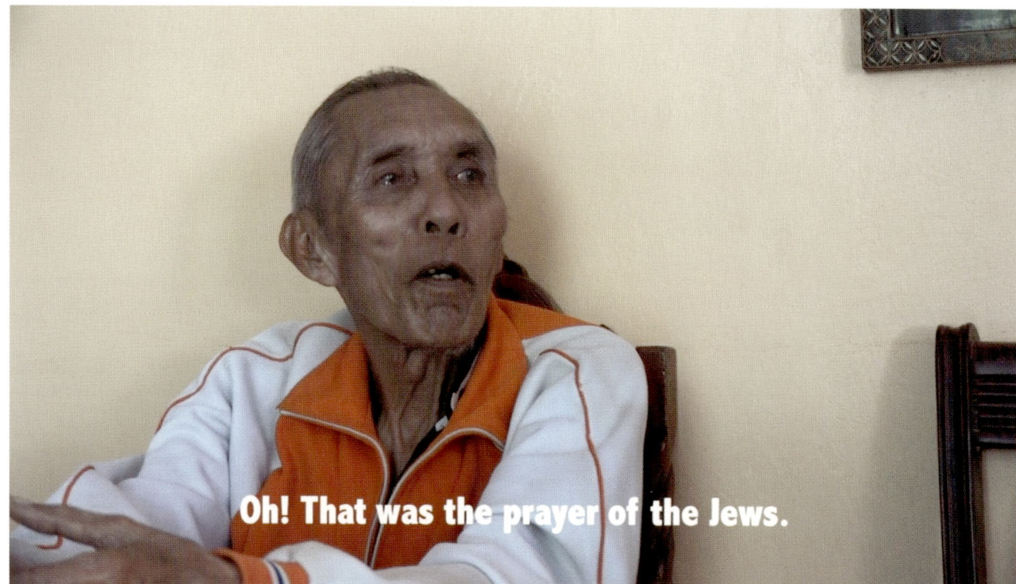

TS: Next, I asked Lolo Meling, your great grandfather's younger brother.

Threese: When Mamay was small, she saw and heard her great grandfather Ambrosio saying a different prayer.

Lolo Meling Dicdiquin: Oh! That was a prayer of the Jews.

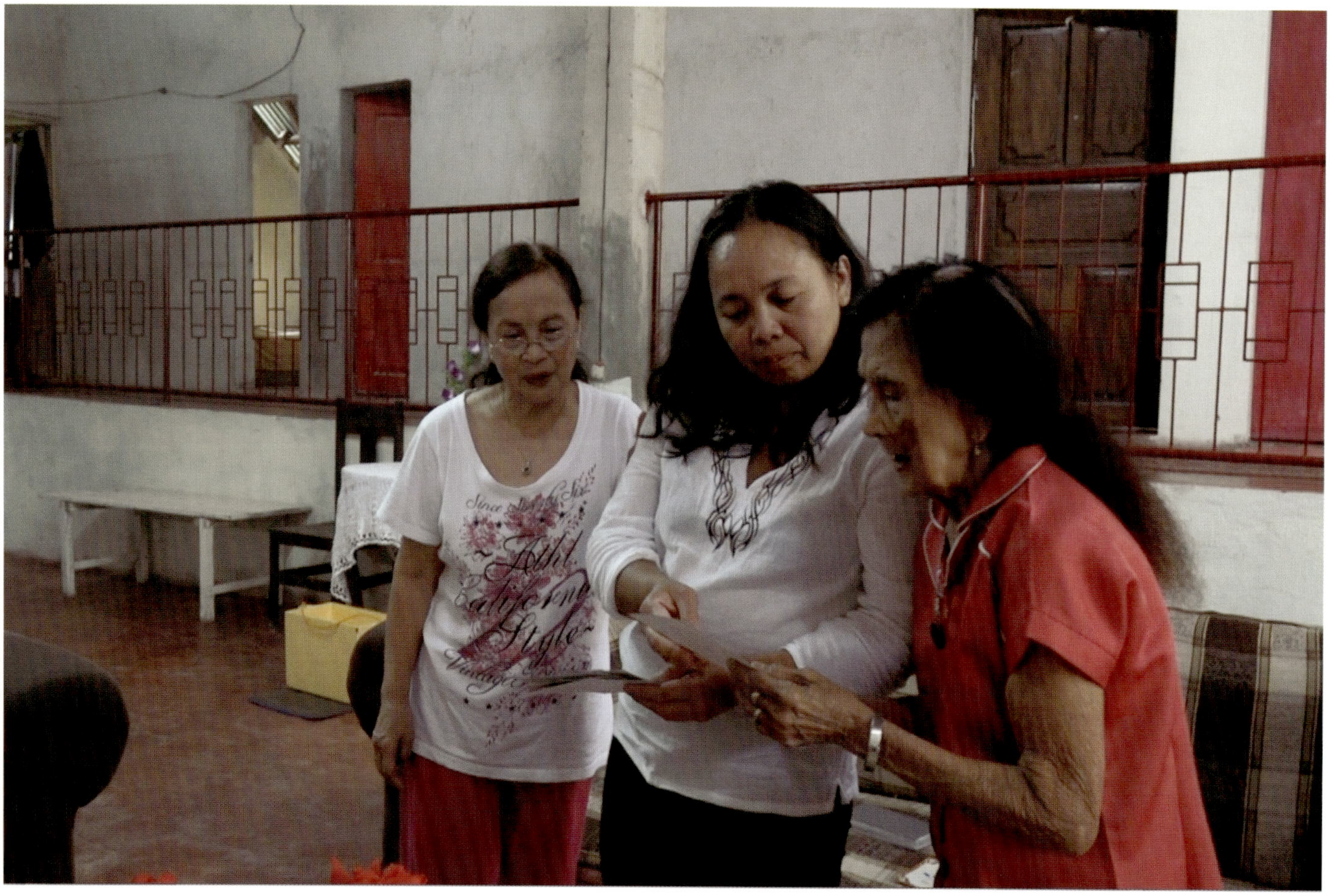

TS: Then, when we were looking at old photos with Auntie Guiling, she remarked that the family's commitment to education came from being Jewish.

CM: Next year, maybe you'll attend your sister's Seder and ask the four questions.

Manlapay's annual school-wide athletic competition began with a parade and featured organized sports such as badminton and volleyball, however, many of the students (including John Carlos) seemed more interested in playing local children's games such as dampa (involving rubber bands) and sticker.

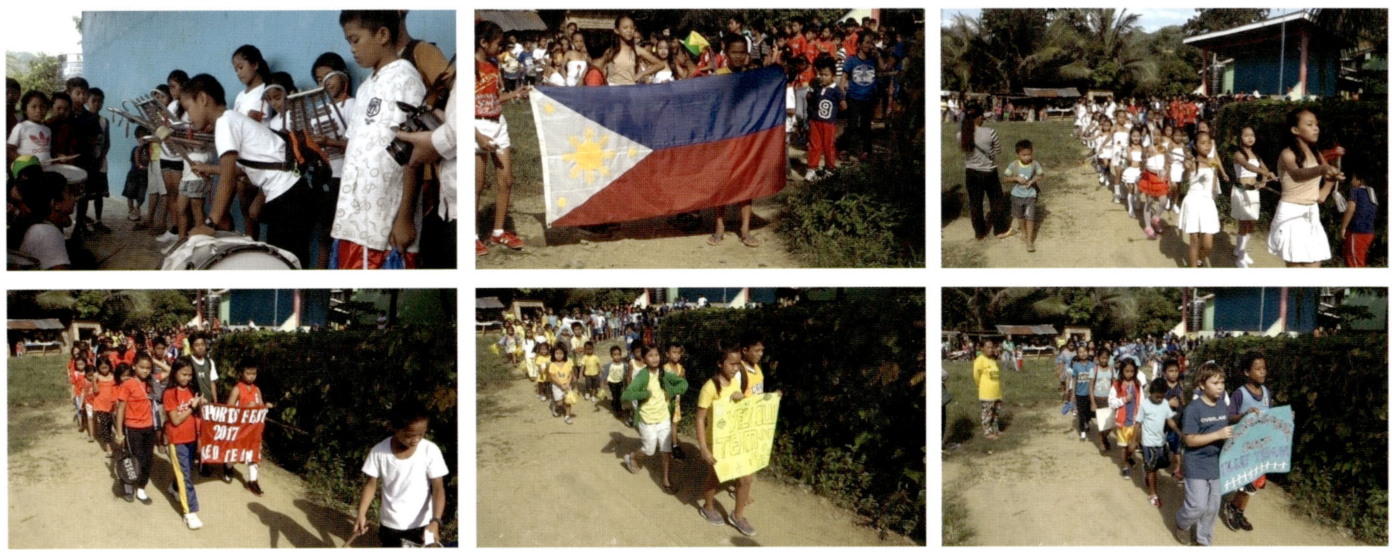

TS: Our stay in Manlapay ended with a school-wide athletic competition.

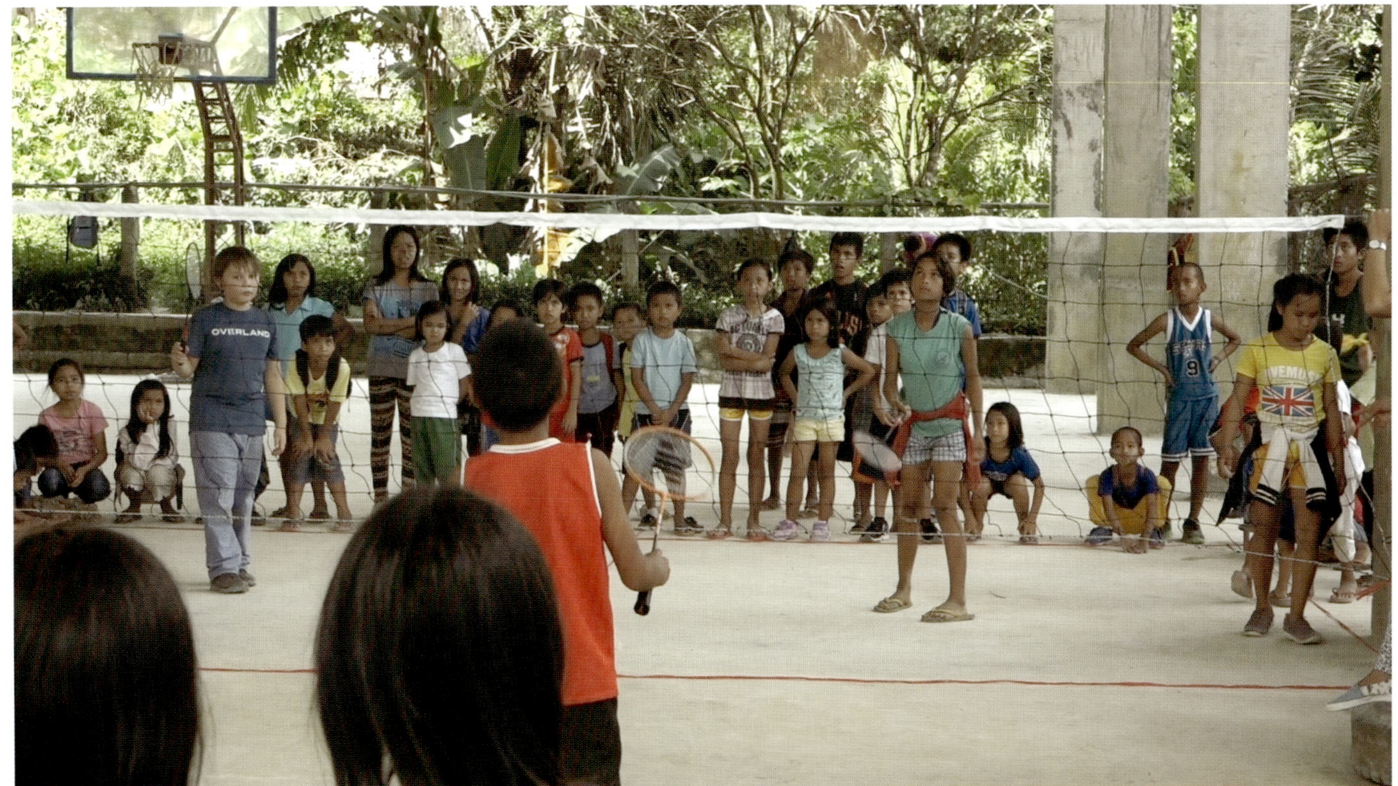

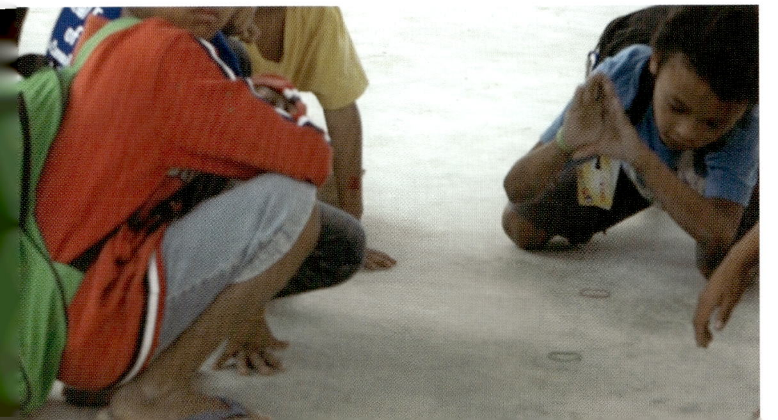

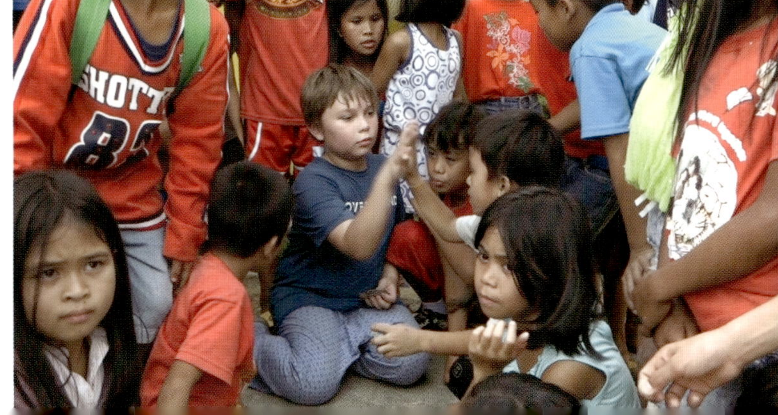

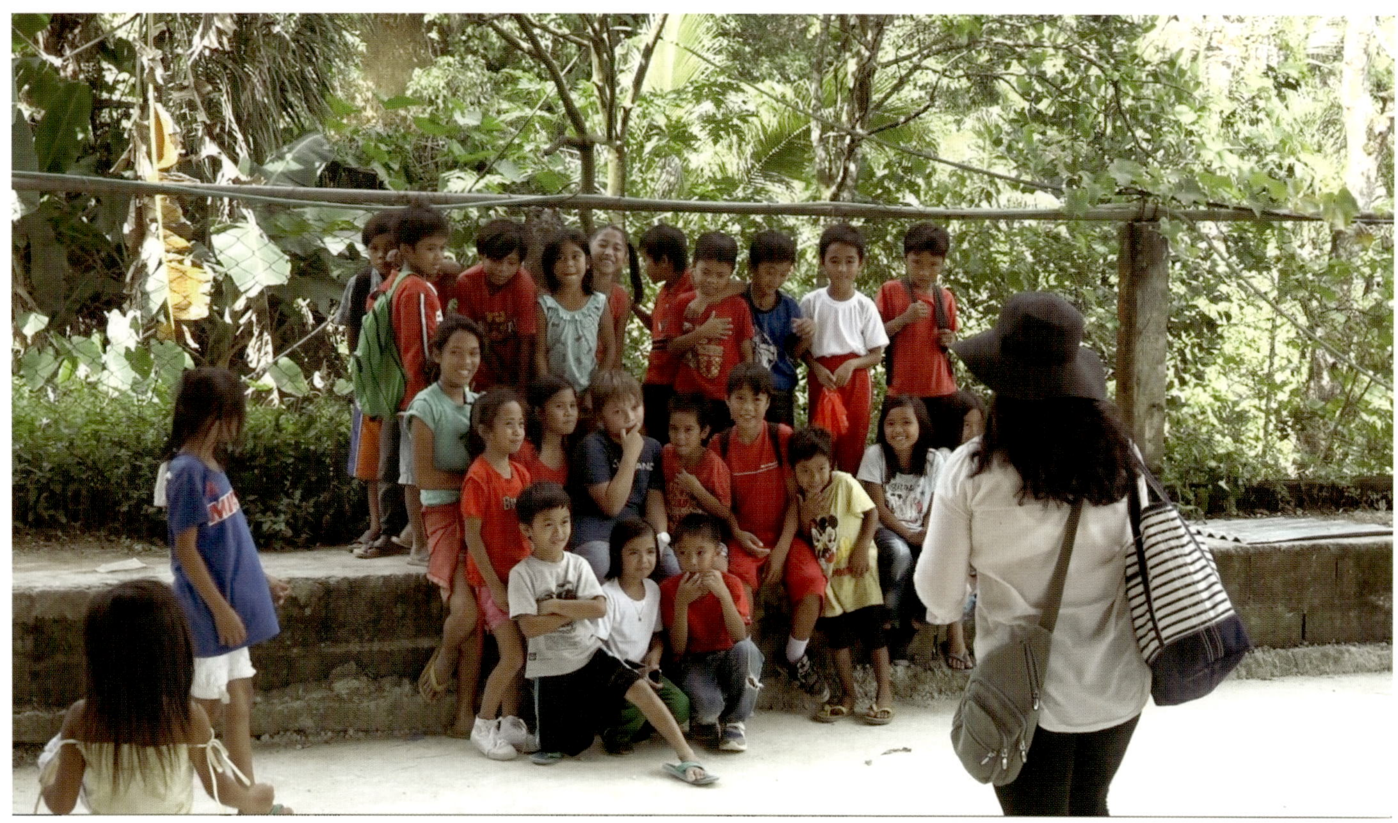

TS: We were about to head home, but first there was one last stop we had to make.

We traveled to Davao, Mindanao, to meet Victor Gross and his family—an encounter that proved to be the perfect conclusion to our documentary. For me, the trip was part of a much longer personal journey in which I gradually came to feel at home in the Philippines. In the process of making this film we had talked with many family members and with friends who had become family. Now we went to visit a family we had never met but with whom we had developed a profound, if imaginary, connection. Victor's father, Edward Meyer Gross, was a New Yorker who spent the last forty-four years of his life in the Philippines. He and his first wife, the Filipina actress Titay Molina, made the first feature films in the Philippines. Philippine film scholars had characterized him as an agent of American imperialism, but I saw it otherwise. Titay Molina was part of a world-wide wave of women filmmakers, and Edward Meyer Gross provided the political cover that allowed her and their Filipino colleagues to produce a remarkable series of nationalistic films (not all Americans in this period wanted to turn the Philippines into a U.S. colony). Were we not some modern-day version of this couple? Were they not our historical counterparts? This I knew: When we were in the Philippines I took my cues from Threese (including her admiration for Rodrigo Duterte, president of the Philippines). I suspect that E. M. Gross did the same. Making this documentary was a way—perhaps the only way—to find out more about E. M. Gross and his family. Edward Gross (E.M. Gross's grandson) met us at our hotel and drove us to the family compound a few miles away.

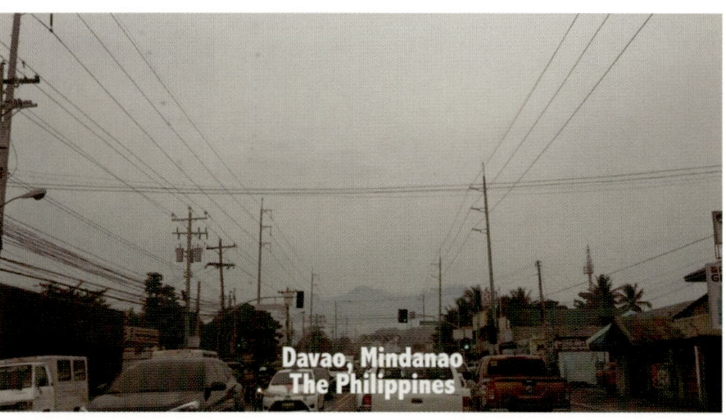

Threese: Is that Mount Apo?

Edward Gross: That's … on the far end is Mount Apo.

TS: Thanks once again to the Internet, we were on another blind date, this time between two families.

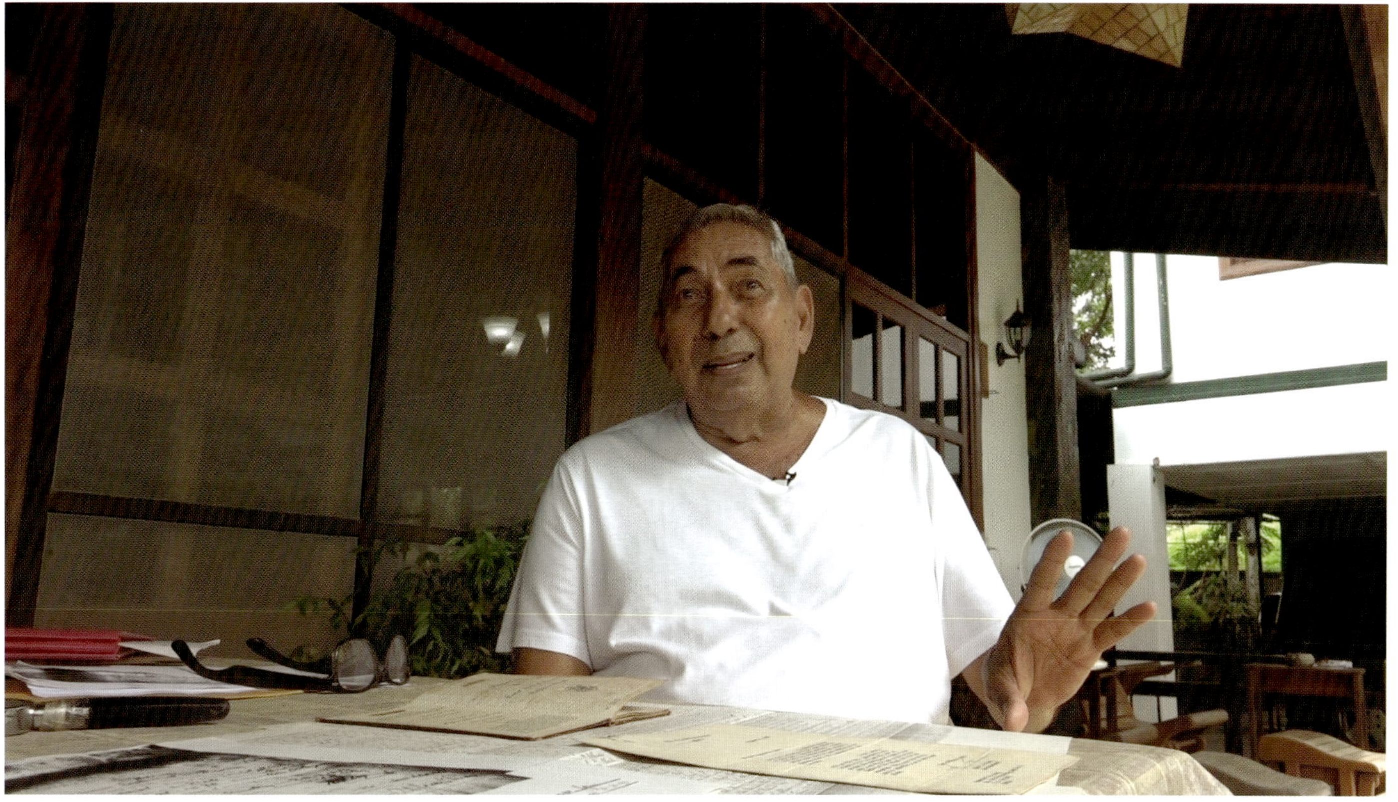

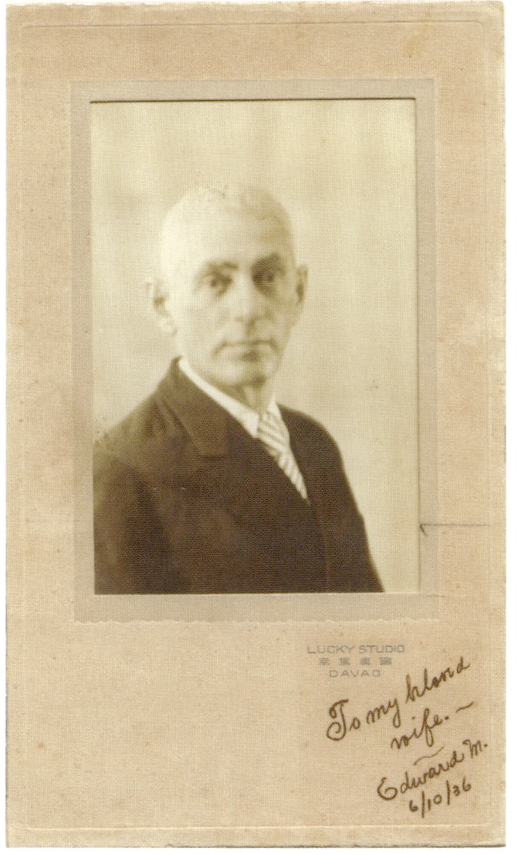

Victor Gross: The nickname "Titay"—the legal name was Antonia Molina, who was his leading lady in the film…in the pictures. They got married, and I don't even know the year she died, but they were childless. And one way or the other, I don't know the circumstance, but married or not married, my mom lived together with Dr. Gross. In the beginning my father had two girls—Perla and Mary, born 1937 and 1938. Then, at that time, he said, "It was enough. Two girls, enough." Until the war, when he was confined to quarters, that I accidentally came about. Which was in 1943.

When I was a baby this was when the Japanese started to lose the war, and they took all the Americans here in Davao and loaded them on a boat, on the top deck, and they used that boat to regroup all the Japanese, to regroup in Manila for the last stand. When my father was taken away we became defenseless. We survived from the river—food from the river. We had eels, fresh shrimp. But my mother remembers that if she had gone out with her friends—her friends were all killed by the Japanese when they were in the mountains…when they stayed hidden. So, she said, had we moved out with them we also would have also been all killed.

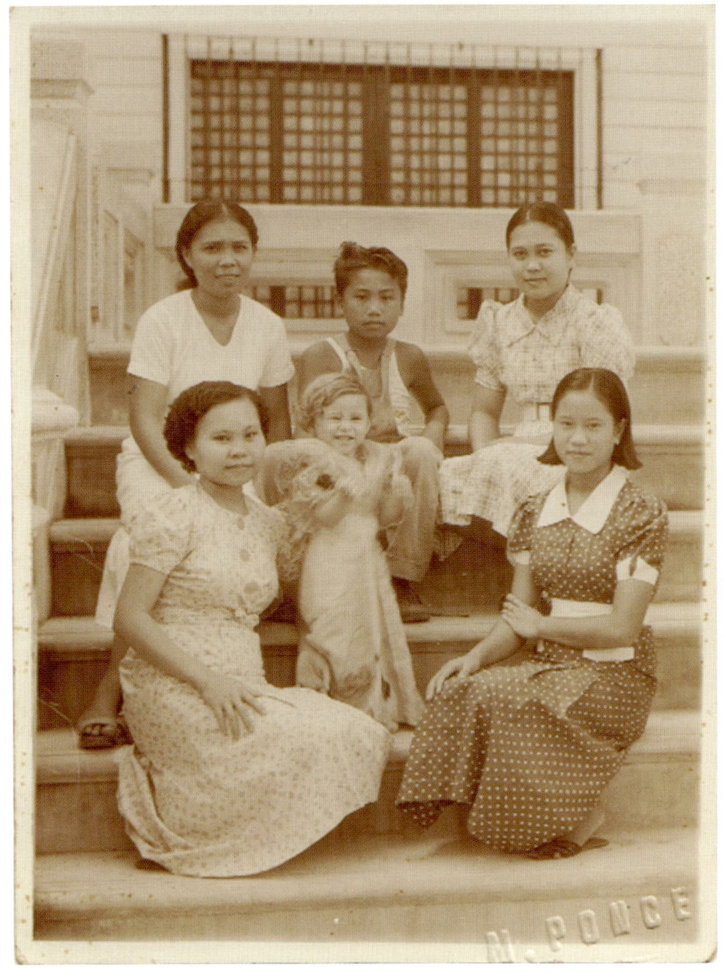

Susie Gross (lower left) with daughter Perla Gross.

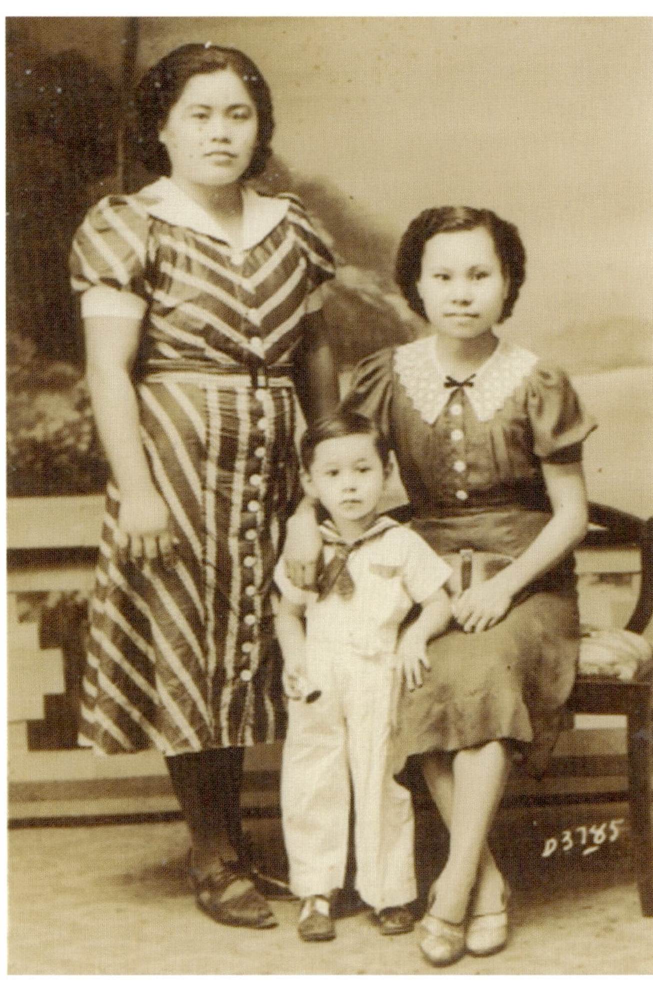

Victor with his yaya and mother Susie.

Victor: What we know is, the brother of Titay Molina is Professor Antonio Molina, who was the Dean of Music at a university in Manila. He kept communications with my mom after the war. In fact, he took my two sisters to Manila to have them study there with him.

Charlie: Do you remember your father at all?

Victor: No. I don't. Well, what stuck in my mind is: I got spanked because he had a diesel engine that was driving a small generator and I was getting dirt and was pouring it over the generator. No. He died in November 1946.

Charlie: So just a few months after Independence.

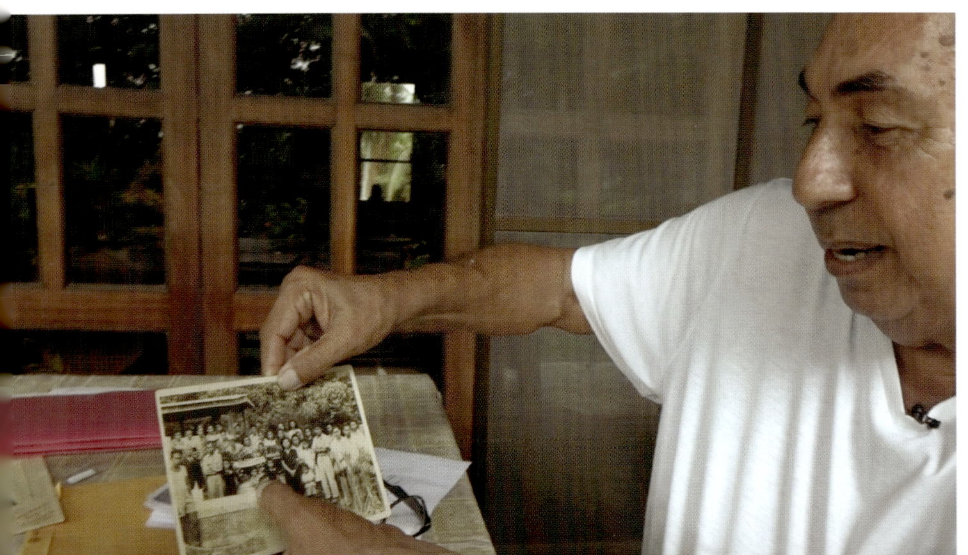

Victor: I have a picture here of his death. Oh, there we go. This is the last photo, when he was buried. I am here. This is Perla, my eldest sister. This is Mary.

Threese: And your mom is?

Victor: I was there, in the middle. That's my mom.

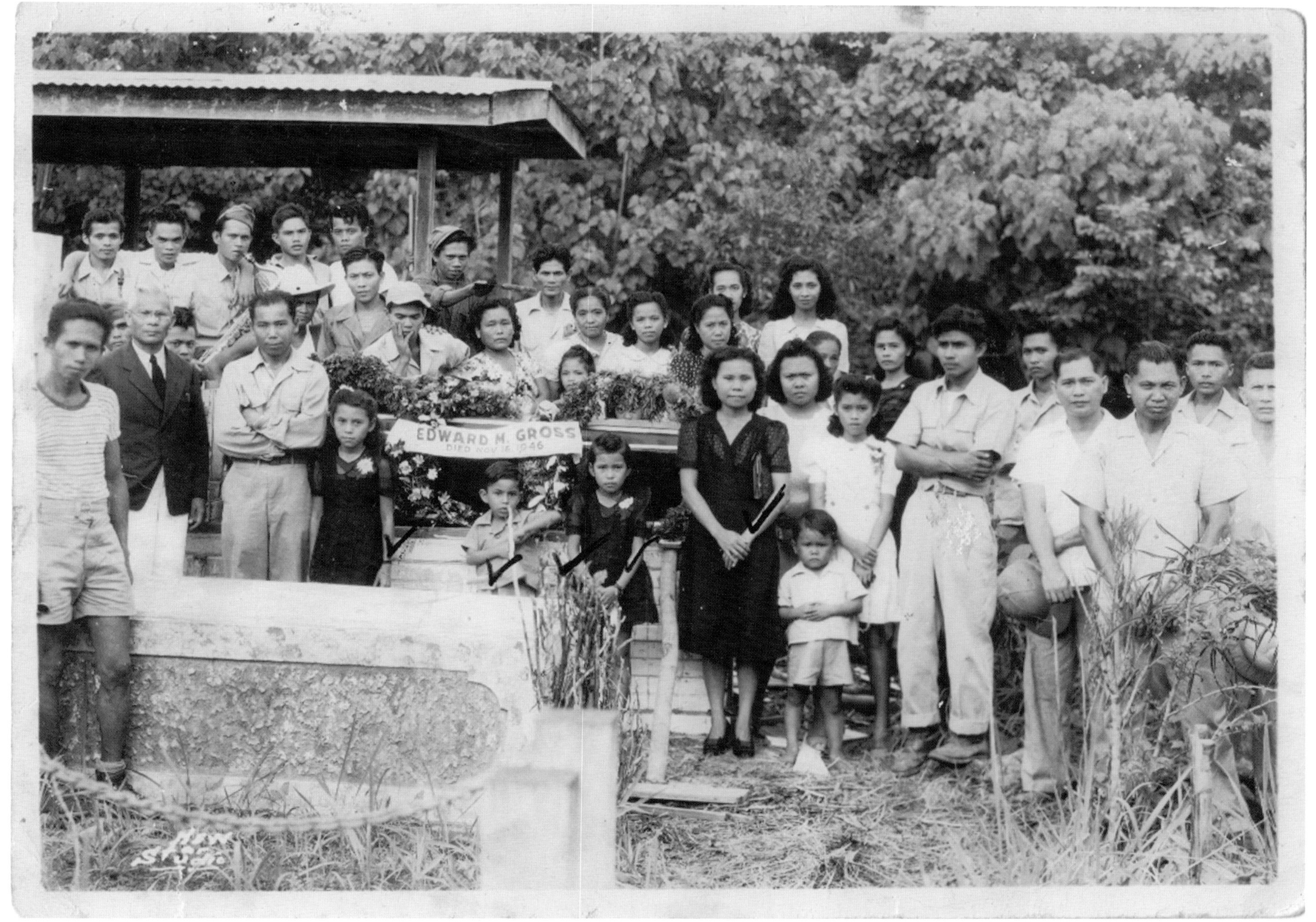

EDWARD M. GROSS

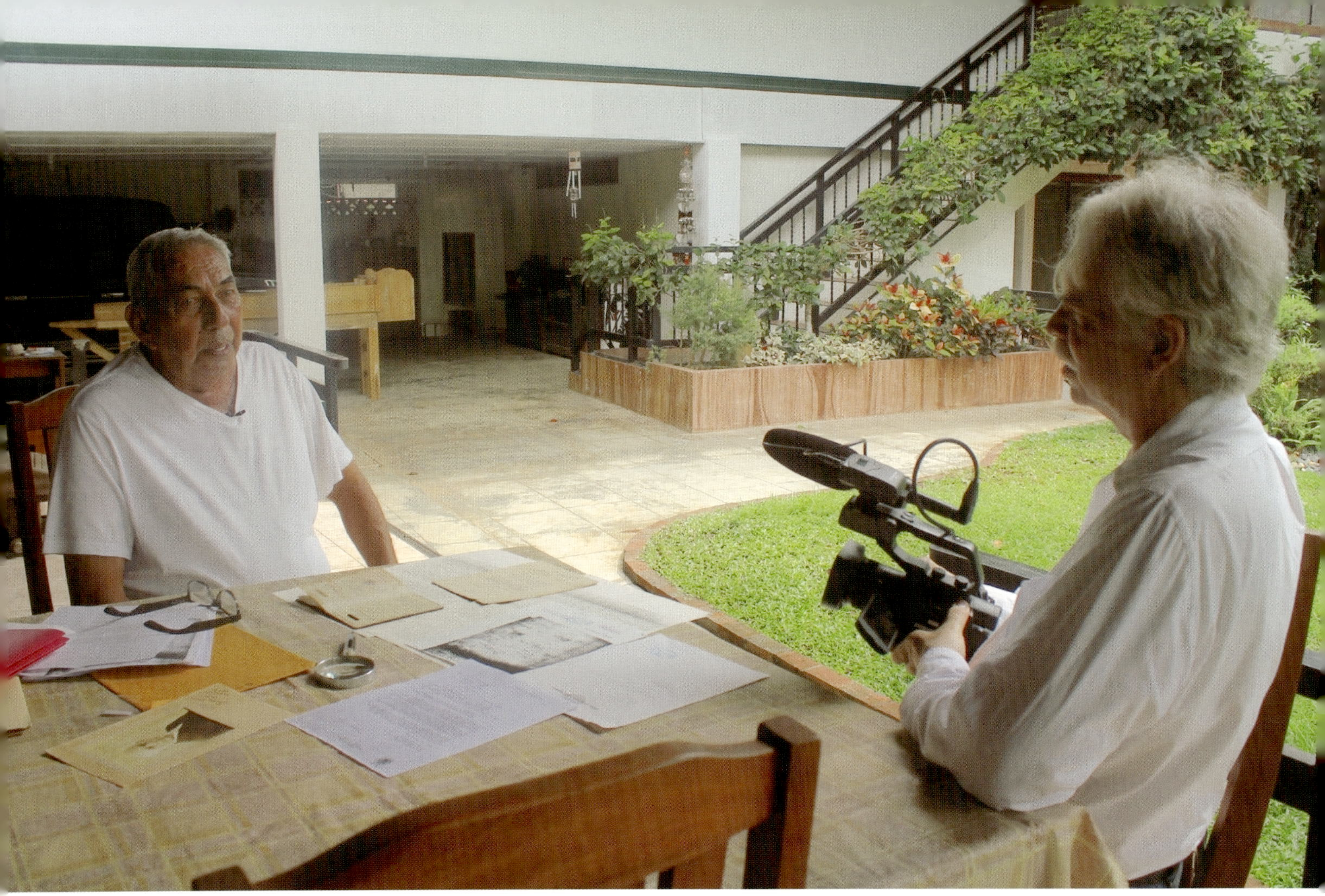

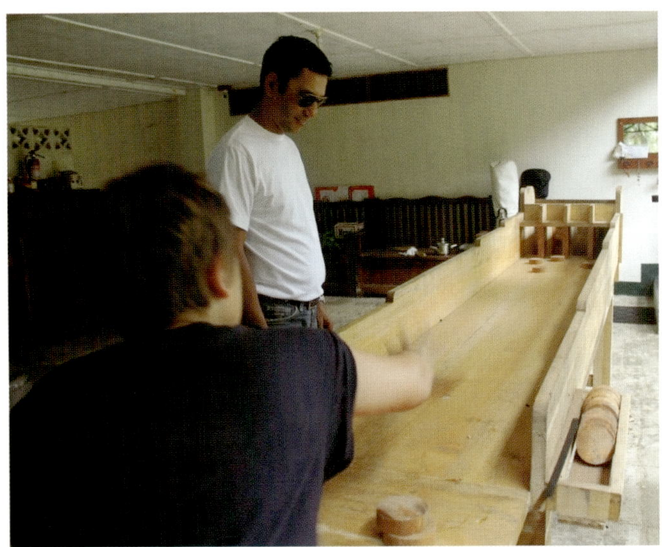

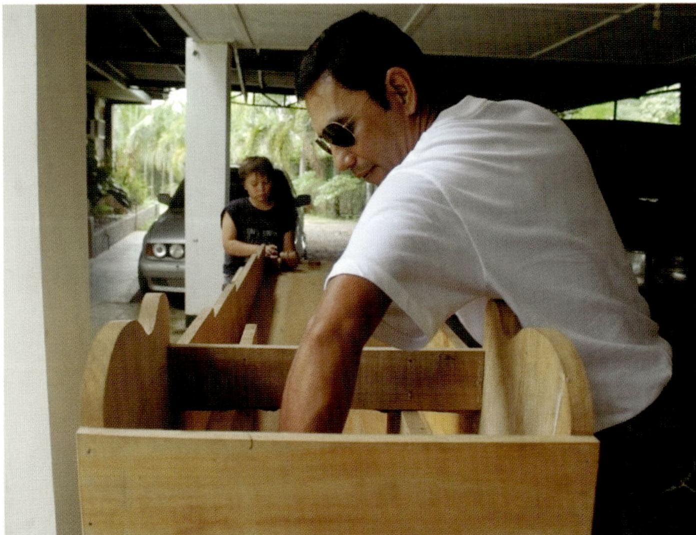

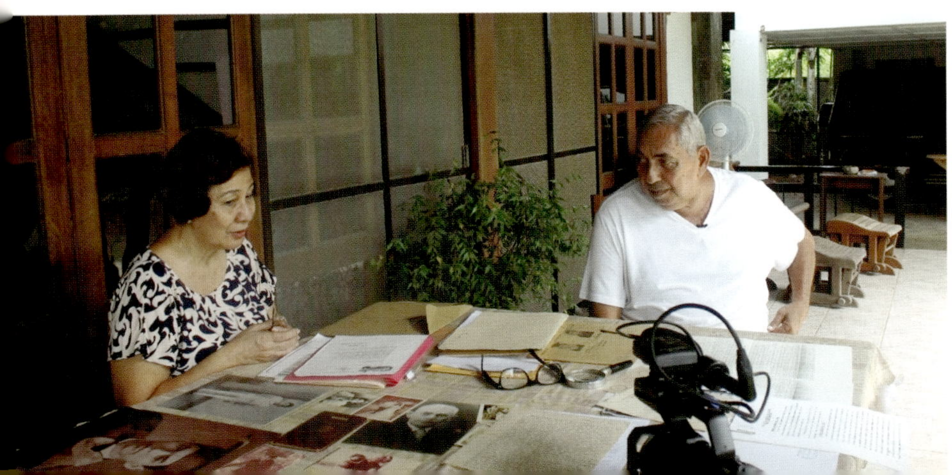

TS: During the interview you played shuffleboard with Edward Gross, who was named after his grandfather. Victor's wife Jade, joined the conversation, and then Victor showed us the woodworking business he had started. It was now run by his son, John, and daughter, Emy.

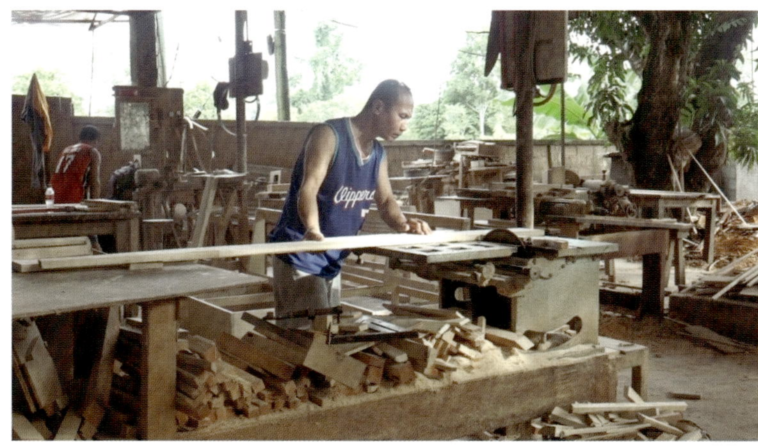
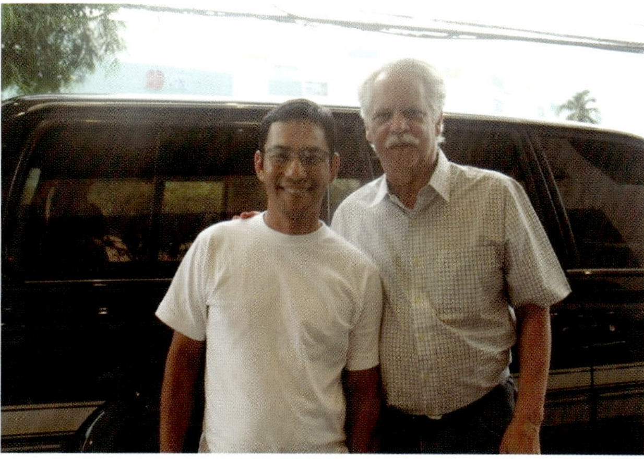

CM: Our visit was coming to an end. We took some final photographs, including one of me and the filmmaker's namesake.

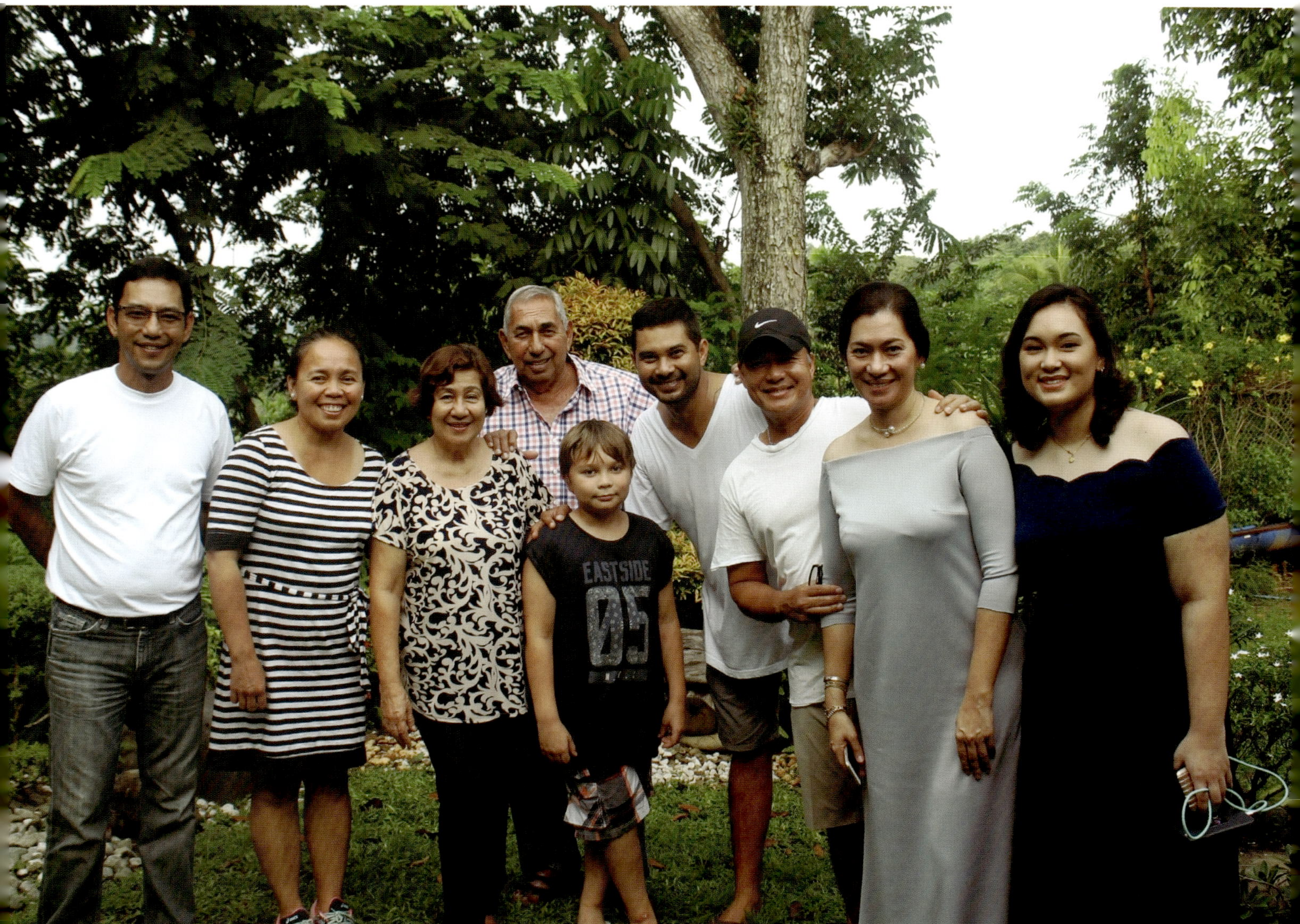

TS: Then the unexpected happened. Emy returned with her daughter, known as Gabrielle Gross, who had been singing at a wedding. Then Emy's husband and Gabrielle's father, Chad Borja, appeared—the famed singer of my youth.

CM: Suddenly we were being treated to our own private concert. Edward Meyer Gross's passion for music had continued across generations.

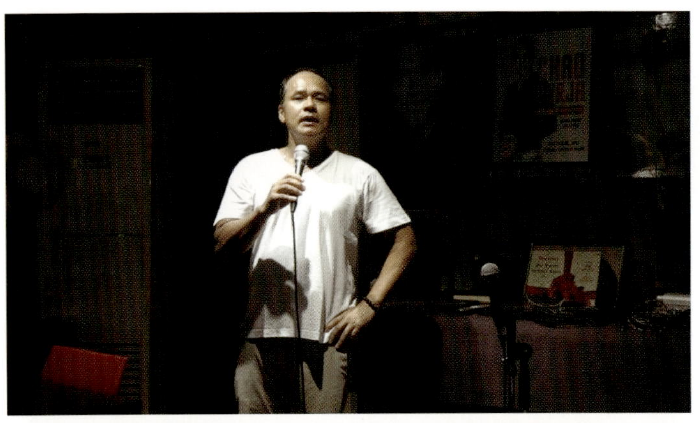

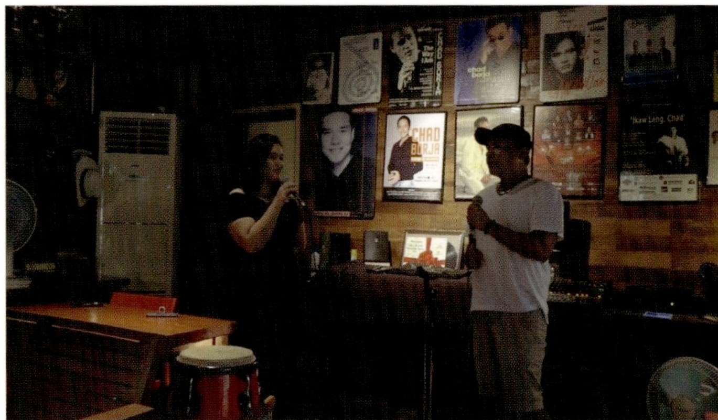

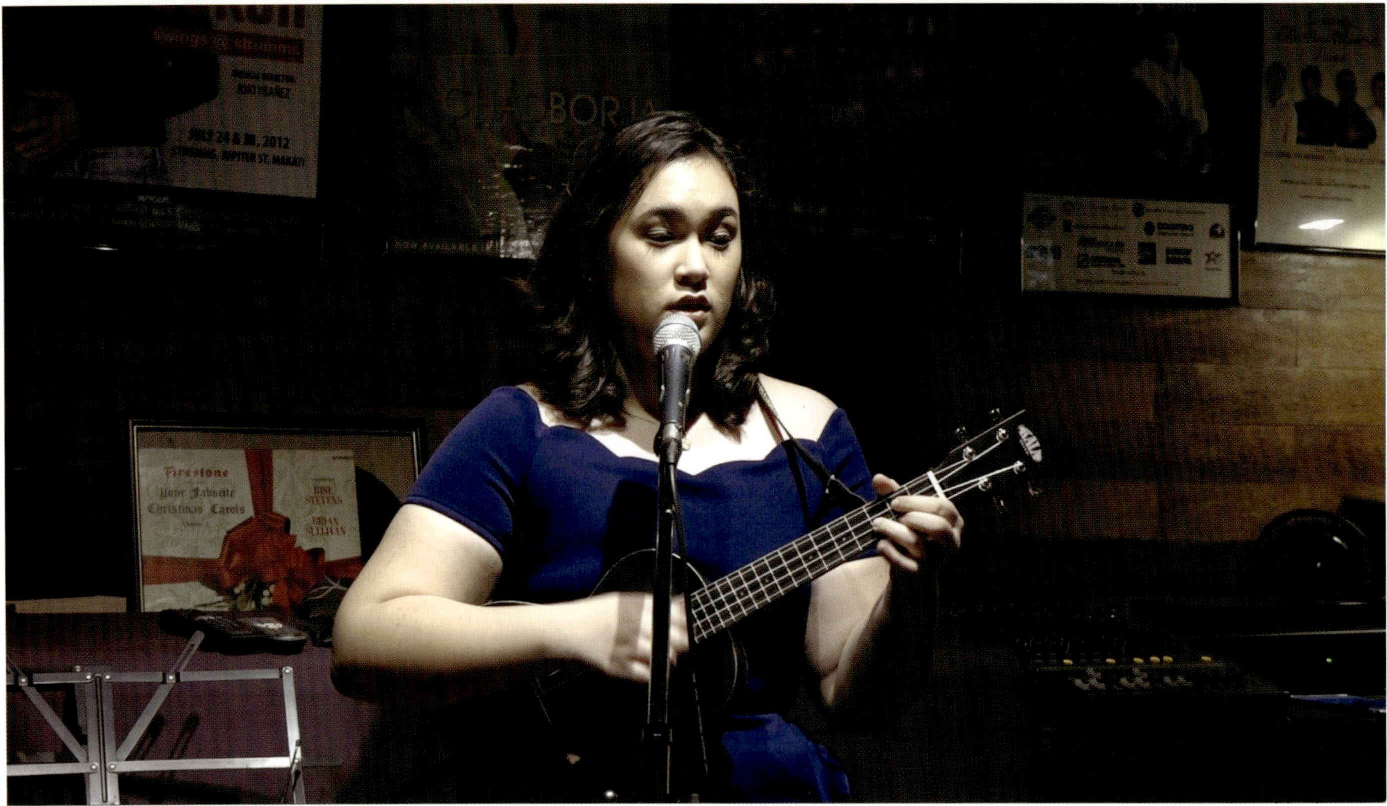

Chad Borja sings an excerpt of "I Left My Heart in San Francisco"; Chad Borja and Gabrielle Gross sing an excerpt of "Solo Saxophone" from Miss Saigon*; and then, Gabrielle Gross sings a song that she wrote:*

"A Song Inspired by You.*"*

"Talk to him," they say.
"Just say hi, it's not that hard."
Introduce yourself
They say "There's nothing in your way."
I kinda shrug it off
And tell myself it's nothing serious.

So, what am I doing twelve o'clock at midnight
Wide awake and thinking of you?
What am I doing twelve o'clock at midnight
Wide awake and thinking of you.

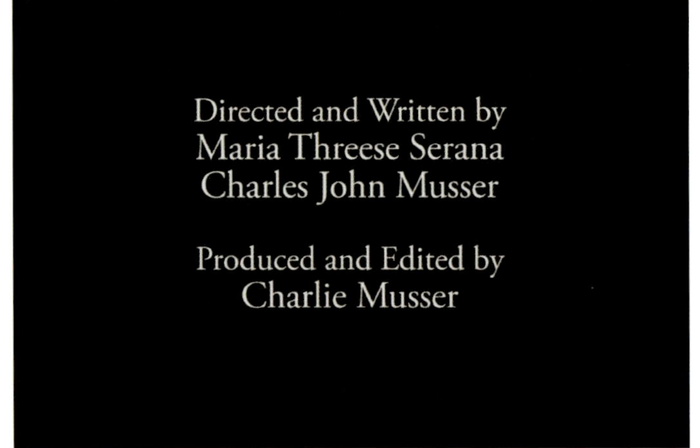

"I'll talk to him," I say
I'll just say Hi, it will be just fine.
It's easier said than done.
I'm not like them, no not at all.

There's this one thing in the way.
It starts with "No," ends with "self-confidence."
Once more I shrug it off.
Convince myself I am not wasting my time.

So, what am I doing twelve o'clock at midnight
Wide awake and thinking of you?
What am I doing twelve o'clock at midnight
Wideawake and thinking of you?

Oh, silly me,
Here we go again
Here come the butterflies
And there's a grin.
Call me crazy to suppose
that maybe you'd like to get to know me.

Oh, what a face you have
There's something about you
I just can't explain.
But it's too late
I've lost my chance.

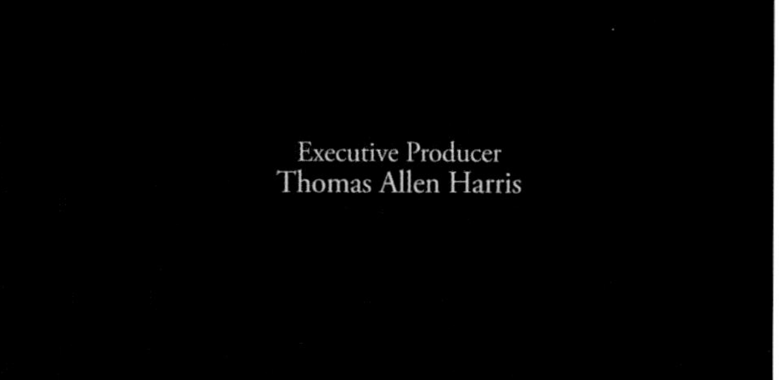
Executive Producer
Thomas Allen Harris

Co-producers
Lorna Johnson
Nick Deocampo

Co-director
Lorna Johnson

INTERVIEWEES

Teraii Maria Serana
Marilyn Keach Bernart
Paolo Cherchi Usai
Lorna Johnson
Victoriano Bejagan
Vanessa Toulmin

CINEMATOGRPAHY

Threese Serana
Charles Musser
Tram Luong
Masha Shpolberg
Lorna Johnson
Wills Glasspeigel
Hannah Zeavin

INTERVIEWEES

Nick Deocampo
Ferdinand F. Klebold
Juan Dicdiquin
Meling Dicdiquin
Ashish Avikunthak
Victor Gross
Thomas Elsaesser

MUSIC

A Song Inspired by You
Performed by Gabrielle Gross
Music and Lyrics by Gabrielle Gross
Ivory Music & Video

This film is
dedicated to

Antonia Molina
and
Edward Meyer Gross

Pioneers of
Filipino Cinema

Maybe I'll see you again if fate allows it
And this time I won't be so afraid.
Yes, maybe I'll see you again
If fate allows it
But for now, a memory is all I have.

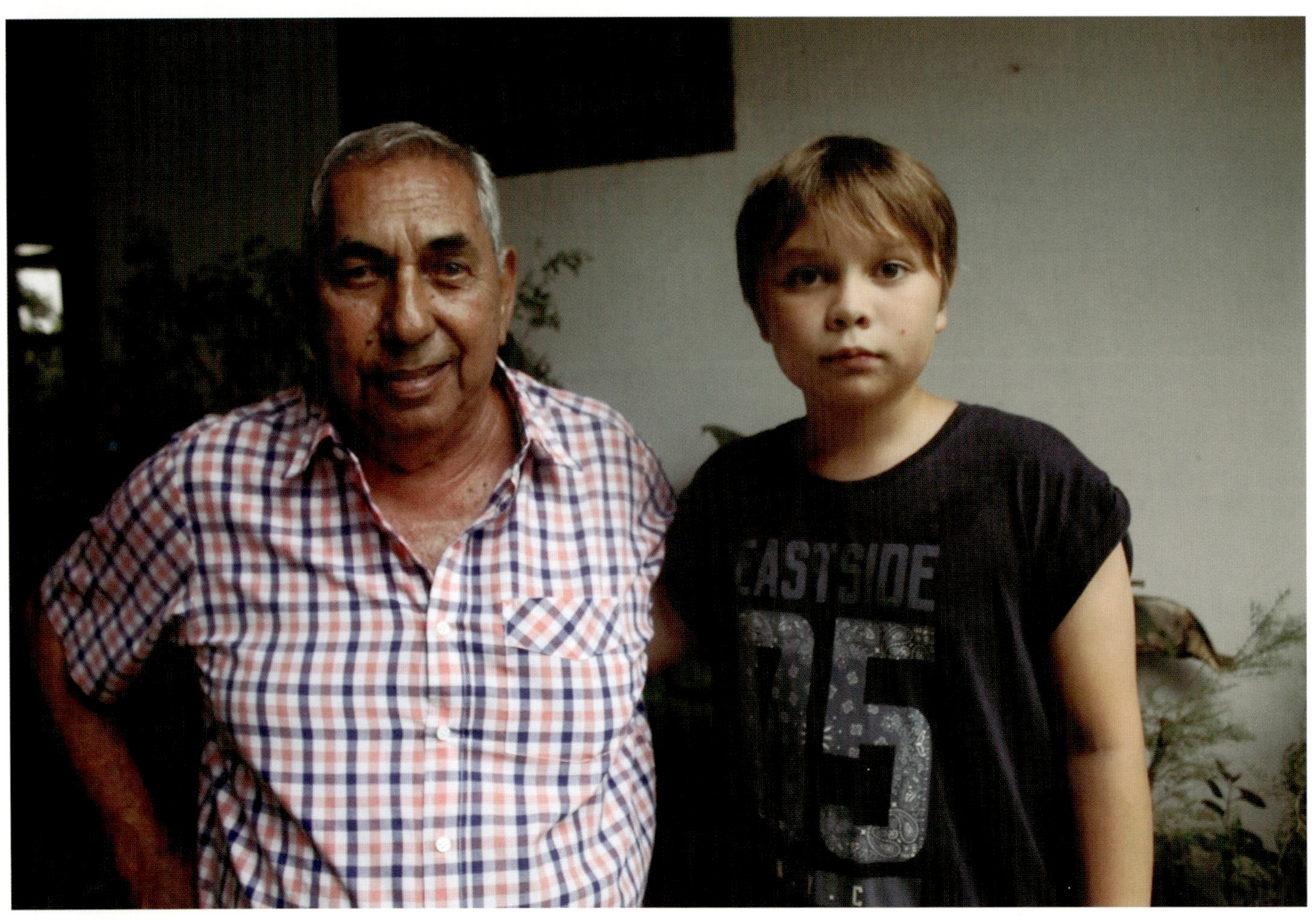

A portrait of my son together with the son of Edward Meyer Gross.

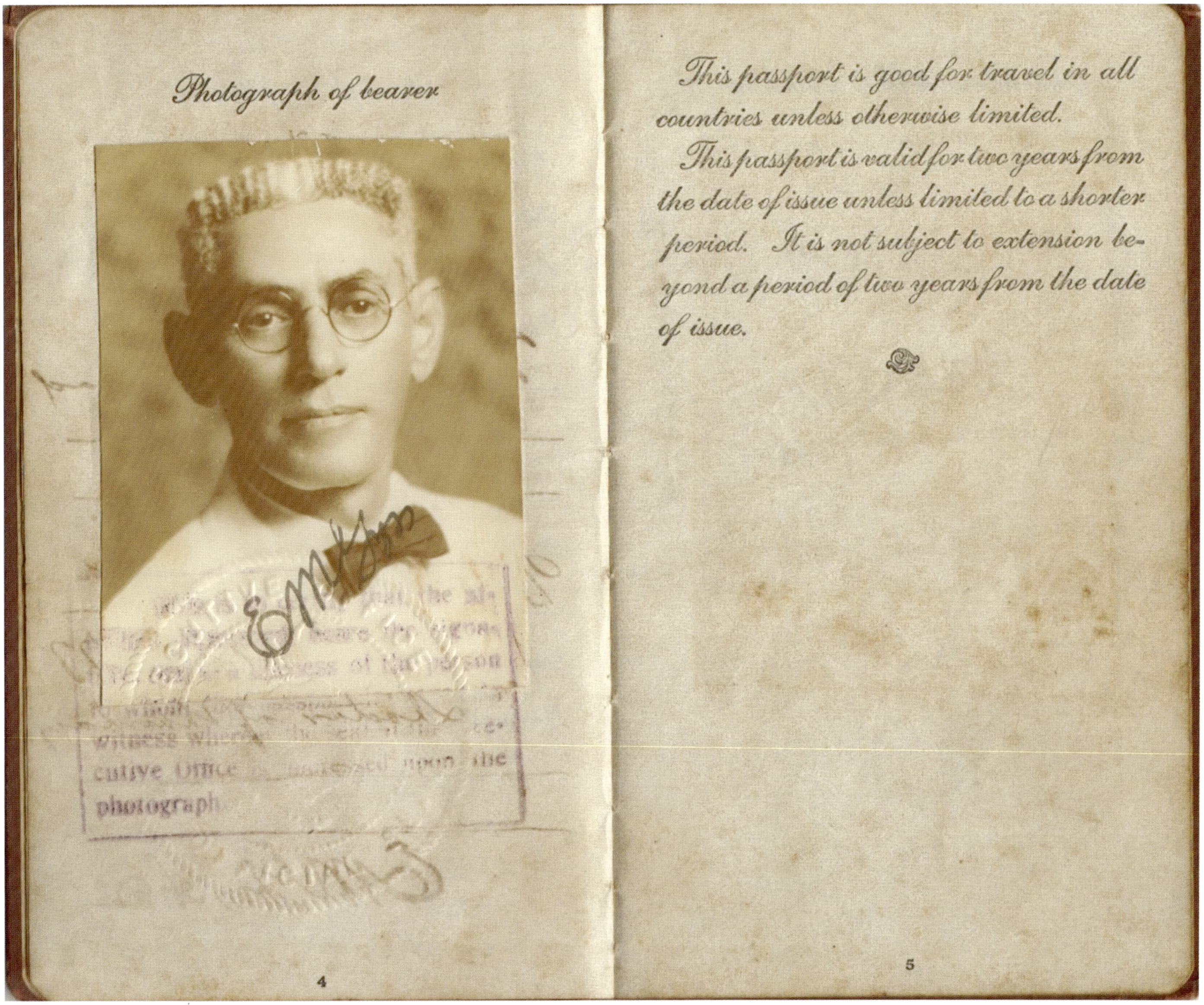

Photograph of bearer

This passport is good for travel in all countries unless otherwise limited.

This passport is valid for two years from the date of issue unless limited to a shorter period. It is not subject to extension beyond a period of two years from the date of issue.

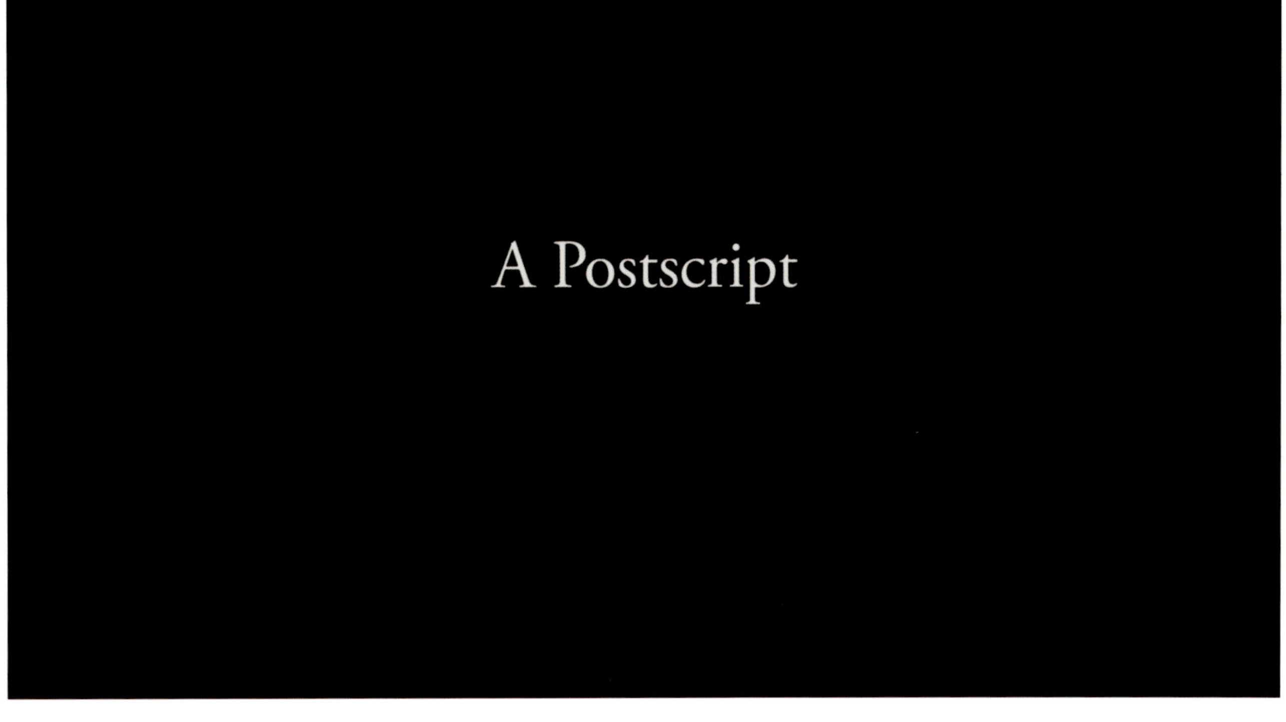
A Postscript

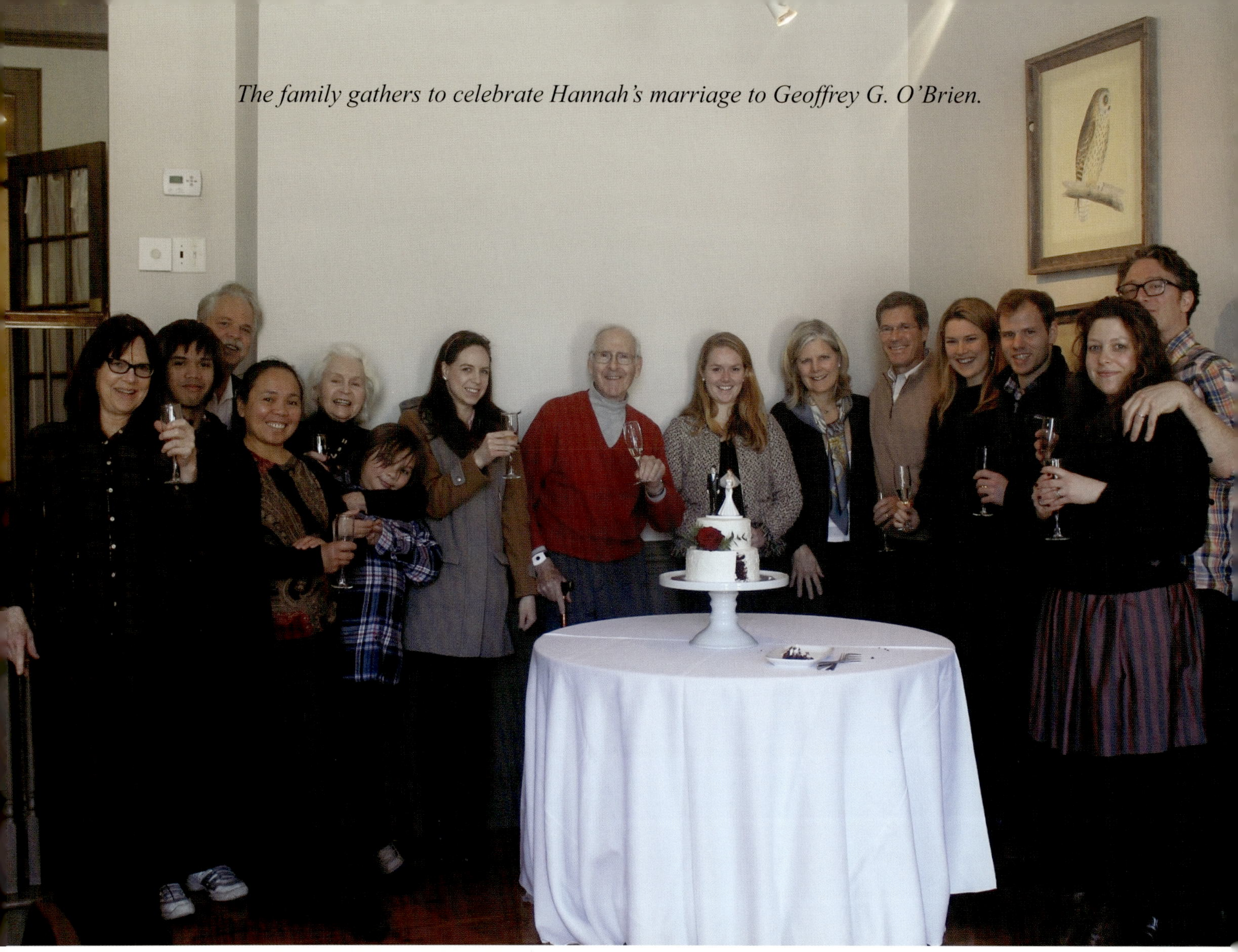

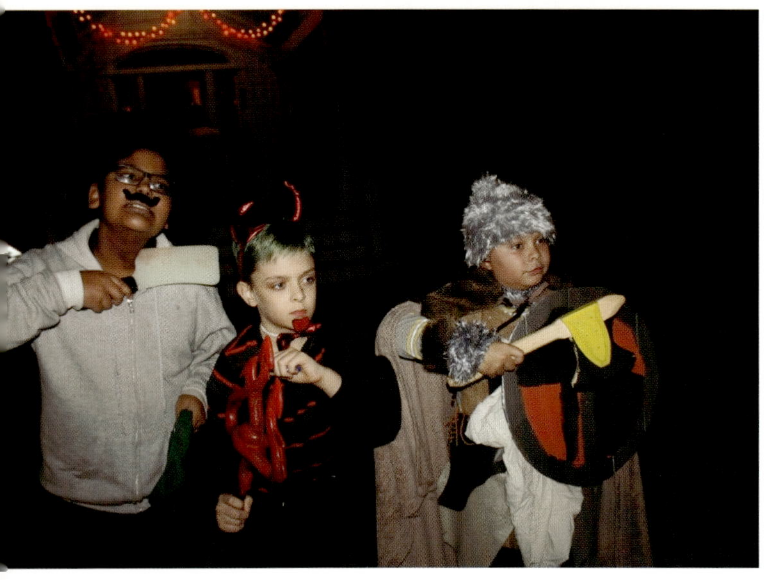

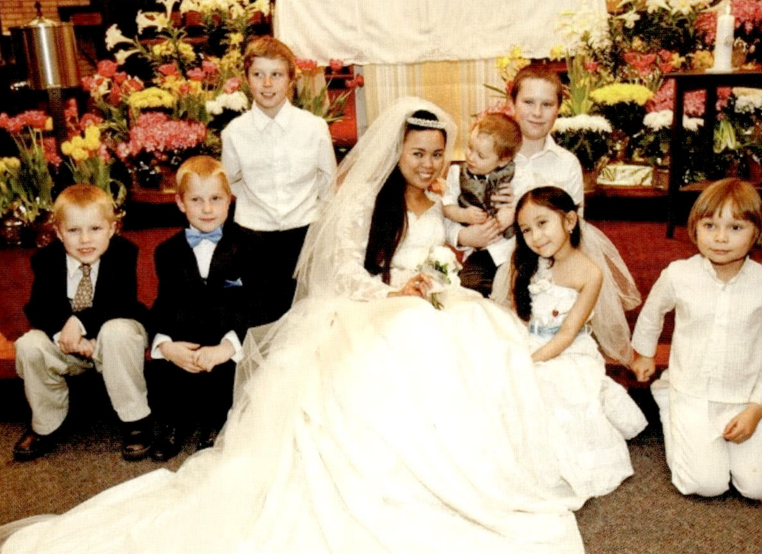

TS: This family album has left out many things. Friends and family members have fallen by the wayside. Your oldest friend Ahad and your neighborhood pal Seamus. Your Tita Kat's wedding, where you were a ring bearer, and your Uncle Warren, who saved you from an onrushing car.

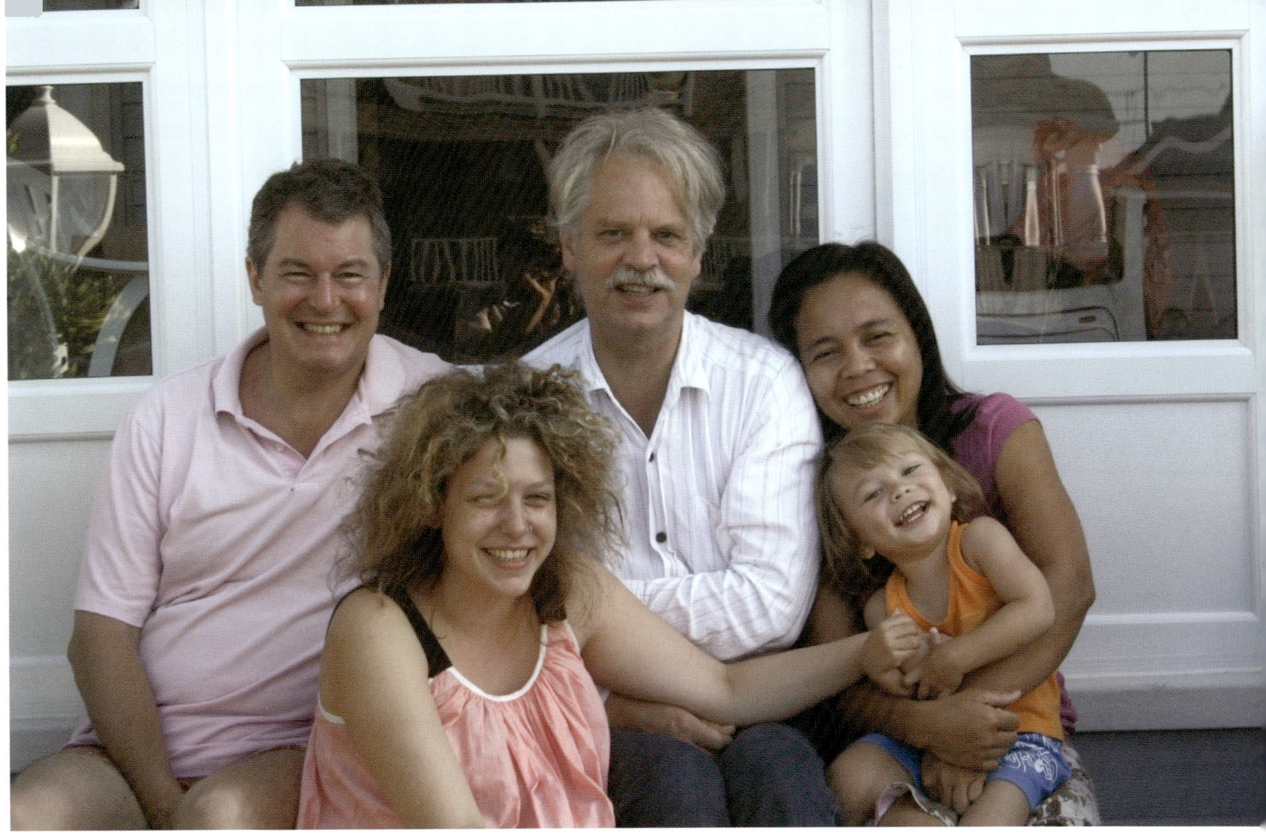

CM: Much has been left unsaid, as well—the usual family squabbles and painful secrets.

Thomas Elsaesser had just finished a documentary about his family, **The Sun Island (*2017*), *when I interviewed him.***

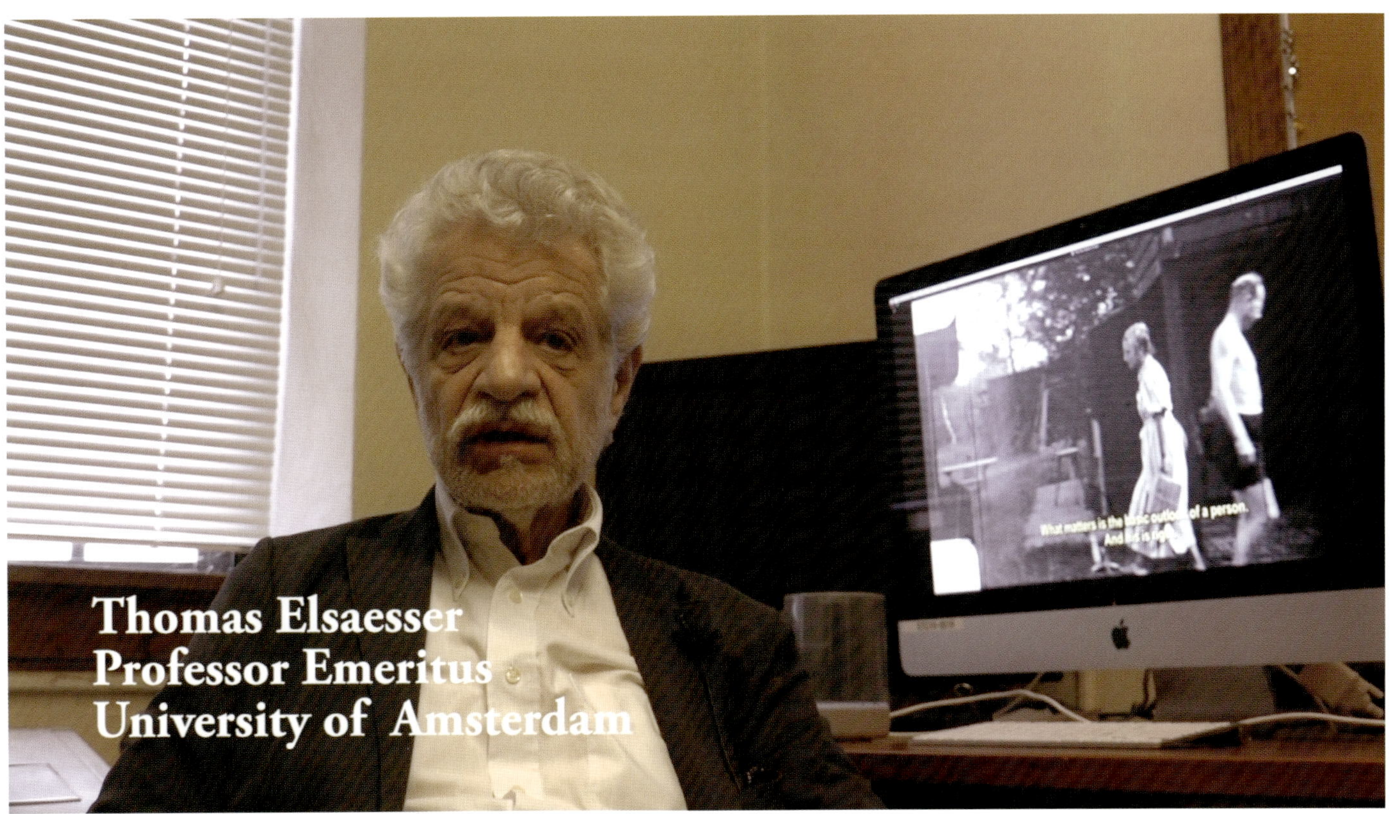

CM: As my friend Thomas Elsaesser has remarked about the photo album:

Thomas Elsaesser: Sometimes they reveal very hidden stories that even those who participated weren't fully aware of. And sometimes, of course, they are more the Sunday edition of the lives of family members and they screen out, or leave out, what is more troublesome or more problematic.

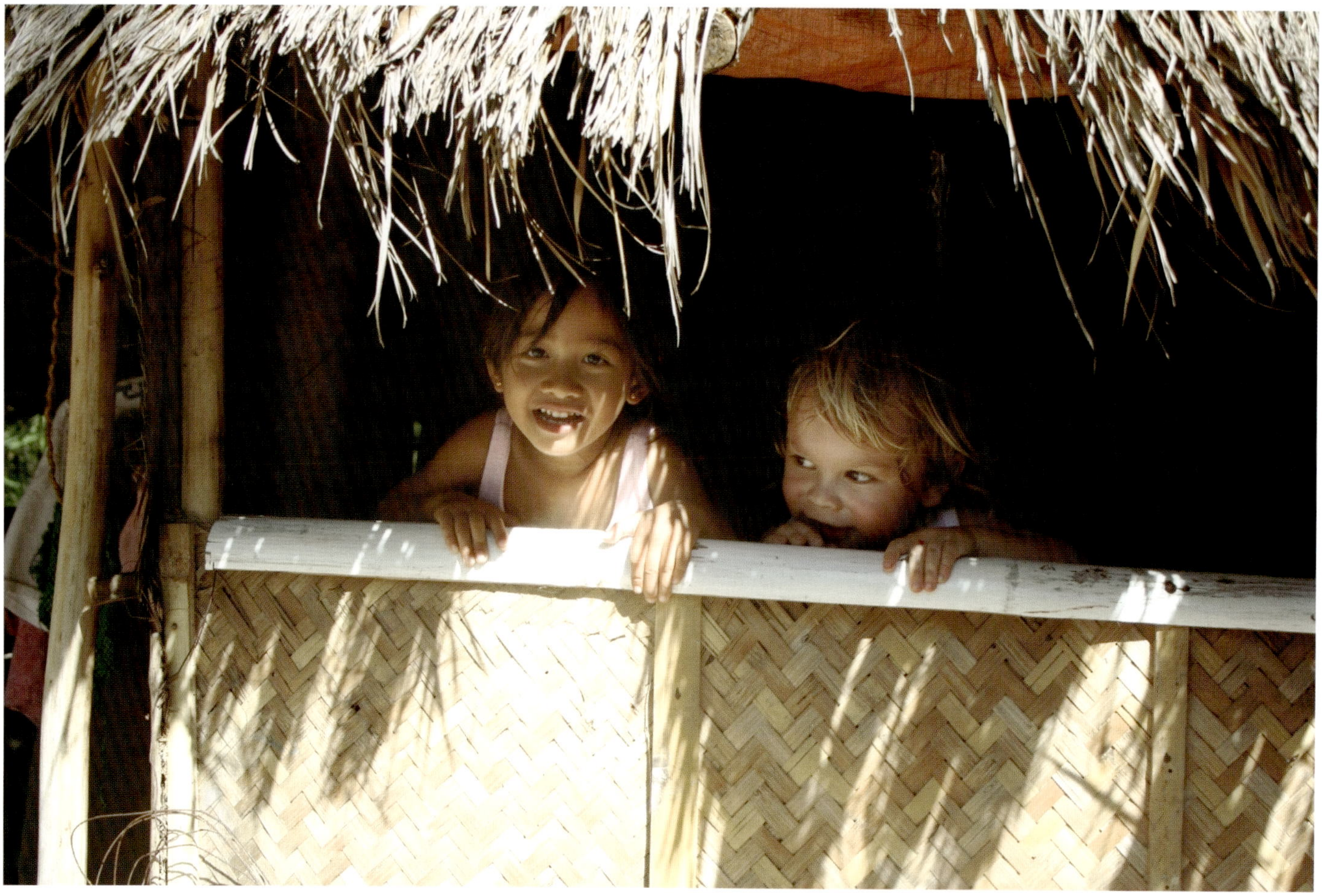

CM: And so, despite our best intentions, this family album may differ very little from the one that my mother kept while I was growing up. Will the silences and omissions overpower what we have shown—and told? You'll be the judge of that—perhaps not now, but in the decades ahead.

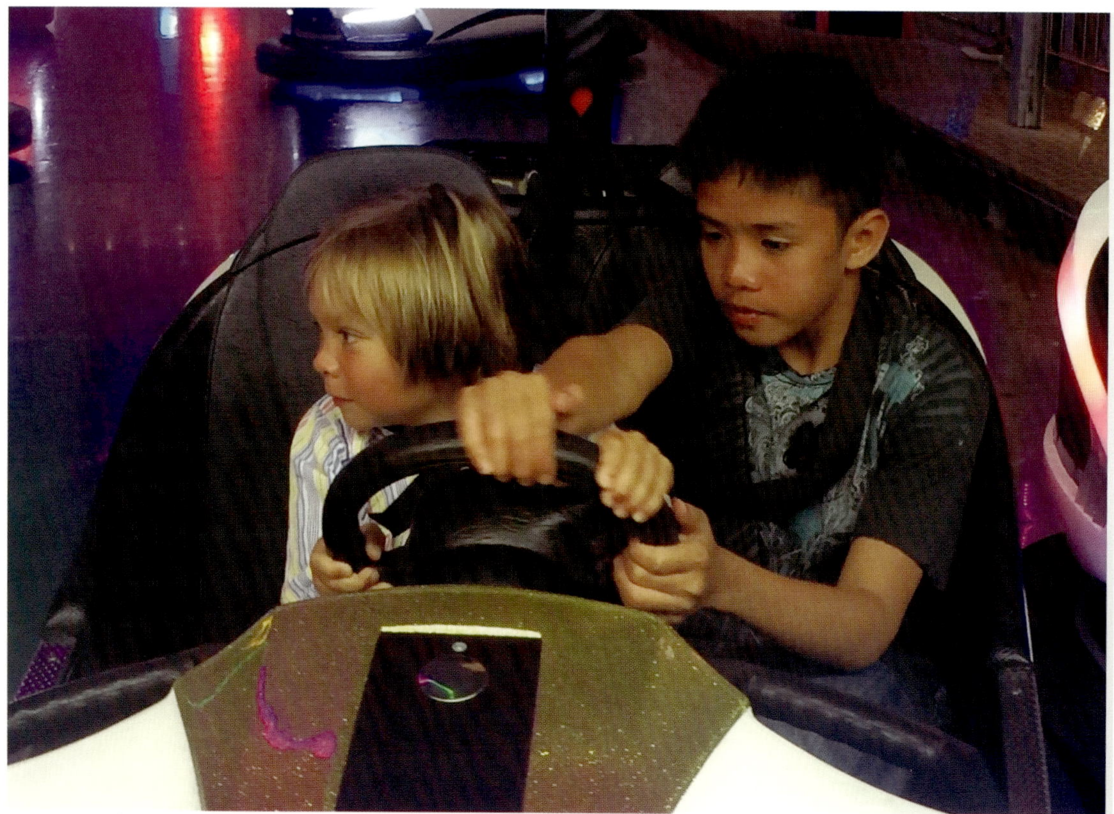

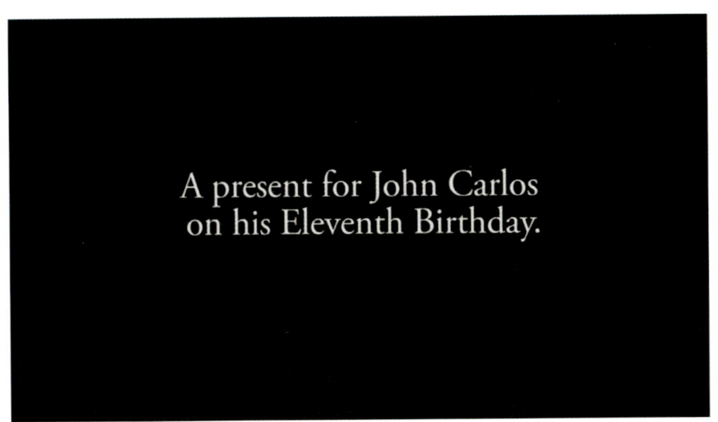

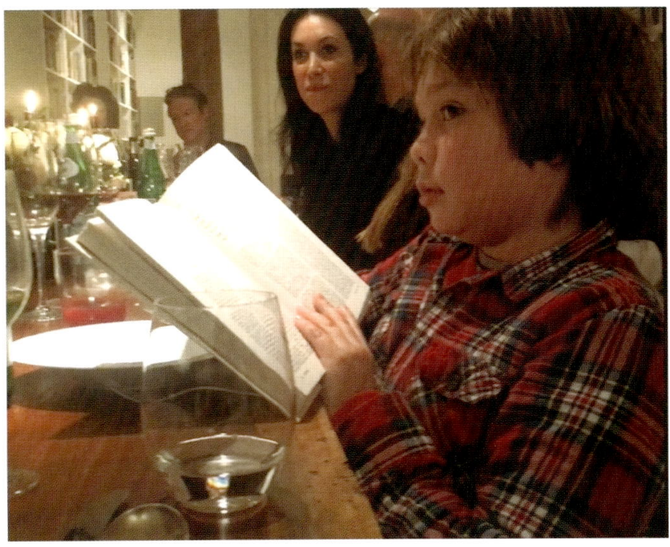

March 31, 2018. John Carlos reading the Four Questions at Hannah's Seder.

FEATURING: Rosario "Mamay" Serana, Jane Musser Nelson, Nancy Musser Klebold, Robert John Musser, various John Mussers, Grace Winter Greene Musser, Lei-Marie Ruschell, Jennifer & Branko Hodzic, Liza Abenion Nevitt, Noah Johnson Frizell, Josh Glick, Masha Shpolberg, Maria Pinango, Domingo Medina, Ashwini Deo, Iravati Chadha, Simone Medina, Patrick Hermann, Geoffrey G. O'Brien, Hannah Grace Zeavin Musser and Binhi Chua Serana.

WITH: Ernesto De Pedro, Gordon Nelson, Elizabeth Nelson, Sarah Nelson, Paul Musser, Ginger Musser, Rene Martel, Anne Martel, Cheerful Catherine Serana McGuinness, Psyche Jade Serana, Darling Rose Sheena, Matthan Serana, Lynne Zeavin, Hadley Zeavin, Barbara Allen, Ahad Anzari, Seamus Blau, Warren Bierwirth.

PHOTOGRAPHY: Anonymous, Yarda Jergens Keach, Marilyn Keach Musser, Robert Musser, Nancy Musser Klebold, Moon Moon Serana, Charles Musser, Anne Kern, Susan Hart, David Coombs, Ellis Rosenber, Paolo Jacob, Vanessa Toulmin, Richard Frizell, Ashish Chadha and Domingo Medina.

Edison film frames: Edison National Historic Site, Motion Picture; Broadcasting and Recorded Sound Division, Library of Congress; Museum of Modern Art. "An auto-da-fé of the Spanish…," engraving by Bernard Picart: Wellcome Collection; map "Maris Pacifici" (1589), by Abraham Ortelius, used for endpapers with details also appearing internally: Wikipedia Commons.

Special Thanks: Worthington Hooker Elementary School, Donner Photographic Lab, Filipino American Family Association, Mowel Fund Film Institute, National Fairground and Circus Archive; Motion Picture, Broadcasting and Recorded Sound Division, Library of Congress; The Orphan Film Symposium; Le Giornate del Cinema Muto.

Special Thanks: Patrick Hermann, Evelyn Robles-Rivas, Anna Marra, Wills Glasspiegel, Greg Johnson, John Lucas, Gorman Bechard, David Schwartz, Charles Lyon, Seth Fein, Katherine Germano, Alexis Krasilovsky, Dan Streible, Jane Gaines, Laura Poitras, Laura Wexler, Dudley Andrew, Francesco Casetti, Lee Faulkner, Sandra Luckow, Livio Jacob, Piera Patat, Jay Weissberg, David Robinson.

With assistance from members of Digital Diaspora Family Reunion Workshop, The Yale Digital Media Center for the Arts, Film & Media Studies Program, and members of Documentary Film Workshop.

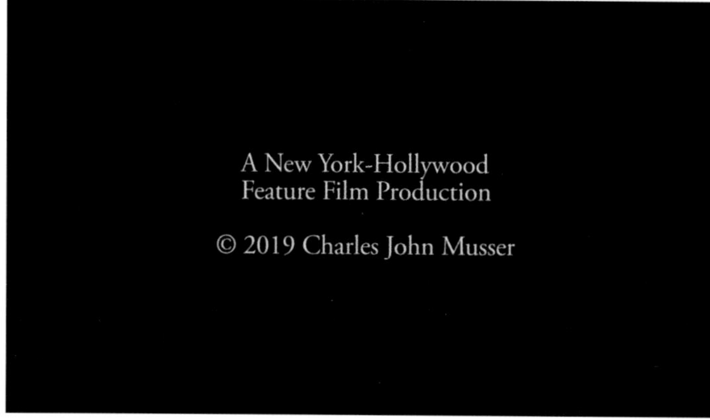
A New York-Hollywood
Feature Film Production

© 2019 Charles John Musser

Biographies

Biographies of Contributors

Charles Musser (producer, director, writer & editor) worked for two years as First Assistant Editor on Peter Davis's Oscar-winning documentary *Hearts and Minds* (1974). His debut documentary, *An American Potter* (1976), on Gerry Williams, won a Blue Ribbon at the American Film Festival, Best in Category Fine Arts, at the San Francisco Film Festival, and other awards. It was followed by *Before the Nickelodeon: The Early Cinema of Edwin S. Porter* (1982), which premiered at the New York Film Festival and internationally. With *Before the Nickelodeon: Edwin S. Porter and the Edison Manufacturing Company* (1991), this was part of a book-film project. That book was also part of an informal trilogy that includes *The Emergence of Cinema: The American Screen to 1907* (1990), which won the Jay Leyda Prize in Cinema Studies and the Katherine Singer Kovacs Prize for best book in Film, TV and Video Studies, among other awards. Establishing himself as a leading scholar of American silent film, Charlie published the catalog raisonné *Edison Motion Pictures, 1890-1900: An Annotated Filmography* (1997) and *Oscar Micheaux and His Circle: African American Filmmaking and Race Cinema of the Silent Era* (2001), co-edited with Pearl Bowser and Jane Gaines. Most recently he authored *Politicking and Emergent Media: U.S. Presidential Elections of the 1890s* (2016). Charlie returned to documentary filmmaking with *Errol Morris: A Lightning Sketch* (2014), which premiered at the Big Sky Documentary Film Festival. He is Professor of Film & Media Studies, Theater Studies, and American Studies at Yale University, where he teaches courses on documentary and film historiography.

Threese Serana (director & writer) taught Philippine History and Political Science at the University of the Philippines-Cebu before moving to the United States. She also worked in community development and was a journalist for *The Freeman,* and online editor at *Sunstar*—two of Cebu's oldest newspapers—often reporting on film, culture and politics. Threese recently finished her M.A. in Environmental Education and is preparing to work as a certified public school teacher in New Haven, CT.

Lorna Ann Johnson (co-director & co-producer) is an award-winning filmmaker. Her film *My Wolverine* received the Jury Award at the 5@5 Program at the Mill Valley Film Festival, and Best Experimental Film from the National Black Programming Consortium. Her documentary *Freedom Road* (2004), which profiles women prisoners in a memoir writing workshop, has been broadcast nationally, screened internationally and is currently distributed by Women Make Movies. *Just Another War* (2007), a documentary chronicling the impact of war on three women, has been screened at the Athens Film Festival in Ohio and the Montreal International Human Rights Film Festival. *About Love*—a film which looks at love lost, love found and love hoped for—was screened at the 2012 Reelsisters Film Festival in Brooklyn, New York. Lorna is currently completing the documentary *Seven Square Miles,* about a violence reduction program in Trenton, NJ. She is an Associate Professor in Communications Studies at The College of New Jersey, where she teaches courses on filmmaking and African Diaspora Cinema.

Thomas Allen Harris (executive producer) is a filmmaker and artist whose work illuminates the human condition and the search for identity, family, and spirituality. His deeply personal films—*VINTAGE – Families of Value* (1995), *É Minha Cara/ That's My Face* (2001), and *The Twelve Disciples of Nelson Mandela* (2005)—have received critical acclaim at numerous international film festivals. His most recent feature film, *Through a Lens Darkly: Black Photographers and the Emergence of a People* (2014), which looks at the ways photographic representations serve as tools of representation and self-representation through history, has won over seven international awards including the 2015 NAACP Image Award for Outstanding Documentary Film. His latest short film, *About Face: The Evolution of a Black Producer* (2017), had its premiere on World AIDS Day at the Whitney Museum of American Art and over 100 institutions worldwide, as part of Visual AIDS' 28th annual Day With(out) Art. In 2009, Thomas founded Digital Diaspora Family Reunion, LLC *(*DDFR*)* a socially engaged transmedia project that has incorporated community organizing, performance, virtual gathering spaces, and storytelling into over 45 unique audio-visual events in over 30 cities. To date, DDFR has brought over 3,000 people together in live events and gathered in excess of 30,000 images, sharing content through social media, television, articles, newspapers, and radio, receiving over 70 million impressions worldwide. He is bringing DDFR to national TV with *Family Pictures USA*. Thomas currently teaches in Film and Media Studies and African American Studies at Yale University.

Nick Deocampo (co-producer) has been making prizewinning film and video documentaries for more than thirty years, covering varied themes from life under the military dictatorship to film history and the environment. His breakthrough film, *Oliver* (1983), is considered a classic in Philippine documentary. *The Philippines: A Legacy of Violence* (1990) won a prize at the Brussels International Film Festival. He was commissioned by The Nippon Foundation to make the six-hour documentary series on the Asian environment, *Cross Currents: Journey to Asian Environments* (2011). He is presently producing a ten-hour documentary series on the one-hundred-year history of cinema in the Philippines, a series that already includes the colonial cycle in Philippine cinema, covering the Spanish, American and Japanese occupations. Nick has authored and edited several books on cinema history including *Short Film: Emergence of a New Philippine Cinema* (1985); *Beyond the Mainstream: The Films of Nick Deocampo* (1997), which received the National Book Award for Screenplay from the Manila Critics Circle; *Lost Films of Asia* (2006); and *SineGabay: A Film Study Guide* (2008), winner of the National Book Award from the Manila Critics Circle. He is currently working on a five-volume history of Philippine cinema. Its first installment is *Cine: Spanish Influences on Early Cinema in the Philippines* (2003), which won another National Book Award. The two subsequent volumes are: *Film: American Influences on Philippine Cinema* (2011) and *Eiga: Cinema in the Philippines during World War II* (2016), The next two volumes will focus on the histories of alternative Philippine cinema and the Philippine movie industry. Nick is currently an Associate Professor at the U.P. Film Institute College of Mass Communication at The University of the Philippines–Diliman.

Laura Wexler is the author of *Tender Violence: Domestic Visions in an Age of U. S. Imperialism* (University of North Carolina Press, 2000), which received the Joan Kelley Memorial Prize of the American Historical Association for the best book in women's history and/or feminist theory. She co–authored *Pregnant Pictures* (Routledge, 2000) with photographer Sandra Matthews. With Laura Frost, Amy Hungerford and John MacKay, Laura edited a special issue of the *Yale Journal of Criticism* on Interpretation and the Holocaust. Her many other publications on photography and American visual culture include recent studies of the writings of Frederick Douglass, and the photographs of La Toya Ruby Frazier. Her current research interests center on family photographs and national memory. Laura is Professor of American Studies and Women's, Gender, & Sexuality Studies. She co-chairs the Women's Faculty Forum at Yale and holds an affiliation with the Film Studies Program, the Program in Ethnicity, Race and Migration, and the Public Humanities Program.

John Lucas (book designer) has worked as a documentary photographer for more than 25 years. John has directed and produced several cutting-edge multimedia projects including collaborative work with poet Claudia Rankine. He also designs her books. In 2014 he completed his first feature-length documentary film, entitled *The Cooler Bandits*, which was awarded Best Documentary at the 2014 Harlem International Film Festival. His work has been exhibited in museums and galleries, both nationally and internationally, including the Brooklyn Art Museum, Cleveland Museum of Art, Redcat (Los Angeles), OK Harris Works of Art (NYC), La Panaderia (Mexico City), and Fieldgate Gallery (London). He is currently a visiting lecturer at Yale, teaching documentary film.

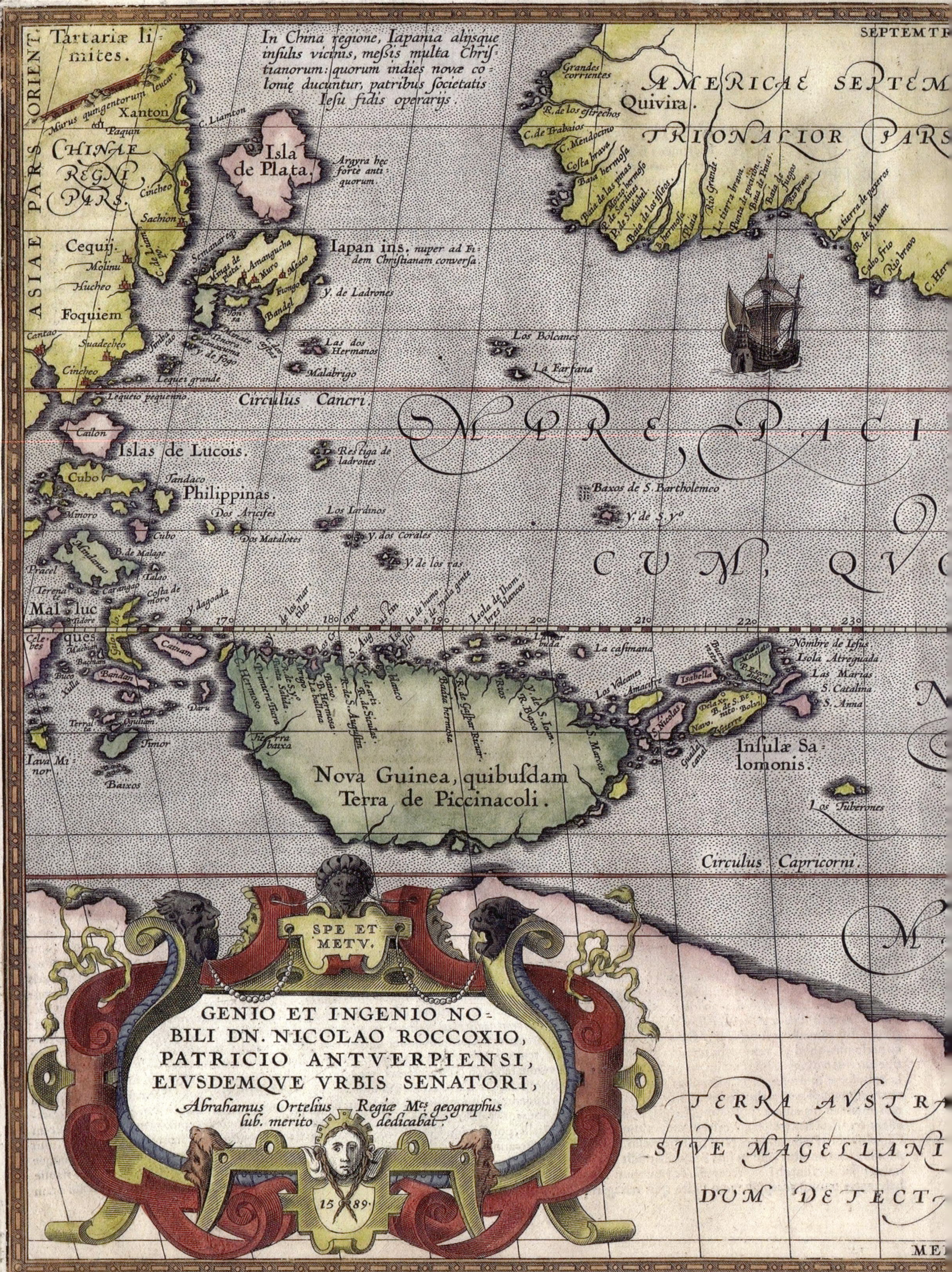

Tartariæ limites.
In China regione, Iapania alijsque insulis vicinis, messis multa Christianorum: quorum indies novæ coloniæ ducuntur, patribus societatis Iesu fidis operarijs.
SEPTEMTR
ASIAE PARS ORIENT.
AMERICAE SEPTEM
Quivira.
TRIONALIOR PARS
Grandes corrientes
R. de los estrechos
C. de Trabaios
C. Mendocino
Costa brava
Baia hermosa
Isla de los pinas
Rio grande
Rio de mai.
Murus quingentorum leucar.
Xanton
Paquin
CHINAE REGNI PARS.
Cincheo
Sachion
C. Liamton
Isla de Plata.
Argyra hæc forte anti quorum.
Iapan ins. nuper ad Fidem Christianam conversa.
Cequij
Molinu
Hucheo
Foquiem
Liampo
Goto
Minga de plata
Amanucha
Muro
Meaco
Fungo
Bandal
Y. de Ladrones
Las dos Hermanos
Malabrigo
Los Bolcanes
La Farfana
Cantao
Suadecheo
Cincheo
Lequio grande
Lequeio pequenio
Circulus Cancri.
MARE PACI
Cailon
Islas de Lucois.
Res tiga de ladrones
Cubo
Tandaco
Philippinas.
Baxos de S. Bartholemeo
Y. de S. y.°
Minoro
Cubo
Dos Arrecefes
Dos Matalotes
Los Iardinos
Y. dos Corales
Y. de los ras
CUM, QUO
Pracel
B. de Malage
Talao
Carangas
Costa de moro
Mal Luc
Tidore
Celebes
190
180
190
200
210
220
230
Cattigara
La casñana
Nombre de Iesus
Isola Atreguada
Las Marias
S. Catalina
S. Anna
Los Volcanes
Amacofre
Isabella
Nova Guinea, quibusdam Terra de Piccinacoli.
Insulæ Salomonis.
Los Tuberones
Circulus Capricorni.
Lava Mor
Baixos
Timor
SPE ET METU.
GENIO ET INGENIO NOBILI DN. NICOLAO ROCCOXIO, PATRICIO ANTVERPIENSI, EIVSDEMQVE VRBIS SENATORI,
Abrahamus Ortelius Regiæ Mtis geographus lub. merito dedicabat.
1589
TERRA AVSTRALIS SIVE MAGELLANICA NONDVM DETECTA.